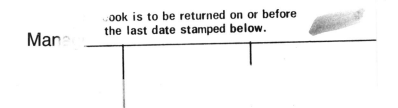

To Katie, Martin, Jane and Theresa

Managing Financial Resources

Michael Broadbent and John Cullen

*Published in association with
the Institute of Management*

the Institute
of Management

FOUNDATION

BUTTERWORTH
HEINEMANN

Butterworth-Heinemann
Linacre House, Jordan Hill, Oxford OX2 8DP
A division of Reed Educational and Professional Publishing Ltd

R A member of the Reed Elsevier plc group

OXFORD   BOSTON   JOHANNESBURG
MELBOURNE   NEW DELHI   SINGAPORE

First published 1993
Reprinted 1994 (twice), 1995, 1996

British Library Cataloguing in Publication Data
Michael Broadbent
   Managing Financial Resources
   I. Title   II. Cullen, John
   658.15

ISBN 0 7506 0669 X

Printed and bound in Great Britain by
Hartnolls Limited, Bodmin, Cornwall

Contents

Series adviser's preface

This book is one of a series designed for people wanting to develop their capabilities as managers. You might think that there isn't anything very new in that. In one way you would be right. The fact that very many people want to learn to become better managers is not new, and for many years a wide range of approaches to such learning and development has been available. These have included courses leading to formal qualifications, organizationally-based management development programmes and a whole variety of self-study materials. A copious literature, extending from academic text-books to sometimes idiosyncratic prescriptions from successful managers and consultants, has existed to aid − or perhaps confuse − the potential seeker after managerial truth and enlightenment.

So what is new about this series? In fact, a great deal − marking in some ways a revolution in our thinking both about the art of managing and also the process of developing managers.

Where did it all begin? Like most revolutions, although there may be a single, identifiable act that precipitated the uprising, the roots of discontent are many and long-established. The debate about the performance of British managers, the way managers are educated and trained, and the extent to which shortcomings in both these areas have contributed to our economic decline, has been running for several decades.

Until recently, this debate had been marked by periods of frenetic activity − stimulated by some report or enquiry and perhaps ending in some new initiatives or policy changes − followed by relatively long periods of comparative calm. But the underlying causes for concern persisted. Basically, the majority of managers in the UK appeared to have little or no training for their role, certainly far less than their counterparts in our major competitor nations. And there was concern about the nature, style and appropriateness of the management education and training that was available.

The catalyst for this latest revolution came in late 1986 and early 1987, when three major reports reopened the whole issue. The 1987 reports were *The Making of British Managers* by John Constable and Roger McCormick, carried out for the British Institute of Management and the CBI, and *The Making of Managers* by Charles Handy, carried out for the (then) Manpower Services Commission, National Economic Development Office and British Institute of Management. The 1986 report, which often receives less recognition than it deserves as a key contribution to the recent changes, was *Management Training: context and process* by Iain Mangham and Mick Silver, carried out for the Economic and Social Research Council and the Department of Trade and Industry.

It is not the place to review in detail what the reports said. Indeed, they and their consequences are discussed in several places in this series of books. But essentially they confirmed that:

- British managers were undertrained by comparison with their counterparts internationally.
- The majority of employers invested far too little in training and developing their managers.
- Many employers found it difficult to specify with any degree of detail just what it was that they required successful managers to be able to do.

The Constable/McCormick and Handy reports advanced various recommendations for addressing these problems, involving an expansion of management education and development, a reformed structure of qualifications and a commitment from employers to a code of practice for management development. While this analysis was not new, and had echoes of much that had been said in earlier debates, this time a few leading individuals determined that the response should be both radical and permanent. The response was coordinated by the newly-established Council for Management Education and Development (now the National Forum for Management Education and Development (NFMED)) under the energetic and visionary leadership of Bob (now Sir Bob) Reid of Shell UK (now chairman of the British Railways Board).

Under the umbrella of NFMED a series of employer-led working parties tackled the problem of defining what it was that managers should be able to do, and how this differed for people at different levels in their organizations; how this satisfactory ability to perform might be verified; and how an appropriate structure of management qualifications could be put in place. This work drew upon the methods used to specify vocational standards in industry and commerce, and led to the development and introduction of competence-based management standards and qualifications. In this context, competence is defined as the ability to perform the activities within an occupation or function to the standards expected in employment.

It is this competence-based approach that is new in our thinking about the manager's capabilities. It is also what is new about this series of books, in that they are designed to support both this new structure of management standards, and of development activities based on it. The series was originally commissioned to support the Institute of Management's Certificate and Diploma qualifications, which were one of the first to be based on the new standards. However, these books are equal'v appropriate to any university, college or indeed company course leading to a certificate in management or diploma in management studies.

The standards were specified through an extensive process of consultation with a large number of managers in organizations of many different types and sizes. They are therefore employment based and employer-supported. And they fill the gap that Mangham and Silver identified – now we do have a language to describe what it is employers want their managers to be able to do – at least in part.

If you are engaged in any form of management development leading to a certificate or diploma qualification conforming to the national management standards, then you are probably already familiar with most of the key ideas on which the standards are based. To achieve their key purpose, which is defined as achieving the organization's objectives and continuously improving its performance, managers need to perform four key roles: managing operations, managing finance, managing people and managing information. Each of these key roles has a sub-structure of units and elements, each with associated performance and assessment criteria.

The reason for the qualification 'in part' is that organizations are different, and jobs within them are different. Thus the generic management standards probably do not cover all the management competences that you may need to possess in your job. There are almost certainly additional things, specific to your own situation in your own organization, that you need to be able to do. The standards are necessary, but almost certainly not sufficient. Only you, in discussion with your boss, will be able to decide what other capabilities you need to possess. But the standards are a place to start, a basis on which to build. Once you have demonstrated your proficiency against the standards, it will stand you in good stead as you progress through your organization, or change jobs.

So how do the new standards change the process by which you develop yourself as a manager? They change the process of development, or of gaining a management qualification, quite a lot. It is no longer a question of acquiring information and facts, perhaps by being 'taught' in some classroom environment, and then being tested to see what you can recall. It involves demonstrating, in a quite specific way, that you can do certain things to a particular standard of performance. And because of this, it puts a much greater onus on you to manage your own development, to decide how you can demonstrate any particular competence, what evidence you need to present, and how you can collect it. Of course, there will always be people to advise and guide you in this, if you need help.

But there is another dimension, and it is to this that this series of books is addressed. While the standards stress ability to perform, they do not ignore the traditional knowledge base that has been associated with 'management studies'. Rather, they set this in a different context. The standards are supported by 'underpinning knowledge and understanding' which has three components:

- Purpose and context, which is knowledge and understanding of the manager's objectives, and of the relevant organizational and environmental influences, opportunities and values.
- Principles and methods, which is knowledge and understanding of the theories, models, principles, methods and techniques that provide the basis of competent managerial performance.
- Data, which is knowledge and understanding of specific facts likely to be important to meeting the standards.

Possession of the relevant knowledge and understanding underpinning the standards is needed to support competent managerial performance as specified in the standards. It also has an important role in supporting the transferability of management capabilities. It helps to ensure that you have done more than learned 'the way we do things around here' in your own organization. It indicates a recognition of the wider things which underpin competence, and that you will be able to change jobs or organizations and still be able to perform effectively.

These books cover the knowledge and understanding underpinning the management standards, most specifically in the category of principles and methods. But their coverage is not limited to the minimum required by the standards, and extends in both depth and breadth in many areas. The authors have tried to approach these underlying principles and methods in a practical way. They use many short cases and examples which we hope will demonstrate how, in practice, the principles and methods, and knowledge of purpose and context plus data, support the ability to perform as required by the management standards. In particular we hope that this type of presentation will enable you to identify and learn from similar examples in your own managerial work.

You will already have noticed that one consequence of this new focus on the standards is that the traditional 'functional' packages of knowledge and theory do not appear. The standard textbook titles such as 'quantitative methods', 'production management', 'organizational behaviour' etc. disappear. Instead, principles and methods have been collected together in clusters that more closely match the key roles within the standards. You will also find a small degree of overlap in some of the volumes, because some principles and methods support several of the individual units within the standards. We hope you will find this useful reinforcement.

Having described the positive aspects of standards-based management development, it would be wrong to finish without a few cautionary remarks. The developments described above may seem simple, logical and uncontroversial. It did not always seem that way in the years of work which led up to the introduction of the standards. To revert to the revolution analogy, the process has been marked by ideological conflict and battles over sovereignty and territory. It has sometimes been unclear which side various parties are on – and indeed how many sides there are! The revolution, if well advanced, is not at an end. Guerrilla warfare continues in parts of the territory.

Perhaps the best way of describing this is to say that, while competence-based standards are widely recognized as at least a major part of the answer to improving managerial performance, they are not the whole answer. There is still some debate about the way competences are defined, and whether those in the standards are the most appropriate on which to base assessment of managerial performance. There are other models of management competences than those in the standards.

There is also a danger in separating management performance into a set of discrete components. The whole is, and needs to be, more than the sum of the parts. Just like bowling an off-break in cricket, practising a golf swing or forehand drive in tennis, you have to combine all the separate movements into a smooth, flowing action. How you combine the competences, and build on them, will mark your own individual style as a manager.

We should also be careful not to see the standards as set in stone. They determine what today's managers need to be able to do. As the arena in which managers operate changes, then so will the standards. The lesson for all of us as managers is that we need to go on learning and developing, acquiring new skills or refining existing ones. Obtaining your certificate or diploma is like passing a mile post, not crossing the finishing line.

All the changes and developments of recent years have brought management qualifications, and the processes by which they are gained, much closer to your job as a manager. We hope these books support this process by providing bridges between your own experience and the underlying principles and methods which will help you to demonstrate your competence. Already, there is a lot of evidence that managers enjoy the challenge of demonstrating competence, and find immediate benefits in their jobs from the programmes based on these new-style qualifications. We hope you do too. Good luck in your career development.

Paul Jervis

Preface

The primary aim of this book is to explain the principles involved in the management of financial resources. In parallel the book also aims to provide practising non-financial managers with an understanding of the terms and techniques of accountancy so they may communicate more easily with and understand financial reports issued by their more accounting-aware colleagues.

The book concentrates on one type of financial information – management accountancy – but draws together concepts from systems analysis, organizational behaviour, marketing and other distinct disciplines to reflect the rich variety which is involved in the management of any limited resource within large organizations. Many accountancy texts for non-financial managers, while technically superb, omit the broader contextual issues this book hopes to provide.

After many years teaching management students we were delighted to be asked by the publisher to provide a text which would reflect a broader approach to the subject of accounting. *Managing Financial Resources* provided an opportunity to share our ideas with a wider audience, using a framework which has proved robust throughout our teaching at various levels.

The book may be used in isolation as *the* course text, but we would encourage you to explore the broader literature in this area while also observing and reflecting upon the way in which financial resources are managed in your own organizations.

At the end of each chapter we have included problems and discussion topics which are highly diverse in nature and requirement. They range from open-ended case studies to problems having particular numerical answers. Suggested answers are offered at the back of the book. While these problems may provide useful areas for discussion, they may be easily supplemented by issues and examples from your own organization, thus bringing freshness and depth to your discussions with fellow students of the principles involved.

The book contains ten chapters – the role of each is explained towards the end of Chapter 1 – using a framework which provides an overview of the relationships between subject areas. Each new chapter refers back to that framework, reminding you of the interrelationships involved. In the appendices at the back of the book are extracts from the published accounts of a public limited company with an analysis of its performance using financial ratio analysis. This method of presentation allows you to read the relevant chapter without interruption, referring to the appendix for further details when required.

Several people have helped in the preparation of this book. We would like to thank the anonymous reviewers, who commented critically and helpfully on the earlier drafts. We are also grateful to Renee Hayes, Adele Bulmer, Margaret Marks and Angela Sharp who somehow converted our original manuscripts into a presentable form. We would also like to thank the authors of some of the end-of-chapter exercises.

Michael Broadbent
John Cullen

1 Introduction: The scope and development of accountancy in the management of financial resources

The aims of this chapter are to:

- Provide a working definition of accounting.
- Consider the historical development of financial accounting and management accounting.
- Compare and contrast financial and management accounting.
- Provide a framework for the study of the management of financial resources and a summary of the contents of this book.

Introduction

The management of financial resources can be considered at many different levels. At the micro level, the individual or organization is interested in how the financial resources available may be best utilized to achieve specific objectives. A 12-year-old boy may be considering the purchase of a mountain bike and how this may be best financed using the resources available: balancing income from his pocket-money, paper round and gifts to achieve the end result. Equally a large multinational or small private company will have to manage their complex financial resources – to acquire new assets, pay employees and other expenditure while providing a return on assets to the owners. At a macro level, the government is interested in the sound financial management of the economy, by adopting political policies which ensure returns to their supporters, and the nation at large. At whatever level, the basic raw material for such management is information.

The sophistication and detail of the information maintained will largely depend upon the size and complexity of the organization and on legal requirements. While the 12-year-old boy may retain details of his financial transactions within his head, as he matures he will have to record transactions and maintain records for insurance, taxation and legal reasons, to name just three. As an individual he will need to have an idea of his assets (things he owns) and his liabilities (money owed to others) so he can decide how best to finance new purchases of assets or help with his everyday budgeting. Because his financial affairs are relatively simple he is unlikely to need assistance in maintaining financial records, as decisions will be unique to him.

Any organization, whether a large multinational company or a local tennis club, will be required to maintain a set of financial records. This is because the money involved, while legally belonging to that organization, will have been loaned to or invested by individuals in it. At the annual general meeting of any organization the presentation of the annual accounts is a common feature of that meeting regardless of an organization's size. The annual accounts represent a financial summary of the transactions made by that organization during the year, known as an *income statement*, and the financial affairs at the year end, known as the *balance sheet*. The annual accounts are usually accompanied by an auditor's report which states if the financial statements presented to the meeting represent a true record.

Similarly, for a limited company, the management, usually through the board of directors, owe a duty to individuals who have either lent money to the company or bought shares in that company. In a similar manner to a tennis club, the information is summarized annually in the form of published accounts, which contain various statements of a financial nature and reports by the company auditors and directors. While legal requirements may necessitate information to be recorded, management practice also necessitates the maintenance of records.

The financial information of a small organization may be recorded primarily for legal reasons, as an organization grows in size the financial information becomes more complex, often including several tiers of management, or different branches or divisions within a company. Once professional managers are required because of an organization's size then information becomes a crucial ingredient of management practice. Records must be maintained for decision-making, planning and control purposes over and above those required by legislation.

Information exists at different levels within organizations, either within the formal administrative mechanisms or within the informal ones, it may be held within a paper filing system, a computerized file or within the minds of individual employees. This text is particularly concerned with the storage, use and interpretation of financial data with regard to the management of an organization in meeting both the objectives of that organization and its external interested parties.

Such a financial focus must be considered within the broader context of other information which is critical to understanding organizations. The storage and presentation of financial data either within organizations or about organizations is known as *accountancy*, which attempts to use a financial information system to help control and assist in the economic decision-making process relating to that organization.

Objective of accountancy

To develop an objective for accountancy by observing what accountants do would be a lengthy and time-consuming process, as they are involved in a broad range of tasks all relating to the way financial data is recorded and applied. It would be better to approach the objective by considering the output of accountants' labour, the provision of financial reports. Early ideas about the objectives of such reports concentrated on the issue of ensuring that organizational assets were correctly accounted for to the owners of that organization. However, over time the objective of finance reporting has broadened; a 1975 UK report put forward this definition:

> ...to communicate economic measurements of and information about the resources and performance of the reporting entity useful to those who have a reasonable right to such information. (Corporate Report, 1975)

While another American definition gives more idea of the processes included in such reporting:

> The process of identifying, measuring and communicating economic information to permit informed judgement and decisions by the users of the information. (AAA, 1966)

Both the above definitions provide a basis for the study of the management of financial resources either using accounting information produced for users within an organization, say a budget holder, or for accounting information prepared for external users, say shareholders or creditors. These general ideas can be applied to the two main branches of accounting, which are financial reporting and management accounting. At this stage it will be sufficient to state that financial reporting provides information to users of that information who are external to that organization, while management accounting provides information to decision-makers within that organization. Before an analysis of the different roles of these two branches of accounting is presented it may be useful to consider their recent historical development, as this will also provide a useful backdrop to other areas of study.

The following section provides a brief history of accounting, the initial part explaining the development of financial accounting and its links with company legislation, while the latter views the development of management accounting through management's requirements for information.

A recent history of accounting

The Industrial Revolution in Britain and elsewhere brought about the replacement of domestic traditional crafts with methods of production housed in large factories, which required substantial capital investment. Because of the size of funds required for this capital investment it was often the case that a large number of individuals would be required to provide the capital, as no one such individual was sufficiently wealthy. The process of bringing individuals together to invest in a single entity was legally difficult until the passing of the Joint Stock Companies Act in 1844. The *shareholders* (also called *stockholders*), or the individuals owning a share of the business, delegated the use of their money to directors and managers who were employed to run the business on their behalf. As already stated, the managers therefore owed a duty to protect the interests of their shareholders, and to operate on their behalf.

A further Act in 1855 enabled groups of individuals to form companies which had separate legal identities to their shareholders and which possessed limited liability. These two developments meant that by 1856 directors of companies owed duties of care to the shareholders who owned the business and a responsibility to meet the claims of creditors as they fell due. It was not until 1907 that companies had to file their audited balance sheet, a statement of assets and liabilities at the year end, with the Registrar of Companies, but an 1857 Act did require proper books of account to be kept, the appointment of auditors to report on the accounts and the preparation of a balance sheet for the formal annual meeting of shareholders.

The 1928 Companies Act required the presentation of an income statement known as a *profit and loss account* to shareholders, but it was not until 1948 that this statement had to be filed with the Registrar of Companies. The 1948 Act also required the audit to be carried out by professionally qualified persons rather than from the body of shareholders.

The 1967, 1981 and 1989 Companies Acts have greatly expanded the accounting disclosure requirements of registered companies and have specified how such accounts should be presented to comply with the EC Fourth and Seventh Directives. Companies must now display how profits have been calculated, including the policies adopted, and information on the valuation of the assets held within the company and presented in the balance sheet at the year end.

The accounting profession itself has introduced a system of self-regulation whereby accountants preparing financial reports for external users must adopt the Statement of Standard Accounting Practice (SSAP) as prescribed. If they fail to do so the independent auditors will qualify the audit report within the accounts indicating where such practices have been breached.

The development of financial reporting has been involved with the information requirements of external users, with legislation being particularly concerned with shareholder and creditor protection, and the content of the balance sheet, providing a statement of assets and liabilities and the profit and loss account, providing a statement of profitability. (These will be developed fully in Chapter 2.) The emphasis is very much upon asset valuation and profit calculation as both of these are important measures of financial performance by external users.

With the developments of financial accounting came those of management accounting. There is some debate whether they developed in parallel or whether management accounting was derived from the inadequacy of financial accounting information for managers' requirements. Johnson and Kaplan (1987) argue that management accounting has a long history and was not a product of financial reporting. Indeed Johnson (1972) has found evidence to suggest that sophisticated internal management accounting systems existed in some large firms as early as the mid-nineteenth century.

The traditional view of the history of management accounting is that it developed primarily for the costing and pricing of products and the valuation of assets at the year end, particularly stocks and work-in-progress. This cost accounting emphasis is rather a narrow view. While no historian is denying its existence, evidence is emerging of much broader information bases for management decision-making and their links with management accounting.

Chandler (1962, 1977) suggests that management accounting was crucial to the development of the giant firms which grew from early beginnings in the mid-nineteenth century to become very large companies by the early part of the twentieth century. Management accounting information was used not only to determine prices but to assess how different parts of the business were performing, focusing on efficiency through the use of company resources.

Other advances in company efficiency had been promoted by the engineer managers, like F.W. Taylor, who from around 1880 aimed to improve the production process by standardizing jobs and processes as much as possible, with the objective of minimizing costs.

By the early twentieth century companies like Du Pont, American Tobacco and General Electric (US) were using management accounting to assess divisional performance by adopting measures like return on capital employed and developing budgeting techniques to coordinate the flow of goods to their customers.

Even in health care Chapman (1921) recommended that:

> . . . one of the first principles of properly recording hospital finances is to set up a chart of accounts that will reflect the individual departmental performance of the various units of the hospital, so that comparable

periods may be analysed against one another, to note the performance of these periods.

While early management accounting may have a history of rapid development, in 1987 Johnson and Kaplan argued that management accounting had lost its relevance to modern day manufacturing and that the techniques and ideas developed early in the twentieth century were still being used in an unmodified form today. Subsequent chapters of this book present both traditional ideas and modern developments within management accounting, hopefully repudiating the Johnson and Kaplan argument.

It is important to stress that the historical development of management accounting is not a product of legislation or accounting standards but a dynamic process to meet the needs of managers in the tasks of decision-making and the control of operations within the firm. This distinction between financial reporting and management accounting will be emphasized in the next section.

Financial and management accounting compared

Accounting, the process of providing information to relevant users for economic decision-making, will vary in emphasis with regard to the user's needs and the regulatory framework within which it has to be presented. The information base used to prepare these different statements may be common to both management and financial accounting; it is the aggregation and emphasis placed upon the information which separates the two.

The aim of financial accounting is to provide a recording system which fulfils the requirements of the Companies Act 'to keep proper books of account' in the terminology of the 1844 act, and to use this information to produce financial reports that are published in accordance with current legislation and standards, for external users. The objective is to produce financial reports that provide reliable measures of profit and asset measurement for the period in question using historic data.

Management accounting aids management in decision-making and control within the firm; the information provided may be using historic data but the emphasis is on future (budgeted) data. The framework for presentation may be specific to particular managers as no legislative or accounting standard requirements have to be fulfilled. Table 1.1 illustrates the differences between the two.

The dominant requirements of both legislation and standards for financial reporting have meant that users' needs for specific information may be neglected. Emphasis is very much on producing data which is comparable between companies rather than being specific to any particular user requirements. Management accounting

Table 1.1 *Financial and management accounting compared*

	Financial accounting	Management accounting
Data	Historic	Future and historic
Users	External	Internal management
Decision-making	By external uses	By internal management
Cost base	Historic	Future
Legislation/standards	Yes	No
Objective	Profit and asset measurement	Aids management decision-making and control

by its very nature should meet the specific requirements of the management team and distinguishes between cost accounting and management accounting (Figure 1.1). The former considers historic (or ex post) data to cost and price products and place values on stock and work-in-progress. The latter uses historic and future (ex ante) information to provide management with a base to plan, control, coordinate, communicate and motivate others within the firm.

The two streams within management accounting can be traced back to the origins of the discipline. The cost accounting side was developed to support the requirement of financial reporting by providing valuations for stock and work-in-progress at year and period ends. The management accounting stream is part of the expertise of functional management and has developed from various disciplines. The two streams of management accounting are not obvious today, as information technology has made the costing less time-consuming freeing up management accountants to develop their advisory role to management on the financial resources within an organization.

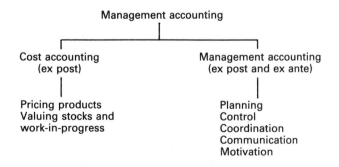

Figure 1.1 *Management accounting and cost accounting*

Public sector reporting practices

While a short summary of the historical development of accounting may be presented for the private sector, no such attempt will be made for the public sector, which includes organizations as diverse as British Rail, central government, local government, the National Health Service and the British Broadcasting Corporation. While each has to provide evidence of sound financial management to the population at large, the backgrounds of such organizations vary greatly. They are products of a variety of social, political and legal characteristics, but they all have one factor in common – their outputs are not easily measured and consequently their financial statements are mainly concerned with inputs rather than financially measurable outputs.

Public sector reporting practices were very much concerned with the recording and verification of finances rather than the internal management of financial resources. Public sector finances were managed by professionals in their fields: doctors, policeman, educationalists, etc. and the financial accountability was overseen by a treasurer; the emphasis was on financial reporting style records. In the UK since the early 1980s there has a been a dramatic change in this sector, the most visible outcome being the privatization of some large public utilities, but the services that remain within the sector have gone through a programme of change requiring value for money through measures of economy, efficiency and effectiveness. These changes have shifted the emphasis to the management of financial resources from that of recording financial transactions. The role of the accountant within the public sector is increasingly that of the management accountant.

In demonstrating the management of financial resources this book has attempted to balance ideas and issues from both the public and private sectors of our economy. In doing so, it provides insights into the way in which private sector techniques are being developed and employed within the public sector.

A framework for the study of accounting

The following framework has been developed by the authors while teaching on certificate and diploma level management programmes. It offers a sufficiently simple construct to provide a structure for the initial study of accounting, while also supplying a model to understand complex interrelationships as your studies develop. The framework is illustrated in Figure 1.2 and will be referred to again at the beginning of each new chapter. It will be useful to explain each box in the diagram in turn before considering the relationships between each one.

Most organizations are involved with the production of goods or

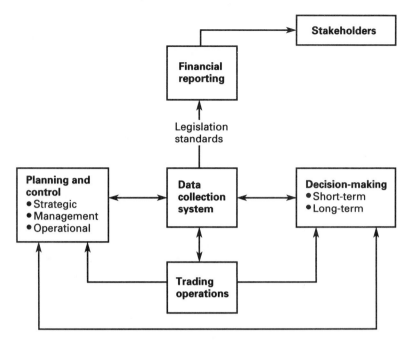

Figure 1.2 *A framework for the study of accounting and the managing of financial resources*

the delivery of a service. The method by which this is done may be highly complex, it may include several processes to complete the product, and require support activities from marketing, personnel, administration, research and development departments etc. to complete and deliver the product or service. However complex or however simple, the *trading operations* box represents the total activities of the firm.

The *data collection system* is the process whereby information about operations and anything related to them is recorded. As previously stated, this information may be formally recorded within an accounting system or management information system while some will almost invariably be held informally by managers. The accounting system will record economic transactions that have taken place to enable the operations either to be initiated for a new firm, or to continue for an existing one. The data collection system will include records of stock levels, manpower, wages and salaries, receipts from customers, payments to suppliers etc. The accounting system records such transactions through a process known as double entry book-keeping which can be traced back to the twelfth century. The data may be classified in a variety of ways, but financial accounting recognizes two types, a debit and a credit, and the logic of this process means total debit entries must equal total credit entries, hence the phrase 'balancing the books' and the 'balance sheet'.

The *financial reporting* box represents the reports prepared by financial accountants for the external stakeholders of the firm; represented by the *stakeholders* box.

The two remaining boxes *planning and control* and *decision-making*, represent the domain of management accountants, of those who provide information to management for the process of decision-making, planning and control. The techniques adopted and the information selected from the data collective system will depend on the circumstances and management requirements.

Having briefly outlined the nature of each box it would be useful to consider the constituent parts relating to financial accounting and management accounting respectively. The financial accounting route is illustrated in Figure 1.3

The operations of the business are regarded as economic transactions, recorded as such in the data collection system and summarized for presentation in the financial report for stakeholders. The data collection system is not used to provide management with information on how to manage but is seen as a legal requirement to maintain accounting records and provide information for external reporting. The stakeholders receive information in prescribed format as specified by legislation and current accounting standards.

Financial accounting will be developed in Chapter 2, when the main statements within published financial reports will be considered with regard to the users of such statements and their objectives. The main financial reports are the balance sheet and profit and loss account which are provided annually by companies. Chapter 3 will

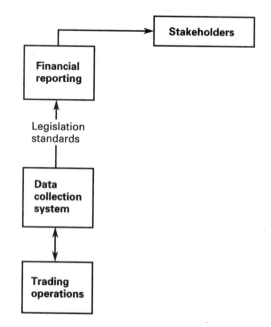

Figure 1.3 *Financial accounting*

analyse the information contained within the published financial reports to develop ratios which may be used to compare the performance of companies, in a similar manner to the methods of financial analysis used within the City of London.

Extracts from the published accounts of a quoted limited company are presented in Appendix B, with a full ratio analysis, for those interested in such detail.

The management accounting route is presented in Figure 1.4. This process is more complex as it includes the accountant's contribution to the management process within the firm, whose objective, in a profit-seeking company, is to provide a level of profit or return measured by the financial reporting route, that is considered adequate by the stakeholders investing in the business. The process within the firm includes techniques and procedures which have been developed and modified over long periods of time. In fact, as management techniques and styles have developed so too has the contribution that management accountants could be asked to make to the management process. These developments within management have come from a variety of sources; for example, economics has contributed ideas about investment in assets, sociology has made managers view their relationships with employees and among employees change, operational research has provided mathematical techniques to help the scheduling of work, computer science has assisted in the way information is processed and stored. The list could go on, but it is these highly diverse contributions to management that make the task of managing so challenging.

To return to the management accounting route, the main boxes are planning and control and decision-making. These two are very much part of the same process as any decision must involve planning the consequences of such a decision, and then controlling or monitoring the developments from that decision against the plan devised. Within this text the decision-making and planning and control aspects will be separated for ease of understanding, as the techniques within each part can be quite complex.

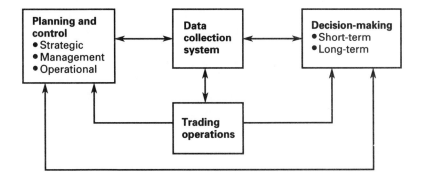

Figure 1.4 *The management accounting route*

Chapter 4 will consider the way the data collection system can contribute to management decision-making, planning and control. Within this chapter the nature of cost within an organization will be analysed and developed to provide a basis for subsequent chapters.

Chapter 5 will develop the ideas of planning and control through traditional concepts of budgets and budgeting control, developed from a general model of control. The text will then consider more technical aspects of control in Chapter 6, with the introduction of standard costing which can be traced back to the engineer-managers of the late nineteenth century.

Chapter 7 develops ideas of decision-making for short-term decision-making. It introduces techniques about cost behaviour first developed in Chapter 4, and applies them to a variety of situations. Chapter 8 also looks at decision-making, but for long-term projects, and applies techniques from economics to the management of financial resources. Because such a process relies heavily upon future estimates then it is useful to consider risk and uncertainty within the decision-making process for these longer-term decisions.

Chapter 9 develops ideas presented from the decision-making process, and aspects of Chapter 4, about cost classifications to apply to the pricing decision within the firm. Quite clearly such a process will have to consider not only the financial resource implication of such a decision but also the marketing impacts, as price is only one variable within the marketing mix.

The final chapter will bring together all the issues raised in the text to consider broad issues of performance appraisal for the firm as a whole, using ideas from Chapters 2 and 3, external reporting and assessment of company performance, and the management accounting techniques introduced in subsequent chapters. This chapter will also consider performance of different parts of a firm and develop concepts that may be useful to monitor and control activities which may be highly diverse, and which may have conflicting objectives and interests both in the long and short term.

The balance of the chapters between financial accounting and management accounting is deliberate. The emphasis of this book is very much on the management of financial resources. While an understanding of the financial reporting practices to external stockholders, presented in Chapters 2 and 3, is essential, it is the internal management process which warrants the greater emphasis. As managers, or potential managers yourselves, it is useful to understand published financial reports, but not the complex accounting process which aggregates data to produce them. It is more important for you to understand the internal management process and how management accounting may aid you in the provision of efficient and effective management, hence the seven chapters devoted to this area of study.

Throughout the text we must always remember that information is the resource to be managed and nurtured − without it the management process would collapse. The management of financial resources must use information to provide a mechanism for enabling this process to be carried out effectively and efficiently, but good decision-making and control must not rely exclusively on financial information, but must be seen in the broad context of management.

The decision-making and control process may be considered as a rational process, which naturally flows from objective-setting, through choices between alternatives, and the measurement of outcomes against those envisaged in the objectives. A fuller version of this is given in Figure 1.5.

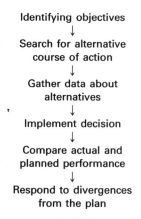

Identifying objectives
↓
Search for alternative
course of action
↓
Gather data about
alternatives
↓
Implement decision
↓
Compare actual and
planned performance
↓
Respond to divergences
from the plan

Figure 1.5 *The decision-making and control process*

While individual stages of such a process may be hard to recognize within organizations, nevertheless they will be present in some form or another. Because financial resources are so critical to the well-being of an organization, such decision processes may be more obvious within the management of such resources, particularly within profit-seeking organizations whose objectives are much clearer than those of their not-for-profit counterparts.

Summary

Accounting has been defined as:

> The process of identifying, measuring and communicating economic information to permit informed judgements and decision by users of information. (AAA, 1966)

It is clearly to this subject area the management of financial resources must turn, but in doing so, it not only provides opportunities it also provides problems. Accountancy like any profession has its own vocabulary; the terminology and expressions used are particular to the subject. This immediately creates problems of interpretation and understanding. This text aims to provide you with a basis not only for understanding the techniques and terminologies but also to provide a vehicle that will aid the communication process between managers and accountants. All are in the same game, the management of an enterprise, whether it is using manpower, machines or financial resources.

This introductory chapter has provided a framework from which to proceed with your studies on the management of financial resources. It has drawn heavily from ideas put forward by the accounting literature.

After reading this chapter you should be able to:

- Define accounting.
- Understand the brief history of accounting.
- Compare and contrast the differences between financial and management accounting.

References

AAA (American Accounting Association) (1966) *A Statement of Basic Accounting Theory*, AAA, Sarasota, Fla

AAA (American Accounting Association) (1975) Report of the Committee on Concepts and Standards for External Financial Reports, *Accounting Review Supplement*, **XLX**

Chandler, A.D. (1962) *Strategy and Structure*, MIT Press, Boston, Mass.

Chandler, A.D. (1977) The *Visible Hand: The Managerial Revolution in American Business*, Harvard Business Press, Cambridge, Mass.

Chapman, F.E. (1921) Hospital accounting as basis for hospital analysis. *Modern Hospital*

Corporate Report (1975) Accounting Standards Steering Committee, London

Johnson, H.T. (1972) Early cost accounting for internal management control: Lyman Mills in the 1850s. *Business History Review*, Winter

Johnson, H.T. and Kaplan, R.S. (1987) *Relevance Lost: The Rise and Fall of Management Accounting*, Harvard Business Press, Cambridge, Mass.

Further reading

Arnold, J. and Hope, T. (1990) *Accounting for Management Decisions*, 2nd edn, Prentice Hall, Englewood Cliffs, NJ, Chapters 1, 2

Glautier, M.W.E. and Underdown, B. (1991) *Accounting Theory and Practice*, 4th edn, Pitman, London, Chapters 1, 2 and 3

Jones, R. and Pendlebury, M. (1992) *Public Sector Accounting*, 3rd edn, Pitman, London, Chapters 1 and 2

Problems and discussion topics

1 The following is an extract from the published Annual Accounts of the International Food, Drink and Leisure Group.

> We continue to develop our strength in the marketplace through the ownership of leading international brands, creativity in new product development, skilful retailing and innovative hospitality concepts.

CORPORATE OBJECTIVES

- To provide our shareholders with above-average returns from our core activities by building upon our long-term record of growth in profits, earnings-per-share and dividends.
- To satisfy the existing and emerging requirements of our world-wide customers and consumers by providing high quality goods, services and hospitality.
- To ensure a good work environment for our employees avoiding unfair discrimination, recognizing their contributions and encouraging their initiative.
- To enrich the community, principally through our capacity to create wealth but also through selective direct support of enterprise, education and charities.
- To conduct our business with due consideration of its impact upon the environment.

Do you consider these objectives compatible with one another and how might that company communicate the success of achieving these objectives to its stakeholders?

2 Either for the organization where you work, or an organization that you are familiar with, obtain the published Annual Report and answer the following questions after familiarizing yourself with its contents.

(a) In what ways do you find the information contained to be useful to you as an employee or interested party?
(b) What additional information would you find useful to be included?

3 Either for an organization where you work or an organization that you are familiar with, consider the following.

> How does accounting affect the way you do your job, and does this have positive or negative benefits for you as an individual and for the organization as a whole?

2 External financial reporting: Published company accounting statements

The aims of this chapter are to:

- Outline the users of published accounting information.
- Provide an understanding of the major accounting statements published by companies – the balance sheet, the profit and loss account and the cash flow statement (the latter replacing the fund flow statement from 1992 onwards).
- Illustrate the concepts and conventions adopted in preparing published accounting information.

Introduction

The recording of financial information within an enterprise is a natural part of good business practice. The enterprise may be a charity, a local authority, a sports and social club or a multinational business. Regardless of its objective, size and legal structure management must ensure the financial transactions of that enterprise are duly recorded. Company legislation requires directors of companies to maintain books of accounts and to report on the activities of that company on an annual basis through a published statement known as the *annual report and accounts*. Company legislation has been supplemented by accounting standards (SSAPs) which provide quite detailed rules and procedures of how the accounting statements within such documents are to be presented and what specific information is required to be disclosed within them.

Figure 2.1 illustrates the flow of information from operations through the data collection system or the financial books of account in this case, and how this information is refined for the requirements of legislation and accounting standards into the published *external financial reports*. These are provided annually for the organization's stakeholders, who may be defined narrowly as creditors and shareholders for companies, or broadly as any interested or potentially interested party in the organization.

The way financial transactions are collected, recorded and stored

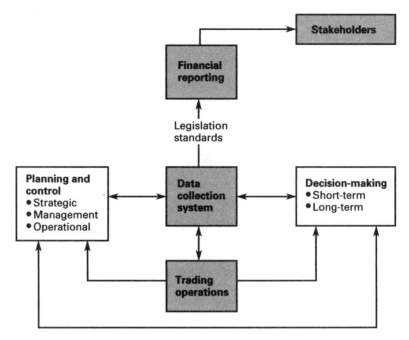

Figure 2.1 *External reporting*

within the data collection system is known as *double entry book-keeping*. This process recognizes the dual aspect of any transaction by utilizing debit entries for assets and expenses and credit entries for liabilities, equity and income. It also ensures that aggregate amounts recorded as debits exactly equal aggregate amounts recorded as credits – the balancing of the books. The detail of this process is not relevant to this text, but it is sufficient to say that the book-keeping system is capable of handling all the financial transactions of an enterprise.

The process by which the books of account within the data collection system are converted into external financial reports is a product of the concepts and conventions of accounting which have been developed in a pragmatic way and which are now included within Company Law. The annual report and accounts for companies provide three basic statements of a financial nature for each year. They are:

- Balance sheet at the year end
- Profit and loss account for the period
- Cash flow statements for the period

with supporting notes and schedules.

Each of the above has particular requirements for presentation and it is the aim of this chapter to understand the layout and nature of such statements, the users or stakeholders who might find such statements useful, and the underlying rules which govern the particular way such statements are prepared and presented.

In addition to the three accounting statements outlined above, the annual report and accounts must also contain a *director's report* and an *auditor's report*, while most also contain the optional *chairman's report*.

Users of financial published reports included within the annual report and accounts

Chapter 1 showed how the legal emphasis for providing financial information about a company was biased towards the shareholders and creditors, which is a narrow interpretation of stakeholders. Shareholders need this information to ensure managers are acting in the best interests of the shareholders and protecting their investment within the company. Creditors require such information because companies, being separate legal entities, have 'limited liability' for their debts, so necessitating creditors to seek periodic information about the solvency of the company. Company legislation has traditionally sought to protect the interests of these two user groups, while in the modern commercial environment other broader user groups may also require periodic information.

This broader approach to users was adopted by the Corporate Report (1975), which took the view that financial reports should recognize a responsibility not only to users who are recognized by the legal requirements but to those groups 'who have a reasonable right to information' where the activities of an organization impinge or may impinge on the interests of that user group. The Corporate Report then went on to list seven such groups which ought to be considered when preparing the general purpose external published financial reports.

Chapter 1 did not clearly specify the objectives of each external user; this was deliberate as the aims and objectives of such users may be highly varied. Employees may wish to know the level of profit for wage bargaining purposes, while the Inland Revenue may use the same figure for taxation computations. External financial reports are prepared and presented adopting the notion that generalist information may be useful to most users. This is known as the data orientation approach. While management accountants producing internal information can easily ask fellow managers what information they specifically require to base economic decisions upon; this is known as the decision-maker's approach. A switch from data orientation to a decision-maker's approach for external reporting would be impossible, for the host of external users who 'might have a reasonable right' to information each has a slightly different objective in mind, consequently the general statement.

The stated objective of financial reporting was to aid economic decision-making. So, as each user group is considered in turn a list of decisions relevant to them is included to provide an idea of why the Corporate Report (1975) considered such groups worthy of inclusion. A summary is presented in Table 2.1 after each group has been considered in detail.

User groups specified by the Corporate Report are:

1 Existing and potential shareholders
2 Existing and potential creditors
3 Employees
4 Analyst-advisers
5 Business contacts
6 Government
7 The general public

1 *Existing and potential shareholders* Information is required by existing shareholders to help make decisions involving the retention or disposal of their shareholdings, while potential shareholders will require information to aid in the decision to acquire shares in that particular company. Such information should be comparable from company to company, so this group can analyse the performance of any company's management team with that of another. The information required will relate to past profits and dividend levels which may give an indication of future returns. The published report and accounts is only one information source for this group, there are others which are more informative and timely for the decisions they may need to make. In particular, share prices are quoted daily in good newspapers as is detailed comment on company performances and prospects. The annual report and accounts only provides a guide to past performance; the decision whether to hold, buy or sell a share very much depends on its current price relative to the expected future returns from any particular company when compared to similar returns at a comparable risk level.

The information within the published accounts is a product of legislation which requires management to account for the company's assets and performance each year to its owners. It is not particularly relevant for decisions regarding the trading of shares.

2 *Existing and potential creditors* This group includes those who have made or may make long-term or short-term loans to the company, and those who are owed money by the company in the normal course of trade, by supplying goods and services on credit to the company.

Long-term creditors will be considering the security of their loan to the company and the potential of the company to service the loans, that is, meet interest payments when they fall due; and repay the loan at the due date. Such creditors will be concerned with the long-term viability of the company for the repayment in the longer term and current performance and liquidity for the ability to pay the interest charges. The greatest threat to such creditors is failure of the company, as the nature of limited liability may mean the loan is not repaid in full.

Short-term creditors, either loan or trade, are concerned with the ability of the company to repay that debt and the likelihood of future business.

In Chapter 3, on ratio analysis, we will be considering the usefulness of the annual report and accounts to establish confidence for those user groups by considering such issues as the way in which the company is financed and the share of profit available for this group through interest payments.

3 *Employees*　Such a group is concerned with security of employment, future job prospects and the ability to pay wages and salaries. The published accounts do not really provide useful data to meet these requirements, as the information is presented in aggregate for the whole company, while such information may be more useful on a plant by plant basis. However, company profitability in its aggregate form may be useful for collective bargaining purposes.

4 *Analysts and advisers*　This group is highly varied in nature: it includes stockbrokers, pension fund investment managers and city analysts. All are providing a service directly to their clients about the investment in a particular company or indirectly through the press to advise the general public on investment matters. Such a group should have considerable skill in reading and understanding the published annual report and accounts and therefore should be capable of meeting their clients' specific needs, or advising in a general way.

It is argued, that the existence of such a group of experts reading the accounts and commenting upon the performance of any company aids the flow of information to less sophisticated stakeholders and, therefore, provides the market for shares with a sound information base upon which investors can make informed judgements.

5 *Business contacts*　This is a very broad group including suppliers, customers, competitors and potential predators who may be considering the acquisition of the company from its current shareholders.

Suppliers will be looking for continuing and increasing trade with the company, subject to the ability to pay, while customers will wish to be assured of the continuation of supply at existing levels or at increased levels if they wish to expand.

The latter two parties in this group, competitors and potential predators, will be looking at the published annual report and accounts for very different reasons: they will be attempting to use this information for their own advantage, which may be to the detriment of the company. While the disclosure of financial information may provide a basis for further investigation by such parties, it will not, in itself, provide sound evidence for action.

6 *Government* This user has many interests in any particular organization and the corporate sector in particular. Various local and central government departments will want to ensure each company is complying with current legislation, in the form of corporation tax, value added tax, training programmes, contracts of employment, pollution control etc.

The financial information produced by companies is used particularly for assessing taxation levels on company profits.

7 *The general public* Again this is a very broad user group. It has status because companies are using resources from the community in the form of materials, manpower, energy etc., and using the economic infrastructure of the nation to supply goods and services. It is only reasonable for such a group to have access to information which measures the efficiency of an organization in using these resources.

It is quite interesting that the seven user groups specified by the Corporate Report fail to include company management. This is quite deliberate as it is argued that such a group will have detailed knowledge of the activities, financing and performance of a company from internal sources, the aggregate nature of the published accounts will add nothing to their knowledge.

Having considered the seven groups and their areas of interest it is not surprising to conclude that the published report and accounts of companies are attempting to be all-purpose documents that meet the differing needs of specific user groups. In reality the reports are not designed for any particular users' specific needs but simply provide data which is required by legislation and accounting standards, augmented by additional information which the company decides to make available, hence the data orientation approach. In terms of the Corporate Report, current published accounts may fall short of meeting the needs of the users specified.

The Corporate Report in listing the users also suggested the enlargement of company accounts to include the following additional statements:

1 A statement of value added.
2 An employment report.
3 A statement of money exchange with the government.
4 A statement of transactions in foreign currency.
5 A statement of future prospects.
6 A statement of corporate objectives.

The recommendations for these additional statements have not been

Table 2.1 *User groups and their areas of interest*

1 *Existing and potential shareholders*
   (a) whether to buy or sell shares
   (b) whether to buy a new issue of shares (e.g. a flotation or rights issue)
   (c) how to vote in a takeover or merger
   (d) how to vote at the annual general meeting
   (e) current and future dividend levels and ability to pay
   (f) how share price has moved/will move
   (g) how shares compare with alternative investments
   (h) management efficiency (stewardship)
   (i) future prospects (for income and capital growth)

2 *Existing and potential creditors* (including a lending bank)
   (a) security available and the way money is used
   (b) overall levels of borrowing (capital gearing)
   (c) ability to meet interest payments in cash
   (d) buy or sell long-term loans at the right price
   (e) ability to meet loan repayment in cash

3 *Employees*
   (a) security of employment
   (b) future job prospects
   (c) ability to pay wages
   (d) collective bargaining power
        (i) wage settlement
        (ii) terms of employment
   (e) overall performance
   (f) management efficiency
   (g) profits; bonuses; share schemes

4 *Analysts and advisers*
   (a) stockbrokers − who advise investors
   (b) credit rating agencies − who advise potential creditors
   (c) journalists − who inform the reading public
   (d) trade unionists − who advise employees

5 *Business contacts*
   (a) suppliers − ability to pay debts; value as a long-term customer
   (b) customers − deliver goods; maintain after sales service
   (c) competitors − profit margins; future developments (new operating
        sites, research and development, diversification); 'trade secrets'
   (d) another company planning a takeover or merger − similar interest to
        shareholders; past record and style of operation

6 *Government*
   (a) as a creditor
   (b) as a customer
   (c) as a custodian of public money and the public interest at both national
        and local levels

Table 2.1 *Continued*

(d) contribution of company to economic well-being, employment, exports etc.
(e) ability to pay taxes (VAT, excise duties, PAYE, NI, corporation tax, capital taxes, rates etc.)
(f) compliance with taxation and company laws
(g) statistical information (production, sales, employment, investment, imports/exports, political and charitable donations, research etc.)

7 *The general public* (taxpayers, consumers, political groups, environmentalists etc.)
(a) role as employer
(b) role in local economy
(c) discharge of social responsibilities
(d) attitude to environmental policies
(e) contribution to national wealth

consolidated into legislation, consequently companies can choose on an individual basis if they wish to supply such statements. The majority do not, consequently financial reporting is highly dependent on the traditional statements of the balance sheet, profit and loss account and cash flow statements (replacing the fund flow statement from 1992 onwards), to which we now turn.

Principal accounting statements

It is not the purpose of this text to provide its readers with the detailed methodology of recording financial transactions within the books of account, but to provide an understanding of the principal financial statements presented within the annual report and accounts. The principal statements are:

- Balance sheet
- Profit and loss account
- Cash flow statement

Balance sheet

This provides a summary of the assets owned by a company at a point in time, usually the year end, and the claims against those assets. As a company has a separate legal entity it is simple to visualize it owning assets, but at the same time recognizing that the company and its assets are owned by its shareholders in the form of equity capital. So, for a company having no borrowings or liabilities to creditors, the balance sheet would be simple:

$$\text{Assets} = \text{Equity capital}$$

If the company borrowed funds or bought goods on credit, it would be liable to repay these amounts in future. Hence claims to outsiders, that is other than shareholders, are known as liabilities. The balance sheet equation therefore becomes more complex:

$$\text{Assets} = \text{Equity capital} + \text{Liabilities}$$

A simple balance sheet is shown below for a newly formed company.

Simple balance sheet for the Abel Company Ltd

	£
Assets	
Freehold property	61,500
Plant and equipment	5,700
Stock	6,500
Cash at bank	1,300
	75,000
Equity capital	
60,000 £1 shares	60,000
Liabilities	
Bank loan	15,000
	75,000

There is an infuriating logic about balance sheets – they always balance. This is because of the double entry book-keeping process by which financial accounting records transactions, a process designed to maintain the balances of the balance sheet.

If the Abel Company bought further stock for £600 in cash, two things would happen: the stock would rise to £7,100 (£6,500 + £600) and the cash at bank would fall to £700 (£1300 – £600). The balance sheet would maintain its equilibrium.

	£	Adjustment	£
Freehold property	61,500		61,500
Plant and equipment	5,700		5,700
Stock	6,500	+ 600	7,100
Cash at bank	1,300	– 600	700
	75,000		75,000
60,000 £1 shares	60,000		60,000
Bank loan	15,000		15,000
	75,000		75,000

Had the stock been acquired on credit, then the cash would be unaffected but another liability would be created to record the indebtedness to the supplier. The stock figure would rise as before. So the balance sheet this time would look like this, again maintaining its equilibrium:

	£	Adjustment	£
Freehold property	61,500		61,500
Plant and equipment	5,700		5,700
Stock	6,500	+ 600	7,100
Cash at bank	1,300		1,300
	75,000		75,600
60,000 £1 shares	60,000		60,000
Bank loan	15,000		15,000
Creditors	nil	+ 600	600
	75,000		75,600

Similarly, if the company sold its entire stock of £7,100 for £10,100, so making a profit of £3,000, and the customer promised to pay in 10 days the balance sheet after the transaction would look like this, again maintaining its equilibrium:

	£	Adjustment	£
Freehold property	61,500		61,500
Plant and equipment	5,700		5,700
Stock	7,100	− 7,100	nil
Debtors	nil	+ 10,100	10,100
Cash at bank	1,300		1,300
	75,600		78,600
60,000 £1 shares	60,000		60,000
Profit to date	nil	+ 3,000	3,000
Bank loan	15,000		15,000
Creditors	600		600
	75,600		78,600

Quite clearly the recording of each transaction by amending the balance sheet for each financial event is going to be highly repetitive and time consuming, consequently the transactions are separated into the groupings already mentioned: assets, liabilities, equity, expenses and income. The first three, assets, liabilities and equity, comprise balance items, while the latter, expenses and income, can be netted off against one another to produce a profit or loss for the period.

The balance sheet is an accounting statement showing the financial position of a business at a particular point in time. It shows the source of the money (the liabilities and equity) and what the business owns (assets) at a single point in time, for example at the close of business on 31 December 1992. The assets are usually subdivided into fixed assets, these being held by the business for more than a year, and current assets, those which are constantly changing and only held in the business for less than a year. The fixed assets usually comprise of land, buildings, plant and equipment etc., while current assets are such items as stock (inventory), debtors, bank balance and cash.

Just as assets are divided between fixed and current on the basis of length of holding, usually one year, then liabilities are divided into long-term, amounts owing for longer than one year, and current liabilities, those items which will be paid during the current year.

A simplified balance sheet for the Abel Company Ltd as at the end of this period is presented below.

	£	£
Assets		
Fixed	67,200	
Current	11,400	78,600
Equity		
Share capital and		
retained profits	63,000	
Liabilities		
Long-term	15,000	
Current	600	78,600

It follows the balance sheet formula presented earlier but now has sub-classification of items. The original formula:

Assets = Equity capital + Liabilities

can now be expressed in greater detail as:

Fixed assets (FA) + Current assets (CA) = Equity capital (E) + Long-term liabilities (LTL) + Current liabilities (CL)

or, in short form:

FA + CA = E + LTL + CL

Current liabilities (CL) are conventionally deducted from current assets (CA); together they represent the funds available to finance the current, day-to-day, activities of the business. The resulting figure is known as working capital (WC):

Current assets (CA) − Current liabilities (CL) =
Working capital (WC)

So returning to the equation above, it now becomes:

Fixed assets (FA) + Working capital (WC)
= Equity capital (E) + Long-term liabilities (LTL)

or, in short form:

FA + WC = E + LTL

This is one of the popular presentations used for published company balance sheets. The other moves long-term liabilities to the other side of the equation:

FA + WC − LTL = E

The latter stressing the ownership concept of shareholders through their equity claim.

The balance sheets of the Abel Company Ltd would then become:

	£
Fixed assets	67,200
Working capital	10,800
	78,000
less Long-term liabilities	15,000
	63,000
Equity − share capital	
and retained profits	63,000

Profit and loss account

This statement brings together the expenses and income from the data collection system to provide an accounting statement showing the profit earned or loss incurred by a business during a specific period of time.

The recording and logic behind such a statement is that:

Income − Expenses = Profit

The profit adds to the wealth of the business and is therefore reflected in an increase in equity which may be paid out as a cash dividend or retained in the business increasing the equity part of the balance sheet by adding to retained profits.

The way in which a profit and loss account for a particular period should be presented is specified in the Companies Act and follows the following layout:

Profit and Loss Account for the year ended 31.12.92 for Bethsa plc

	£m
Turnover (sales)	1,590
less Cost of sales (cost of goods sold)	1,315
Gross profit	275
less Other expenses	46
Profit before interest and taxes (operating profit)	229
less Interest charges	18
Profit before tax	211
less Taxation	72
Profit after tax (available for distribution)	139
less Dividends	47
Net increase in retained profits	92
Retained profits at 31.12.91	216
Retained profits at 31.12.92	308

In preparing a profit and loss statement it is important to 'match' the items of income (in this case turnover or sales) with the costs used up (expenses) which generated that income. Quite complex rules are necessary to ensure the income and expenses of one year are accounted for in the profit and loss of that year, rather than the year after or before. It is essential that a full year's income is matched with a full year's expenses to provide a realistic time-based measure of profits; quite clearly 53 weeks of income and 52 weeks of expenses would give a misleading picture of profitability.

In the profit and loss account presented above the income figure is represented by the *turnover* or *sales* figure. That is the value of goods sold or services provided in that period which have been invoiced; it is not the amount of money received from sales or services in that year. By adopting this approach the profit and loss account may be accounting for sales which are not paid for at the year end, but it is assumed payment will be made by those credit customers in the near future. Invoices sent to customers and remaining unpaid are known as *debtors* and appear in the year end balance sheet as current assets.

The remainder of the profit and loss account itemizes expenses by type; this assists the user of the accounting statement to compare expenses incurred by this company with other companies and provides a level of detail which may give an insight into the management of the company.

The first type of expense is *cost of goods sold*, which is the value of

items which have been inputs in creating the goods sold or services
provided during the year. For a retailer costs of sales would include
the cost price of the goods sold during the year, while for a manufacturer it would include the raw materials used up, the labour cost
and the manufacturing cost of these sales. The cost of goods sold
must be 'matched' with the turnover (sales) figure to include only
those costs which relate to that turnover. For example, a retailer may
have an opening stock of goods at the beginning of the year, made
purchases throughout the year, and be left with a closing stock of
goods at the year end. It is important that the costs are matched
with turnover to give a figure for 'cost of goods sold'. The turnover
(sales) in the year may include goods purchased in that year and
goods purchased in the previous year but unsold at the start of the
year (opening stock), but cannot include the closing stock as this
remains in the business at the year end, and cannot be an expense
of generating that turnover. The closing stock may well be sold in
the following year and become an expense of that year to be matched
against the turnover of the next year. A simple illustration may
help, which relates to Bethsa plc:

	£m	£m
Turnover (sales) during the year		1,590
Purchases during the year		1,190
Opening stock at beginning of year		345
Closing stock at year end		220

Would be reported as:

	£m	£m
Turnover		1,590
less cost of goods sold:		
Opening stock	345	
Purchases	1,190	
	1,535	
less closing stock	220	1,315
Gross profit		275

This adjustment for opening and closing stocks explains the necessity
of stock-taking procedures at the year end, which should ensure the
matching of turnover and cost of goods sold is consistent each year.
The closing stock figure would be reported in the balance sheet at
the year end as a current asset, while the opening stock would have
been taken from the previous year's closing balance sheet.

The *other expenses* are much easier to explain, as the matching
process is largely done using the calendar to decide which expenses
are relevant to a particular year − 12 months' turnover must be
matched with 12 months' expenses. If an expense has only had a

cash outlay relating to 9 months of the year, then an estimate must be made of the remaining 3 months unpaid and included in the profit and loss account to give a 12-month charge. Equally, expenses relating to the following year paid in advance must be excluded from the current profit and loss account.

'Other expenses' include such items as rent, rates, electricity, selling and distribution expenses, administrative expenses etc. Unlike cost of goods sold these expenses do not relate directly to the inputs obviously creating the goods sold but are more related to the expenses required to provide an infrastructure in which such trading can proceed.

The *operating profit* (or profit before interest and taxes) provides a measure of the efficiency of the company. It compares inputs (expenses) and outputs (turnover) which can be presented as a ratio. This idea of measuring efficiency through ratio analysis will be developed in Chapter 3.

Interest charges are the specific expense related to how the business was financed, interest being the annual expense of having liabilities which are interest-bearing, like bank loans, debentures and the like.

Taxation is the Inland Revenue's charge for the year. The level will vary with profits earned, capital investment policies, dividend policy etc. The taxable profit figure when computed is likely to be different from that stated in the profit and loss account as the Inland Revenue has a series of rules which provide allowances and charges for different expense items. While corporation tax is currently at 33%, the taxation figure is unlikely to be exactly 33% of profit before taxation.

Once taxation has been charged, the remaining profit is available to shareholders, either to be paid as a dividend or retained within the business for future expansion.

Cash flow statement

This statement replaces the fund flow statement from 1992 onwards and provides a different view of the activities of the business from that revealed by the balance sheet and profit and loss account. The view adopted asks two basic questions:

How did the business generate cash?
Where did the cash go?

In answering these questions the statement does not need to consider the matching problem associated with the balance sheet and profit and loss account, it is simply an analysis of cash in and cash out.

The cash flow statement lists the inflows and outflows of cash for the period under the following headings:

● Operating activities

- Returns on investments and servicing of finance
- Taxation
- Investing activities
- Financing activities

and this results in the change in cash balance for the year. The reason such a format was introduced was to provide information not supplied on the other two statements so assisting users of financial statements to make judgements on the relationship between profit and cash flows for a particular business.

Cash from *operating activities* are the net cash effects of operating or trading activities and represent the net increase or decrease in cash resulting from operations shown in the profit and loss account. Quite clearly such flows should be positive if the business is generating sufficient cash to continue trading.

Returns on investments and *servicing of finance* are the receipts of cash resulting from the ownership of an investment, while the cash outflows represent the payments to providers of finance to the business. The cash inflows will include interest and dividends received while the outflows will include interest and dividends paid.

The cash flow relating to *taxation* will be the cash inflows and outflows relating to transactions with the Inland Revenue.

Cash flows from *investing activities* will relate to the disposal and acquisition of fixed assets including investments in subsidiary companies.

The cash flows relating to *financing activities* summarize the receipts from and repayments to external providers of finance. Receipts will include the cash from issuing shares and loans, while the payments will relate to the repayment of loans and the purchase and cancellation of shares.

The decrease or increase in cash or cash equivalents for the year is simply the difference between cash resources at the beginning of the year compared to those at the end.

A detailed cash flow statement is presented below.

Cash flow statement for the year ended 31.3.1992 for Cathod plc

Operating activities	£m	£m
Cash flow from customers		2,059.8
Cash payments to suppliers	(1,037.4)	
Cash payments to employees	(433.8)	
Other cash payments	(247.5)	1718.7
Net cash flow from operations		341.1
Returns on investments and servicing finance		
Interest received	18.9	
Interest paid	(59.2)	
Dividends received from associated companies	19.6	
Dividends paid	(72.7)	

Net cash outflow from return on investments and servicing of finance		(93.4)
Taxation paid		(59.0)
Investing activities		
Purchase of tangible fixed assets	(343.9)	
Purchase of subsidiaries	(131.0)	
Sale of tangible fixed assets	118.8	
Sale of trade investments	9.3	
Net cash outflow from investing activities		(346.8)
Net cash outflow before financing		(158.1)
Financing activities		
Issue of ordinary share capital	(11.6)	
Issue of loan capital	(164.7)	
New short-term loans	(9.7)	
Loan capital repaid	32.6	
Net cash flow from financing activities		(153.4)
Decrease in cash or cash equivalents		(4.7)
		(158.1)

Note: Comparable year's figures are not presented

Having considered the three main accounting statements we turn to the underlying concepts and conventions adopted in their preparation.

A detailed presentation of the accounts of W.H. Smith is represented in Appendix B. However, copies of other companies' published annual reports are available in libraries and are well worth reading to acquaint yourselves with such statements.

Accounting concepts and conventions

The users of published accounting information are highly varied, each requiring slightly different information about a company. We have already seen that accounting statements may only meet general needs, rather than the specific needs of each individual user group. We have also considered an outline of the development of accounting reporting practices and the way in which accounting has developed in a practical way since before the Industrial Revolution. This section links these two themes by introducing a set of rules upon which users can rely through the adoption of 'good practice' by accountants over time.

The rules adopted, known as concepts and conventions, still allow accountants to have freedom as to which rules to adopt and how they should be interpreted. While Statements of Standard Accounting Practice (1971 to 1991), Financial Reporting Standards (1991 onwards) and the Companies Acts do restrict the freedom of choice they still allow some flexibility, so that accounting information does not become so highly regulated that it cannot develop and evolve to meet new practices and requirements of users.

A framework of concepts and conventions

Concepts may be thought of as the basic 'rules upon which accounting is based', while conventions are of a more ethical nature. If concepts are thought of as the rules that provide a framework for the game, then conventions can be considered to be the issues that govern how the rules are interpreted.

Quite clearly both concepts and conventions are important in the game of financial reporting; the audience (users) must understand the rules and the interpretation of them if they are to understand and enjoy the game.

Glautier and Underdown (1991) suggest that accounting concepts can be thought of as filters restricting the data into and out of the accounting process, while conventions determine how that data may be viewed. Figure 2.2 demonstrates this approach by using the filters to select which data is allowed into the accounting process and then again for the data which is published in the form of annual reports to users.

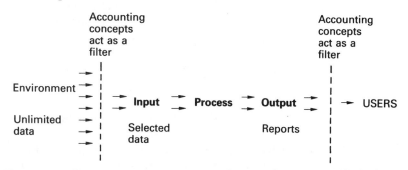

Figure 2.2 *Concepts as filters for data. Source: Glautier and Underdown, 1991*

The following framework proposed by Dyson (1991) for the study of the concepts and conventions of accounting may not be universally adopted but does provide a structure which may assist in the process of understanding the issues involved.

Dyson classifies the concepts and conventions of accounting as follows:

What should be recorded   – entity
     – periodicity
     – going concern/continuity

How it should be recorded	– money measurement
	– historic costs
	– realization
	– accruals/matching
	– duality
How the concepts should be followed (the conventions)	– prudence/conservatism
	– consistency
	– objectivity

The four fundamental concepts laid down in Standard Statement of Accounting Practice Number 2 (SSAP2) are going concern/continuity, accruals/matching, prudence/conservatism and consistency, and must be adopted by the preparers of accounts, unless a clear indication is otherwise given.

What should be recorded?

These rules deal with the amount and type of information that users may require, and specifically deal with what should be recorded.

Entity concept

This is the practice of distinguishing the affairs of the business from the personal affairs of its owner(s), in that the financial transactions of a business are completely separate from those of its owner(s). In a limited company the distinction between the business and its owners should be fairly obvious, but in the case of a sole trader or partnership confusion may arise because such enterprises have no separate legal identity from their owners, and are known as *unincorporated businesses*.

The origin of this rule can be traced back to the fifteenth century where wealthy individuals employed managers, or stewards, to run a business or manage an estate on their behalf. The stewards then had to account for the funds granted to the business or estate by its owner by preparing statements which provided evidence that the assets and any extra wealth generated had been safeguarded for the owner. Such a statement is the forerunner of the modern balance sheet which states that the business is liable to repay the assets of the business to its owner.

A simple example would be Mr Jones trading as a butcher. The balance sheet of Mr Jones the butcher would only include the business assets and liabilities of that enterprise, and the profit and loss account of Mr Jones the butcher would only relate to the income and expenses of that enterprise. Household purchases made by Mr Jones would be excluded from such statements.

Periodicity

Accounting will divide a business's life into regular defined periods of time, which is usually a year for external reporting. This rule can again be traced back to the fifteenth century steward who would report at regular intervals about the affairs entrusted to him by the owner of the business or estate.

The idea of annual reports for limited companies has grown from custom and practice, and is now enshrined in company and taxation legislation. Such an arbitrary period may not be particularly useful as it may run contrary to the activities of that enterprise. For example, a large contractor may be constructing a dam or power station for a customer which may take several years to complete; the insurance syndicates at Lloyds of London report on a three-yearly basis, arguing a single year is not sufficient time to measure their liability to claimants.

Going concern (continuity) concept

Accounting will assume that the entity will continue in existence for the foreseeable future unless there is information to the contrary. This convention is particularly important for the value placed upon the assets of an enterprise. Fixed assets are normally valued at cost less an allowance for depreciation, rather than their current realizable value if sold. Should the enterprise cease trading the assets would have to be sold, consequently accounting assumes the enterprise will continue and the fixed assets used in that business for future periods.

This approach to accounting links the contribution made by assets to current and future profit generation rather than the immediate cash benefits available from selling the assets and ceasing trading.

How should it be recorded?

As already noted, the previous concepts state what should be recorded, while the following measurement concepts explain how that information should be recorded.

Money measurement concept

Accounting will, of necessity, confine itself to facts measurable in monetary terms. Money is an ideal means of converting economic data into a common unit, but may neglect important aspects of a business in that conversion and aggregation process. Accounting does not pretend to include all matters which are of significance to an entity.

The balance sheet of an organization does not record the skill of the workforce, the quality of management, the competitive advantage over competitors etc. While these strengths may be reflected in the level of profit, they are not specifically included within the accounting process.

Historic cost concept

Accounting will record transactions at their original (historic) cost, and use this figure as a basis for future reporting purposes. While this represents an extension of the money measurements concept, it raises a basic problem. The historic cost of an asset is not an indication of the current value of that asset because it ignores both the changes in the general purchasing power of money and changes in the specific value of such assets.

This is the most controversial of all the accounting concepts and conventions and there have been several attempts to change the rules to allow for the effect of inflation when preparing accounting information, but the issue is so complex that no generally accepted system of doing so has emerged.

A balance sheet fixed assets section contains the following information:

Fixed assets	At cost	Depreciation to date	Net book value
Land	100,000	–	100,000
Buildings	175,000	25,000	150,000
Plant and equipment	390,000	137,000	253,000

The detail of the transactions that generated the above figures highlights the problem with the historic cost convention. The land was bought in 1965 and currently has a value of nearly £750,000. One building was acquired at the same time for £10,000 and would cost £325,000 to replace now. The other building was constructed last year at a cost of £165,000. To add the original costs together (£10,000 + £165,000) does not provide a true reflection of value. The figure in the balance sheet is more an accident of when assets were acquired rather than a measure of worth.

The plant and equipment has been acquired ever since the founding of the company in 1965, some being scrapped and replaced while other pieces have been kept. The plant and equipment, like the buildings, are depreciated each year, in that a proportion of their original cost is charged against profit each year. The depreciation figure is a product of the original historic cost and does not reflect an accurate charge for the use of comparable assets hired from an external contractor.

The historic cost rule is therefore particularly important to fixed assets valuation because depreciation is seen as the charging of the original cost against successive periods expected to benefit from the asset, and not as an attempt to reflect the present values for the usage of these assets.

The problem is lessened in the case of current assets because sale in the near future is the whole point of holding such assets, so such long-term inconsistencies in value are not created.

Realization concept

Accounting will recognize revenue at the point when value is transferred to a third party, and something, also of value, received in exchange, either payment or the right to receive payment. Accounting needs a transaction to trigger the recording process, without it there is no certainty of the money measurement. Commercial law deems a contract to have been established and the same practice is used for accounting. If goods are bought or sold on credit, with payment being promised in the future, accounting will deem this to be a transaction.

This rule impinges on the valuation of fixed assets because it implies that no increase in the value of an asset can be recognized as a profit or gain until the asset is sold. This helps justify the inclusion of fixed assets at their historic cost which was the objective amount paid for them and it is considered prudent to leave them in the accounts at this figure.

Accruals/matching concept

Accounting will set the cost of resources used up by an activity, or in a period, against the income from the activity of that period. We have already seen the product of this rule when considering the profit and loss account earlier in this chapter. It relates to the matching of income with expenses to generate profit and not the matching of cash received with cash expended to measure profit, and also the accruing of income and expenses to fit into the period in question by ensuring a full period's costs are present in the accounts.

The rule is important because of the need to report the results of an entity with a continuous existence in arbitrary time periods. The results of succeeding periods would neither be consistent nor comparable if this rule was not observed.

Duality concept

Accounting will view every transaction as having a twofold effect on the position of a business as recorded in the accounts. This approach ensures the balancing of the balance sheet and provides a control mechanism for the recording of data in the form of double entry book-keeping.

How the concepts should be followed (the ethics or conventions)

It might be thought that by observing all the above concepts it would be impossible to arrive at different levels of profit: this is simply not so. Different accountants could use the same basic data, observe the same concepts and still obtain different results. The concepts still leave scope for subjective judgements by accountants, and it is the following ethical conventions that require accountants to follow the letter and the spirit of the basic rules.

Prudence/conservatism convention

Accounting must not anticipate profit and should provide for all foreseeable losses, and when faced with two or more methods of valuing an asset, the accountant should choose that method which gives the lesser value.

This convention is an interpretation of the realization concept, which states all profits must be realized by a transaction, and the cost concept, which states assets must be held at acquisition cost. The provision for all known losses may give an over-pessimistic approach, but it is consistent.

Consistency convention

Accounting aims to provide data which can be used for comparisons over time, and therefore the treatment of similar items should be consistent from one year to the next. A change in the way a company values stocks and work-in-progress may result in increased profits but would sacrifice comparability over time. If circumstances change, it is permissible to adopt new rules, or interpret old rules differently, the effect of such a change should be highlighted and quantified, with a statement of the change in policy.

Inter-company comparisons are made difficult by the adoption of different rules by different companies. While accounting treatments within a company must be consistent, it does not mean consistency is required across several companies.

Objectivity convention

Accountants should use the minimum of bias and subjectivity. Historic cost accounting implies objectivity because assets are recorded as the amount actually paid for them; the figure is real, objective and can be proved by documentary evidence. Other items may be less objective, the valuation of stock for instance may involve the decision to scrap certain items and give them a zero value. The accountant must attempt to be objective in this decision, and not be swayed by management. This is not a simple task, but if optional decisions are possible, accountants should fall back on to the prudence concept of accounting for all anticipated losses.

Concepts and conventions in practice

The above concepts and conventions are much criticized as relying for their authority on being accepted by practising accountants, and having no coherent theory of accounting to underpin them. While criticism can be levelled at any of the concepts, it is the historic cost one which is most criticized. A lay person studying a balance sheet will wish to attribute 'value' to the assets included, but this is not the case, their balance sheet figure is only an estimate of the unexpired portion of their original cost.

The major limitations of accounting concepts and conventions can be summarized by saying they cannot embrace a complete, accurate, up-to-date picture of the complexities of business within the accounting statements. Accountants are aware of these problems and in an attempt to overcome them notes explaining the accounting policies adopted within the accounts are attached to the accounting statements.

Illustration 2.1 The affairs of Fred

Day 1 Fred is made redundant. He uses £100 cash to purchase 100 books at £1 each and sells 50 of them for £2 each for cash. He rented a market stall for the day which cost £5. Fred's wife and child left the matrimonial home promising never to return.

Day 2 Fred sells a further 20 books at £2 each on credit to Bill, who collects the books from Fred's house. Fred learns that books of this type would now cost him £1.25 and could be sold in Newcastle for £2.50.

Day 3 Fred bought a van for £50 to carry his stock of books to various markets. He estimates the van will last 5 working days and then have a scrap value of £5.

Also during the day he sells a further 10 books at £2 each for cash and pays market expenses of £7.

Calculate for each day of trading:
  (a) The profit or loss.
  (b) A cash flow statement.
and
  (c) Draw up a balance sheet at the end of each day's trading.

Day 1 Profit and loss statement

	£
Sales	
(50 books × £2)	100
Opening Stock	nil
Purchases	
100 book × £1	100
	100
Closing stock	
50 × £1	50 50
Gross profit	50
Expenses	5
Profit for day	45

Day 2 Profit and loss statement

	£
Sales	
(20 books × £2)	40
Opening Stock	50
Purchases	nil
	50
Closing stock	
30 × £1	30 20
Gross profit	20
Expenses	nil
Profit for day	20

Day 1 Cash flow statement

	£
Opening balance	100
Cash inflow from	
cash sales	100
	200
Less cash outflow for	
purchases	100
Rental	5 105
Closing balance	95

Day 2 Cash flow statement

	£
Opening balance	95
No cash transactions	
Closing balance	95

Day 1 Balance sheet

	£
Opening equity	100
Profit for day	45
	145
Stock of books	50
Cash	95
	145

Day 2 Balance sheet

	£
Opening equity	145
Profit for day	20
	165
Stock of books	30
Debtor – Bill	40
Cash	95
	165

Day 3 Profit and loss account

	£
Sales 10 × £2	20
Opening stock	30
Purchases	nil
	30
Closing stock	20 10
Gross profit	10
Less expenses	7
depreciation	9 16
Loss for day	(6)

Day 3 Cash flow statement

		£
Opening balance		95
Cash inflow		
from sales		20
		115
Cash outflow		
Van	50	
Market	7	57
Closing balance		58

Day 3 Balance sheet

		£
Opening equity		165
Loss for day		(6)
		159
Van	50	
Less depreciation		
to date	9	41
Stock of books		20
Debtor − Bill		40
Cash		58
		159

While the affairs of Fred are straightforward, in business terms the financial reporting of his transactions adopting accounting concepts and conventions as presented above filters out information, makes assumptions and implies an accuracy that is not present.

Entity:	Fred's business is separate from Fred's domestic household.
Periodicity:	Fred's transactions are accounted for each day, giving a standard basis for comparison.
Going concern:	We have assumed the business will continue trading.
Money measurements:	Only money transactions have been recorded.
Historic costs:	Each transaction has been recorded at its historic cost.
Realization:	While the stock of books may have different values elsewhere, no further valuation has been included as this would not be transaction-based, but the sale to Bill was accounted for assuming Bill will pay.
Accruals:	Sales and cost of sales have been matched carefully, making sure unsold stock items

are excluded. The van is depreciated over its useful life at £9 per day so spreading its cost over its period of usage.

Duality:	The balance sheet balanced.
Prudence:	No increased value was taken for the books.
Consistency:	Each day's transactions were treated in the same manner.
Objectivity:	Only objectively measured transactions have been accounted for, although the van's future usage and value must be a product of a subjective judgement.

Summary

This second chapter has considered the users of published financial statements, outlined the main statements presented and the underlying concepts and conventions upon which those statements are based.

After reading this chapter you should be able to:

● List the main users of published financial information and provide reasons for their interest.
● Understand the basic layout of the balance sheet, profit and loss account and cash flow statement.
● Be aware of the fundamental concepts and conventions of accounting.

In the next chapter the basic statements described so far will be developed and used for comparisons for both intra- and inter-company performances with the use of accounting ratios.

References

Corporate Report (1975) The Accounting Standards Steering Committee, London
Dyson, J.R. (1991) *Accounting for Non-Accounting Students*, 2nd edn, Pitman, London
Glautier, M.W.E. and Underdown, B. (1991) *Accounting Theory and Practice*, 4th edn, Pitman, London, Chapter 11

Further reading

Glautier, M.W.E. and Underdown, B (1991) *Accounting Theory and Practice*, 4th edn, Pitman, London, Chapters 4, 5, 9 and 10
Laughlin, R. and Gray, R.H. (1988) *Financial Accounting: Method and Meaning*, VNR International, London, Chapters 7 and 11

Problems and discussion topics

1 In January Erika Gladwell decided to convert her large vegetable
plot into a market garden specializing in herbs and flowers. She
injected £10,000 in cash from her savings and fenced off the land.
The following relates to transactions for the first six months of
trade up to the end of June.

Payment to fencing contractor	1,850
Purchase of herb plants	970
Purchase of petrol rotavator	2,050
Purchase of petrol driven harrow	1,000
Purchase of manure and fertilizer	690
Purchase of seeds	500
Purchase of small van	7,000
Sales to local health store – herbs	2,900
Sales to florist	4,800
Van and rotavator expenses paid	760
Wages to casual handyman	650
Cash withdrawn for personal use £100 per week	2,600

At the end of June Erika considered things were going quite well
until she received a bank statement indicating she was £370
overdrawn. To allay fears she jotted down the following statement, justifying her success.

Income statement for period up to 30 June

	£	£
Income		
Herbs	2,900	
Others to be harvested	3,600	6,500
Flowers	4,800	
Others to be cut	4,000	8,800
		15,300
Expenses		
Fencing	1,850	
Herb plants	970	
Van etc. expenses	760	
Manure and fertilizer	690	
Wages	650	
Loss in value for van	300	
Loss in value for rotavator	nil	
Loss in value for harrow	nil	
Seed purchases	500	5,720
Net profit		9,580
Cash withdrawals		2,600
Profit after drawings		6,980

She also estimated £780 for the value of standing crops unsold at 30 June.

Having visited her bank manager Erika was appalled by his condescending attitude about her income statement and has asked you to explain why it is incorrect and to redraft the statement in accordance with recognized accounting concepts and conventions.

2 The profit and loss accounts and balance sheets below refer to two football clubs, for the same financial year. To avoid inter-club conflict their names will be disguised.

	Pembroke City	Pembroke United
Balance sheets	*£000*	*£000*
Fixed assets	3,092	12,783
Current assets	490	203
Current liabilities	(2,165)	(2,563)
	1,417	10,423
Less long-term loans	68	1,743
	1,349	8,680
Shares capital	363	6,430
Revenue reserves	986	2,250
	1,349	8,680

Profit and Loss Accounts		*£000*	*£000*
Gate receipts		1,787	1,053
Other match receipts		1,087	633
		2,874	1,686
Less expenses			
Wages		1,459	929
Ground expenditure		217	64
Interest		111	293
Other expenses		833	1,287
		2,620	2,573
Profit before player transfers		254	(887)
Player purchases	2,007		
Player sales	95	1,912	n/a
Profit/(Loss) for year		(1,658)	(887)

Pembroke United capitalizes the cost of new players acquired on the transfer market and depreciates this cost over the life of their contracts. The fixed asset figures reflect this accounting policy. Pembroke City does not capitalize its players but accounts for player acquisition and disposal as an expense or revenue for the particular year.

You are required to consider these two accounting treatments and justify each using the concepts and conventions of accounting.

3 Tracey and Melanie both started retail businesses on 1 January. During the year that followed the two friends undertook identical business transactions as follows:

>   1 Purchased equipment on 1 January for £400,000.
>   2 Paid research and development expenditure of £50,000.
>   3 Purchased stock as follows:
>   1 January 2,000 units at £50 each
>   1 May 2,000 units at £100 each
>   4 Sold stock as follows:
>   30 September 2,000 units at £150 each
>   5 Incurred other expenses of £50,000.

The two retailers use different conventions of calculating profit as follows:

Depreciation: Tracey uses straight line depreciation over five years, Melanie uses straight line depreciation over ten years.

Research and development: Tracey writes off R&D over a ten year period. Melanie writes off expenditure in the year in which it is incurred.

You are required to:
  (a) Prepare income statements for Tracey and Melanie for the year ended 31 December.
  (b) Say which policies you consider best reflect the matching and prudence policies.

3 Assessment of company performance

The aims of this chapter are to:

- Explain why financial ratios are appropriate for analysing company performance.
- Develop financial measures which will assist in the analysis of a company's liquidity, profitability, efficiency and investment through ratio analysis.
- Apply the ratios to evaluate company performance using inter- and intra-company comparisons.
- Consider the ratios used by financial markets in assessing company performance.
- Consider the limitations of ratio analysis in general and the particular effect individual company accounting policies may have on this analysis.

Introduction

The external financial statements considered in Chapter 2 were the end product of an accounting data collection and accumulation process. Information had been filtered and moulded by the set of measurement rules known as the concepts and conventions, supported by the Statements of Standard Accounting Practice (SSAP) and Company Law to produce the financial statements contained in the annual report and accounts. While the balance sheet, profit and loss account and cash flow statement of a particular company may be used for its particular stakeholder groups, they provide information in isolation from other companies, and a limited comparison of performance over time (usually the current year's results and the previous year's for comparison purposes).

The broad aim of this chapter is to provide tools of analysis which will aid comparison between companies (inter-firm comparison) and within a company (intra-firm comparison) over time.

The area of study for this chapter is illustrated in Figure 3.1. The figure illustrates the flow of accounting data to the stakeholders. We have already considered that this data is not specifically designed for particular user needs, but is highly general in nature. In this chapter we will attempt to develop and adapt the information to be

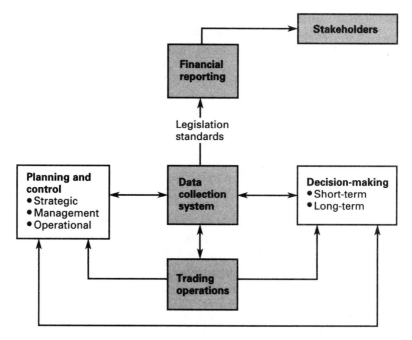

Figure 3.1   *Financial ratio analysis*

more user-specific. The accounting ratios presented will provide measures of profitability, liquidity, efficiency and investment which may be useful for the evaluation of opportunities available to stake-holders whether for conventional financing, trading or employment reasons. The provision of comparisons between companies through accounting ratio analysis should aid the economic decision-making process which was put forward as a major aim of financial reporting.

The need for accounting ratios

The calculation and presentation of ratios is a method of relating one number to another, so as to draw inferences about the position or performance of an activity. In doing so it is possible to control for size, time and other differences, so making results comparable.

A hotel located in Sunderland reported that 106 rooms were occupied during a particularly rainy week in March. While this data may be useful, it could easily be enhanced by comparing the rooms occupied with those available. If only 106 rooms were available, it represents a 100% occupancy rate, but if 424 rooms were available it represents a 25% occupancy rate. The 106 room occupation cannot be compared with a similar hotel in the city, as each is of a different size, but the occupancy rate, the ratio of rooms let to rooms available, can be compared. So with accounting ratios the provision of a ratio or scaling process enables comparisons to be made more easily.

In 1992 Aquasuck Ltd, a swimming pool cleaning and maintenance company, reported a profit after tax of £300,000. While this may be interesting, there is no indication of whether it represents good or bad performance, or more specifically how does it compare with the expected profit for the year or the previous year's profit level. For investment purposes a stakeholder in Aquasuck Ltd will also require a comparison between the performance of this company with others in the same cleaning field. This need for comparison, often between companies and across years, suggests that some sort of scaling activity would be useful, so relative performance between different-sized organizations may be calculated, and that there is a need to standardize data to make comparisons so derived much easier and more worthwhile.

If Aquasuck Ltd had reported profits of £200,000 in 1990 and £250,000 in 1991, then the £300,000 in 1992 represents an improvement relevant to past performance, but this assumes the resource base has remained constant. Quite clearly, if capital employed had doubled between 1990 and 1992, the £300,000 would represent a drop in efficiency over time.

If the £300,000 represented a 10% return on capital employed (£3m invested in service capacity) and the average performance for such companies is 7%, then Aquasuck Ltd is achieving results above the industry average. If average returns for the industry were 16%, stakeholders may be asking questions of management about their level of efficiency. Had Aquasuck Ltd been quoted on the Stock Exchange (i.e. a public limited company, plc) then shareholders may consider selling their shares in this company and re-investing elsewhere, and therefore the marketability of shares fuels the requirement by stakeholders to have comparable company performance data. These are some illustrations of the development and need for accounting ratios.

The ratios presented in this chapter are not meant to be totally comprehensive but do provide an indication of the more important ones used for financial analysis, while the ratios used by City analysts are presented in more detail.

Points to remember when calculating and using ratio analysis

1   *A ratio is only meaningful when it is compared to another ratio.* Knowing that a particular company has a profitability ratio of 16% is not useful in isolation.

2   *Any ratio is only as accurate as the figures from which it was derived.* The validity of comparing ratios from one period to another to establish trends will be affected by inflation, changes in accounting policies adopted by the company and seasonal patterns for half-yearly reports.

Consider the following results extracted from a company's published accounts:

	Year 1	Year 2
	£000	£000
Turnover	1,270	1,370
less Cost of sales	907	997
Operating profit	363	373
Fixed assets	2,574	4,574
Current assets	2,795	2,609
	5,369	7,183
less Current liabilities	832	904
Capital employed	4,537	6,279

If two traditional ratios were calculated, one representing a profitability measure and the other an efficiency measure, the following would result:

	Year 1	Year 2
Operating profit/sales	28.5%	27.2%
Return on capital employed Operating profit/capital employed	8.0%	5.9%

Clearly performance in Year 2 is worse than Year 1. While sales have increased in monetary terms (from £1,270 to £1,370), if inflation were running at 10% then sales of £1,397 (£1,270 × 1.10) would have been required to keep pace. The cost of sales figure represents a 10% increase in cost from one year to the next, but overall profitability has declined.

The return on capital employed figure of 5.9% in Year 2 represents a significant fall. While the profits have hardly changed, the capital employed has risen significantly, particularly the fixed asset figure. This may represent a major acquisition of fixed assets or the revaluation of the existing ones. In the former case the fall in return is quite serious as more assets are being used less efficiently, while the latter just represents a restatement of asset values, making year-by-year comparison invalid.

3 *Inter-firm comparisons using accounting ratios will only be valid if the same accounting policies are adopted in preparing the accounts.* So such issues as stock valuation and fixed asset depreciation policies can make comparisons very difficult.

4 *Ratios adopted for inter-firm comparison need not be restricted to accounting information.* Efficiency ratios using a much broader range

of data may be particularly useful. For example, in retailing turnover per employee is a useful ratio; while in the National Health Service cost per patient bed may be appropriate.

While ratios must be used with care, they do provide a useful form of performance analysis, and it is to the accounting ratios themselves we now turn. They will be presented under the headings of liquidity, profitability, efficiency and investment ratios, but before a detailed presentation of the first group of ratios it would be useful to consider the trade cycle of a typical firm (Figure 3.2).

Figure 3.2 shows, on a day-to-day basis, the working capital requirements of a business. Working capital has already been defined in Chapter 2 as current assets less current liabilities, which means the funds needed to allow the manufacture of products or delivery of services until debtors (customers) have paid for the goods or services. The longer the time period between the purchase of raw materials and receipts from the sale of finished goods the greater the need for working capital. A business without working capital and cash liquidity cannot survive in the short term, no matter how healthy its long-term profitability projections may look.

The faster the flow of funds around the trade cycle the lesser the requirement for significant amounts of working capital. A super-market may receive cash from its customers only days after delivery from its suppliers, and before subsequent payment; while a house

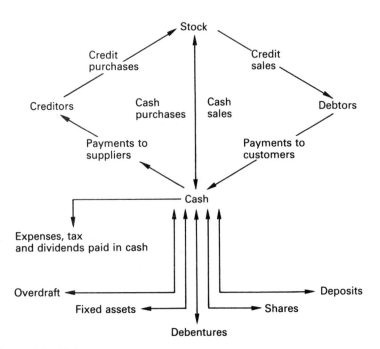

Figure 3.2 *The trade cycle*

builder may have to finance a development for several months before a subsequent purchaser is found and then several weeks before the contract of sale is signed and the cash received. Quite clearly these timings have an effect on cash, which is also known as liquidity, and it is to the liquidity ratios we now turn. We will use the accounts of Zeda plc which appear below for demonstrating the calculations involved.

Profit and loss account for the year ended 31 December for Zeda plc

	19×2	19×1
	£m	£m
Turnover	735	755
Cost of sales	431	481
Gross profit	304	274
Distribution costs	189	172
Administrative expenses	31	30
Operating profit	84	72
Interest	12	8
Profit on ordinary activities before taxation	72	64
Tax on ordinary activities	23	20
Profit on ordinary activities after taxation	49	44
Extraordinary items	28	2
Profit for the financial year	77	46
Dividends	25	19
Retained profit for the year	52	27
Earnings per share (basic)	45.3p	40.7p

The 50p nominal value shares are currently quoted on the Stock Exchange at £4.06.
Zeda is a very large retail company having outlets serving motoring, building, gardening, decorating and other DIY pursuits.

Balance sheets as at 31 December for Zeda plc

	19×2	19×1
	£m	£m
Fixed assets		
Tangible assets	182	169
Investments	20	9
	202	178
Current assets		
Stock	166	137
Debtors	41	42
Cash in hand	76	62
	283	241

Creditors: falling due in one year		
Trade creditors	137	126
Taxation	16	11
Proposed dividend	15	12
Bank loans and overdrafts	28	20
	196	169
Net current assets	289	250
Creditors: falling due after more than one year		
Loans	109	124
	180	126
Capital and reserves		
Called up share capital	54	54
Share premium account	26	26
Revaluation reserve	28	26
Profit and loss account	72	20
	180	126

Liquidity ratios

Trade creditors allowing credit to a business will be interested in the ability of the business to settle the indebtedness within the normal terms of trade allowed. Such creditors will be anxious about settlement as they normally have no special legal recourse if the business fails and consequently will be unwilling to allow credit to a business which is running into financial difficulties.

The risk associated with trade creditors is increased if large sums are owed by small firms as these perish quickly in difficult trading periods, while larger firms are more robust in weathering such downturns in the market.

There are two major ratios which are significant in measuring the all-important liquidity of a business, they are:

1 The current ratio
2 The acid test (or quick) ratio

Both can be calculated from balance sheet figures. The *current ratio* is the ratio of current assets to current liabilities, expressed as follows:

$$\frac{\text{Current assets}}{\text{Current liabilities}}$$

Zeda has current assets of £283m (£241m) and current liabilities of £196m (£169m), giving a current ratio of 1.44 (1.43). This means that if all short-term creditors demand their money immediately then their claims could be met 1.44 times (1.43 times) if the current assets could be converted into cash immediately. While this is clearly unreasonable it does give an indication of liquidity, because under normal trading circumstances short-term creditors are unlikely to demand immediate payment. Accounting textbooks often state that a current ratio of 2.1 is adequate, but such generalizations are not useful, as highly efficient businesses may be able to reduce stocks, by applying just-in-time techniques, and reduce debtors by cash trading without affecting financial stability.

The *acid test ratio* gives a better measure of liquidity as it eliminates stock, the least liquid asset (that is, the most difficult to convert into cash quickly) from the current ratio, so providing a measure of the most liquid assets against short-term claims. The ratio is expressed as follows:

$$\frac{\text{Current assets} - \text{stocks}}{\text{Current liabilities}}$$

Zeda has current assets of £283m (£241m) which includes stocks of £166m (£137m), giving an acid test ratio of 0.60 (0.62). Zeda is a very large retail company and clearly has the ability to trade with what would be considered to be a weak acid test ratio, this is because its sales income is mainly in cash, while its creditors are supplying goods in credit terms. Accounting text books claim an acid test ratio of 1.1 to be ideal, but again this varies from industry to industry.

It is quite common for small, fast-growing companies to have weak current and acid test ratios, because long-term finance is difficult to acquire. Such companies tend to use the credit granted by suppliers as a basis for expansion. Quite clearly this is a dangerous ploy, as it means liquidity is very short, but successful companies should grow out of this problem by attracting long-term finance and reducing the reliance on trade credit.

Profitability ratios

Users of accounts will wish to know how much profit a business has generated relative to the previous year and relative to other enterprises in the same industry. There are many profitability ratios, some relating capital employed to the profit figure, while others relate profit to sales levels. The former relate different profit measures to different balance sheet (or capital) investments within the business.

Return on capital employed

This is a very common measure of profitability both for external assessment of companies' performance and for internal assessment of the efficiency of management. (This latter point will be developed in Chapter 10 and the problems associated with its use.) It measures the return on the total capital of the business regardless of how it is financed.

Considering Zeda plc, the total capital is calculated as follows:

	19×2 £m	19×1 £m
either:		
Fixed assets	202	178
Current assets	283	241
	485	419
less Current liabilities	196	169
	289	250
or:		
Shareholder investment	180	126
Creditors falling due after more than one year	109	124
	289	250

Both calculations recognize the total capital employed in the business and must be related to a profit measure which does not discriminate between returns to shareholders and loan capital separately. Such a measure is *operating profit*, as it represents total profits before interest, the return to loan capital, is deducted. Zeda plc has an operating profit of £84m (£72m) giving a return on capital employed (ROCE) of 29% (29%).

Returns to shareholders' funds

Shareholders' funds are also known as equity investment and for Zeda plc are £180m (£126m). This calculation can be related to any profit figure which relates solely to the equity investment within the company. It may be expressed before or after taxation, or before or after extraordinary items. Because the extraordinary items, which are expressed net of taxation, relate to activities which are not considered to be part of the ordinary activities of the business, they are often excluded from ratio analysis as they represent unusual, one-off items which may obscure the true performance if included.

Common returns to shareholder funds are expressed as follows:

$$\frac{\text{Net profit on ordinary activities before tax}}{\text{Shareholders' funds}}$$

$$\frac{\text{Net profit on ordinary activities after tax}}{\text{Shareholders' funds}}$$

For Zeda plc the ratios are as follows:

	19×2	19×1
Before tax	40%	51%
After tax	27%	35%

Because of the large extraordinary item in 19×2 'profit for the financial year' to shareholder investment would not be a useful ratio to compute, as it would invalidate any trend within the ratios.

Profits to sales ratios

The other profitability ratios relate profits to turnover (sales). It is quite common to compute several such ratios in an attempt to relate different profit calculations to sales. Common ones are:

$$\text{Gross profit percentage} = \frac{\text{Gross profit}}{\text{Turnover}}$$

which measures trading profits before other expenses.

$$\text{Operating profit percentage} = \frac{\text{Operating profit}}{\text{Turnover}}$$

which measures profits after all operating expenses.

$$\text{Net profit percentage} = \frac{\text{Profit on ordinary activities before tax}}{\text{Turnover}}$$

which gives an indication of net return, on the sales turnover.
For Zeda plc the figures are as follows:

	19×2	19×1
	%	%
Gross profit ratio	41.3	36.3
Operating profit ratio	11.4	9.5
Net profit ratio	9.8	8.5

If a full analysis is required it is quite common to relate the first few lines of the profit and loss account to turnover so giving percentage figures rather than absolutes. If this is done for Zeda plc the result is as follows:

	19×2		19×1	
	£m	%	£m	%
Turnover	735	100.0	755	100.0
Cost of sales	431	58.7	481	63.7
Gross profit	304	41.3	274	36.3
Distribution expenses	189	25.7	172	22.8
Admin. expenses	31	4.2	30	4.0
Operating profit	84	11.4	72	9.5
Interest	12	1.6	8	1.0
	72	9.8	64	8.5

At this stage we are getting a much clearer picture of the profitability of Zeda plc. The cost of sales percentage has decreased from Year 19×1 to 19×2 giving an increased gross profit percentage but on a smaller sales figure. The two expense costs have increased relative to sales which may indicate opportunities for efficiencies in the future.

Efficiency ratios

These relate to the management of the capital employed figure in the balance sheet. The capital employed figure is the aggregation of fixed and current assets less any current liabilities, and ratios are available for items within these broad classes of asset and liability.

We will first consider the current assets and current liability ratios, which when combined give a measure of working capital management. All the ratios in this grouping relate a balance sheet item to a related profit and loss account figure and then express it as a ratio relative to an annual figure. It may be useful to consider stock in detail and then relate a general rule to debtors and creditors.

Stock efficiency is measured by how large the year end stock figure is compared to the cost of sales during the year expressed in days. For Zeda plc the closing stock figure is £166m (£137m) whilst the cost of sales is £431m (£481m). If the stock turnover figure is calculated then the stock figure has changed on average £431m/ £166m (£481m/£137m) times during the year, i.e. 2.596 times (3.511 times). If this is standardized to daily figures it becomes 365 days ÷ 2.596 i.e. 141 days (104 days). The result of this calculation means that closing stock figures represent 141 (104) days of sales at cost price. To shortcut the calculation the stock turnover is given by:

$$\frac{\text{Stock}}{\text{Cost of sales}} \times 365$$

Similarly, debtors turnover is given by:

$$\frac{\text{Trade debtors}}{\text{Sales}} \times 365$$

and creditors turnover by:

$$\frac{\text{Total creditors}}{\text{Total credit purchases}} \times 365$$

It is customary to use average stock (the simple average of opening and closing figures), average debtors and average creditors figures.

The creditors turnover figure is difficult to compute because credit purchases are not always available in published accounts, so cost of sales may be used as a proxy. If the figures are calculated for Zeda plc, using year end figures and the proxy for creditors turnover, the results are as follows:

	19×2 days	19×1 days
Stock turnover	141	104
Debtors turnover	20	20
	161	124
Less creditors turnover	116	96
Working capital turnover	45	28

Clearly the Zeda plc stock turnover has decreased quite dramatically, reflecting the drop in turnover. Debtors turnover has remained static at 20 days. Remember Zeda plc is a retailer so debtors would be expected to be a small percentage of sales, the majority of which will be on cash terms. The 20 days debtors turnover relates to all sales not just credit sales and therefore gives an indication of trends rather than a figure that represents a credit period for debtors. The creditors turnover has increased, creditors are now being paid after a four month credit period rather than the 96 days (three months) of the previous year. Overall working capital turnover is taking an extra 17 days, which must be financed in some way.

Having considered the working capital efficiency ratios we now turn to the fixed asset efficiency ratio known as *fixed asset turnover ratio*. It is calculated by dividing turnover by fixed assets, i.e.

$$\frac{\text{Turnover (sales)}}{\text{Fixed assets}}$$

The logic behind such a ratio is that fixed assets should generate sales and then profits. Relating the two together gives a rough indication of efficiency.

If fixed assets turnover is computed for Zeda plc, the turnover is £735m (£755m) while the fixed tangible assets were £182m (£169m), giving a figure of 4.04 times (4.47 times). Clearly fixed asset utilization has fallen over the two year period.

Before moving on to the investment ratios it may be useful to put together the ratios already presented in a format which relates efficiency ratios and profitability ratios together. It is known as the *pyramid of ratios*.

Pyramid of ratios (Figure 3.3)

While such a pyramid has no formal established layout it does provide an insight into the way accounting ratios are derived and how they fit together. While many ratios are excluded from the pyramid, those included do give management and investors a guide to overall company performance in terms of efficiency and profitability.

The first profitability ratio which gives an indication of overall performance relates operating profit to capital employed, known as return on capital employed (ROCE). It was defined as:

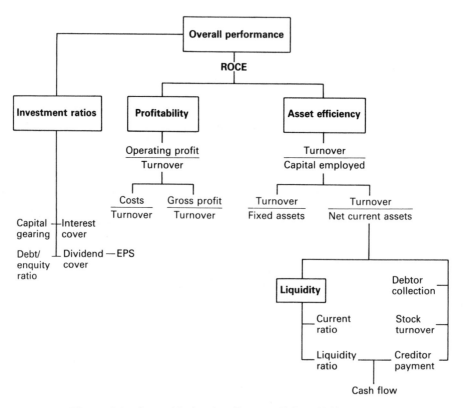

Figure 3.3 *Pyramid of ratios (Source: Kyle, 1992)*

$$\frac{\text{Operating profit}}{\text{Capital employed}}$$

It can be subdivided into the two ratios which form the second line of the pyramid:

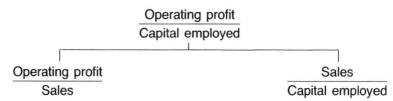

Also:

$$\frac{\text{Operating profit}}{\text{Sales}} \times \frac{\text{Sales}}{\text{Capital employed}} = \frac{\text{Operating profit}}{\text{Capital employed}}$$

So if the ROCE is thought to be unsatisfactory it is possible to investigate both sides of the pyramid, that relating to return on sales (profitability) and that relating to asset utilization (efficiency). After the second line of the pyramid, known as the 'Du Pont Equation', the strict mathematical logic of the pyramid collapses but it still provides a framework for performance analysis.

The next part of the chapter introduces ratios which are used by the analysts in conjunction with those already calculated to provide an insight into long-term solvency and performance relative to current share prices.

Investment ratios

While we have already considered the two short-term liquidity ratios, current ratio and acid test ratio, the stock market analysts and providers of long-term finance generally require a measure of long-term solvency known as *capital gearing* in the UK, or *capital leverage* in the United States.

The solvency, or survival, of an organization will be related to its ability to meet short-term liabilities from creditors as they fall due. This short-term ability may be affected by decisions concerning long-term funding. If an individual or company borrows large sums of money for repayment in the future, the short-term liquidity will reflect the interest payments, whether annual, bi-annual or monthly, and the eventual repayment of the loan. The ratio of finance raised from borrowing and that raised from shareholders is crucial to understand the overall financial risk of any enterprise.

There are a number of ways of expressing the capital gearing of a company. The two most common ones are the long-term loans to equity capital ratio, and the long-term loans to total capital employed. For Zeda plc the figures are:

$$\frac{\text{Long-term loans}}{\text{Shareholder funds}} = \frac{£109m}{£180m} = 61\% \ (98\%)$$

$$\frac{\text{Long-term loans}}{\text{Capital employed}} = \frac{£109m}{£289m} = 38\% \ (50\%)$$

High capital gearing may lead to high levels of interest payments per annum. This will be less of a problem if the operating profits are stable over time. However, gearing may be advantageous as benefits can accrue to shareholders from some level of borrowing, but at what level is subject to much debate. A highly geared company (with a longer percentage of borrowed capital) means as profits rise, the providers of the borrowed capital continue to receive the same interest payments so leaving an increased proportion of profits for shareholders. This idea of 'gearing up' shareholder returns considers the ratio of profits available to shareholders compared to lenders of finance. While the financial gearing ratio measures balance sheet gearing, the idea of *interest cover* considers the ratio of interest to operating profit.

$$\text{Interest cover} = \frac{\text{Operating profit}}{\text{Interest changes}}$$

For Zeda plc the figures are 7 times (9 times), which means interest payments of 7 times (9 times) their current level could be sustained by the current level of operating profits.

We will return to financial gearing again after we have developed the more commonly quoted financial ratios found in good daily newspapers and financial periodicals.

Stock market ratios

One of the most important items of information for a shareholder will be the *earnings per share* (EPS) figure, which is presented at the foot of the profit and loss accounts for all Stock Exchange listed companies. The figure is calculated by comparing the earnings (profits) attributable to shareholders for the current year, divided by the number of shares in issue for that year. The figure for Zeda plc was quoted as 45.3p (40.7p), which was calculated by taking the

$$\frac{\text{Profit on ordinary activities after taxation}}{\text{Number of shares in issue}} = \frac{£49m}{108m \text{ shares*}} = 45.3p$$

* Zeda plc has £54m of called up share capital but the shares have a nominal value of 50p giving 108 million shares in all.

The EPS calculation ignores extraordinary items in the profit and loss account, so comparisons can be made on a year-by-year basis not distorted by unusual events of any particular year. The EPS figure serves as a good measure of the profits generated by management which accrue to shareholders. Some of the profit may be paid out as a cash dividend directly to shareholders while some of this profit may be held in the business for reinvestment and expansion purposes.

While the EPS is not quoted in the financial press, it forms the basis of two important ratios. The first is the *dividend cover ratio* which gives an indication of the profit paid out as dividends from that available. The dividend cover ratio is calculated by comparing the earnings per share with the dividend share. For Zeda plc the EPS was 45.3p (40.7p) while the dividend per share is £25m/108m shares = 23.1p (17.6p) giving a dividend cover of 1.96 times (2.31 times). Like the interest cover ratio, the dividend cover gives an indication of how many times over the dividend could have been paid from earnings (profits) available. It also gives an indication of the earnings (profits) retained by the company.

The other ratio derived from the EPS figure is the *price earnings ratio* (P/E ratio) which is calculated by:

$$\frac{\text{Market price of the share}}{\text{EPS}}$$

For Zeda plc the current market price of the ordinary share is quoted at £4.06 giving a P/E ratio of 8.96. This figure indicates that shareholders are willing to pay a multiple of 8.96 of current earnings to acquire a share in Zeda plc for £4.06. In fact the P/E ratio is often referred to as an *earnings multiple*. The reciprocal of the P/E ratio is the *earnings yield*, which gives an indication of the earnings (profits) relative to the market price of shares, for Zeda plc it is 11.15%.

The final Stock Exchange ratio is the *dividend yield*, which is computed as follows:

$$\frac{\text{Dividend per share}}{\text{Market price of the share}}$$

For Zeda plc the figure is 5.69%. This indicates shareholders are receiving a cash return of 5.69% on their investment. If the earnings yield and dividend yield are compared, it provides a clear indication of the level of profits being held by management for reinvestment within the company. It also checks back to the dividend cover, as dividing the earnings yield by the dividend yield gives the dividend cover figure (11.15%/5.69% = 1.96 times).

If the figures for Zeda plc were presented in a *Financial Times* format they would look like this:

STORES

Stock	Notes	Price	+ or −	19×1–19×2 High	Low	Mkt Cap £m	Yld Gr's	P/E
Zeda 50p		406	+2	406	296	438	7.6	8.9

Let us work through the columns one by one.

- *Stock*, this is the name of the stock, in this case Zeda. It may be followed by the nominal value of its share, but this is not of great importance to the shareholders, it is column 2, the price, which is of real significance.
- *Price*, which is the price at which the shares ceased trading at the end of business on the previous day. It represents a mid price, between what shares can be purchased for and sold for. For example, Zeda shares may be bought for 409p but sold at 403p. The difference in the figures is called the 'turn'.
- *+ or −* gives the mid price change from the previous day's trading.
- *High* and *Low*   The price of the 'stock', showing the highest and lowest prices reached during the calendar year (this data straddles up to 16 months in the early part of the year and is switched to the current year around the time of the Spring Budget). This information is designed to put some perspective on the share price, particularly when compared with movements in the rest of the same sector.
- *MKt Cap £m*   The market capitalization is the price of the share currently quoted multiplied by the number of shares in issue. So for Zeda it is 108m shares × £4.06 = £438m.
- *Yld Gr's* is a shorthand form of saying dividend yield, but the yield is expressed before the basic rate of income tax. For Zeda plc the figure quoted is 7.6% which represents the dividend per share grossed up for the basic rate of tax, which is 25%, i.e. 23.1p × 100 ÷ 75 = 30.8p, and divided by the current share price 30.8/406 = 7.6%. You may find this grossing up for taxation strange, but it is thought better to quote the gross figure from which particular tax payers can adjust for their specific taxation rates, rather than assuming investors are all basic rate tax payers.
- *P/E*   This is the price earnings ratio, which we have already calculated as being 8.96.

The figures quoted are updated in the *Financial Times* on a daily basis, adjusting for share price changes and for earnings changes. The former is a straightforward adjustment, while the latter takes the figure for the previous 12 month period, by including interim figures for half-yearly results.

Illustration 3.1 Financial Times daily London share service

FOOD RETAILING

	Notes	Price	+ or –	1992 high	low	Mkt Cap £m	Yld Gr's	P/E
■ASDA _____		25½	+1½	*42	22½	568.6	11.4	6.5
■Albert Fisher _____		34	−1½	83	34	204.0	14.7	3.6
Appleby W'ward _____		258	−2	288	223	14.4	4.5	12.6
■Argyll _____		326	+5	*372	273	3,650	4.0	13.5
■Ashley _____		15	___	51	13	21.1	‡	2.1
8¼ p Net Cv Pf _____		57	−1	87	57	8.00	19.3	—
Brake Bros _____		343	−7	439	343	157.8	2.2	14.4
■Budgens _____		33	___	45	32	53.6	—	—
Cullen's _____		25	___	38	25	6.54	2.7	φ
Dairy Farm S _____		72	___	97	66½	1,179	3.3	15.3
Dumas _____		8#	___	26	8	0.92	—	19.8
Farepak 10p _____		238	___	275	234	53.8	2.8	φ
■Fyffes 1 £ _____		80	___	*93	73	223.3	1.7	12.5
■Geest _____		343	___	440	315	244.9	3.1	13.0
Greggs _____		407m	___	470	388	45.1	4.6	11.2
Hunter Saphir _____		44	___	61	43	10.8	7.6	—
■Iceland _____		481	−9	536	412	416.1	2.4	13.9
■Kwik Save _____		642	−8	669	514	988.8	3.1	14.0
■Low (Wm) _____		180	−1	286½	169	95.7	6.2	6.5
M & W _____		87	___	106	87	13.3	3.4	10.7
■Merchant Retl _____		9½	−¾	*33	9½	8.60	15.4	9.0
■Morrison (W) _____		125	+4	*130	83½	879.1	0.7	φ
5¼ pc Cv Pf _____		211	+1	225	155	98.4	3.3	—
■Nurdin P"k _____		150	−1	186	144	186.3	4.9	9.9
■Park Food _____		124m	−1	153	78⅝	64.3	3.4	φ
■Sainsbury (J) _____		437	+5	476	337	7,704	2.7	17.3
Shoprite _____		507	−5	569	291	71.3	1.0	—
■Tesco _____		242	+6	*296	215	4,702	3.5	12.1
■Thorntons _____		164	___	210	162	104.5	2.9	13.2
Wardell Robts 1 £ _____		63	___	111	57	14.0	6.3	8.6
Watson & Phep _____		225	___	357	223	77.3	7.6	9.6

Source: Financial Times: London Share Service 14 August 1992

Summary of financial ratios

Liquidity ratios

$$\text{Current ratio} = \frac{\text{Current assets}}{\text{Current liabilities}}$$

$$\text{Acid test (quick) ratio} = \frac{\text{Current assets} - \text{stocks}}{\text{Current liabilities}}$$

Profitability ratios

$$\text{ROCE} = \frac{\text{Profit before interest and tax (operating profit)}}{\text{Capital employed}}$$

$$\text{Return to shareholders (pre tax)} = \frac{\text{Net profit on ordinary activities before tax}}{\text{Shareholders' funds}}$$

$$\text{Return to shareholders (post tax)} = \frac{\text{Net profit on ordinary activities after tax}}{\text{Shareholders' funds}}$$

$$\text{Gross profit ratio} = \frac{\text{Gross profit}}{\text{Turnover}}$$

$$\text{Operating profit ratio} = \frac{\text{Operating profit}}{\text{Turnover}}$$

$$\text{Net profit ratio} = \frac{\text{Profit on ordinary activities before tax}}{\text{Turnover}}$$

Efficiency ratios

$$\text{Stock turnover} = \frac{\text{Stock (or average stock)}}{\text{Cost of sales}} \times 365$$

$$\text{Debtors turnovers} = \frac{\text{Debtors (or average debtors)}}{\text{Turnover}} \times 365$$

$$\text{Creditors turnovers} = \frac{\text{Trade creditors}}{\text{Total credit purchases}} \times 365$$

(NB: Total credit purchases is not available from published accounts, so cost of sales is used as a proxy.)

$$\text{Fixed asset turnover} = \frac{\text{Turnover}}{\text{Fixed assets}}$$

Investment ratios

$$\text{Gearing (either)} = \frac{\text{Long term loans}}{\text{Shareholders' funds}}$$

$$\text{Gearing} = \frac{\text{Long term loans}}{\text{Capital employed}}$$
(or)

$$\text{Interest cover} = \frac{\text{Operating profit}}{\text{Interest charges}}$$

Stock market ratios

$$\text{EPS} = \frac{\text{Profit on ordinary activities after taxation}}{\text{Number of shares in issue}}$$

$$\text{Price earnings} = \frac{\text{Market price of share}}{\text{EPS}}$$
(P/E ratio)

$$\text{Dividend Yield} = \frac{\text{Dividend per share}}{\text{Market price of share}}$$

The use of accounting ratios for inter-firm comparison

While accounting ratio analysis does provide a technique that can be applied to intra-firm and inter-firm comparisons, there are inherent problems in the application of such a technique. The problems arise mainly from the different methods of interpreting the basic concepts and conventions of accounting as presented in Chapter 2. For intra-firm comparison over time (like that using the Zeda plc figures), if the methods of accounting have been held constant then useful year-by-year comparisons can be made. Using ratio analysis for inter-firm comparison is more problematic as different companies in the same industry may use different interpretations of the basic concepts and conventions of accounting. These different interpretations are known as *accounting policies*.

Accounting policies

In Chapter 2 we considered the concepts and conventions of accounting and how these were augmented by accounting standards and legislation to provide a common basis for financial reporting. While this may be the case, there is the opportunity for companies to adopt different accounting bases or policies which comply with the requirements of the concepts and conventions, accounting standard and legislation. The adoption of specific accounting policies by a company is the result of judgement by the management of that company to adopt those accounting policies which they consider most appropriate in the preparation of that company's financial accounts.

Accounting policies affect the value placed on fixed assets. The following three examples highlight the issues involved; there are more.

1   Using the historic cost convention, fixed assets are recorded in the accounts at their original cost. To spread the cost of a long-term asset over its useful life fixed assets are depreciated which creates a charge for the use of that asset in the profit and loss account. There are several methods of charging depreciation, but consideration of just two methods, straight line and reducing balance, will illustrate the problem of inter-firm comparability. Consider the following example:

Two companies acquire identical assets at the same point in time, costing £10,000 each. Company X decides to provide for depreciation using the straight line method over a 10 year period. The annual change for depreciation will be £1,000 p.a. Company Y decides to provide for depreciation using the reducing balance method providing depreciation on a 25% reducing balance. The depreciation in each year of usage will vary as follows:

Original cost	10,000	
depreciation Year 1	2,500	(25% × 10,000)
Written down value Year 1	7,500	
depreciation Year 2	1,875	(25% × 7,500)
Written down value Year 1	5,625	
depreciation Year 3	1,406	(25% × 5,625)
Written down value Year 3	4,219	
etc.		
etc.		

If a comparison between the companies is made in Year 2, then the balance sheet values will be as follows:

	Company X	Company Y
Original cost	10,000	10,000
Depreciation to date	2,000	4,375
Net book value	8,000	5,625

Quite clearly, any ratio involving these values, namely capital employed and fixed asset turnover, will produce very different figures, not because of different efficiency and profitability levels but solely because of different accounting policies. Similarly the charge for the use of the assets in the profit and loss accounts will be different and make all the profitability ratios uncomparable.

Even if the companies had adopted the same accounting policy for depreciation they could have been based on different estimated asset lives or different percentages for the reducing balance method.

2   Fixed assets revaluation is a policy adopted by some companies, particularly the revaluation of land and buildings on a periodic basis:

If the balance sheet of a company is as follows:

	£m	£m
Fixed assets Land and buildings		0.9
Equipment and plant		1.3
		2.2
Current assets	1.9	
less Current liabilities	0.8	1.1
		3.3
Ordinary share capital	1.0	
Retained profit	0.7	
	1.7	
Long-term loans	1.6	3.3

after the revaluation of the land and buildings to £2.6m, the balance sheet appears to be strengthened by increasing the value of equity in relation to debt finance as follows:

	£m	£m
Fixed assets Land and buildings		2.6
Equipment and plant		1.3
		3.9
Current assets	1.9	
less Current liabilities	0.8	1.1
		5.0
Ordinary share capital	1.0	
Retained profit	0.7	
Revaluation reserve	1.7	
	3.4	
Long-term loans	1.6	5.0

The revaluation reserve is not available for distribution as it represents an unrealized gain but it makes the finance gearing reduce as follows:

	before revaluation	*after revaluation*
$\dfrac{debt}{equity}$ ratio	94%	47%

Quite clearly the adoption of such an accounting policy makes inter-company ratio analysis very different and often misleading.

3 If a property development is being undertaken by, say, a major retail company building a new store, then a common accounting policy is to charge the interest on the money borrowed to finance the development against the cost of the fixed asset being created, rather than charge the interest through the profit and loss account

as normal. This increases the value of the fixed asset and avoids charging interest in the year it accrues so increasing profits during the development period.

These three examples provide an insight into the way accounting policies can affect the asset valuation and the reported profits of an organization. The more cynical amongst you may see these as a way of 'window dressing' the accounts to show the managers in a favourable light to their shareholders.

Illustration 3.2   Extracts from the annual report and accounts Central Independent Television plc, 1990

Note 1   Accounting policies
  (A) *Basis of preparation of accounts* The accounts on pages xx–xx have been prepared in the expectation that the group will be awarded the East, West and South Midlands Region Channel 3 broadcasting licence with effect from 1 January 1993.
  They have also been prepared in accordance with applicable accounting standards and under the historical cost convention except for owned plant, equipment and motor vehicles which are revalued each year to current cost having regard to price indices published by the Central Statistical Office.
  (B) *Basis of consolidation* The Group accounts consolidate the accounts of the company and its subsidiary companies and associated undertakings. The Group's share of the results of associated undertakings is based on unaudited accounts for the periods ended 31 December.
  A separate profit and loss account for Central Independent Television plc is not presented.
  (C) *Programmes and film rights* The costs of the Group's own productions and purchased film rights are wholly written off on first transmission. Untransmitted programmes, including programmes in the course of production and the rights to films not yet transmitted, are carried forward at cost less such amounts as are necessary to reduce these assets to their estimated realizable value.
  (D) *Foreign currencies* Transactions denominated in foreign currency are translated at the rate of exchange ruling at the date of the transaction. At the balance sheet date all monetary assets and liabilities denominated in foreign currencies are translated at the rates contracted to settle the transactions. In the absence of such contracts the rate ruling at the year end is used.
  The results of foreign subsidiaries and associated undertakings are translated at the average rate for the year. Exchange

differences arising from the translation of the opening net investment in foreign subsidiaries and associated undertakings are taken to reserves. Other exchange differences are taken to the profit and loss account.

(E) *Intangible fixed assets and depreciation* Licence renewal costs are carried forward in the expectation that the broadcasting licence will be renewed on 1 January 1993. Depreciation will be provided during the life of the new licence.

(F) *Tangible fixed assets and depreciation* Depreciation is calculated on cost or valuation on a straight line basis at the following annual rates so as to write down the value of the assets to an estimated residual value over their expected useful lives:

Technical and other equipment 20%

Short leasehold improvements over the period of the lease.

(G) *Finance leases* Assets held under finance lease agreements are included in tangible fixed assets and are amortized in accordance with the Group's depreciation policy. Outstanding obligations due under the leases, net of finance charges allocated to future periods, are included in creditors. The finance element of the rental payment is charged to the profit and loss account over the term of the lease.

(H) *Operating leases* Amounts falling due under operating leases are treated as expenses chargeable to the profit and loss account on an accruals basis.

(I) *Deferred taxation* Provision is made, using the liability method for taxation deferred by capital allowances on fixed assets, eligible programmes and other timing differences to the extent that the Directors consider that a liability will arise or an asset will be realized in the foreseeable future.

(J) *Pensions* The Group operates a contributory defined benefit pension scheme covering the majority of its permanent employees. The pension fund is administered by trustees and is accounted for separately from the Group's finances. The Group's contributions are paid in accordance with actuarial advice and are charged so as to spread the cost of pensions over the expected remaining service lives of current employees.

No doubt comparability of performance between companies will be enhanced if the accounting data for different companies is produced using the same accounting policies. While legislation and SSAPs help in this endeavour, there are still opportunities for different interpretations of the same economic event and the accounting treatment that results.

Inter-firm comparison

Published data is available by industry grouping published by the Centre for Interfirm Comparisons Limited. This organization aggregates and analyses data provided by its subscribing members, so that industry indices of performance may be established, not only for accounting ratios but other management issues. Copies of this are available in most libraries.

The Stock Exchange also provides sector performance figures for companies quoted on the exchange. It is presented on a daily basis in the *Financial Times* and is known as the 'FT − Actuaries Share Indices'. It provides earnings yields dividend yields, and P/E ratios by industry sector.

Summary

This chapter has dealt in detail with the reasons for ratio analysis and the methods of computing accounting ratios for inter-firm and intra-firm comparison. The ratios were presented under the headings of liquidity, profitability, efficiency and investments ratios.

The latter part of the chapter gave illustrations of some of the problems of ratio analysis by considering how different accounting policies can dramatically alter the asset and profit levels of a company.

After studying this chapter you should be able to:

- Explain why accounting ratios are useful for analysing company performances.
- Calculate accounting ratios relating to liquidity, profitability, efficiency and investment.
- Apply the ratios to inter-firm and intra-firm comparisons.
- Understand the Stock Exchange data supplied in the *Financial Times*.
- Understand the effect of accounting policies on ratio analysis.

Further reading

Glautier, M.W.E. and Underdown, B. (1991) *Accounting Theory and Practice*, 4th edn, Pitman, London, Chapter 15

Laughlin, R. and Gray, R.H. (1988) *Financial Accounting: Method and Meaning*, VNR 1988 International, London, Chapter 8

Rickwood, C. and Thomas, A. (1992) *An Introduction to Financial Accounting*, McGraw Hill, Maidenhead, Chapter 29

Problems and discussion topics

1   The naive interpretation of many financial statistics implies that 'higher is better, lower is worse'. However, such a sweeping generalization is incorrect. For example, a high current ratio may imply an unwarranted build up of stocks and work-in-progress, and this may be a sign of an unfavourable situation in the future.

For each of the following statistics you are required to give an example of a high value that might not be interpreted favourably (or might have unfavourable connotations as well as a favourable interpretation).

(a)   E.P.S.
(b)   Return on capital employed
(c)   Return to shareholders' funds
(d)   Net income to sales
(e)   Current ratio
(f)   Acid test ratio
(g)   Debt–equity ratio
(h)   Times interest covered

2   The following data relates to the student numbers (Table 1) and financial data (Table 2) of four universities.

Table 1   *Full-time equivalent (FTE) student numbers*

Conversion factors		H	L	S	T
1.00	Full-time	2,437	4,517	3,908	3,961
0.90	Sandwich	2,216	1,306	3,975	3,731
0.40	Part-time (day and evening)	951	1,385	1,412	1,050
0.20	Evening only	16	403	141	147
		5,620	7,611	9,436	8,889

H = Halifax University; L = Leek University; S = Southsea University; T = Thorne University.

Table 2   *Summary: Actual expenditure 1987–1988 (£'000)*

Expenditure heading	H	L	S	T
Academic staff	10,062	12,550	15,149	14,710
Professional and other academic support staff	3,233	3,557	5,822	4,833
Premises	3,139	2,756	4,079	4,124
Supplies and services	1,749	1,279	2,381	2,703
Transport	278	312	565	647
Establishment expenses	1,027	1,166	1,104	1,120
Agency services	38	–	182	(33)
Miscellaneous expenses	325	334	719	483
	19,851	21,954	30,001	28,587
Miscellaneous income	(327)	(332)	(330)	(450)
Catering services (net deficit)	46	228	315	200
Residences (net deficit)	245	132	631	183
Debt charges and other provisions	2,949	1,893	3,349	2,656
Redundancy and other premature retirement compensation	222	729	642	508
Total expenditure	22,986	24,604	34,608	31,684

(a) Using the data provided above, which university do you consider to be the most efficient?
(b) Which areas of expenditure do you consider worthy of investigation for each one?
(c) What factors do you consider would make comparisons between such institutions difficult or meaningless?

3   The details given below are a summary of the balance sheets of four companies engaged in different industries.

	A %	B %	C %	D %
Land and buildings	10	2	57	5
Other fixed assets	17	1	13	73
Stocks and work-in-progress	44	–	16	1
Trade debtors	6	77	1	13
Other debtors	11	–	2	5
Cash and investments	12	20	11	3
	100	100	100	100
Capital and reserves	37	5	55	50
Creditors: over one year	12	5	6	25

Creditors: under one year				
Trade	32	85	24	6
Other	16	5	15	11
Bank overdraft	3	–	–	8
Total capital employed	100	100	100	100

The activities of the four companies are as follows:

1 Operator of a chain of retail supermarkets
2 Lorry transport operator
3 Commercial bank with a network of branches
4 Contractor in the civil engineering industry

You are required to:
(a) State which of the above activities relate to which set of balance sheet details, giving a brief summary of your reasoning in each case.
(b) State what you consider to be the major limitations of ratio analysis as a means of interpreting accounting information.

4 The summarized accounts of Ragidem plc are shown below:

Group consolidated profit and loss accounts (£m)

	1988	1989	1990	1991	1992
Turnover	220	264	294	314	327
Operating profit	30	32	34	39	43
Add interest receivable	1	1	1	1	1
	31	33	35	40	44
less Interest payable	7	7	10	12	16
Profit before tax	24	26	25	28	28
less Taxation	7	7	6	9	9
	17	19	19	19	19
Extraordinary items	2	–	1	–	1
	19	19	20	19	20
Dividends	5	6	6	7	8
Retained earnings	14	13	14	12	12

Group consolidated balance sheets (£m)

	1988	1989	1990	1991	1992
Ordinary share capital (£1 par value)	45	45	45	45	45
Reserves	74	87	101	113	125
	119	132	146	158	170

16% unsecured loan (1990–93)	20	20	15	10	5
10% debenture (1993)	18	18	18	18	18
Bank loan–variable rate (note 1)	–	4	11	29	41
Capital employed	£157	£174	£190	£215	£234
Land, buildings, plant etc. (note 2)	87	106	112	112	116
Long-term investments	8	8	8	8	9
Fixed assets	95	114	120	120	125
Stock	80	96	100	109	125
Debtors	59	60	74	91	111
Cash	9	23	16	–	15
Current assets	148	179	190	200	251
Creditors	34	47	49	55	61
Tax payable	9	8	10	11	12
Dividends	5	6	6	7	8
Short-term loans	38	58	55	32	61
Current liabilities	86	119	120	105	142
Net assets employed	£157	£174	£190	£215	£234

Note 1: This loan is renegotiated each year, the current date for repayment is 1996.
Note 2: Capital expenditure has been contracted amounting to £30m for the year 1993.

	1988	1989	1990	1991	1992
Average share price Ragidem (pence)	380	420	378	370	320
Average P/E ratio for the industry	10	10	14	15	18

You are required to:
Prepare a report commenting on the main features of the financial performance of Ragidem plc.
  (i) Present suitable ratios which highlight the main features of the financial performance of Ragidem plc.
  (ii) Prepare a report commenting on these features.

4 Cost classification

The aims of this chapter are to:

- Introduce the idea of a data collection system.
- Provide an understanding of the way the data collection system can contribute to management decision making, planning and control.
- Introduce the idea of cost objects.
- Describe the ways that costs can be classified.
- Describe how costs, both direct and indirect, can be charged to products.
- Distinguish between absorption costing and marginal costing.
- Introduce the ideas of quality costing, activity based management and strategic management accounting.

Introduction

We are now going to concentrate on the management accounting issues within organizations. The issues involved in management accounting are illustrated in Figure 1.4 which is derived from the outline of the book represented in Figure 4.2. This particular chapter is concerned with the data collection system and how it can contribute to management decision-making and planning and control. In this chapter the nature of cost within an organization will be analysed and developed to provide a basis for subsequent chapters.

Cost objects

The key to understanding management accounting is to recognize that costs are classified in many different ways depending upon the purpose for which the information is to be used. The purpose is determined by the activity being undertaken and a useful way of looking at this is to talk about *cost objects*. A cost object is any activity for which a separate measurement of cost is desired. For instance, if you want to know the cost of a particular product, the cost object is the product. If you want to know the cost of running a ward in a hospital, the cost object is the ward. In today's competitive

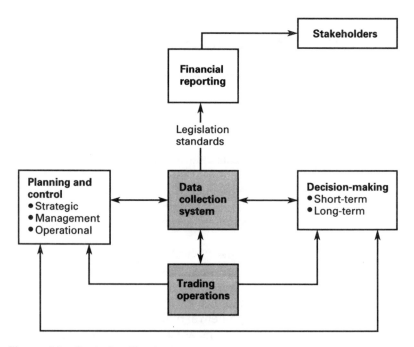

Figure 4.1   *Cost classification*

environment it is becoming important for management accountants to produce cost information about competitors. While this can be very difficult, the cost object in this case is the competitor.

At this early stage, it is also important to realize that information about cost objects may be required for different reasons. For example, the cost of a product may be required for either decision-making purposes or for stock valuation purposes. In each case the cost of the same product may be stated differently because of the end use to which the information is being put. For decision-making purposes you may decide to use the marginal cost of the product. For stock valuation purposes you may decide to use full absorption cost. The terms *marginal cost* and *full absorption cost* will be explained later. At this stage, it is simply important to recognize that the way the cost is analysed for a particular cost object will depend on the management task involved. Is the information about the cost object being provided to enable managers to make a decision; or is it to enable them to plan and control; or is it to enable them to value stock? Management accounting is therefore concerned with cost objects, and the provision of information about these cost objects to enable managers to carry out their different management tasks.

Classification of costs

The data collection system accumulates costs and classifies them into certain categories such as labour, material or overhead costs and then allocates these costs to cost objects. Whatever cost object is selected as the focus of attention, some costs will be direct (in the sense of being traceable to the cost object) while others will be indirect. A particular cost item can only be termed direct or indirect once the cost object has been specified. We have therefore introduced another classification of costs, i.e. direct and indirect costs.

Direct and indirect costs

Initially we will consider the cost object to be a product. Direct costs are costs which can be traced in full to the product. Conventionally direct costs can be further subdivided into direct materials, direct labour and direct expenses.

Direct materials consist of all those materials which can be physically identified with a specific product. For example, wood used to manufacture a table can easily be identified as part of the product and therefore can be classified as direct materials. Alternatively, materials used for the repair of a machine which is used for the manufacture of many different tables are classified as indirect materials. These items cannot be identified with any one specific product because they are used for the benefit of all products. However, it is important to note that not all items of materials that can be identified with a specific product are classified as direct materials. For example, the screws used in the manufacture of a particular table can be identified specifically with the table, but because the cost is likely to be insignificant the expense of tracing such items does not justify the possible benefits from calculating the more accurate product costs. Therefore, in this case the screws would be classified as indirect materials.

Direct labour consists of those labour costs which can be specifically traced to or identified with a particular product. Examples of direct labour costs include the wages of employees who assemble parts into the finished product, or machine operatives engaged in the production process. In contrast, the salaries of factory supervisors or the wages paid to staff in the stores department cannot be specifically identified with the product and thus form part of the indirect labour costs. The wages of all employees who do not work on the product itself but who help in the manufacturing operation are classified as indirect and part of the manufacturing overhead cost.

Other direct costs are called *direct expenses*. The cost of hiring a machine for producing a specific product is an example of a direct expense. Although other direct expenses are uncommon, it is important that all indirect expenses are carefully examined to see whether it is possible to reclassify some of them as direct expenses. A low level of indirect costs means that there is less difficulty in absorbing the costs subsequently into a product.

Absorption of costs into a product

Having briefly identified costs into their direct and indirect categories it is now useful to look at the way these costs are charged to products. In doing this we can introduce the idea of a coding system which forms a basic requirement for any cost classification system. We will also look at the role that cost centres play in charging costs to products. In a later chapter we will be discussing the concept of responsibility accounting and the idea of responsibility centres. Responsibility centres may be classified in accordance with the responsibilities undertaken by the centre managers. They can be cost centres, revenue centres, profit centres, investment centres or strategic business units. Figure 4.2 shows a cross-section of responsibility centres in a manufacturing organization.

As mentioned earlier, we are currently concentrating on *cost centres* and it is sufficient at this stage to say that a cost centre is a responsibility centre where the manager assumes responsibility for costs. Using terminology already developed in this chapter, a cost centre is in fact a cost object. Cost centres can be quite small, e.g. one person or one machine, or quite large. There may be a series of cost centres within a department, or a whole department may be a cost centre. Once cost centres have been set up for an organization, it is then necessary to set up a system which charges costs to the cost centres.

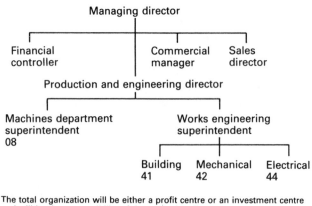

The total organization will be either a profit centre or an investment centre and will be the responsibility of the managing director.

The sales director will have both revenue and cost centres under his control although these are not highlighted in the snapshot of an organization chart shown above.

The machines department superintendent is responsible for cost centre number 08.

The works engineering superintendent is responsible for three cost centres – cost centre number 41 (building), cost centre number 42 (mechanical) and cost centre number 44 (electrical).

Figure 4.2   *Responsibility centres in a manufacturing organization*

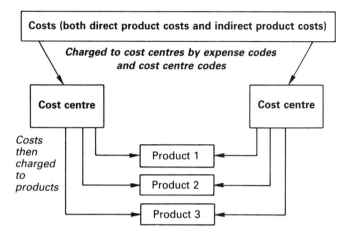

Figure 4.3 *Charging costs to units of product*

Cost centres have an important role to play in the provision of costing information within organizations. Initially cost accounting is concerned with the accumulation of costs on the basis of cost centres. The costs can then be subsequently charged to units of product in order to provide product cost information. Figure 4.3 shows this process in very simplified form.

A basic requirement for accumulating at these two levels is an appropriate coding system that charges costs to identified cost centres and products. Cost accounting procedures require that all source documents are coded by reference to cost centres initially, before they can be attached to individual products. Costs need to be charged to cost centres using cost codes and expense category codes. An example of these codes is shown in Figure 4.4. Actual costs can then be charged to the appropriate cost centre and expense category within that cost centre.

Having described the system of charging costs to cost centres, through a coding system, we will now go on to concentrate on the charging of these costs to products. Direct labour, direct materials and direct expenses can be charged directly to a product using the appropriate expense code and product code. This process is shown in Figure 4.5.

Indirect costs (commonly referred to as overhead costs) cannot be charged directly to a product and as a result it is necessary to use a system of overhead absorption in order to charge products with an appropriate share of overhead costs. Overhead absorption relies on the allocation and apportionment of overhead costs to cost centres. It is important to note that there are two different types of cost centres present in this process:

Service cost centres – these are not involved in the actual manufacturing process, but provide services to the manufacturing cost centres

Cost centre code	Cost centre description
01	Raw materials
02	Cleaners
04	Personnel department
08	Machines department
11	Quality control department
22	Stores department
37	Canteen
41	Works engineer – building
42	Works engineer – mechanical
44	Works engineer – electrical

Cost centre	08 Machines

Expense Category	*Expense Code*
Labour	001
Salaries	030
Natural gas	150
Electricity	160
Depreciation	230
Consumables	252

Therefore salaries cost in the canteen is coded 37 030.
Therefore depreciation cost in the machines cost centre is coded 08 230

Figure 4.4 *Cost centre coding in a manufacturing organization*

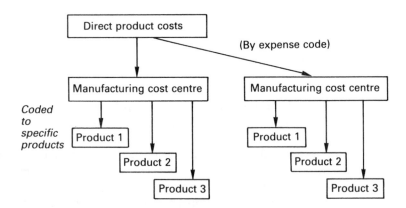

Figure 4.5 *Coding to specific products*

and facilities for the factory as a whole. Examples of service cost centres are maintenance, stores and canteen.
Manufacturing cost centres – these are involved in the manufacturing process, such as a machines department.

Overhead costs are charged to both manufacturing and service cost centres by either allocation or apportionment. *Allocation* is where overhead costs can be specifically related to the cost centre. For example, the costs of the canteen staff are direct costs as far as the canteen is concerned but indirect costs as far as the product goes. Examples of overheads which may be allocated are indirect labour, indirect materials and depreciation. *Apportionment* is where overhead costs are incurred for the benefit of many cost centres and cannot be specifically related to one particular cost centre, for example business rates. Elaborate systems have been developed for apportioning overhead cost between the various cost centres but in the main these are very arbitrary.

Having accumulated overhead costs to both service and manufacturing cost centres, the next stage is to apportion service cost centre costs to the manufacturing cost centres on some 'fair' basis. The apportionment of service cost centre costs to manufacturing cost centres results in the accumulation of all overhead costs into the manufacturing cost centres. The next stage is to calculate overhead absorption rates for the manufacturing cost centres, which then allows for products to be charged with an appropriate amount of overhead expense. The process of charging overhead costs to products is shown in Figure 4.6. An example of this process is shown in Illustration 4.1.

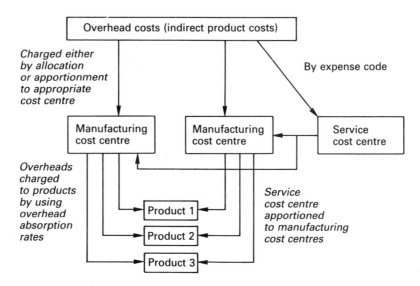

Figure 4.6 *Charging for overheads. As a result of procedures shown in Figures 4.5 and 4.6, products 1, 2 and 3 have now been charged with their direct costs and an appropriate share of overhead costs*

Illustration 4.1 Charging overheads to products

The annual budgeted production overhead costs for a factory with two production departments (Machine Shop and Assembly) and one service department (Stores) are as follows:

	£	£
Indirect wages and supervision		
Machine Shop	100,000	
Assembly	60,000	
Stores	20,000	
		180,000
Indirect materials		
Machine Shop	90,000	
Assembly	30,000	
Stores	5,000	
		125,000
Rent		40,000
Light and heat		20,000
Insurance for machinery		15,000
		380,000

The following information is also available:

	Machine Shop	Assembly	Stores
Area occupied (sq m)	10,000	5,000	5,000
Book value of machinery (£)	100,000	50,000	–
Direct and indirect materials issued by the stores department (£)	300,000	100,000	–
Budgeted machine hours – machine department		26,000	
Budgeted direct labour hours – assembly		6,000	

An overhead analysis sheet would be prepared which shows the allocation, apportionment and overhead absorption rate calculations:

> **Stage 1**   Allocation and apportionment of overhead costs to cost centres

Item of expenditure	Basis of apportionment	Machine Shop £	Assembly £	Stores £
Indirect wages and supervision	Allocation	100,000	60,000	20,000
Indirect materials	Allocation	90,000	30,000	5,000
Rent*a	Apportion by area	20,000	10,000	10,000
Light and heat*b	Apportion by area	10,000	5,000	5,000

Insurance for machinery*c	Apportion by book value of machinery	10,000	5,000	—
		230,000	110,000	40,000

Stage 2	Apportion service cost centre costs to manufacturing cost centre

Stores*d	Issues of materials from stores department	30,000	10,000	(40,000)
		260,000	120,000	—

Stage 3	Work out overhead absorption rates

Number of machine hours	26,000	
Number of labour hours		6,000

Overhead absorption rates

Machine shop – machine hours overhead absorption rate	£10 per machine hour	
Assembly – direct labour hours overhead absorption rate		£20 per direct labour hour

Stage 4	Apply production overhead cost to products

Product A spends 3 hours in the Machine Shop and 1 hour in Assembly. Production overheads charged to a unit of Product A would therefore be:

	£
Machine Shop 3 × 10	30
Assembly 1 × 20	20
	50

Notes
*a Rent – the budgeted rent cost is £40,000 and the factory covers 20,000 square metres. The cost per metre is therefore £2 and apportionment of rent costs would be as follows:

		£
Machine Shop	10,000sq m × £2 =	20,000
Assembly	5,000sq m × £2 =	10,000
Stores	5,000sq m × £2 =	10,000

*b Light and heat – the budgeted light and heating cost is £20,000 and the factory covers 20,000 square metres. The cost per metre is therefore £1 and apportionment of the light and heating cost would be as follows:

		£
Machine Shop	10,000sq m × £1 =	10,000
Assembly	5,000sq m × £1 =	5,000
Stores	5,000sq m × £1 =	5,000

*c Insurance for machinery – the budgeted insurance cost is £15,000 and the book value of the machinery is £150,000. The cost per £ of book value is therefore £0.10 and apportionment of the insurance costs would be as follows:

		£
Machine Shop	£100,000 × £0.10 =	10,000
Assembly	£50,000 × £0.10 =	5,000

*d Apportionment of stores department costs to the two manufacturing cost centres – the budgeted overhead cost for the stores department has been worked out at £40,000. Apportionment will be based on the value of the direct and indirect materials issued by the stores department to the two manufacturing cost centres. The total value of material issued is £400,000 and therefore the cost per £ of material issued is £0.10. Apportionment of the stores department costs is as follows:

		£
Machine Shop	£300,000 × £0.10 =	30,000
Assembly	£100,000 × £0.10 =	10,000

Illustration 4.1 highlights the process of charging production overhead costs to products. A number of the issues involved in this process will be referred to later in the book. Critics of the approach used here suggest that activity based costing is a better way of charging overhead costs to products. Activity based costing will be discussed later in this chapter and in more depth in Chapter 7. Overhead absorption rates are used in variance analysis and this is an issue we will pick up in Chapter 6. Chapter 9 deals with pricing, and the use of full costs in pricing decisions will be dealt with in that chapter.

It is important to note at this stage that overhead absorption rates are normally worked out on the basis of budgeted costs and budgeted activity. The differences between budgeted overhead costs and actual overhead costs are dealt with at the cost centre level in the form of variance analysis. This is an issue we will deal with later when we look at budgeting. It is also important to note that what we have described above is the calculation of a full absorption product cost. For decision-making purposes it may be more useful to calculate a product cost based on marginal costing. This is an issue we will deal with later.

Fixed, variable, semi-variable and semi-fixed costs

Having concentrated on direct and indirect costs and the use of cost centres, it would now be useful to have a look at another way of classifying costs. The knowledge of how costs behave is important for the tasks of decision-making and planning and control within an organization. For these purposes costs can be classified as being variable, fixed, semi-variable and semi-fixed. In the long run it can be argued that all costs are variable and this particular point has been argued strongly by Johnson and Kaplan (1987). However, we will concentrate on a short timescale and an activity level which is within the relevant range.

A cost is *fixed* if, within a specified period of time, it does not change in response to changes in the level of activity. Total fixed costs are constant over all levels of activity (within relevant range) whereas unit fixed costs decrease proportionally with the level of activity.

A *variable* cost is one that changes in response to changes in the level of activity. Variable costs vary in direct proportion to the volume of activity, that is, doubling the level of activity will double the total variable cost. Total variable costs are therefore linear and a unit variable cost is constant.

In order to illustrate the concept of fixed and variable costs, we will use the example of running a car. The road fund licence for a car is a fixed cost since the total cost remains the same irrespective of the number of miles travelled. Petrol costs are variable since the amount of petrol used varies directly with the number of miles travelled.

Semi-variable costs include both a fixed and a variable element. For example, a telephone bill contains a fixed standing charge and a variable charge based on the number of units dialled. A *semi-fixed* cost or stepped cost is one where the cost remains constant for a range of activity; then, when the activity increases still further the cost will take a step upwards. The example usually used to illustrate this is that of a factory or office supervisor. Up to a certain level of activity one supervisor is sufficient. However, if the activity and therefore number of people being supervised increases, it will probably be necessary to employ another supervisor. There will therefore be a stepped increase in supervisory costs.

A graphical presentation of cost behaviour is shown in Figure 4.7.

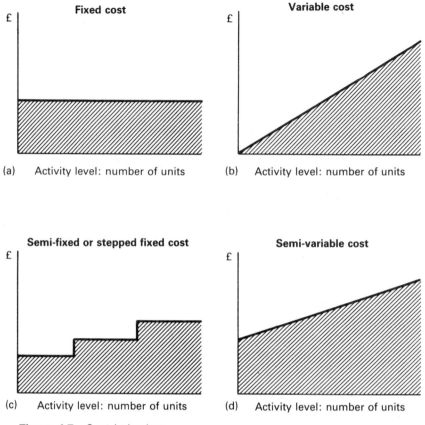

Figure 4.7   *Cost behaviour*

Another way of classifying costs, which is closely linked to the idea of cost behaviour, is in terms of relevant costs. In fact, in order to extend the discussion we can talk about relevant costs and revenues.

Relevant costs and revenues

The concept of *relevant costs and revenues* is particularly important for decision-making. Relevant costs and revenues are only those which will be affected by a decision. Costs and revenues which are independent of a decision are obviously not relevant and need not be considered when making that decision. The relevant financial inputs for decision-making purposes are therefore future cash flows which will differ between the various alternatives being considered. These costs and revenues are also often referred to as *incremental* or *differential* costs and revenues.

Costs that have already been incurred are not relevant to a particular decision. Costs that have already been committed, even though they may not yet have been paid, are not relevant to the decision. This is because those costs will have to be met irrespective of the decision taken. The same principle applies to revenues.

It is important to note that a relevant cost may be one that changes with the level of activity, or it may not be. Therefore it is wrong to assume that relevant costs are exclusively composed of variable costs. Costs classified as fixed can be relevant, providing they are future costs which differ between alternatives.

It is not always easy to identify relevant costs and revenues since this kind of information is not easily extracted from the accounting records of a company. This is particularly true when we are calculating opportunity costs. An *opportunity cost* is a cost which measures the opportunity that is lost or sacrificed when the choice of one course of action requires that an alternative course of action be given up. Opportunity costs occur only when there are scarce resources. We will be looking at the issue of relevant costs and revenues in more detail in Chapter 7.

In order to identify yet another classification of costs, we will return to the idea of responsibility accounting. We introduced the idea of responsibility centres earlier in this chapter and Figure 4.2 illustrated a cross-section of responsibility centres in a manufacturing organization. Costs and revenues allocated to responsibility centres should be classified according to whether they are controllable or non-controllable by the manager of the responsibility centre.

Controllable and non-controllable costs

The objective behind classifying costs into controllable and non-controllable elements is to help managers plan and control. The concepts of responsibility and control are very closely linked. A *controllable* cost may be defined as a cost which the manager of a particular cost centre can control. If the manager of the responsibility centre has no control over the occurrence of a cost, then the cost should be classified as *non-controllable* as far as the manager of that cost centre is concerned. It is important to classify costs in this way in order to be able to evaluate a manager's performance fairly. It is unreasonable to evaluate a manager's performance on things he cannot control. The same also applies to revenues and profits.

If we return to Figure 4.2, it is important to note that controllability and responsibility issues are important at all levels within the hierarchy. The total organization depicted in the diagram could be either a profit centre, an investment centre or a strategic business unit and will be the responsibility of the managing director. It is just as important at this level to classify costs and revenues into controllable and non-controllable elements. This is particularly so if the organization is part of a large group and the headquarters staff make some of the decisions (e.g. on capital investments over a certain amount). It is also important to note that non-controllable costs at one level in the hierarchy may be controllable by somebody at a different level. For example, the machines superintendent in Figure 4.2 may not have any control over wage negotiations but the production and engineering director may have.

We have now looked at several different classifications of costs (direct/indirect; fixed/variable; relevant costs and benefits; controllable/uncontrollable costs) and it is now our intention to discuss the terms absorption and marginal costing.

Absorption versus marginal costs

At this stage it is useful to identify the difference between the terms marginal and absorption costing. *Absorption costing* is a system of costing which charges fixed costs as well as variable costs to cost objects. This system was illustrated in Figure 4.6 when all overhead costs were absorbed into the product, together with the direct costs illustrated in Figure 4.5. In a *marginal costing* system only variable costs are charged to cost objects and fixed costs of the period are written off in full against the aggregate contribution, contribution being sales value less variable costs. It is argued that the special value of marginal costing is in decision-making.

Illustration 4.2 provides an example of the two different ways of presenting cost information.

Illustration 4.2   Absorption versus marginal costing

The following information is available for a firm producing and selling a single product.

Budget:	
Production units	24,000
Sales units	24,000

	£000s
Direct materials	132
Direct labour	132
Direct expenses	–
Variable production overhead	48
Fixed production overhead	144
Variable selling and administration overhead	24
Fixed selling and administration overhead	96

The product is sold for £30 per unit.

Using the two formats, the budgeted unit data and the budgeted profit and loss account would be set out as follows:

Marginal costing

(1) Unit data

	£	£
Selling price		30
Variable costs		
Direct materials	5.50	
Direct labour	5.50	
Direct expenses	–	
Variable production overhead	2.00	
Variable selling and administration overhead	1.00	
		14
Contribution per unit		16

Absorption costing

(1) Unit data

	£	£
Price price		30
Production cost of sales		
Direct materials	5.50	
Direct labour	5.50	
Direct expenses	–	
Variable production overhead	2.00	
Fixed production overhead	6.00	
		19
Gross profit		11
Selling and administration costs		
Variable selling and administration overheads		1
Fixed selling and administration overheads		4
Net profit per unit		6

(2) Profit and loss account

	£000's	£000's
Sales revenue		720
Variable costs		
Direct materials	132	
Direct labour	132	
Direct expenses	–	
Variable production overhead	48	
Variable selling and administration overheads	24	
		336
Contribution		384
Fixed costs		
Fixed production overhead	144	
Fixed selling and administration overhead	96	
		240
Net profit		144

(2) Profit and loss account

	£000's	£000's
Sales revenue		720
Production cost of sales		
Direct materials	132	
Direct labour	132	
Direct expenses	–	
Variable production overhead	48	
Fixed production overhead	144	
		456
Gross profit		264
Selling and administration costs		
Variable selling and administration overhead	24	
Fixed selling and administration overhead	96	
		120
Net profit		144

Illustration 4.2 is a simple example which highlights the two different approaches to costing systems. Absorption costing is also often referred to as *full costing*, while marginal costing is also often referred to as *variable costing*. We will be using these terms later in the book when we look at short-term decision-making (Chapter 7) and pricing (Chapter 9).

For external reporting purposes, SSAP 9 requires absorption costing to be used, since the cost of stocks must include all production overheads irrespective of whether they are fixed or variable. It is important to note that selling and administration costs would not be included in the stock valuation. However, for internal management purposes either system of costing can be used. The system to be used depends on the purpose for which the information is required, a point made earlier but repeated because it is fundamental to understanding the role of management accounting within organizations.

Having identified all the traditional classifications of costs, we are now going to introduce some additional classifications and ideas which are not very often found in traditional textbooks dealing with the management of financial resources. The first of these is a classification based on quality costs.

Quality costs

Another useful classification of costs, which links in with the desire to improve quality within organizations, is a classification into different types of quality costs. There is a recognition within all organizations that quality is of prime importance. In this time of 'world class performance', organizations need to be offering both world class products and world class service. The total quality management initiatives need to be recognized in management accounting information systems. One way of doing this is to classify costs into different types of quality costs.

CIMA identify the following classification of quality costs:

Cost of ensuring and assuring quality, as well as loss incurred when quality is not achieved. Quality costs are classified as prevention cost, appraisal cost, internal failure cost and external failure cost. (BS6143)

The different types of quality costs are defined as follows:

* *Prevention cost* − the cost incurred to reduce appraisal cost to a minimum. Prevention costs include: quality planning; design and development of quality measurement, test and control equipment; quality review and verification of design; calibration and maintenance of quality measurement, test and control equipment; calibration and maintenance of production equipment used to evaluate quality; supplier assurance; quality training; quality auditing; acqui-

sition, analysis and reporting of quality data; quality improvement programme.

- *Appraisal cost* – the cost incurred, such as inspection and testing, in initially ascertaining the conformance of the product to quality requirements. Included in appraisal costs are: pre-production verification; receiving inspection; laboratory acceptance testing; inspection and testing equipment; materials consumed during inspection and testing; analysis and reporting of test and inspection results; field performance testing; approvals and endorsements; stock valuation; record storage.
- *Internal failure cost* – the cost arising from inadequate quality before the transfer of ownership from supplier to purchaser. Included here are the cost of scrap, rework, retest, reinspection and redesign. Also included are: replacement and repair; trouble-shooting or defect/failure analysis; fault of sub-contractor; modification permits and concessions; downgrading; downtime.
- *External failure cost* – the cost arising from inadequate quality discovered after the transfer of ownership from supplier to purchaser. Included under this category are the cost of claims against warranty, replacement and consequential losses, and evaluation of penalties incurred. Also included are complaints; concessions; loss of sales; recall costs; product liability.

Illustration 4.3 provides an example of quality cost headings in a hospital. Recent changes in the National Health Service (NHS) have meant that hospitals are looking closely at the cost of quality in health care. The illustration highlights two different types of quality costs which can be related to our definitions discussed above. *Costs of conformance* relates to our definitions of prevention costs and appraisal costs. Costs of *non-conformance* relates to our definition of failure costs. Blades (1992) suggests that, in order to satisfy customers' requirements and provide 'value for money', it is vital for the organization to identify, measure and control the costs of quality. The basic argument is that more money spent up front on prevention measures will reduce the overall costs of quality since failure costs will fall in excess of the additional amounts spent on prevention. Blades (1992) makes the comment that failure costs in the NHS can have both massive financial and social costs.

Illustration 4.3 Quality costing in a hospital (Source: Blades, 1992)

With the recent National Health Service (NHS) reforms in the UK, hospitals are looking closely at the cost of quality in health care.

Cost of quality in health care
Costs of conformance in the NHS (low cost)

- Training on quality
- Administration
- Auditing
- Promoting quality
- Undertaking consumer surveys
- Planning for quality
- Writing procedures and specifications for quality

Costs of non-conformance in the NHS (high cost)

- Complaints
- Litigation
- Latrogenic disease (medically induced injury)
- All activities that are not performed correctly (e.g. poorly organized meetings, trying to get through on the telephone, and high staff turnover)

A theme of this book is the need to link management control systems to the strategies being followed by the organization. An organization following a quality strategy needs a management control system which reflects this. A system of cost classification which identifies costs into different categories of quality cost is one way of doing this. The next area to look at is activity based management.

Activity based management

Activity based management is a concept that will be introduced on numerous occasions throughout the book. The concept initially came into prominence with the development of activity based costing by Cooper and Kaplan (1988). Activity based costing concentrates on the need to make a more realistic allocation of overhead costs to products. It emphasizes the requirement to obtain a better understanding of the behaviour of overhead costs, and thus ascertains what causes overhead costs and how they relate to products. Cooper and Kaplan argue that activity based costing addresses the real issues of how and why overheads are being spent. The key is to identify the cost drivers for these overhead costs. The task is to understand, first, which activities are being delivered by these organizational overhead resources; second, what are the unit costs associated with delivering these activities; and, third, which products are using these activities and how many units they are using. Cooper and Kaplan (1988: 97) emphasized the strategic nature of activity based costing:

> Indeed, activity based costing is as much a tool of corporate strategy as it is a formal accounting system. Decisions about pricing, marketing, product design, and mix are among the most important ones managers can

make. None of them can be made effectively without accurate knowledge of product costs.

There has been a lot of debate about the merits of activity based costing and this debate will be covered in Chapter 7. Activity based costing literature has tended to concentrate on the use of the technique for improved product costing. However, product costing is not its only use and it can be argued that concentration on this aspect has led to much of the criticism of the technique. Emphasis should be placed on the role that 'activity management' can play in the planning and control of costs within organizations. This particular role will be introduced in Chapter 6.

The strategic nature of activity based management has been referred to in this section and it is to the strategic nature of accounting that we will turn next.

Strategic management accounting

A theme of the book is that management accounting provides information which helps managers to plan, control and take new decisions. Another theme of the book is the need to link strategy and control systems together. Strategic management accounting is a new development within management accounting which emphasizes the need for management accounting to become more externally focused to enable the enterprise to look outwards to the final goods market (Bromwich and Bhimani, 1989). Simmonds (1981: 26) described strategic management accounting as:

> The provision and analysis of management accounting data about a business and its competitors for use in developing and monitoring the business strategy, particularly relative levels and trends in real costs and prices, volume, market share, cash flow and the proportion demanded of a firm's total resources.

It is the idea of relativity which is key to the understanding of the role that accountants can play in the process. Contact with postgraduate management students in the past few years would suggest that some management accounting systems are still concentrating on internal matters. These internal concerns are important and are well documented in this book. However, it is also important that we signal the need for accounting information to play an important role in the strategic development of organizations. Reference to the ideas of strategic management accounting and continual reference to the importance of non-financial measures of performance should reinforce this point.

Summary

This chapter has been concerned with the data collection system and the way it can be used to contribute to management decision-making and control. As part of the data collection system we have also introduced the concepts of quality costing, activity based management and strategic management accounting. After reading this chapter you should be able to:

- Understand the purpose of a data collection system within an organization.
- Identify different cost objects within an organization.
- Recognize the different ways in which costs are classified depending upon the purpose for which the information is to be used.
- Allocate and apportion overhead costs to cost centres and calculate simple overhead absorption rates.
- Understand the difference between absorption costing and marginal costing.
- Understand the basic ideas behind quality costing, activity based management and strategic management accounting.

In the next chapter we will develop the ideas of planning and control within organizations and concentrate on the process of budgeting.

References

Blades, M. (1992) Healthy competition. *The TQM Magazine*, April, pp. 111–13
Bromwich, M. and Bhimani, A. (1989) *Management Accounting: Evolution Not Revolution*, Chartered Institute of Management Accountants, London
CIMA Terminology (1991) Chartered Institute of Management Accountants, London
Cooper, R. and Kaplan, R.S. (1988) Measure costs right: Make the right decisions. *Harvard Business Review*, September/October, pp. 96–103
Johnson, H.T. and Kaplan, R.S. (1987) *Relevance Lost: The Rise and Fall of Management Accounting*. Harvard Business School, Boston, Mass.
Simmonds, K. (1981) Strategic management accounting. *Management Accounting*, April, pp. 26–9

Further reading

Dale, B.G. and Plunkett, J.J. (1991) *Quality Costing*, Chapman and Hall, London
Drury, C. (1992) *Management and Cost Accounting*, 3rd edn, Chapman and Hall, London, Chapters 2 and 4
Ward, K. (1992) *Strategic Management Accounting*, Butterworth-Heinemann in association with the Chartered Institute of Management Accountants, Oxford

Problems and discussion topics

1 (a) Define the term 'cost object'.
   (b) Distinguish between direct and indirect costs and discuss the factors which should influence whether a particular cost is treated as direct or indirect in relation to a cost object.
   (c) Identify different cost objects within your own organization, or an organization that you are familiar with, and ascertain which costs are direct and indirect in relation to those cost objects.

2 The annual budgeted production overheads for a factory with two production departments (Machine Shop A and Machine Shop B) and one service department (Stores) are as follows:

	£	£
Indirect wages and supervision		
Machine Shop A	150,000	
Machine Shop B	100,000	
Stores	30,000	
		280,000
Indirect materials		
Machine Shop A	100,000	
Machine Shop B	50,000	
Stores	10,000	
		160,000
Rent		60,000
Light and heat		30,000
Insurance for machinery		20,000
		550,000

The following information is also available:

	Machine Shop A	Machine Shop B	Stores
Area occupied (sq m)	20,000	5,000	5,000
Book value of machinery (£)	60,000	20,000	–
Issues of direct and indirect material from stores (£)	350,000	200,000	–
Budgeted machine hours			
Machine Shop A	36,000 machine hours		
Machine Shop B	9,500 machine hours		

You are required to:

(a) Determine the budgeted overhead absorption rate for Machine Shop A.

(b) Determine the budgeted overhead absorption rate for Machine Shop B.

(c) Calculate the production overheads which would be charged to Product X if the product spent 6 hours in Machine Shop A and 3 hours in Machine Shop B.

3 In your own organization, or for an organization with which you are familiar, attempt to identify quality costs and analyse these quality costs into prevention, appraisal and failure costs.

5 Planning and control

The aims of this chapter are to:

- Provide an understanding of the general control model.
- Illustrate the relationship between the general control model and planning and control within organizations.
- Develop the idea of management control with particular emphasis on budgeting.
- Provide an understanding of the purposes of budgeting.
- Outline the various stages in the budgetary process.
- Provide illustrations of budgeting from both public sector and private sector organizations.
- Demonstrate that budgeting is a behavioural process as well as a technical process.

Introduction

In this chapter we will be looking at the role of planning and control within organizations. The areas of study for this chapter are shown in Figure 5.1.

All organizations, whether they be public or private sector, are concerned with issues of planning and control. It is, in fact, very useful before looking at these issues in depth, to set the scene by highlighting a couple of fairly recent developments in the public sector.

Local management of schools

The 1988 Education Reform Act paved the way for schools to be given delegated budgets with the amounts being available to a school mainly dependent on pupil numbers. The Act stated that the governing body of any school which has a delegated budget:

(a) shall be entitled, subject to any provisions made by or under the scheme, to spend any sum made available to them in respect of the school's budget share for any financial year as they think fit for the purpose of the school: and (b) may delegate to the head teacher, to such an extent as may be permitted by or under the scheme, their power under paragraph (a) above in relation to any part of that sum.

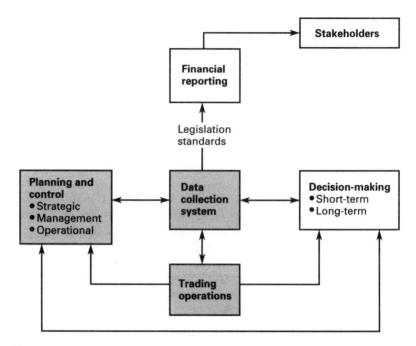

Figure 5.1 *Planning and control*

A failure to manage the budget correctly may result in the school governing body losing its right to a delegated budget. This move to delegated budgets has had a dramatic impact on schools.

GP fund holding

Working For Patients (1989) announced the government's proposals to offer large GP practices the opportunity to manage a budget out of which they are responsible for securing a wide range of hospital and primary care services on behalf of their patients. The belief was that practice budgets offer GPs an opportunity to improve the quality of service on offer to patients, to stimulate hospitals to be more responsive to the needs of GP's and their patients and to develop their own practices for the benefit of their patients. Fund holding practices are completely free to shift expenditure within the year between the individual components of the total budget. Any savings generated can be spent at the practice's discretion on improving their practice and offering more and better services to their patients. Practices are also permitted to overspend in any one year by up to 5% of budget. However, a corresponding reduction is made in the budget for the following year. If the overspend is due to changed circumstances of the practice, the practice may ask for a budgetary review. If a practice overspends in excess of 5% or consistently overspends at a lower level, the Family Health Services Authority will initiate an audit.

Both these public sector developments have given rise to much heated debate. The concept of budgeting has been placed in the public domain and the potential benefits and possible concerns about budgeting have been well debated. We will return to these issues later in the chapter but it would now be useful to go back to the beginning in order systematically to develop the area of planning and control within organizations.

General control model

We can start by looking at a general control model. Consider any system which has inputs and outputs. It may be a complex one, like a business organization, or a simple one like a heating system controlled by a thermostat. There are four essential conditions that must be satisfied before any process can be said to be controlled.

- We must know what we want to achieve, and set objectives.
- We must measure outputs and decide whether or not we are achieving our objectives.
- We must be able to predict the effect of any action we may take to alter or control the processes.
- We must be able to correct any deviations away from our objectives.

These conditions will now be applied to a simple input–output system or process in order to build the model (Figure 5.2). First we set objectives and then we add a way in which the outputs are measured and compared to the objectives. This is illustrated in Figure 5.3. It may be that when we compare outputs to objectives we find a great difference between what we wanted to achieve and what is actually happening. We must build a model that can enable us to predict what will happen if we are not meeting our objectives. This means that any actions we take to bring outputs and objectives back in line will be the correct ones. If we cannot predict the result of our actions, then problems can only be solved by trial and error. The action we take may remedy the situation, but it is important fully to understand why. Figure 5.4 shows a predictive model of the process with an evaluation stage at which it is decided which alternative action is superior.

Up to this stage we have taken no action to remedy the deviations from the desired objective. The diagram is completed by linking the corrective action decided upon and the inputs, as illustrated in Figure 5.5.

Figure 5.2 *Simple input–output process*

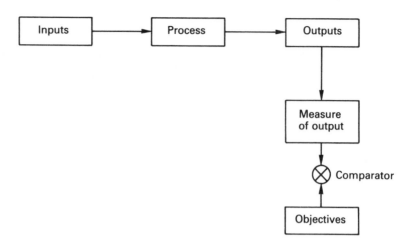

Figure 5.3 *Measurement of output and comparator introduced*

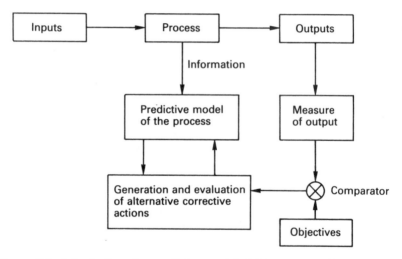

Figure 5.4 *Introduction of a predictive model of the process with an evaluation stage*

The general control model which has been built here has been developed from the science of cybernetics. Textbooks often illustrate this cybernetic model by reference to a thermostat. The thermostat is then used to introduce the ideas of planning and control within business and public sector organizations. However, it is important to realize that there are complications in an organization setting which do not exist in the world of the thermostat. Examples of these differences are:

- Measurement errors exist in attempting to report the results of a period of an organization's activities. These arise from the many problems of periodic accounting measurement.

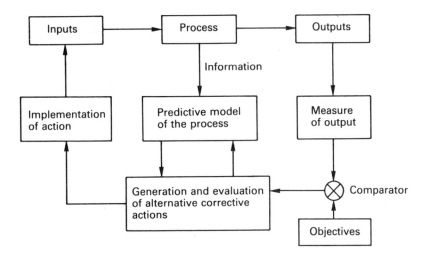

Figure 5.5 *Implementation of action*

- Reported results may be distorted as they are processed and aggregated by individuals.
- Predetermined standards may be inappropriate to conditions that prevail during the period under consideration since unpredictable changes may have occurred since plans were made.
- Corrective responses cannot be selected with certainty. Managers do not always have suitable alternatives available and cannot be sure of the effects of particular actions.
- Responses may not be implemented in the manner managers intend; neither human motivation nor business success is perfectly predictable.
- The thermostat treats the system to be controlled as independent of other systems. The elements, departments and functions of a business organization are interrelated.
- Reports in organizations do not work continuously like the thermostat but operate at discrete periodic intervals. As a result, corrective action may be severely lagged allowing matters to get further out of control. In addition, it assumes that the conditions which led to results reported for the past period continue in the period to which corrective action is applied. This assumption may be invalid in the dynamic business environment.

In an attempt to deal with the uncertainties in the environment, the concept of single and double loop learning has been introduced into the academic literature.

Single and double loop learning

In single loop learning the only corrective action that takes place is to ensure that the original objective is met. If the environment is

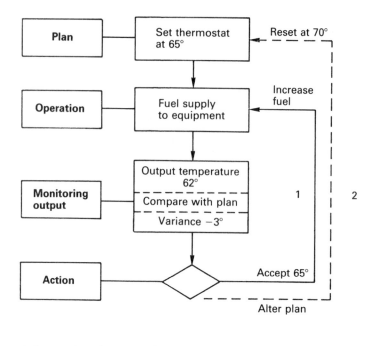

1 Automatic action: closed system ———— feedback
2 Human intervention: open system — — — feedback

Figure 5.6 *Feedback in a control system* (CIMA Terminology, 1991, p. 71). *A control system which operates without outside intervention (as the solid arrow lines) is termed a* closed system *and one that requires periodic outside adjustments to the planned or actual inputs an* open system *(dotted lines)*

fairly unstable, it may be necessary actually to change the objective since it becomes impossible to meet the original objective. This changing of the original objective is known as double loop learning. This is illustrated in simplistic form in Figure 5.6. In this particular diagram, single loop learning is demonstrated when the fuel is increased in order to reach the 65° temperature. If conditions outside have got much cooler and the occupants of the house decide that the temperature required (i.e. the objective) needs to be higher, then the objective is changed (new temperature 70°). This changing of the objective, in recognition of external changes in the environment, is an example of double loop learning.

We have again gone back to the thermostat to illustrate issues relating to planning and control. In using this analogy, it is important that we remember the differences, which have already been highlighted, between an organization and a thermostat. However, the analogy is useful and organizations need to recognize that changing environments may necessitate either a change in plan to meet the original objective, or a change in the original objective. The impact of such a change in the objective needs to be recognized. For example, a reduction in the target profit in a year may have an impact on the future capital investment programme of the organization.

Having looked at the development of a general control model, we will now turn our attention to planning and control issues within organizations.

Application of the general control model to organizations

A useful starting point is to look at the CIMA definitions of planning and control.

> *Planning* – the establishment of objectives, and the formulation, evaluation, and selection of the policies, strategies, tactics and action required to achieve these objectives.

> *Control* – the continuous comparison of actual results with those planned, both in total and for separate sub-divisions, and taking management action to correct adverse variances or to exploit favourable variances.

These definitions are presented in diagrammatic form in Figure 5.7.

From these two definitions it is obvious that the two processes are linked together. Controls cannot exist without plans and the more complete and integrated plans are, the more effective controls can be. There is no way that managers can determine whether their organizational unit is accomplishing what is desired and expected unless they are aware of the expectations in the first place. Another prerequisite of a control system is some form of organization structure. As briefly referred to in Chapter 4, organization responsibility must be clear and well defined. Responsibility centres were introduced in Chapter 4 and will be discussed later in this chapter.

Having looked at basic models of planning and control, we are now going to look at the nature of management control systems within organizations, and the role that budgets play within the overall management control system.

Management control system

A useful starting point is to look at a framework of planning and control which was introduced by Robert Anthony in 1965.

Anthony framework of planning and control

Strategic planning is the process of deciding on objectives of the organization, on the resources to be used to achieve those objectives

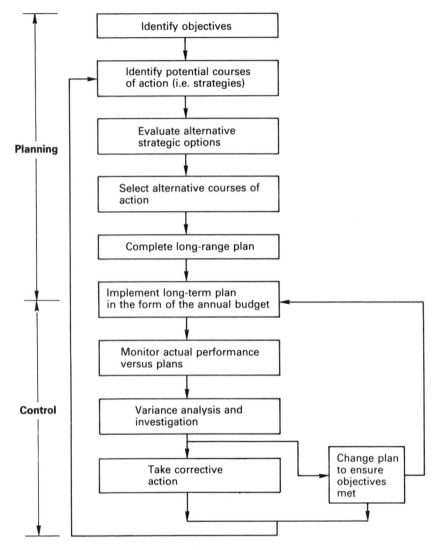

Figure 5.7   *Planning and control*

and the policies that are to be used to govern the acquisition, use and disposition of those resources.

Management control is the process by which management assures that the organization carries out its strategies, i.e. ensures that resources are obtained and used efficiently and effectively in the accomplishment of the company objectives.

Operational control is the process of assuring that specific tasks are carried out efficiently and effectively.

In looking at an organization's overall planning and control system, it is important that strategic objectives, different strategies, long-range plans and annual budgets are all linked together and that, as a result of feedback mechanism, information is fed back to the planning process.

Cost centre – where managers assume responsibility for costs

Revenue centre – where managers assume responsibility for revenues

Profit centre – where managers assume responsibility for both costs and revenues

Investment centres – where managers assume responsibility for both profit and investment. This therefore includes responsibility for capital investment decisions as well as working capital decisions

Strategic Business Unit – where managers assume responsibilities for profit, investment and their own strategic development. It is usual for Strategic Business Units to focus on a particular market segment or product group. It is also likely that a Strategic Business Unit will face specific competitors which may not be shared with any other Strategic Business Units within the organization

Figure 5.8 *Responsibility centres*

In this book we are particularly concentrating on the management control system. The management control system consists of a structure or design of relationships among things and a process or set of activities that the system does. The management control structure focuses on various types of responsibility centres as described in Chapter 4 (cost centres, revenue centres, profit centres, investment centres or strategic business units). Figure 5.8 illustrates the differing responsibilities associated with each type of responsibility centre.

The management control process involves both formal and informal communication and interaction between managers. Informal communication occurs by means of memoranda, meetings and conversations. Formal management control consists of programming, budgeting, reporting and analysis.

In the introduction to this chapter we looked at two developments in the public sector which centred around the use of budgets. Budgets are an important part of the planning and control function within organizations. In Anthony's terms, budgets are an important part of the management control system. Budgets are in fact the vehicle for implementing the strategic and long-range plans of an organization. We will now concentrate on the budgeting process within organizations.

Budgeting

In concentrating on the budgeting system we will be applying the general control model discussed earlier to the budget reporting system within an organization.

A budget is defined as follows:

A plan expressed in money. It is prepared and approved prior to the budget period and may show income, expenditure, and the capital employed. (CIMA definition)

This in some ways is a fairly narrow definition of a budget since budgets will include both financial and non-financial information.

Empirical evidence underscoring the importance of qualitative and non-financial measures in manufacturing activities is mounting. Management accountants can therefore no longer ignore information that is not expressible in financial terms. Data on product quality, customer satisfaction, delivery efficiency, vendor reliability, machine integrity and the contribution of workers to the enterprise all become crucial factors for managing in an increasingly competitive and rapidly changing product market. Evidence is emerging that where internal accounting systems do not reflect these important changes factory managers are beginning to ignore accounting numbers completely. (Bromwich and Bhimani, 1989: 94)

While most of the discussion on non-financial measures refers to the performance measurement stage, it is important that these issues are also discussed at the planning stage.

Budgets are produced in all organizations, whether they are small, large, private or public sector. They are important and are produced for the following reasons:

- To *compel* planning − by having a formal budgeting procedure, managers are forced to consider organizational objectives and ways in which those organizational objectives can be achieved. Budgets are in reality the 'action plan' for the long-range plans produced by organizations.
- To *coordinate* the activities of the various parts of the organization and to ensure that the parts are working together. The budget process forces managers to think of the relationship of their function or department with others in the organization.
- To *communicate* plans to the various responsibility managers. The budget setting process is an important avenue of communication between the different levels of management within an organization.
- To *motivate* managers to work towards the organizational objectives. Once the budget is approved, the various responsibility managers know what is expected of them.
- To *control* activities − the budget provides a yardstick against which the performance of the organization can be compared. Through the comparison of actual versus budget, variances can be identified and corrective action taken where necessary.
- To *evaluate* the performance of managers.

It is important to recognize that budgeting within organizations can be fraught with difficulties. These difficulties are mainly of a behavioural nature and will be dealt with later in the chapter.

Having identified the purpose of budgeting, we will now go on to look at the stages in the budgetary process and will then use a case study to illustrate the various stages.

Stages in the budgetary process

A number of stages can be identified in the preparation of plans and budgets:

- Stage 1   Identification of
  - key objectives of the organization for the coming year;
  - external changes likely to affect the organization. These must be communicated to the budget-holders in order that these managers know what overriding factors to consider when preparing their budgets.
- Stage 2   Determination of key or limiting factors. Every organization has some factor which limits its growth. In most cases this is the volume of sales or the number of customers and the amount of manufacturing plant available. This key factor has significance for planning and budgeting. It may be that one of these key or limiting factors may be so important that the entire plan may need to be built around it. This is then called the *principal budget factor*.
- Stage 3   Preparation of an initial sales forecast. This is undertaken by:
  - asking the sales manager to estimate the potential sales for each product under his or her control;
  - using mathematical and statistical techniques to establish the most profitable sales mix.
- Stage 4   The preparation of an initial budget, which will include a production budget, direct labour budget, production overhead budget, selling and distribution budget, capital expenditure budget and cash budget.
- Stage 5   Negotiation of budgets with superiors.
- Stage 6   The coordination of these initial budgets, usually by the organization's financial staff, in order to ensure that there are no inconsistencies between them.
- Stage 7   After any necessary alterations to remove inconsistencies, the initial budgets are consolidated into a master budget, which is set out in the form of a budgeted profit and loss account, cash flow forecast and balance sheet.
- Stage 8   Approval of this master budget by the board of directors or the appropriate top policy-making body within the organization.
- Stage 9   Ongoing review of budgets.

It must be realized that planning and budgeting is not a mechanistic process, but a dynamic and iterative process involving every manager within the organization. The involvement of all managers will allow their expertise to be properly used and will provide a strong motivational force.

It is important that an organization realizes that planning and budgeting is a management function not an accounting function. The organization's financial staff will provide a wealth of financial data to assist decision-making and will probably provide the planning and budgeting coordinator, but budget-making involves all of the organization's managers.

In larger organizations, a budget committee, made up of the heads of the main functions of the organization, may discuss and set the plans and budgets. In many smaller organizations this may not be appropriate and a less formal system may be established.

In order to understand this process in an organizational setting, we will now look at an illustration of the budgetary process in one particular company.

Case study

This case study is based on a company making glass containers. The Northcott factory is part of Rainbow Glass Limited which is a subsidiary of Rainbow Group plc. Rainbow Glass reacted to deteriorating market conditions by making each of the glass factories into profit centres. The factories were given a high level of autonomy and the sales function within the company was decentralized. Each of the glass factories was given its own sales team under a Director of Sales. The finance function at each factory was considerably strengthened with a Financial Controller being appointed for each factory and several financial and management accountants being appointed at each factory. Centralized production planning was disbanded in favour of decentralized planning at each of the factories. The result was a significant increase in senior staff at the factories with a corresponding reduction at Head Office. Each of the factories became a company in its own right with a considerable amount of autonomy. The only restrictions were in terms of large capital investment, financing and group profit requirements. This case study is based on one of these autonomous factories, Northcott factory. The budgetary process at Northcott factory is outlined under the headings identified above for the stages in the budgetary process.

Illustration 5.1 The budgetary process in a glass container company

A 1993 budget would be produced to cover January 1993 to December 1993. The Stages in the budgetary process would be as follows.

Stage 1	Key objectives of the organization for the coming year External changes likely to affect the organization

The long-range plan acts as the focal point for the preparation of the budget. A long-range plan produced in May 1992 covering the years 1993–7 would provide an indicator of the key objective requirements for the 1993 budget. Key objectives would relate to issues such as profit, sales volumes, market share, manning levels, cash and capital expenditure requirements. Both group and glass finance teams provide information on general economic factors which are likely to affect the budget for the Northcott factory.

Stage 2   Determination of key or limiting factor

The sales team identify total sales forecasts and the production team, known production constraints. Production facilities are matched up with sales requirements to determine whether the limiting factor relates to sales requirements or production facilities.

Stage 3   Preparation of initial sales forecast

The sales team then produce a detailed sales forecast by bottle. The process is as follows:

- The sales team forecast the number of bottles to be sold during the year by bottle and then these sales are valued at 1 January 1993 prices.
- The sales team forecast the expected selling price increases throughout the year and the value of these increases is added to the basic sales price.
- Quantity discounts are taken into account and the net result is the budgeted sales volume and value.

Stage 4   Preparation of an initial budget, which will include a production budget, direct labour budget, production over- head budget, selling and distribution budget, capital expenditure budget and cash budget

---

This is an extensive part of the budgeting process. As indicated in Stage 1, production facilities need to be matched up with sales forecasts in order to decide on the production volume budget (in volume terms) for the year. Once the production volume budget for the year has been decided then costs are calculated for that level of production. In the glass company costs are calculated for items such as raw materials, melting fuel, packaging materials, labour, repair materials, rent and rates, heating and lighting, distribution, consumables and other costs.

There is a considerable amount of participation in the budget-setting process at Northcott factory. In July 1992 the finance department sends out requests for particular information from managers and superintendents with a targeted date of mid-September for completion. For example, with respect to labour costs for a superintendent's cost centre, the superintendent would be asked to supply manning and overtime requirements (subject to review by the Northcott executive and within long-range plan guidelines). Finance would then carry out detailed calculations with respect to labour costs.

The factory finance team has developed a computer spreadsheet package for constructing the budget. The package is especially useful in terms of the calculation of individual budgets, phasing, alterations because of constant review and the consolidation of various expense categories and cost centres.

Stage 5   Negotiation of budgets with superiors

As part of Stage 4, a budget is developed for each cost centre by expense category. Discussions take place between different levels of a particular functional area. For example, we can refer back to a section of Figure 4.2 which was presented in Chapter 4.

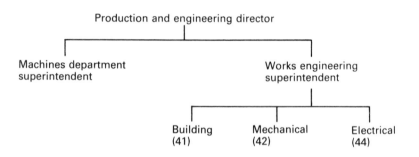

Budget discussions would take place between different levels of the production and engineering function about budgets that were being produced. It is important to realize that this would be an ongoing process with continuous discussions taking place during the budget-setting process.

Stage 6   Coordination of these initial budgets

The finance department at Northcott acts as the focal point for the budget-setting procedures at the factory. While there is considerable participation by all managers in the budget-setting process, the finance department issues all the relevant documents, collates information coming back from managers and superintendents, carries out detailed financial calculations on non-financial data, initiates required meetings and consolidates all of the information.

Stage 7   Initial budgets are consolidated into a master budget, which is set out in the form of a budgeted profit and loss account, cash flow forecast and balance sheet

---

At Northcott, the initial budgets are consolidated into a master budget by the finance department. The master budget at Northcott is quite extensive and includes:

Commentary — a two page commentary on the budget which summarizes key points from the rest of the master budget document.
Risks and opportunities — a listing of risks and opportunities identified by the management team.
Trend of key data — incorporating both financial and non-financial data. It includes a comparison between a forecast for the present year (1992) and the 1993 budget.
Profit and loss account — includes a comparison between forecast for the present year (1992) and the 1993 budget.
Summary of variances — identifying reasons for cost differences between the 1992 forecast and the 1993 budget.
Cashflow and closing balance sheet information — includes a comparison between a forecast for the present year (1992) and the 1993 budget.
Sales volumes and values — includes a comparison between a forecast for the present year (1992) and the 1993 budget.
Production statistics (non-financial) — includes a comparison between a forecast for the present year (1992) and the 1993 budget.
Capital expenditure budget — includes a comparison with the long-range plan.
Manning and overtime figures — includes a comparison between a forecast for the present year (1992) and the 1993 budget.
Technical improvements — new developments and an indication of their impact on budget cost figures.
Cost price increase assumptions.
Manufacturing assumptions — non-financial data.

It is important to note that the forecast for 1992, mentioned in a number of the items in the master budget, relates to the latest forecast for 1992 and not the original budget for 1992 which had been set some considerable time ago.

Stage 8   Approval of the master budget by the board of directors or the appropriate top policy-making body within the organization

---

The master budget document is presented to the Northcott board for discussion and review. The review may ask for further amendments to be made to the submitted budget and the finance team would coordinate such amendments after discussions with the appropriate managers and superintendents. Once the Northcott board has approved the budget (target date of mid-November 1992) it would then be sent to the Glass Board for approval. The Glass Board would consider the submission from the Northcott factory, alongside submissions from the other glass factories, and consult Group Board. Amendments may be requested by the Glass Board and these would again be coordinated by the finance team at Northcott after discussions with the appropriate managers and superintendents. Once the amendments had finally been made, the finance team at Northcott would issue the budgets to the management team at the factory. A budget would be issued to each cost centre superintendent or manager. The budget is phased on a 52-week year and presented on a 4/4/5 basis (i.e. period 1 is 4 weeks, period 2 is 4 weeks, period 3 is 5 weeks). The Northcott board will be given a copy of the final master budget. The target date for issuing 1993 budgets is mid-December 1992.

Stage 9   Ongoing review of budgets

Once the year has started, monthly (on a period basis) budget performance reports are issued to the appropriate managers. Meetings take place on the basis of these reports to discuss performance against budgets. Since circumstances tend to change, revised forecasts will be produced on a quarterly basis during 1993. Budgeting is seen as a continuous and dynamic process within the organization.

Illustration 5.1 describes a typical budget-setting process within a large organization. There are several key points coming out of the description. First of all, the illustration provides ample evidence that budgeting should involve the whole management team. Later in the chapter we will talk about the behavioural aspects of budgeting and, as part of this, will discuss the role of participation. While there has been some debate about whether participation will work in all situations, most observers feel that participation in budget-setting is a prerequisite for a meaningful budget. Linked in with the idea of participation, the illustration also provides evidence of the interactive nature of the budget-setting process. Continuous review meetings took place within the organization before the final budget was set.

Illustration 5.1 also provides evidence of the important role that management control structure plays in the budget-setting process. Responsibility centre managers submit information to the finance team concerning their particular responsibility area. Total budgets are built up as a consolidation of responsibility centre budgets. Once final budgets have been agreed the responsibility centre budgets are issued to the managers or superintendents concerned. Once the budget year has started, monthly budget performance reports are issued to the responsibility centre managers and these provide a comparison between actual and budgeted performance.

The glass container company used a lot of non-financial data in the master budget report and this provides an illustration of the point referred to earlier by Bromwich and Bhimani (1989). The master budget document included information on product quality targets, customer satisfaction targets, efficiency targets, other manu-facturing assumptions and comments on market share. To repeat an earlier point, while much of the discussion on non-financial measures refers to the performance measurement stage, it is important that these issues are discussed at the planning stage.

The final point to be made about Illustration 5.1 is that it also provides a passing reference to what was earlier classed as double loop learning. Stage 9 of the budgetary process at Northcott factory refers to revised forecasts being produced on a quarterly basis during 1993. While the intention of this revision process is to change plans as the year progresses in order to ensure that the factory meets its original budgeted profit target, it may become necessary as the year progresses to change the target in recognition of circum-stances that have changed considerably in the external environment.

Having looked at a case study that explains the budget-setting process, it is not our intention in this book to provide a very detailed example of the calculations involved in the setting of the budget. However, it is worth including one particular example which gives a feel for some of the calculations which may take place. It also links this chapter with Chapter 2 in the sense that an output of the budgeting process, as part of the master budget, would be a budgeted profit and loss account and a budgeted cash flow statement. The conventions used in the preparation of these statements were covered in Chapter 2 and therefore no explanation of them will be undertaken here. Illustration 5.2 provides both the data and the final budget reports for Thurbro Ltd.

Illustration 5.2   Thurbro Ltd (ACCA source)

Thurbro Ltd make and sell a single product, product A. The following information is available for use in the budgeting process for the year to 31 December 1993.

(1) Sales

> Selling price £20 per unit
>
> | Sales volume | Units |
> |---|---|
> | Quarter 1 1993 | 6,000 |
> | Quarter 2 1993 | 4,000 |
> | Quarter 3 1993 | 3,600 |
> | Quarter 4 1993 | 5,600 |
> | Quarter 1 1994 | 4,800 |

(2) Stock levels

> | At 31 December 1992: | Finished product A | 1,500 units |
> |---|---|---|
> | | Raw material X | 3,500 kilos |

Closing stocks of finished product A at the end of each quarter are budgeted as a percentage of the sales unit of the following quarter as follows:

> At the end of quarters 1 and 2 − 25%
> At the end of quarters 3 and 4 − 35%

Closing stock of raw material X is budgeted to fall by 300 kilos at the end of each quarter in order to reduce holdings by 1,200 kilos during 1993.

(3) Product A unit data

> | Material X | 4 kilos at £1.60 per kilo |
> |---|---|
> | Direct labour | 0.6 hours at £3.50 per hour |

(4) Other quarterly expenditure

> | | Qtr 1 | Qtr 2 | Qtr 3 | Qtr 4 |
> |---|---|---|---|---|
> | | £ | £ | £ | £ |
> | Fixed overhead | 45,000 | 48,000 | 47,000 | 50,000 |
> | Capital expenditure | | 50,000 | | |

(5) Forecast balances at 31 December 1992

> Debtors £40,000
> Bank balance £22,000
> Bad debts provision £2,000

Creditors' materials £9,600
Fixed assets (at cost) £500,000

(6) Cash flow timing information
    (a) Sales revenue: 60% receivable during the quarter of sale, 38% during the next quarter, the balance 2% being expected bad debts.
    (b) Material X purchases: 70% payable during the quarter of purchase, the balance of 30% during the next quarter.
    (c) Direct wages, fixed overhead and capital expenditure: 100% payable during the quarter in which they are earned or incurred.
(7) Fixed assets are depreciated on a straight line basis of 5% per annum, based on the total cost of fixed assets held at any point during the year and assuming nil residual value.
(8) All forecast balances at 31 December 1992 will be received or paid as relevant during the first quarter of 1993.
(9) Stocks of product A are valued on a marginal cost basis for internal budgeting purposes.

Using the information given above, the following budgets have been prepared for 1993.

Cash budget for the year to 31 December 1993

	Qtr 1 £	Qtr 2 £	Qtr 3 £	Qtr 4 £
Balance brought forward	22,000	41,546	1,404	(9,667)
Receipts:				
Debtors				
Previous quarter	38,000	45,600	30,400	27,360
Current quarter	72,000	48,000	43,200	67,200
Total receipts	110,000	93,600	73,600	94,560
Payments:				
Creditors for materials:				
Previous quarter	9,600	10,416	7,344	8,803
Current quarter	24,304	17,136	20,541	23,498
Wages	11,550	8,190	9,786	11,172
Fixed overhead	45,000	48,000	47,000	50,000
Capital expenditure		50,000		
Total payments	90,454	133,742	84,671	93,473
Balance carried forward	41,546	1,404	(9,667)	(8,580)

Workings carried out in order to produce cash budget:
1 Production units of finished goods per quarter

	Qtr 1	Qtr 2	Qtr 3	Qtr 4
Closing stock	1,000	900	1,960	1,680
Sales	6,000	4,000	3,600	5,600
	7,000	4,900	5,560	7,280
Opening stock	1,500	1,000	900	1,960
Production quantity required	5,500	3,900	4,660	5,320

e.g. Closing stock Qtr 1 = 4,000 sales units (Qtr 2) x 25%
= 1,000 units

2   *Purchase of raw materials per quarter (kilos)*

	Qtr 1	Qtr 2	Qtr 3	Qtr 4
Closing stock	3,200	2,900	2,600	2,300
Production (at 4 kg/unit)	22,000	15,600	18,640	21,280
	25,200	18,500	21,240	23,580
Opening stock	3,500	3,200	2,900	2,600
Material purchases	21,700	15,300	18,340	20,980

e.g. Production material requirements Qtr 1 = 5,500 production units
× 4 kg per unit = 22,000 kg
Closing stock Qtr 1 = 3,500 − 300 = 3,200 kg
Qtr 2 = 3,200 − 300 = 2,900 kg

3   *Cost of material purchases*

	Qtr 1	Qtr 2	Qtr 3	Qtr 4
Material purchases (kg)	21,700	15,300	18,340	20,980
@ £1.60 per kg	1.60	1.60	1.60	1.60
Cost of material purchases (£)	34,720	24,480	29,344	33,568

4   *Creditors for material payments*
e.g. Quarter 2
Payments from previous quarter = 34,720 × 30% = 10,416
Payments from present quarter = 24,480 × 70% = 17,136.

5   *Direct wages budget*
e.g. Quarter 1
Production units × number of hours per unit × rate per hour
5,500 × 0.6 × 3.50 = £11,550

6 Sales budget

	Qtr 1	Qtr 2	Qtr 3	Qtr 4
Sales volume (units)	6,000	4,000	3,600	5,600
Selling price per unit (£)	20	20	20	20
Sales value (£)	120,000	80,000	72,000	112,000

7 Receipts from debtors

e.g. Quarter 2

Receipts from previous quarter £120,000 x 38% = 45,600
Receipts from present quarter   £80,000 x 60% = 48,000

93,600

Budgeted profit and loss account for the year to 31 December 1993

	£	£
Sales revenue (19,200 x £20)		384,000
Variable cost of sales (19,200 x £8.5)		163,200
Contribution margin		220,800
Less fixed costs		
Fixed overhead	190,000	
Depreciation	27,500	
Bad debts written off and provision increase	7,680	
		225,180
Budgeted net loss		(4,380)

Workings carried out in order to produce budgeted profit and loss account:

1 Variable cost of sales

	£ per unit
Variable material x cost per unit = 4 kilos at £1.60 per kilo =	6.4
Variable labour cost per unit = 0.6 hours at £3.50 per hour =	2.1
	8.5

2 Depreciation

5% × (£500,000 + £50,000) = £27,500

3 Bad debts written off and provision increase

2% × annual sales budget = 2% × £384,000
= £7,680

In Illustration 5.2, the cash budget has been presented on a quarterly basis. Many organizations would in fact produce this data on a monthly basis, the reason being that organizations need to have a good understanding of the pattern of receipts and payments since extra finance may have to be raised in certain months or quarters. For example, in Thurbro Ltd the cash situation deteriorates in quarter 3 and the company is faced with an overdraft situation. It needs to ensure that there is an overdraft facility available at the bank for the organization. If an overdraft facility is not available it may have to look at the timing of some of the cash flows to ensure that the cash situation remains positive. Cash flow management is an important aspect of organizational life, as it is in private life, and budgets enable organizations to predict problem situations in advance. Obviously, as the year progresses, environmental circumstances may change and this is the reason that organizations such as Rainbow Glass (Northcott: Illustration 5.1) have introduced the idea of regular forecasting as the year progresses. Any organization, whether it be public, private or voluntary sector, needs to ensure that it produces plans for cash management and monitors those plans against actual figures as the year progresses.

Illustration 5.2 also includes an example of a budgeted profit and loss account. The important aspect to note here is that, while we referred back to the requirements stipulated in Chapter 2 in the introduction to this particular example, the layout of internal budget documents does not have to comply with any external requirements. For internal purposes, the layout of the budget information needs to be in a style which is most useful to the managers of the organization. For instance, the profit and loss account in Thurbro has been presented in a way which differentiates between fixed and variable costs. The profit and loss statement identifies contribution and values stocks at marginal cost. While this is not acceptable for external published financial reports, it is perfectly acceptable for internal management budget statements. This also applies to the layout of budgeted cash flow statements.

Having looked at examples from private sector organizations, we will now go on to look at budgets in the public and voluntary sector.

Budgeting in non-profit-making organizations

As was shown earlier in this chapter, budgets play a very important role in organizations that are not set up to make a profit. Organizations such as schools, churches, local authorities, GP surgeries, hospitals and central government bodies all have to prepare budgets and are subject to the control aspects of budgeting. There is always extensive public debate about the impact of budgets on local authority spending and hospital spending. There are both similarities and differences between budgeting for private sector organizations and budgeting for public sector and charitable organizations. The available resources for financing the proposed level of public service should be sufficient to cover the total costs of such services. Funding may come from grants, taxes or some commercial activity within the organization.

Traditionally in non-profit-making organizations there has been a concentration on inputs (i.e. control of expenditure). The budgetary control process has concentrated on comparing actual cash inputs with budgeted cash inputs. Critics have suggested that, in the past, such organizations tended to calculate budgets using an *incremental budgeting* approach. Incremental budgeting takes the current level of activities as given and adjustments are made for any changes that are expected to occur during the new budget period. Criticisms of this approach are based on the fact that it perpetuates any past inefficiencies since current activities are taken as given and not challenged. Systems such as zero base budgeting have been suggested as an improvement on incremental budgeting.

Zero base budgeting (ZBB) rejects the traditional incremental approach. Basically ZBB involves setting up a system whereby the manager must justify every budget request and rationalize why the money must be spent at all. Alternative ways of carrying out activities are investigated and cost/benefit criteria are used when considering the alternatives. Priorities are determined and resources are allocated in accordance with these priorities. The principle at the centre of zero base budgeting is that the current level of activities must not be taken as given: the present base level must be questioned and alternatives sought. In many ways there are similarities between zero base budgeting and activity based management, which was introduced in Chapter 4 and will be developed further in both Chapters 6 and 7. Activity based management is based on the philosophy that managers can only manage costs by managing the activities that cause the costs. Zero base budgeting similarly attempts to use activity identification in order to improve the nature of budgeting within an organization. A strictly theoretical approach to ZBB may be very time consuming but many organizations who use the system tend to adopt a partial approach. Such a partial approach maintains the basic principle of zero base budgeting while reducing the level of detail involved.

People who work in the public sector will recognize that vast changes have taken place within this sector during the past ten years. While attention is still given to inputs, there is now increased awareness of the need to look at outputs and appropriate measures of performance. The term 'accountable management' has become an important concern of public sector managers. A particular turning point was the Financial Management Initiative in 1982. Its purpose was to promote in each central government department an organization and system in which managers at all levels have (Cmnd 8616, 1982, Para 13):

- A clear view of their objectives and means to assess and, wherever possible, measure outputs or performance in relation to those objectives.
- Well-defined responsibility for making the best use of their resources, including a critical scrutiny of output and value for money.
- The information (particularly about costs), training and access to expert advice which they need to exercise their responsibilities effectively.

The considerable reforms which have taken place since 1982 in the public sector all embody an approach to management and control which is similar to that propounded by the Financial Management Initiative.

One of the particular characteristics of the public sector is that there is often no direct link between the service being delivered and the payment for the service. However, in the new market based philosophy of the local management of schools and GP fund holding there is an attempt to link clients and funds. In schools for instance, budgets are allocated on the basis of pupil numbers and therefore the more children a school can attract, the larger the budget will be for that school. Diminishing numbers of pupils will result in smaller budgets and the obvious reduction in the money available for the school. Illustration 5.3 briefly identifies the nature and mechanics of local management of schools.

Illustration 5.3   Local management of schools

Local management of schools was introduced by the Education Reform Act 1988. A large proportion of the education budget of a local authority is now delegated to individual schools through formula funding. The process of delegation is as follows:

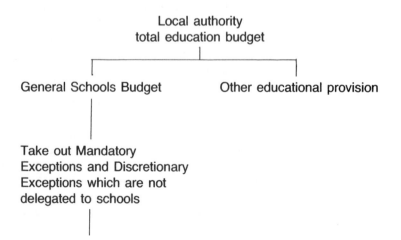

Local authority
total education budget

General Schools Budget

Other educational provision

Take out Mandatory
Exceptions and Discretionary
Exceptions which are not
delegated to schools

Aggregated Schools
   Budget (ASB)

Delegated to schools
with each school
receiving its budget
share — 80% of ASB
has to be allocated
according to pupil
numbers

The Aggregated Schools Budget is delegated to individual schools by formula funding. The formula used may be complex and have several parts:
(a) Base allocation — each type of school may have a lump sum irrespective of its size.
(b) Variable allocation — a school may receive a lump sum depending on its size.
(c) The formula allocation — after the base/variable allocations have been taken from the Aggregated Schools Budget, the remaining resources are distributed by the formula.

The formula allocates resources to schools through a series of sub-formulae. Each budget head has its own sub-formula which distributes a certain amount of resources to each school. The sum from each budget head is aggregated to form the school's total allocation and therefore its budget. This total allocation for a school is known as the budget share.
   A typical primary school in a typical local authority would receive funding through this formula for the following budget headings:

Staffing: Teachers
   Nursery nurses
   Non-teaching assistants/clerical assistants
   Midday supervisors
   Caretakers
   Short-term staff absence
Curriculum: Capitation
   Social disadvantage
   Swimming
Premises: Internal painting
   Minor repairs
   Rates
   Rents
   Water/sewage
   Refuse

Energy
Caretaker costs
Cleaning
Grounds maintenance

The formula allocation includes weightings awarded to the different age ranges of the pupils at the school. Let us now look at an example of the formula being used:

1993/94 Budget: Primary School
1   Teachers

	£
Primary base allocation	16,000
Infants 50 x £1,000	50,000
Juniors 50 x £1,000	50,000
	116,000

Note: There are 50 infant children and 50 juniors at the school. The age weighted pupil unit (AWPU) is £1,000 per pupil. £116,000 is the amount which would appear under the budget heading 'Teachers' for this particular school.

2   Non-teaching assistants/clerical assistants

	£
Primary base allocation	1,000
Infants 50 × 1.75 × £30	2,625
Juniors 50 × 0.80 × £30	1,200
	4,825

Note: The age weighted pupil unit (AWPU) is £30 per pupil. 1.75 represents the weighting for infant children. 0.80 represents the weighting for junior children. £4,825 is the amount that would appear under the budget heading 'Non-teaching assistants/clerical assistants' for this particular school.

Schools are therefore cash limited and they must not plan to overspend their budget. Virement is allowed between different budget headings but the school must obviously meet its educational requirements. The balance at the end of a budget year can be carried forward into next year's budget regardless of whether it is a surplus or a deficit. If overspending does occur at a particular school the local education authority can offer increased financial training to the governing body. As a last resort, where it is considered that adequate financial control is not taking place, the provision of a delegated budget may be withdrawn from a school.

The importance of pupil numbers for a school has hopefully been demonstrated in Illustration 5.3. Current legislation requires that 80% of the Aggregated Schools Budget for a local authority is allocated to schools on the basis of pupil numbers. It is important to note, however, that with changes in legislation the likelihood is that this percentage figure may be even higher in future years.

It can in fact be argued that the amount allocated to individual schools through formula funding represents income to that school. It is then up to that school to ensure that its spending on the running of the school does not exceed the income it has received through formula funding. Virement is allowed between budget heads, but it is important to note that educational standards will have to be met. Statistics on national curriculum tests and external examinations will be published in order to ensure that schools are maintaining educational standards while at the same time keeping within budgeted spending limits.

As mentioned earlier, recent developments in the public sector have focused on the need to attempt to measure the outputs of such organizations. British Rail, schools, local authorities and hospitals are all required to produce output type information. This issue of output measurements will be developed further in Chapter 10.

In this chapter we have seen that budgeting can be fraught with difficulties. Most of these difficulties are of a behavioural nature and it is to this area that we now turn.

Behavioural issues

At an early stage in this chapter, we recognized the differences between a control system in an organization and the workings of a thermostat, and that many of these differences related to the fact that organizations were basically groups of people. Emmanuel, Otley and Merchant (1990) emphasize that the technical aspects of budgeting are fairly straightforward whereas the behavioural issues relating to budgeting are much more complex. The critical problems arise out of how managers use the information provided by the budget system, and how the effects of such use feed back on the information that is entered into the budget. It is useful to consider this area under a number of different headings.

Management use of budgets

Dew and Gee (1973) indicated that many managers considered that the budgetary information with which they were provided was not very useful, and it was frequently ignored. To account for this they tested the following conditions, which were considered necessary for an effective system of budgetary control:

- Management's authority and responsibility must be clear — in Dew and Gee's study this condition was not always satisfied. We have already emphasized the need to have a very comprehensive and clear set of responsibility centres within the organization.
- Managers must accept their budgets and consider them to be attainable — Dew and Gee discovered that participation improved the attitude of middle managers towards control information. A considerable amount of work has been undertaken with regard to the level of targets used in budgets. The consensus view seems to be that the highest level of performance is achieved by setting the most difficult specific goals which are acceptable to a manager, the key point being that the budget is difficult but attainable. A consequence of this is that, from a control point of view, negative variances may sometimes occur and the way in which these variances are dealt with is very critical. This is an issue we will return to later.
- Budgetary control information must be understood by the managers — managers included in the study tended to be unhappy about the way in which budgetary information was presented. There was no flexibility in terms of presentation and all reports tended to be in a similar format. Dew and Gee suggested that formats needed to be flexible in order to meet the requirements of different managers. For instance, some managers may prefer some of the information in graphical form.
- Training in budgetary control must be effective — the study suggested that managers looked for personal contact with accountants in order to understand the meaning of budgetary information.
- Managers must understand the aim of budgetary information — the study by Dew and Gee suggested that many managers were suspicious about the role of budgets and tended to look at the process in a fairly negative way.

Participation

Dew and Gee (1973) found that participation in the budget-setting process improved the attitude of middle managers to the control process. The fact that managers have been involved in setting the budget makes it more likely that they will accept it. The acceptance of a budget target is crucial to the success or failure of a budgeting system. There is a large amount of literature on the impact of participation on budgeting systems and performance, and some of it is contradictory. However, there is reasonable consensus on a number of points concerning the benefits of participation.

- As mentioned already, managers who participate in the budget-setting process are more likely to accept targets than if they are imposed.
- Managers who participate are likely to have a more positive attitude towards the organization as a whole. Participation can also lead to greater job satisfaction and higher levels of self-esteem.
- Budgets should be more accurate since the managers who have the greatest knowledge of local conditions and difficulties will have been involved in the setting of the budget.
- Participation should decrease the likelihood of information distortion and manipulation. Some people may argue, however, that, at the budget-setting stage, it is more likely that budgets will be more biased (e.g. introduce slack into budgets) since the managers, whose performance may be judged on their ability to meet the budget, will be involved in setting the budget. The key point here is the way that the information is used in evaluating managerial performance; this issue will be picked up later.

As indicated by the last point, there has been a lot of debate about the role of participation in the setting of budgets. Participation may not work in all situations and with all personality types. Participation may not always improve performance for the organization since standards may be lowered. Some organizations who claim to use participative budgeting are not really using it since the work completed by lower level managers is ignored and replaced by figures produced by senior managers. This has been referred to as *pseudo-participation* and is in fact more demotivating than a situation where no participation takes place at all.

Budgets as targets

Hofstede (1968) suggested that the highest level of performance is achieved by setting the most difficult specific goal which will be accepted by the manager concerned. Stedry (1960) suggested that the formulation of a specific target improved performance. However, he added that the precise effect is determined by the way in which the target influences the participant's own goals or 'levels of aspiration'. Emmanuel, Otley and Merchant (1990) indicate that the crucial feature of targets seems to be that they must be accepted by the person to whom they are assigned.

Budgets as forecasts

It is important to recognize that budgetary biasing may take place when budgets are being prepared in organizations. Budgetary biasing is usually associated with people introducing slack into their budgets so that they can achieve their targets more easily. However, there is also evidence that managers operating in tough environments may bias their estimates in the opposite direction and set themselves budgets that they are unlikely to achieve. The reasoning behind this is that managers may be feeling insecure because of past poor performance and feel that by promising improvement, they would gain immediate approval despite the risk of future disappointment.

Lukka (1988) found evidence of both forms of budgetary biasing in the organization he looked at. The important message for organizations is that they need to try to understand the reasons why this biasing is taking place. It may be because of the way that budgets are used in performance evaluation within organizations, and this is the next issue we will deal with.

The use of budgets in performance evaluation

As mentioned earlier, budgetary control systems are often viewed very negatively. The authors have been involved with groups of part-time postgraduate students who have expressed similar negative reactions to budgetary control systems. The major problem seems to be associated with the way in which the budgetary control information is used in performance evaluation. This was studied in detail by Hopwood (1976), based on observations in a manufacturing division of a large US company. Three distinct styles of using budget and actual cost information in performance evaluation were observed and were described as follows.

- Budget constrained style – evaluation is based on the ability of the responsibility manager continually to meet the budget on a short-term basis. This criterion of performance is stressed at the expense of other valued and important criteria. Budget data is therefore used in a rigid manner in performance evaluation.
- Profit conscious style – the performance of the responsibility manager is evaluated on his or her ability to increase the general effectiveness of his or her unit's operations in relation to the long-term goals of the organization. The accounting data must be used with some care and in a rather flexible manner, with the emphasis for performance evaluation on contributing to long-term profitability.
- Non-accounting style – accounting data plays a relatively unimportant part in the supervisor's evaluation of the responsibility centre head's performance.

The three styles of evaluation are distinguished by the way in which extrinsic rewards are associated with budget achievement. In the rigid (budget constrained) style there is a clear-cut relationship; not achieving budget targets results in punishment, whereas achievement results in rewards. In the flexible (profit conscious) style, the relationship depends on other factors; given good reasons for overspending, non-attainment of the budget can still result in rewards, whereas the attainment of a budget in undesirable ways may result in punishment. In the non-accounting style, the budget is relatively unimportant because rewards and punishment are not directly associated with its attainment.

Negative reactions to budgets often result from the use of the budget constrained style of budgeting identified by Hopwood and the introduction of slack into budgets is often associated with this rigid style of budgeting.

The reader should now be aware that budgeting within organizations is quite complex from a behavioural perspective. The designers and participants need to recognize these complexities in order to create a budgeting system which helps the organization to achieve its objectives.

Summary

This chapter has been concerned with planning and control issues within organizations. The chapter opened by highlighting two recent developments in the public sector in the area of budgeting. Local management of schools and GP fundholding provide illustrations of the move towards accountable management in the public sector. The chapter then went on to introduce the idea of the general control model and demonstrate the relationship between this general control model and organizational planning and control. Particular emphasis has been placed on management control and the role of budgeting as an important part of the management control system. The reasons for budgeting within organizations were addressed together with an outline of the various stages in the budgetary process. Illustrations of budgeting were provided from both the private sector and the public sector. The final part of the chapter dealt with the behavioural aspects of budgeting. Budgeting is not just a technical process, and managers need to appreciate that budgeting must be considered in an organizational context. After reading this chapter you should be able to:

- Describe the general control model.
- Explain the relationship between the general control model and planning and control systems within organizations.
- Explain the differing responsibilities associated with different types of responsibility centres.
- Describe the purposes of budgeting.
- Explain the different stages in the budgetary process.
- Provide illustrations of budgeting from both the public sector and the private sector.
- Prepare a simple budgeted cash flow statement and profit and loss account.

- Appreciate the need to consider the behavioural aspects of budgeting.

Now we will go on to consider further aspects of the budgetary process. The next chapter will concentrate on budgetary control and introduce the idea of standard costing. There will also be discussion of activity based budgeting.

References

Anthony, R.N. (1965) *Planning and Control Systems: A Framework for Analysis*, Division of Research, Harvard Graduate School of Business, Boston, Mass.

Bromwich, M. and Bhimani, A. (1989) *Management Accounting: Evolution not Revolution*. Chartered Institute of Management Accountants, London

CIMA Terminology (1991) Chartered Institute of Management Accountants, London

Dew, R.B. and Gee, K.P. (1973) *Management Control and Information*, Macmillan, London

Emmanuel, C., Otley, D. and Merchant, K. (1990) *Accounting for Management Control*, 2nd edn, Chapman and Hall, London

Financial Management Initiative (1982) Cmnd 8616, HMSO, London

Hofstede, G.H. (1968) *The Game of Budget Control*, Tavistock Institute, London

Hopwood, A.G. (1976) *Accountancy and Human Behaviour*, Prentice Hall, Englewood Cliffs, NJ

Lukka, K. (1988) Budgetary biasing in organisations: theoretical framework and empirical evidence. *Accounting, Organisations and Society*, 13, (3), 281–301

Stedry, R.C. (1960) *Budget Control and Cost Behaviour*, Prentice Hall, Englewood Cliffs, NJ

Further reading

CIMA (1992) *Financial Management within GP Practices*, Chartered Institute of Management Accountants, London

Lawton, A. and Rose, A. (1991) *Organization and Management in the Public Sector*, Pitman, London

Wilson, R.M.S. and Chua, W.F. (1993) *Managerial Accounting: Method and Meaning*, 2nd edn, Chapman and Hall, London, Chapters 3 and 8

Problems and discussion topics

1 CALSCO Ltd*

Crane and Lifting Services Co Ltd (CALSCO Ltd) is an autonomous wholly owned subsidiary of a multinational engineering company. Most of its annual sales of £30 million and profits of £3 million are earned from crane testing and repair services. Other work includes the factoring of parts and equipment, converting cranes to remote control and hiring out lifting gear.

* This case was written by A.F. Coad, J. Cullen and P.D. Johnson, Sheffield Hallam University.

CALSCO Ltd has 28 branches which are located close to their markets in major industrial towns and cities throughout the United Kingdom. The branches are coordinated by a small head office situated on the outskirts of Sheffield.

A typical branch employs a branch manager, a sales representative, an engineering draughtsman, a technical clerk, a site services co-ordinator, several engineers and their mates. Each engineer and mate team has a van which carries spare parts and is used to travel to site to perform crane testing, repair and conversion work. Each branch manager is responsible to an operations director at Head Office.

Head Office houses the directorate and centralized marketing and finance functions. An abridged organization chart is given in Figure 1.

CALSCO's board of directors sets great store by the company's budgeting and performance monitoring system. By the end of October each year the board agrees a budget for the following year. Mike Collins, 44, the company's Managing Director and a qualified chartered accountant, describes the budgeting process in this way:

> At CALSCO, we believe in a bottom-up style of management. Each branch is regarded as a business in its own right. The board does *not* produce a long-term strategic plan to be adhered to by branch managers. We expect *them* to develop their own strategies, consistent with the needs of their customers. Of course, we at head office have a clear picture of where the business is going. But, apart from decisions such as where to open a new branch, company strategy arises out of the process of sanctioning initiatives proposed by branch management.
>
> Our approach to management relies heavily on an effective budgeting and performance monitoring system. At this company, budgeting is not a pie in the sky exercise performed by ivory tower accountants. Budgets are not imposed by head office. Each branch manager submits his annual budget which states, in some detail, what his performance will be in the forthcoming year. We encourage branch managers to set themselves challenging targets. Of course, there are times when branch managers fail to set their sights at a sufficiently high level. However, the directors are highly involved in the business and can usually spot such ploys. Branch managers know that we take a dim view of them if they attempt to set themselves easy targets. Such circumstances result in substantial dialogue between members of the board and the branch manager concerned. We never impose arbitrary alterations to branch budgets. However, our objective in this dialogue is to get the branch manager to move his budget towards what we feel is a reasonable challenge. In most instances they do this. But, it is important to emphasize that it is the branch manager who alters his budget. Only in this way is personal commitment achieved.
>
> Once a branch manager's budget has been agreed, it effectively forms a contract between him and the board of directors.

Mike Keys, 42, Director of Finance and a qualified management

CALSO Ltd, Organization chart

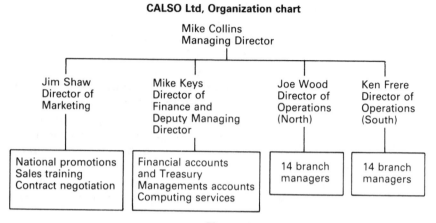

Figure 1

accountant, comments on the role of the management accounts department:

> My management accounts team comprises two qualified management accountants, a clerical supervisor and two cost clerks. They perform a pivotal role in our management control system.
>
> For example, during our budgeting exercise, which usually lasts for six weeks each autumn, they issue timetables and procedures documentation to our branch managers and are available to give them advice both on the completion of their budgets and on the financial implications of their proposals. However, budgeting is a managerial, not an accounting exercise. The branch managers may obtain financial advice from our accounts department and operational advice from their colleagues and directors, but the budgets they submit are *their own*.
>
> Submitted budgets are collated by the management accounts clerk. The first draft of the master budget is produced around the middle of October. All 28 branch budgets are summarized using a computer spreadsheet package. Our spreadsheet model demonstrates how the combined branch budgets affect overall profits, cash flows and returns on investment.
>
> When the budgets are collated, we hold the first meeting of the budget review committee. This committee includes myself, the two operations directors and the marketing director. It is our task to judge the branch budgets, having regard to market potential, branch resources and the levels of profitability expected by our holding company. We can usually spot budgets where branch managers have set themselves easy targets. In those circumstances, we arrange to discuss the budget with the manager concerned to encourage him to revise his expectations. Occasionally, we think that managers are too optimistic with their budget. Such budgets are allowed to stand (for control purposes) because we believe that if a manager aspires to a very high level of performance, it isn't our job to discourage him. However, for the purposes of *planning* cash flows and submitted budgets to our holding company, we revise optimistic

budgets downwards. The spreadsheet model of company budgets is indispensable here. It allows us to produce a number of 'what if' scenarios based upon different assumptions of branch performance.

Discussions between budget review committee members and branch managers are usually completed by the end of October. A full board meeting is then held to formally accept the branch and master budgets. The branch budgets then effectively become a contract between the branch and Head Office.

During the year, monthly management accounts are produced. This is not simply a book-keeping exercise. The accounts for every branch are examined in detail to compare performance with the budget, to check the validity of the accounts and to envisage the profitability of all major contracts.

If branch performance is unlikely to meet the budgeted target, the board want to know at the earliest opportunity, together with the reasons why. This necessitates a special relationship between our management accountants and branch managers. On the one hand, managers must have sufficient confidence in accountants to seek their advice on the financial implications of their activities. On the other hand, branch managers recognize that the accountants act as the eyes and ears of the board and often provide the directors with their first indication of unsatisfactory branch performance.

Our management accountants visit company branches throughout the year. These visits are usually arranged at short notice and afford branch managers the opportunity of discussing their progress with a representative from Head Office. In addition, the accountants check the validity of branch accounting systems, the contents and stage of work-in-progress, and the use of petty cash. Our management accounting is so effective that the end-of-year financial accounts are easily produced.

Joe Wood, 51, a qualified Chartered Engineer and Director of Operations for northern branches, explains:

Budgeting is taken very, very seriously. Every branch manager produces a budget, and I usually spend a whole day with each of them discussing their plans.

Once agreed, the budget is sacrosanct. We don't allow branch managers to revise their budgets downwards as they progress through the year. If we encouraged them to admit that they got their plans all wrong, they could shift the problem from their shoulders to ours. We can't make profits at Head Office, if one branch doesn't meet its budget; that puts pressure on other branches, and that's not fair.

If branch results are not as planned, we encourage the managers to look for alternative ways of achieving their targets.

John Nelson, 37, is manager of CALSCO'S Newcastle branch. He joined the company at 16, straight from school. He worked his way up from service engineer's mate to become branch manager five years ago.

The Newcastle branch has a number of very profitable service contracts with engineering firms in the North East. It has achieved its budgeted performance in each of the past five years. John comments:

> I enjoy working for CALSCO. The style of management here suits me. Apart from a couple of visits from management accountants each year to check my accounting systems, Head Office leaves me alone. I'm effectively my own boss.

Trevor Harding, 34, is manager of the Wolverhampton branch. He joined CALSCO three years ago from the company's major competitor, COUBROSCO.

Recession in the engineering sector of West Midland industry has led to the closure of many firms and the loss of a significant percentage of the target market of the Wolverhampton branch. It has failed to achieve its budgeted performance in each of the past two years. Trevor comments:

> The recession has hit the West Midlands very badly. We have lost many regular customers. Despite a lot of hard work here, it has proved impossible to meet budgeted targets.
>
> When it becomes obvious that we're not going to hit our budget, we usually receive a visit from our management accountants. They turn our accounts upside down to check that we've invoiced all possible sales and haven't hidden away some profit in our reserves. It's as if Head Office don't trust us.
>
> I sometimes feel we have too many accountants running the company. At COUBROSCO we have nowhere near the same amount of paperwork. Monthly variance reports are fine, but they don't tell me how to get sales.

Iain Reid, 58, has recently retired. He was formerly manager of CALSCO's Aberdeen branch. He makes the following observations:

> CALSCO's management control system brings both the best and the worst out of branch managers. It allows them a lot of freedom. However, some managers spend time 'massaging' their performance figures to match budgets. For example, if a manager has a good month he may be tempted to invent reserved costs so as to reduce his profits and save them up for a rainy day. Alternatively he may delay invoicing a completed contract, leaving it in work-in-progress.
>
> The managers who leave CALSCO have usually failed to meet budgets or have been found cheating the system. Managers only receive their 20% of salary annual bonus if they hit budgeted targets.
>
> Creative accounting by branch management can waste a lot of time. One manager had a very intricate scheme for improving the margins on completed contracts by re-coding costs to work-in-progress. The accountants eventually found out and he left the company.

You are required to critically evaluate the management control system of CALSCO and discuss what changes, if any, you would recommend.

2   The concept of devolved management has permeated all the way through the public sector. In this chapter there have been examples of delegated budgets in schools and the health service. Changes have also occurred within local authorities and central government organizations. The UK running costs scheme (operating within the Civil Service) started with a report to the Prime Minister in 1983 by the Management and Personnel Office. This report sets out the principles and guidelines for the budgeting, monitoring and controlling of running costs (i.e. revenue costs) and the delegation of responsibility for them. Evidence from the running costs initiative suggests that managers have increased or reduced the resources allocated to particular activities within their overall budget, to reflect peaks and troughs. They have also deferred or dropped activities and replaced activities as priorities have changed. Managers have become increasingly cost-conscious. Some examples of savings and increased cost-consciousness are set out below.

- Introduction of delegated budgeting led to identification of unnecessary costs and consequent reduction in the size of vehicle fleet.
- Through a delegated budget, payments for unused parking spaces were identified and stopped.
- Budgeting encouraged use of more efficient gas/electricity tariff.
- Devolved budgeting has given rise to the removal of unnecessary telephone extensions and reduction in the '9' facility for outside lines.
- The parts of the department to which budgets have been developed now include an assessment of resource implications in their submissions to the top of the office. Previously they needed constant reminders to do so as, even now, do the parts of the department not covered by budgets.
- Budgeting has helped us to develop links between costs and performance – any objective now has to have a price tag.

You are required to discuss the development of delegated budgets within the public sector. The discussion should cover your views as to the positive features of delegated budgets together with any reservations you may have about this development.

6 Standard costing and budgetary control

The aims of this chapter are to:

- Outline the idea of flexible budgeting.
- Explain the links between budgets and standard costing systems.
- Explain how standard costs are set.
- Provide a definition of ideal and attainable standards.
- Explain the concept of variance analysis and provide examples of variance analysis calculations.
- Consider the limitations of traditional variance analysis.
- Develop the idea of activity based budgeting.

Introduction

In the previous chapter we introduced the idea of budgeting and provided illustrations of the budgetary process within organizations. It was stressed in Chapter 5 that budgeting is as much a behavioural as a technical process. This important message needs re-emphasizing since these behavioural issues are of continuing importance as we develop this particular chapter. The area of study for this chapter is shown in Figure 6.1. You will notice this is the same box that we considered in Chapter 5; however, we are now going to concentrate on the control aspects of the budgetary process. As part of this development, we will be looking at the link between budgets and standard costing systems.

Budgetary control systems

At this stage it is useful to look at the CIMA definition of budgetary control:

The establishment of budgets relating the responsibilities of executives to the requirements of a policy, and the continuous comparison of actual with budgeted results, either to secure by individual action the objectives of that policy or to provide a basis for its revision.

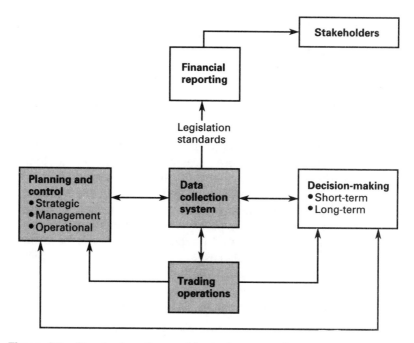

Figure 6.1 *Standard costing and budgetary control*

The budgetary control process therefore requires a comparison between budgeted and actual costs. A useful first stage in this comparison is to prepare a flexible budget which takes into account any difference in activity level between the original budget and the actual costs incurred.

The following data will be used throughout this chapter to illustrate both the flexing of a budget and the calculation of variances.

Illustration 6.1   Budget and actual data for Company X

	Budget	Actual
Sales and production units	10,000	9,000
Selling price per unit	£120	£115
Direct materials		
5 kg at £6 per kg	£300,000	
4 kg at £7 per kg		£252,000
Direct labour		
6 hours at £7 per hour	£420,000	
8 hours at £6 per hour		£432,000
Variable production overhead	£180,000	£200,000
Fixed production overhead	£100,000	£100,000
Profit	£	£
Sales	1,200,000	1,035,000
Direct materials	300,000	252,000

Direct labour	420,000	432,000
Variable production overheads	180,000	200,000
Fixed production overheads	100,000	100,000
PROFIT	200,000	51,000

The major problem with the data presented in Illustration 6.1 is that the actual levels of output (i.e. production and sales) are different from the budgeted levels. In order to provide a meaningful control report it is therefore necessary to flex the budget to take into account the actual level of output. If this flexing does not take place, the control report will be of little value to the manager concerned. In order to flex the budget it is necessary to have an adequate knowledge of cost behaviour patterns within the organization. Cost behaviour was introduced in Chapter 4 and we will be using the notion of fixed and variable costs to flex the budget. Variable costs are flexed to take into account the changing level of output whereas fixed costs are not adjusted for changes in level of output. The flexed budget is calculated as shown in Illustration 6.2.

Illustration 6.2   Original budget and flexed budget

	Original budget		Flexed budget
	£		£
Sales revenue		Sales revenue	
10,000 × 120	1,200,000	9,000 × 120	1,080,000
Direct material		Direct material	
10,000 × 5 kg × £6 per kg	300,000	9,000 × 5 kg × £6 per kg	270,000
Direct labour		Direct labour	
10,000 × 6 hr × £7 per hr	420,000	9,000 × 6 hr × £7 per hr	378,000
Variable production overhead		Variable production overhead	
10,000 × 6 hr × £3 per hr	180,000	9,000 × 6 hr × £3 per hr	162,000
Fixed production overhead	100,000	Fixed production overhead	100,000
PROFIT	200,000	PROFIT	170,000

The next stage in the control process is to provide some variance analysis. Variance analysis is defined by CIMA as: 'The analysis of performance by means of variances. Used to promote management action at the earliest possible stage.' The value of variance analysis comes from an analysis of significant variances, the identification of their causes, and the correction of these causes. Variance analysis can be used to explain the differences between the original budget and the flexed budget. It can also be used to explain the differences between the flexed budget and the actual situation. The original budget, flexed budget and actual figures are shown in Illustration 6.3.

Illustration 6.3 Original budget, flexed budget and actual

	Original budget £	Flexed budget £	Actual £
Sales revenue	1,200,000	1,080,000	1,035,000
Direct material	300,000	270,000	252,000
Direct labour	420,000	378,000	432,000
Variable production overhead	180,000	162,000	200,000
Fixed production overhead	100,000	100,000	100,000
PROFIT	200,000	170,000	51,000

The difference between the original budget and the flexed budget is explained by a *volume variance*.

> Volume variance (using absorption costing)
> Sales volume profit variance   £20,000   (adverse)
> Fixed production overhead
> Volume variance   £10,000   (adverse)
> Volume variance (using marginal costing)
> Sales volume contribution variance   £30,000   (adverse)

The variance calculations will be explained later.

The difference between the flexed budget and the actual figures is explained by price and efficiency variances. These will be dealt with later.

Before continuing with the variance analysis, it is useful at this stage to introduce the concept of standard costing and also to identify the links between standard costing and budgetary control. We will of course return to our example later in the chapter.

Standard costing and budgetary control

Standard costing and budgetary control are similar techniques as both use the concept of management by exception. In standard costing, actual costs are compared to the predetermined standard costs, and in budgetary control actuals are compared with budgeted costs. Any variances that arise will be reported to management, and this will allow the management to decide if they are worthy of investigation and will also provide a trigger which would signal the need for the necessary corrective action.

It is important to note the difference between a standard cost and a budget. Budgets deal with total costs and standards deal with unit costs. Organizations can use both budgetary control and standard cost control within the same overall planning and control mechanism; but standards are only really suitable for organizations or departments where work tasks are built up from repetitive processes, and where inputs can be linked to outputs through a well-understood process. The example used in our illustrations assumes that the two systems are working together.

As mentioned above, standard costing is most suited to an organization whose activities consist of a series of common or repetitive operations. It is therefore relevant in many manufacturing situations since the processes involved are often of a repetitive nature. It is also possible to apply standard costing to non-manufacturing activities where the operations are of a repetitive nature. It cannot, however, easily be applied to activities of a non-repetitive nature, since there is no basis for observing repetitive operations and, as a result, standards cannot be set.

A standard costing system usually operates within the budgetary control system of the organization and the standard costing system provides the detail needed to prepare the budget. This is the way that the budget has been set in the illustrations used in this particular chapter. For example, the direct material budget was calculated by using standards for both price and quantity:

> Standard cost of direct material   £6.00 per kg
> Standard usage of material per unit of output   5 kg
> Budgeted direct material cost = 10,000 units of output × 5 kg per unit of output × £6 per kg = £300,000.

Similarly, the direct labour budget was calculated by using standards for both price and quantity:

> Standard labour cost per hour   £7.00
> Standard labour hours per unit of output   6 hours
> Budgeted direct labour cost = 10,000 units of output × 6 hours per unit of output × £7.00 per hour = £420,000.

Having identified the link between standard costing and budgetary control, it is now useful to look at the way standards are developed.

Establishing cost standards

In Chapter 5 it was suggested that the highest level of performance could be achieved by setting the most difficult specific goal that will be accepted by the manager concerned. CIMA have identified two different levels of standards:

'*Ideal standard* – a standard which can be attained under the most favourable conditions, with no allowance for normal losses, waste and machine downtime. Also known as potential standard.' In practice, ideal standards are unlikely to be achieved and therefore tend to be demotivating to employees because there will always be adverse variances. However, an ideal standard can act as a long-term goal to work to.

'*Attainable standard* – a standard which can be attained if a standard unit of work is carried out efficiently, a machine properly operated or a material properly used. Allowances are made for normal losses, waste and machine downtime.' Attainable standards are less rigorous than ideal standards and provide a fair base from which to calculate variances, but also represent standards that should be achieved. Attainable standards do offer scope for providing a challenging level of activity for employees, particularly if there is an incentive attached to reaching the standard.

Having identified the different types of standard available, the next stage is briefly to outline the mechanisms for arriving at standards for labour and materials.

Direct material standards – these are based on product specifications arrived at from a study of the quantity of materials necessary for each operation. The study should establish the most suitable materials for each product, based on product design and quality policy, and also the optimal quantity that should be used after taking into account any normal or inevitable losses in the production process. This assumes the use of an attainable standard. The standard amount of material required is usually recorded on a bill of materials, with a separate bill of materials being maintained for each product. The standard material product cost is then found by multiplying the standard quantities by the appropriate standard prices. The standard prices are usually obtained from the purchasing department.

Direct labour standards – a time and motion study may be used to set labour standards. The normal procedure for such a study is to analyse each operation in order to eliminate any unnecessary activities and to determine the most efficient production method. The most efficient methods of production, equipment and operating conditions are then standardized. The agreed methods of manufacture are the basis of setting standard labour times. The labour standards must specify the exact grades of labour to be used as well as the times involved. Unavoidable delays such as machine breakdowns and routine maintenance are taken into account when setting the standard time. Again this assumes that an attainable standard is to be used. The agreed wage rate per hour is then multiplied by the standard quantity of hours required per unit of output to arrive at the standard labour product cost.

Setting standards for overheads is more difficult since there is either less, or no direct relationship between overhead costs and unit output. With direct labour and materials, the input unit requirement per unit of output is clearly defined, and can be directly observed and studied in order to set the targets. With variable overheads, the cost of variable resources per unit of output cannot be studied and measured since there is no observable direct relationship between resources required and units of output. In practice, organizations tend to use direct labour hours or machine hours as an activity base for variable overheads. This involves the calculation of a variable overhead absorption rate which is demonstrated later in Illustration 6.4. Fixed overheads are basically independent of any changes in output in the short term, and as a result it is not necessary, for control purposes, to calculate a unit standard cost for fixed overheads. However, if the organization operates an absorption standard costing system, a fixed overhead absorption rate will be calculated and this again is demonstrated in Illustration 6.4. Having dealt with the issue of establishing cost standards, we will now go on to look at variance analysis in more detail.

Variance analysis

As mentioned earlier, variance analysis is used to analyse performance and to promote management action at the earliest possible stage. In Chapter 5 the general control model was developed and an important part of this model is the need to provide feedback in order that corrective action may be taken. Variance analysis fulfils this role within organizations. Managers in charge of a responsibility centre need to be aware of how they are performing against their budget. In our combined standard costing and budgetary control system, variances can be calculated on either an absorption costing basis or a marginal costing basis. These two terms were introduced in Chapter 4. Figure 6.2 shows the variances that can be calculated using absorption costing principles and Figure 6.3 shows the variances that can be calculated using marginal costing principles.

Many of the variances that require calculation are similar under the two different set of principles and the methods of calculating these variances are shown in Figure 6.4. Where there are differences

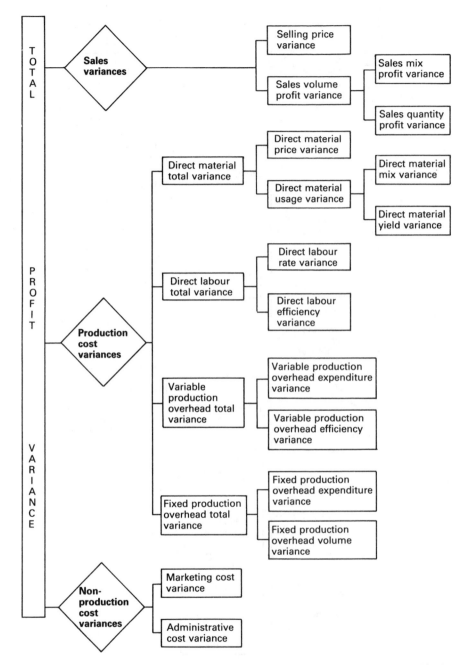

Figure 6.2 *Chart of variances using absorption costing principles* (CIMA Terminology, *1991)*

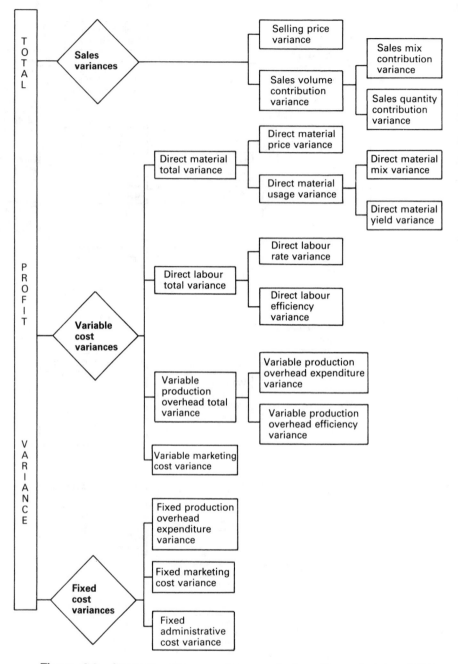

Figure 6.3 *Chart of variance using marginal costing principles* (CIMA Terminology, *1991)*

Material variances
Direct material price variance
(Actual material purchased × standard price) − (Actual cost of material purchased)
Direct material usage variance
(Standard quantity of material specified for actual production × standard price) − (Actual material × standard price)
Direct material total variance
(Direct material price variance) + (Direct material usage variance)

Labour variances
Direct labour rate variance
(Actual hours worked × standard direct labour rate) − (Actual hours worked x actual hourly rate)
Direct labour efficiency variance
(Standard hours of actual production × standard direct labour rate) − (Actual direct hours worked × standard direct labour rate)
Direct labour total variance
(Standard hours of actual production × standard direct labour rate) − (Actual hours worked × actual hourly rate)

Variable production overhead variances
Variable production overhead expenditure variance
(Actual hours worked × standard variable overhead rate) − (Actual cost)
Variable production overhead efficiency variance
(Standard variable production overhead cost of actual production) − (Actual hours worked × standard variable overhead rate)
Variable production overhead total variance
(Standard variable production overhead cost of actual production) − (Actual cost)

Fixed production overhead variance
Fixed production overhead expenditure variance
(Budgeted fixed production overhead) − (Actual fixed production overhead)

Other fixed cost variances
(we have assumed for simplicity purposes that all marketing and administration costs are fixed)
Marketing cost variance
(Budgeted marketing cost) − (Actual marketing cost)
Administrative cost variance
(Budgeted administrative cost) − (Actual administrative cost)

Sales variances
Selling price variance
(Actual sales units × standard selling price) − (Actual sales)

Figure 6.4 *Calculation of variances where there is no difference between the sets of principles*

Using absorption costing
Fixed production overhead volume variance
  (Standard absorbed cost) − (Actual fixed production overhead)
Sales volume profit variance
  (Budgeted sales unit × standard profit per unit) − (Actual sales units × standard profit per unit)

Using marginal costing
Sales volume contribution variance
  (Budgeted sales units × standard contribution per unit) − (Actual sales units × standard contribution per unit)

Figure 6.5 *Calculation of variances where there is a difference between the two sets of principles*

between the two sets of principles, the methods of calculating these variances are shown in Figure 6.5.

It is now necessary to turn back to our example in order to illustrate the calculation of the different variances. As part of the variance analysis it is also possible to provide a reconciliation between the original budgeted profit and the flexed budget profit. A further reconciliation can be provided between the flexed budget profit and the actual profit. All of these calculations and reconciliations are shown in Illustration 6.4.

Illustration 6.4 Variance analysis for Company X including reconciliation between the different profit levels

Using absorption costing

	Adverse £	Favourable £	£
Original budget profit			200,000
Variances			
Sales volume profit			
(1,000 × 20) − (9,000 × 20)	(20,000)		
Fixed production overhead volume			
(9,000 × 10) − 100,000			
	(10,000)		(30,000)
Flexed budget profit			170,000
Variances			
Direct labour rate			
(72,000 × 7) − (72,000 × 6)		72,000	

Direct labour efficiency
(54,000 × 7) − (72,000 × 7)   (126,000)
Direct material price
(36,000 × 6) − (36,000 × 7)   (36,000)
Direct material usage
(45,000 × 6) − (36,000 × 6)   54,000
Variable production overhead
expenditure
(72,000 × 3) − 200,000   16,000
Variable production overhead
efficiency
(54,000 × 3) − (72,000 × 3)   (54,000)
Fixed production overhead
expenditure
100,000 − 100,000   —   —
Sales price
(9,000 × 120) − 1,035,000   (45,000)

	(261,000)	142,000	(119,000)
Actual profit			51,000

Using marginal costing	*Adverse* £	*Favourable* £	£
Original budget profit			200,000
Variances			
Sales volume contribution			
(10,000 × 30) − (9,000 × 30)	(30,000)		(30,000)
Flexed budget profit			170,000
Variances			
Same as in absorption costing	(261,000)		(261,000)
		142,000	142,000
Actual profit			51,000

Notes
(1)   Standard margins per unit

	£	£
Selling price		120
Variable costs		
Direct materials 5 kg × £6	30	
Direct labour 6 hr × £7	42	
Variable production overhead 180,000 ÷ 10,000 units	18	90
Standard contribution per unit		30
Fixed production overhead 100,000 ÷ 10,000 units	10	10
Standard profit per unit		20

(2)   Standard hours of actual production
> 9,000 units × 6 hours per unit = 54,000 hours

(3)   Standard quality of material specified for actual production
> 9,000 units × 5 kg = 45,000 kg

(4)   Variable production overhead absorption rate per direct labour hour
> 180,000 ÷ (10,000 × 6 hours per unit) = £3 per hour

(5)   Standard absorbed fixed production overhead cost
> 9,000 units × £10 per unit = £90,000

Interpretation of the variance analysis

It is not sufficient merely to describe and calculate variances. It is important that the variances are understood by people in the organization and that the calculation of the variances provides useful information for managers within that organization. In our Company X example, there are a number of issues worthy of comment. The first thing to appreciate is that some of the reasons for the variances may be linked. For instance, if we take the *direct material variances* it may be that the company purchased better quality materials which resulted in a favourable *usage variance*. In overall terms, the direct material cost was less for the level of output than anticipated by the standards. There may also be links between the two *labour variances*, but in this case the company actually spent more money on labour costs than anticipated by the standards for the actual level of output. It may be that a lower level of skilled labour was used than anticipated when the standards were set up and this resulted in less efficient use of the labour. The loss of efficiency was also reflected in the adverse *variable production overhead efficiency variance*. The sales situation is also very worrying since both volume and sales price are down. It may be that as a result of a depression, the sales managers decided to drop the selling price in order to stimulate demand. The figures show that this does not appear to have happened. The *volume variances* reflect the difference between the original budget profit figure and the flexed budget profit figure. Once the variances have been calculated and their meaning understood it is then important to complete the exercise by taking any necessary corrective action. As introduced in Chapter 5, this may involve either single or double loop learning. In single loop learning the only corrective action that needs to take place is to ensure that the original objective is met. If the environment is fairly unstable, it may be necessary actually to change the objective since it becomes impossible to meet the original objective. If this is the case, the implications of this change for future planning periods need to be recognized.

Limitations of variance analysis

When considering variance analysis it is also important to recognize the limitations of variance analysis. Variances may arise because the original standards are out of date because of rapid changes in the operating and external environments. If this particular problem is not addressed then variance reports may be full of meaningless information which causes confusion rather than supplying useful management information. In order to address this particular problem, many organizations revise standards and budgets at regular intervals during the year. This means that the standards and budgets are more appropriate and the variance analysis more meaningful. However, the control implications of this need recognizing and managers may become confused about which target they are aiming to achieve.

Overhead volume variances have also been criticized because information which is intended for product costing purposes (i.e. absorption of fixed overheads into cost units) is used as a basis for control information. As illustrated in our Company X example however, the use of marginal costing principles removes the need to calculate a fixed production overhead volume variance. Even if the variance is calculated under an absorption costing system, the important point to remember is that it basically simply provides an explanation, along with the sales volume profit variance, of the impact of volume changes on the original budget. The most recent criticism of traditional variance analysis comes in relation to organizations operating in a just-in-time type of environment. It is argued that, rather than traditional variance analysis aiding organizations who operate just-in-time systems, it actually acts against the interests of such organizations. For instance, it is suggested that traditional efficiency variances encourage production of goods which are not actually required by customers. Material price variances may encourage purchasing managers to buy in bulk even though this may result in higher stocks of raw materials being held. In a just-in-time environment, the key issues with material purchasing are supplier reliability, materials quality, and delivery in small order quantities. Many just-in-time systems depend on long-term contractual links with suppliers, and as a result many have argued that material price variances become less relevant for management control purposes. Scrap factors included in standard costs may result in satisfaction when actual scrap equals standard scrap. This may deter the momentum towards zero scrap levels and the need to get things right first time. There is also a move towards including more non-financial measures in performance reports and this particular issue will be picked up in more detail in Chapter 10.

In the last part of this chapter we continue with this critical look at traditional budgetary control systems by introducing the idea of *activity based budgeting*. The protagonists of this approach argue that, in practice, traditional budgeting systems are lacking in a number of respects.

Activity based budgeting (ABB)

The concept of activity management was introduced in Chapter 4 and the methodology behind it is presented in Figure 6.6. It has been suggested that activity management has an important role to play in the planning and control of organizations.

Before looking at the mechanics of activity based budgeting, it is useful to report on a survey undertaken by Bellis-Jones (1992). He reported that, in a recent survey of senior managers, only 10% of respondents believed conventional budgets, cost centre and variance reporting to be a 'very effective' control mechanism, while over three times this number believed it to be 'poor', particularly in relation to overhead. Interestingly, 80% of the respondents to the survey were in the finance function. Bellis-Jones identified the following reasons for the failure of conventional approaches to budgetary planning and control:

- *Constraint, not control* – conventional approaches to control have suffocated managerial initiative and have run completely counter to the empowering philosophy of total quality and continuous improvement.
- *Based on limited knowledge* – too often managers settle for basing this year's budget on last year's, rather than judging what is right for the business or seeking to improve effectiveness.
- *Compromises in budget-setting* – budgets are generally poor at translating strategy into action. Strategy generally expresses the organizational plan with reference to the operating environment,

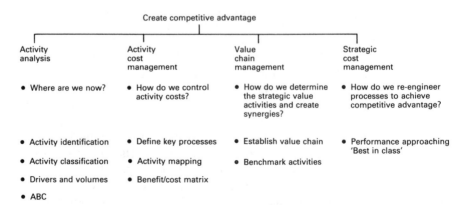

Figure 6.6   *Activity management methodology*

while budget and cost centres are constructed to reflect the hier-archical and functional nature of the structure of the organization and its sub-divisions. The negotiations that take place during the budget-setting process often mean that cuts are made at individual cost centre level without referencing back to the basic strategy of the organization. In the control stage, performance against each budget is examined separately, totally ignoring the cross-functional impact that departments have on each other in practice.

- *Lack of performance measures* – conventional budgets have an over-emphasis on inputs, to the exclusion of outputs. It is still the exception to find useful non-financial measures integrated into the monthly performance reporting package.
- *Too inward looking* – most budgeting processes fail to recognize the crucial role of cross-functional business processes. It is efficient, effective and responsive business processes which provide the foundation of service quality and cost effectiveness. These are rarely recognized in the budgetary process.

Bellis-Jones (1992) suggests that in order to improve matters, organizations need to recognize the following:

- Staff costs are only as fixed as management are prepared to allow, and activities drive cost and can be managed.
- Not all activities add equal value and staff do not usually undertake non-value-added activity for the fun of it: they do so because of the circumstances in which they have been placed by others.
- The majority of activity within a particular department is driven by demands and decisions beyond the immediate control of the budgetholder, upstream in a business process.
- The role of a manager must be to improve the business processes in which his staff have to operate, focusing on the quality of their activities and how such activities link cross-functionally into a business process. Related measures of performance should focus on the factors that drive activities, the quality of the activity under-taken and responsiveness to changing customer requirements.

The theme of ABB and the reasons for developing it were also outlined by Brimson and Fraser (1991). They argued that for management in most companies, improving performance and reducing costs has become a permanent objective and a way of life. However, the formal processes and information systems that support these efforts have remained relatively unchanged. A similar point was made by Johnson and Kaplan (1987) who argued that budgetary control and standard costing systems have been around since the 1920s and have remained relatively unchanged. Brimson and Fraser go on to argue that attempts at improving performance tend to be initiated through a series of one-off exercises and not, as it should be, through a continuous process. They suggest that planning and budgeting should be instruments that support continuous improvement but that, in reality, this is not happening.

They argue that planning usually tackles the issues at too high a level and remains too separate from budgeting. Budgeting, on the other hand, is too much of a financial forecasting exercise and not enough concerned with the allocation and efficient use of resources. They also consider that management reporting places too much emphasis on cost variances and too little, if any, on achievement of output and performance measures. Brimson and Fraser argue that the way forward is to strengthen and integrate the formal, continuing management processes used for planning, budgeting and control. The aims of such processes include:

- Agreeing and communicating business direction.
- Planning best use of resources to achieve the company's strategy and policies.
- Maintaining or increasing profitability.
- Ensuring that customer needs are satisfied.
- Tackling cross-organizational issues.
- Eliminating waste, improving efficiency and reducing costs.
- Harnessing the knowledge and ideas of managers.
- Creating a continuous improvement culture.
- Building a cohesive, committed management team.
- Clarifying manager's roles and responsibilities.
- Agreeing their performance targets.
- Controlling activity performance, as well as costs.

Brimson and Fraser indicate that ABB combines the principles of priority based budgeting, total quality and activity based costing (ABC). Key features of ABB are shown in the Figure 6.7. A key strength of this approach is the activity analysis that takes place. Morrow and Connolly (1991) support the view that budgeting will

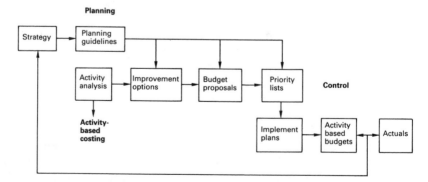

Figure 6.7 *The activity based budgeting process.* (Source: *Brimson and Fraser, 1991*)

improve if it is undertaken on an activity approach. The advantage of this approach, they argue, is that it gives a high profile to the factors that drive resource consumption. From a control point of view the analysis will not be precise, but it will be meaningful.

Morrow and Connolly summarize by saying:

> ...the use of ABC for product costing is leading organizations to have a better understanding of cost behaviour. This opens up opportunities to set and monitor budgets more effectively by taking into account the level of activity and the nature of the cost variability of that activity. Furthermore, this approach can provide a framework to understand the linkage to the decisions which cause cost activities to occur and those which determine the amount of resource needed.
>
> Thus there is a better understanding of cost behaviour and resource consumption. In time, it is likely that these benefits will mean that an activity based approach to both budgeting and reporting will in some organizations replace, rather than supplement, traditional cost reporting when it comes to preparing the budget. (1991: 41)

An interesting illustration of an activities approach is provided by Howes (1992). Howes reported on the provision of management and financial information for hospital nurses. We will make use of some of his findings for a case study.

Case study

Traditionally, financial management of the nursing resource has been through budgetary control of a staff establishment. Variance analysis has concentrated on payroll data with little consideration being given to what nurses have actually been doing.

Little information has been available on why expenditure has been occurring. If there is an overspending on nursing there has been little attempt to discover what it says about the number of patients being treated or the quality of care being delivered. In order to manage effectively, managers need to identify the amount of resources used in caring for each patient.

Within the NHS, resource management initiatives have promoted the delegation of decision-making towards those parts of the organization where the decisions to commit resources are taken. Many hospital units have been restructured into clinical directorates usually based around specialties. A directorate can have an annual budget of several million pounds. To enable the directorate to function efficiently requires a great deal of information about its activity, and systems have been developed for this. Business planning at directorate level will lead to a better understanding of the demand on the service.

It is important that each ward area knows the numbers and types of patients expected during the year. An understanding of the case mix is essential, both locally and corporately, as contracting gets more refined. Everyone must know what the hospital is trying to do, both for the organization as a whole and at individual patient level to determine priorities. There is a 'supply and demand' problem. By managing 'supply' through cash limits without taking any structured action on 'demand', the nursing function may be squeezed resulting in low morale on wards and no guarantee that resources are being best applied.

Nurse costing information is essential for the Clinical Services Manager. A budget statement showing variances between budgeted and actual pay expenditure cannot be related back to patients on the ward. Statistics like cases or bed-days can be included to obtain average costs but this is limited help in explaining variances.

Before costs can be applied to nursing, a cost object must be defined. Past attempts have used 'overall cost per case', 'cost per day' or 'cost per attendance'. In this illustration, a nursing cost object can be attained by building up care plans and developing them into care profiles.

A nursing care plan is a listing of all the interventions required by a patient, showing when and by whom they should be performed. They include general care (e.g. bathing, feeding) as well as activities specific to the treatment of the patient (e.g. administering drugs, monitoring body signs). The sum of the activities a particular patient requires defines that patient's dependency level.

A library of interventions can be collected with standard times and grades of staff for each task. From this library, it is possible to construct a patient care plan. By knowing the expected case mix on the ward, it is possible to aggregate patient care plans to put together a ward plan which reflects demand. Important things to note about care plans are:

- They are designed for each individual patient.
- They incorporate the hospital's approved protocols and define the standards against which the quality of care can be measured.
- They provide data for clinical audit.
- They can be costed.

Costed plans do not guarantee that the total cash required will not exceed the amount available, but managers should be able to negotiate a reconciliation between the two. They can now work towards matching 'supply' and 'demand'.

By defining the grades of nurses in the care plans, realistic establishments can be calculated. It ensures that expensive staff nurse time is not spent on tasks suitable for an auxiliary. Once the nursing care plans have been formulated for the expected case mix, they can be aggregated in different ways. One route is patient-centred and leads to the profile of care. It is useful to clinical staff for monitoring and auditing purposes, and also to senior managers because the profiles can themselves be aggregated into case types or sorted into contracts.

A care profile is an accumulation of the events expected for a patient admitted with a particular diagnosis. The nursing care plan is one element of it. It is a way of defining standards across an entire episode of care and monitoring whether they are being maintained. Profiles should be constructed to be consistent with hospital policies and legal requirements.

A variance analysis is required where standard costs are involved. The main variances are:

- In the number of patients treated – a volume variance in 'demand'
- In the numbers of nurses in post – also a volume variance but in 'supply'.
- In the types of cases seen – this is the case mix variance and is 'demand'.
- In the grades of nurses in post – the skill mix variance, also 'demand'.
- In the salary rates for nurses – a price variance, which is 'supply'.

'Demand' variances can be analysed from the care plans and profiles while 'supply' variances are picked up from the traditional budget statements.

Nursing information should, therefore, in summary form, be part of the case mix database, which must contain for each patient:

- The dependency level.
- The costed time planned for both qualified and unqualified nursing.
- The costed time delivered for both qualified and unqualified nursing.

The activities approach used here has concentrated not only on the resources being used, but also on the work being completed by those resources. It emphasizes the need to look at outputs as part of the budgetary planning and control process. We will return to the ideas of activity based management when we look at activity based costing in Chapter 7.

Summary

The chapter started by looking at the idea of flexible budgeting and the need to take into account the actual level of output. Links between standard costing and budgetary control were identified. We also looked at the different types of standard available and the mechanisms for arriving at standards for labour, materials and overhead. The chapter then concentrated on variance analysis and gave examples of variance calculations which provided a reconciliation between original budget, flexed budget and actual figures. The variances were then interpreted, since variances are of no value without an understanding of why they may have arisen. Limitations of variance analysis were discussed and particular mention was made of the specific limitations relating to firms operating just-in-time systems.

The final part of the chapter dealt with the alternative and fast-developing approach of activity based budgeting. The exponents of ABB argue that traditional budgeting systems are lacking in a number of respects. These views have been presented together with an example of an activities approach offered by Howes (1992). Readers will have their own views on whether the criticisms of traditional budgeting systems presented at the end of this chapter are all valid. The idea of activity based management will be further developed in Chapter 7 through a discussion on activity based costing.

After reading this chapter you should be able to:

- Prepare a flexed budget.
- Understand the term standard costing and recognize the links between standard costing and budgetary control.
- Identify the different types of standard available and the mechanics for arriving at standards for labour, materials and overhead.
- Understand the nature of variance analysis.
- Calculate variances for sales, labour, material and overhead.
- Prepare a reconciliation between original budget, flexed budget and actual figures.
- Debate the limitations of variance analysis.
- Explain the ideas of activity based budgeting and the reasons behind its use.

The next chapter will go on to consider the information required for short-term decision-making within organizations.

References

Bellis-Jones, R. (1992) Budgeting and cost management: a route to continuous improvement. *Management Accounting*, April, pp. 36–8

Brimson, J. and Fraser, R. (1991) The key features of ABB. *Management Accounting*, January, pp. 42–3

CIMA Terminology (1991) Chartered Institute of Management Accountants, London

Howes, J. (1992) Management and financial information for nurses. *Management Accounting*, April, p. 15

Johnson, H.T. and Kaplan, R.S. (1987) *Relevance Lost: The Rise and Fall of Management Accounting*, Harvard Business School, Boston, Mass

Morrow, M. and Connolly, T. (1991) The emergence of activity based budgeting. *Management Accounting*, February, pp. 38–9, 41

Morrow, M. and Hazell, M. (1992) Activity mapping for business process design. *Management Accounting*, February, pp. 36–8

Further reading

Bellis-Jones, R. (1992) Activity based cost management. *Management Accounting Handbook* (ed. C. Drury), Butterworth-Heinemann in association with the Chartered Institute of Management Accountants, Oxford, Chapter 5

Brimson, J.A. (1992) The basics of activity based management. In *Management Accounting Handbook* (ed. C. Drury), Butterworth-Heinemann in association with the Chartered Institute of Management Accountants, Oxford, Chapter 4

Drury, C. (1992) *Standard Costing*, Academic Press in association with the Chartered Institute of Management Accountants, London

Problems and discussion topics

1 A company manufactures one product, and the following information refers to the budget and actual data for that product:

	Budget	Actual
Sales and production units	30,000	28,000
Selling price per unit (£)	280	270
	£'000	£'000
Direct materials		
10 kg per unit at £8 per kg	2400	
252,000 kg at £9 per kg		2,268
Direct labour		
8 hours per unit at £7 per hour	1,680	
196,000 hours at £7 per hour		1,372
Variable production overheads	1,200	1,110
Fixed production overheads	2,100	2,100

You are required to:

(a) Flex the budget to take into account the actual level of output and provide an explanation of the difference between the original budget and the flexed budget.
(b) Provide a variance analysis which explains the difference between the flexed budget profit and the actual profit.

2 Variance analysis is used to analyse performance and to promote management action at the earliest possible stage. The chapter provided illustration of the variances that can be calculated together with a brief interpretation of the possible causes of these variances. It also looked at some of the suggested limitations of variance analysis.

You are required to critically evaluate the system of variance analysis being used in your own organization, or an organization with which you are familiar. For example, does the system of variance analysis currently being used in that organization help to promote the objectives of the organization? Are the standards which the organization uses to compare against actual up-to-date? If the organization does not operate a system of variance analysis, would it be useful for the organization to start operating such a system? If not, explain the reasons why you consider a system of variance analysis is not appropriate for that particular organization. These are just some examples of the types of issues you might raise as part of your critical evaluation.

3   One of the main criticisms of traditional budgeting systems put forward by proponents of activity based budgeting is that tradit-ional systems fail to recognize the crucial role of cross-functional business processes. An activity based management approach can be used in a situation where the cost object is the department or function for which a manager has responsibility. In a wider sense it can also be used where the cost object is the business process, which may cross many functional boundaries. An *activity map* can be drawn to show the linkages between activities within the same or different departments which form the business process. Activity maps can then be annotated with the cost of each activity and, by addition, for the entire process in each department and the total. In order to draw the activity map it is necessary to carry out an *activity analysis*. An activity analysis identifies the activities that take place in the business process and the resources that each activity consumes. It involves inter-viewing the appropriate operational managers involved in the process. In order to ensure that linkages between activities in the business process are identified, it is necessary to ask the person who is responsible for each activity the following questions:

- Who and what triggers the activity to be performed?
- Who are you dependent on in terms of information or product or service flow to enable you to perform the activity?
- What subsequent activities are triggered by the activity?
- Who is dependent on you to enable them to perform an activity?

An example of an activity map (Source: Morrow and Hazell 1992, p. 37) is shown below in Figures 1 and 2. Figure 1 is a simplified version of part of a logistics process. The chart shows all activities that are part of the process of obtaining materials for manufacturing. The horizontal rows indicate the departments involved in the process and the boxes within the chart indicate activities. Figure 2 shows what happens to the activity 'goods inward' when an unexpected consignment is delivered to the store. Activity maps should be annotated with the cost of each activity, but for reasons of space, this has not been done in this

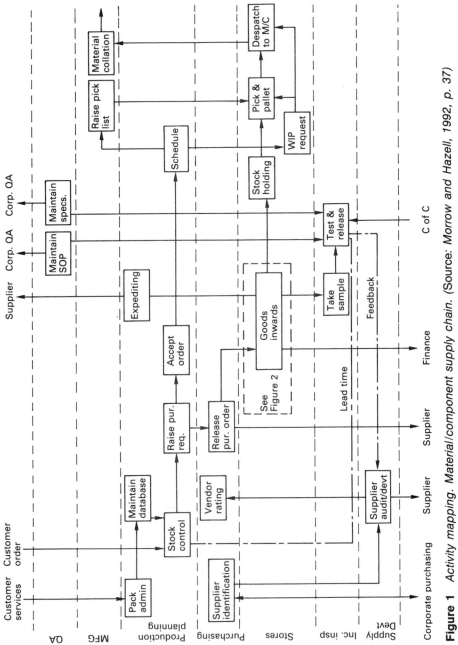

Figure 1 Activity mapping. Material/component supply chain. (Source: *Morrow and Hazell, 1992, p. 37*)

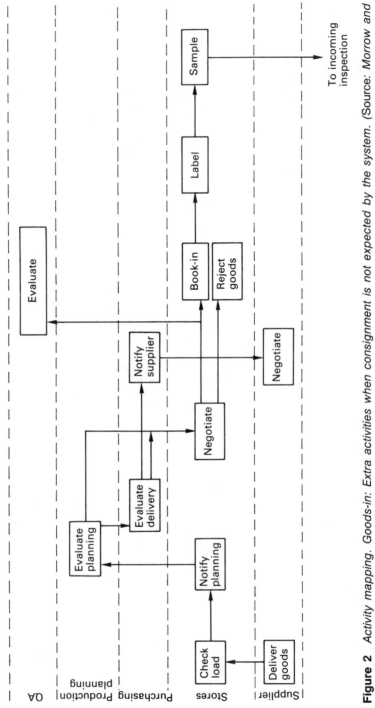

Figure 2 *Activity mapping. Goods-in: Extra activities when consignment is not expected by the system. (Source: Morrow and Hazell, 1992, p. 37)*

particular case. The idea of allocating overhead costs to activity based cost pools will be developed in Chapter 7.

You are required to construct an activity map for a process in your own organization, or an organization with which you are familiar. The process should be one in which you are involved or have been involved. The first stage is to carry out an activity analysis and the information from this analysis can then be used to draw the activity map. You may find it useful, when thinking about the activity analysis, to look at Illustration 7.10 in the following chapter (p. 185).

7 Short-term decision-making

> The aims of this chapter are to:
>
> - Develop the idea of cost-volume-profit analysis.
> - Provide an illustration of cost-volume-profit analysis using mathematical approaches.
> - Provide an illustration of cost-volume-profit analysis using graphical approaches.
> - Apply relevant costing principles to a range of business decisions.
> - Develop the idea of activity based costing.

Introduction

In this chapter we will be looking at the way management accounting information can be used to aid the short-term decision-making process within organizations. The area of study for this chapter is shown in Figure 7.1. The decision-making box in Figure 7.1 covers both short-term and long-term decision-making. The former will be dealt with here while Chapter 8 considers long-term decision-making issues. An understanding of cost behaviour is crucial for both short-term and long-term decision-making and this area was introduced in Chapter 4. Here, we will start by looking at cost-volume-profit relationships.

Cost-volume-profit analysis

Cost-volume-profit (CVP) analysis uses many of the principles of marginal costing and is based on the relationship between sales revenue, costs and profits in the short term and within a range of activity identified as the relevant range. The concept of relevant range is important because CVP relationships are not constant throughout all ranges of output. Cost-volume-profit relationships only hold good over the range of output at which the organization expects to be operating in the near future. The short term is defined as a period up to one year. Therefore, in the short term and where

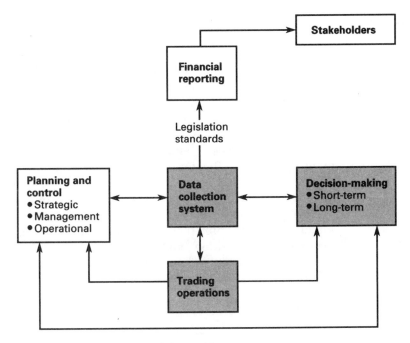

Figure 7.1 *Short-term decision-making*

the changes in activity are relatively small, the principles of marginal costing may be used.

It is useful at this stage to acquaint ourselves with the assumptions that are made when we use CVP analysis. They are as follows:

- All costs can be analysed into fixed and variable elements.
- Fixed costs will remain constant and variable costs vary proportionately with activity.
- Over the activity range being considered, costs and revenues behave in a linear fashion.
- The only factor affecting costs and revenues is volume.
- Technology, production methods and efficiency remain unchanged.
- There is a single product or constant sales mix.
- There are no stock level changes or stocks are valued at marginal costs only.
- The analysis applies to the relevant range only.

This is a fairly comprehensive list of assumptions and many people feel that this over-simplifies complex organizational settings. However, provided that the people both supplying and interpreting CVP information are aware of these assumptions, then CVP analysis can be an important aid to the short-term decision-making process within organizations.

CVP analysis can be presented in both mathematical and graphical form. Initially we will look at the mathematical approach to presenting CVP analysis information.

CVP analysis by formula

The mathematical approach is a quick and flexible method of producing the required information for decision-making. It is also possible to develop computer spreadsheet models which will ease the process of calculation. The mathematical approach uses the formula set out in Figure 7.2, from which it can be seen that an important concept in CVP analysis is the idea of contribution. Contribution is sales revenue less variable costs and this is the key to using most of the formula shown in Figure 7.2. In order to demonstrate the technique of CVP analysis we will apply the formula to data from Smith Ltd. The results are shown in Illustration 7.1.

Having produced the information in Illustration 7.1, it is now important to interpret that information and consider its value for decision-making within Smith Ltd. The first point to note is that every unit produced and sold by Smith Ltd produces a contribution of £10 towards meeting fixed costs. The point at which there is

$$\text{Contribution} = \text{sales price} - \text{variable costs}$$

$$\text{Break-even point (in units)} = \frac{\text{Total fixed costs}}{\text{Contribution per unit}}$$

$$\text{Break-even point (£ sales)} = \frac{\text{Total fixed costs} \times \text{Sales price per unit}}{\text{Contribution per unit}}$$

$$\text{Contribution to sales ratio} = \frac{\text{Contribution per unit} \times 100}{\text{Sales price per unit}}$$

$$\text{Contribution to sales ratio} = \frac{\text{Contribution} \times 100}{\text{Sales revenue}}$$

$$\text{Break-even point (£ sales)} = \frac{\text{Total fixed costs}}{\text{Contribution to sales ratio}}$$

$$\begin{aligned}\text{Level of sales to result in} \\ \text{target profit (in units)}\end{aligned} = \frac{\text{Total fixed costs} + \text{Target profit}}{\text{Contribution per unit}}$$

$$\begin{aligned}\text{Level of sales to result in} \\ \text{target profit (£ sales)}\end{aligned} =$$

$$\frac{(\text{Total fixed costs and target profit}) \times \text{Sales price per unit}}{\text{Contribution per unit}}$$

$$\text{Margin of safety ratio} =$$

$$\frac{(\text{Forecast sales revenue} - \text{Break-even sales revenue}) \times 100}{\text{Forecast Sales Revenue}}$$

Figure 7.2 *Cost-volume-profit analysis by formula*

Illustration 7.1 CVP analysis by formulae

Smith Ltd make a single product and the relevant data is as follows:

Fixed costs per annum		£100,000
Unit selling price	£20	
Unit variable costs	£10	
Forecasted sales units		12,500 units
Capital employed	£150,000	
Target return on capital employed		20%

$$\text{Contribution per unit} = \text{Sales price} - \text{Variable costs}$$
$$= 20 - 10$$
$$= £10 \text{ per unit}$$

$$\text{Contribution to sales ratio} = \frac{\text{Contribution per unit}}{\text{Sales price per unit}} \times 100$$
$$= \frac{10}{20} \times 100$$
$$= 50\%$$

$$\text{Break-even point (in units)} = \frac{\text{Total fixed costs}}{\text{Contribution per unit}}$$
$$= \frac{100,000}{10}$$
$$= 10,000 \text{ units}$$

Two different ways of calculating the break-even point (£ sales):

$$\text{Break-even point (£ sales)} = \frac{\text{Total fixed costs} \times \text{Sales price per unit}}{\text{Contribution per unit}}$$
$$= \frac{100,000 \times 20}{10}$$
$$= £200,000$$

$$\text{Break-even point (£ sales)} = \frac{\text{Total fixed costs}}{\text{Contribution to sales ratio}}$$
$$= \frac{100,000}{50\%}$$
$$= £200,000$$

Level of sales to result in target profit =

$$\frac{\text{Total fixed costs} + \text{Target profit}}{\text{Contribution per unit}}$$

Smith Ltd wanted to make a return on capital employed of 20% and the capital employed figure is £180,000. The profit required to make the 20% return is therefore 20% × £150,000 = £30,000.

$$\frac{\text{Total fixed costs} + \text{Target profit}}{\text{Contribution per unit}}$$

$$= \frac{100,000 + 30,000}{10}$$

$$= 13,000 \text{ units}$$

Level of sales to result in target profit =

$$\frac{(\text{Total fixed cost} + \text{Target profit}) \times \text{Sales price per unit}}{\text{Contribution per unit}}$$

$$= \frac{(100,000 + 30,000) \times 20}{10}$$

$$= £260,000$$

Margin of safety ratio =

$$\frac{(\text{Forecast sales revenue} - \text{Break-even sales revenue}) \times 100}{\text{Forecast sales revenue}}$$

$$= \frac{(250,000 - 200,000) \times 100}{250,000}$$

$$= 20\%$$

Sufficient contribution to meet fixed costs is called the *break-even point*. In Smith Ltd the break-even point is 10,000 units and at that point contribution earned is equal to the fixed costs of the organization. As the name suggests, at break-even point the company makes neither a profit nor a loss. If the organization sells less than 10,000 units it will make a loss. If the organization sells more than 10,000 units it will make a profit. As shown in Illustration 7.1, the break-even point can be stated in either unit terms or sterling terms.

The contribution to sales ratio of 50% means that for every one pound of goods sold the organization will make a contribution of 50 pence. This ratio will remain constant provided there are no changes in the selling price per unit or the variable costs per unit. If either of these changes, then the ratio would have to be recalculated. The contribution to sales ratio of 50% can be used to determine the profit or loss at any particular level of sales. For instance, if Smith Ltd were to sell 12,500 units, the total sales revenue would be £250,000. Using the present contribution to sales ratio of 50%, the contribution generated by this level of sales would be £125,000. Since the fixed costs are £100,000, the profit earned would be £25,000. The contribution to sales ratio is therefore a very useful tool for working out quickly the amount of profit that can be earned from a certain level of sales.

Smith Ltd had decided on a target of 20% return on capital employed. To achieve this, Smith Ltd would be required to make a profit of £30,000. Included in Illustration 7.1 is a calculation that indicates the number of units that need to be sold to achieve this level of profitability. The number of units required to achieve the level of profitability required is 13,000. As you will notice, this is above the forecasted sales level of 12,500 units. Therefore, under the present circumstances, the company will not achieve its required level of return on capital employed. We will return to this particular issue later. The last calculation shown in Illustration 7.1 is one which gives us the margin of safety ratio. This ratio shows the percentage by which the forecasted sales revenue exceeds or falls below the breakeven level of sales revenue. In Smith Ltd, the margin of safety ratio is 20% and this means that sales revenue could fall by 20% before the organization starts making a loss.

Having examined the calculations in Illustration 7.1 based on the original data, it is now useful to go back and look at the problem facing the company with regard to its meeting its target return on capital employed of 20%. In order to meet this target the company would have to increase its sales from 12,500 units to 13,000 units. Since it currently only produces one product, the managers may feel that in the current market conditions the company cannot increase its market share and cannot therefore increase its sales volume by the required amount. It is therefore necessary to consider what other options are open to the company in the short term. The formula outlined in Figure 7.2 can be used to help the decision-making process, and the way that this can be done is demonstrated in Illustration 7.2.

Illustration 7.2 Options using CVP analysis

$$\text{Level of sales to result in target profit (in units)} = \frac{\text{Total fixed costs} + \text{Target profit}}{\text{Contribution per unit}}$$

Each of the options being considered is independent of each other.

The option of reducing fixed costs

Forecasted sales units   12,500
Contribution per unit   £10
Target profit   £30,000

Let X = Total fixed costs

Using formula

$$12,500 = \frac{X + 30,000}{10}$$

$12,500 \times 10 = X + 30,000$

$125,000 - 30,000 = X$

$X = £95,000$

Target return on capital employed of 20% would be achieved if fixed costs were reduced to £95,000.

The option of reducing variable costs per unit

Forecasted sales units   12,500
Target profit   £30,000
Total fixed costs   £100,000
Let X = Contribution per unit
Using formula

$$12,500 = \frac{100,000 + 30,000}{X}$$

$12,500X = 130,000$

$$X = \frac{130,000}{12,500}$$

Contribution per unit = £10.40

Contribution = Selling price − Variable costs (VC)
10.40   = 20 − VC
∴VC   = 9.60

Target return on capital employed of 20% would be achieved if variable costs were reduced to £9.60 per unit.

The option of increasing selling price per unit

This uses the information from the previous option calculation (i.e. reducing variable costs). Contribution per unit needed to meet required return on capital employed is £10.40.

Variable costs per unit £10
Contribution = Selling price (SP) − Variable costs
£10.40 = SP−10
∴ SP = £20.40

Target return on capital employed of 20% would be achieved if selling price was increased to £20.40.

The first option considered was to look at a reduction in fixed costs. In order to meet the required return on capital employed it would be necessary to reduce fixed costs by £5,000. The obvious issue here is whether the organization could reduce fixed costs in the short term since, as the name suggests, these costs are considered to be fixed. One would need to work in the organization to understand the true nature of these costs and whether they could be reduced. It is also important to note that marginal costing assumes that fixed costs are fixed in the short term. However, it does not mean that they are fixed in the longer term and this may be an issue for the organization to look at. The second option considered was a reduction in the variable costs of the organization. In order to meet the required rate of return on capital employed the organization would need to reduce its variable costs to £9.60 per unit. Again the issue is whether this reduction can actually be achieved. Managers within the organization would need to consider the option and the ways in which such a reduction in variable costs could take place. The last option presented in Illustration 7.2 is the level of any selling price increase which would be needed to make the target return on capital employed. As shown by the calculations, the selling price would need to be increased to £20.40 to make the required return. As indicated earlier, the managers may be worried about the state of the market and may feel that it would be difficult to maintain the same sales volume with an increased selling price. However, it is another option for the management team to consider.

It is important to emphasize at this point that the use of CVP analysis indicates the *options* that are available and it is then up to the management of the organization to *decide* whether the options can be achieved. CVP analysis is a tool to aid the management process: it will not take the decisions for the managers. Management in a complex organization is very difficult and there are issues that cannot be built into simple models for decision-making. However, as indicated in the example from Smith Ltd, CVP analysis can help managers in the decision-making process.

CVP analysis is often presented in graphical form and we will now go on to look at this different form of presentation.

CVP analysis in graphical form

The first graph to look at is the *conventional break-even chart* which is shown in Figure 7.3. A break-even chart is one which indicates approximate profit or loss at different levels of sales volume within a limited range. As shown in Figure 7.3, the chart can also be used to quickly identify the break-even point and the margin of safety.

The data from Smith Ltd will now be used to show how this form of graph can be used to analyse specific company situations. The resulting graph is shown in Illustration 7.3. The graph can be used to identify the break-even point and the margin of safety. It can also

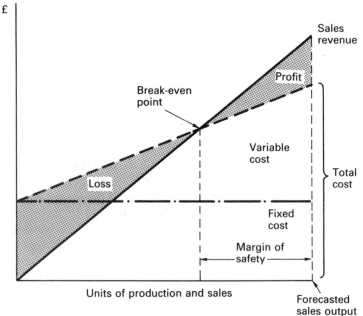

Figure 7.3 *Conventional break-even chart*

Illustration 7.3   Conventional break-even chart for Smith Ltd

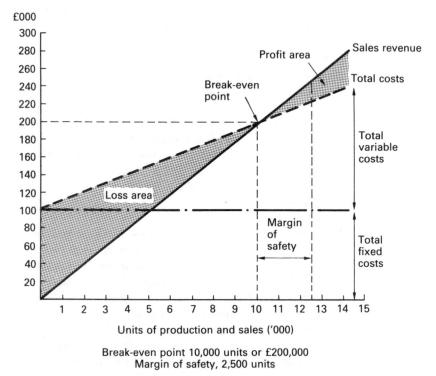

Break-even point 10,000 units or £200,000
Margin of safety, 2,500 units

be used, but not quickly, to identify the profit or loss at any particular volume of sales.

The next graph presented is the *contribution break-even chart*, which is shown in Figure 7.4. The difference between this and the conventional break-even chart is the way in which the cost elements are treated. In the contribution break-even chart the variable cost line is drawn first and then the fixed costs are added. This results in a total cost line which is parallel to the variable cost line. The advantage of this form of presentation, as compared with the conventional break-even chart, is that the total contribution is emphasized in the graph and is represented by the difference between the total sales revenue line and the total variable cost line. As shown in Figure 7.4, the graph can be used to quickly ascertain the break-even point and the margin of safety.

The data from Smith Ltd will now be used to demonstrate how this form of graph can be used to analyse a specific company situation. The resulting graph is shown in Illustration 7.4. The graph can be used to identify the break-even point and the margin of safety. It can also be used, but not quickly, to identify the profit or loss at any particular volume of sales. In addition, the graph can be used to identify the contribution arising from any particular level of sales. For instance, at 10,000 units the contribution is £100,000

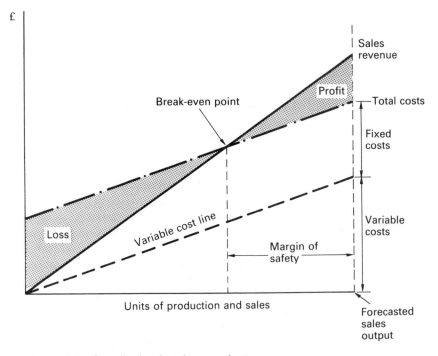

Figure 7.4 *Contribution break-even chart*

Illustration 7.4   Contribution break-even chart for Smith Ltd

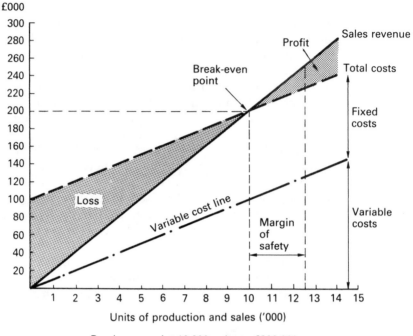

Break-even point 10,000 units or £200,000
Margin of safety, 2,500 units

and this can be found by taking the difference between the sales revenue and variable cost lines at 10,000 units.

Figure 7.5 shows a profit-volume graph. We have already said that the two forms of break-even chart already considered can be used, but not quickly, to identify profit or loss at any given level of sales volume. The profit-volume graph on the other hand does allow easy and quick identification of the amount of profit or loss at any particular volume of sales. It is also very easy to identify the break-even point on this form of graph since it occurs at the point where the profit line intersects the horizontal line.

The data from Smith Ltd will now be used to demonstrate how this form of graph can be used to analyse a specific company situation. The resulting graph is shown in Illustration 7.5. The graph can be used quickly to identify the break-even point and the profit or loss at any given output level. For instance, if Smith Ltd only sold 8,000 units it would make a loss of £20,000. If Smith Ltd sold 12,000 units it would make a profit of £20,000.

When interpreting any of these graphs, it is important to remember the assumptions that underpin CVP analysis. To repeat an earlier point, the information is there to help managers make decisions and not to take the decision for the managers. When managers use

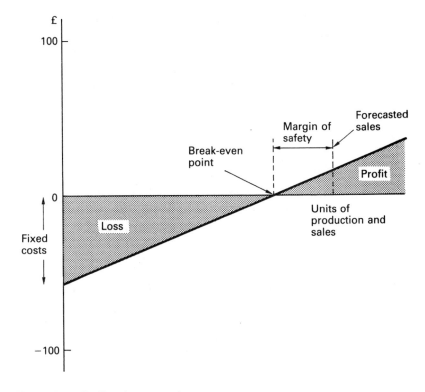

Figure 7.5 *Profit-volume graph*

Illustration 7.5 Profit-volume graph for Smith Ltd

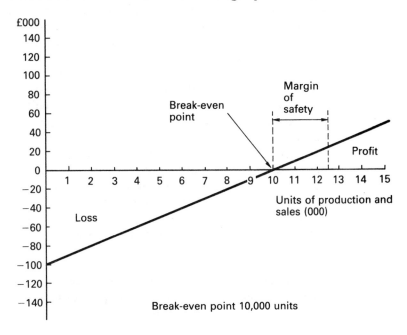

the information for decision-making purposes they must at all times remember the assumptions on which the information is based.

It is possible to show the impact of changes in costs and revenues by drawing additional lines on the charts. An easy way of doing this would be through the use of CVP spreadsheet packages which can quickly show the impact of changes in any of the variables both numerically and graphically. While we have looked at a single product organization, it is possible to bring sales mix issues into the decision-making process. As indicated earlier, CVP analysis assumes either a single product or a constant sales mix. It is possible though, while still maintaining this assumption, to use spreadsheet packages to look at the impact of changes in the sales mix on profitability.

Having looked at CVP analysis, we will now move on to look at the usefulness of relevant costing principles to a range of business decisions.

Relevant costs and revenues for decision-making

The concept of relevant costs and revenues for decision-making was briefly introduced in Chapter 4. Initially, it would be useful to remind ourselves of the key issues identified there. Having done this, we can then go on to look at some illustrative examples.

Relevant costs and revenues are only those which will be affected by a decision. Costs and revenues which will be incurred independent of a decision are not relevant and need not be considered when making that decision. The relevant financial inputs for decision-making purposes are therefore future cash flows, which will differ between the various alternatives being considered. These costs and revenues are often referred to as *differential costs and revenues*.

Implicit in the definition of relevant costs and benefits given above is the fact that costs that have been incurred already are not relevant to a particular decision. Costs that have already been committed, even though they have not yet been paid, are not relevant to the decision. This is because these costs will have to be met irrespective of the decision taken. The same principle applies to revenues.

It is not always easy to identify relevant costs and revenues since this kind of information is not easily extracted from the accounting records of a company. This is particularly true when we are calculating *opportunity costs*. An opportunity cost is a cost which measures the opportunity which is lost or sacrificed when the choice of one course of action requires that an alternative course of action be given up.

Coulthurst and Piper (1986) provide a useful way of identifying relevant costs and benefits within an organization (Figures 7.6, 7.7, 7.8). They argue that their framework provides clarity to the definition of relevant costs and benefits.

Having defined the nature of relevant costs and benefits, we can now go on to look at some examples of illustrate the points made. Illustration 7.6 provides an example of where a relevant cost approach can be used to help the decision-making process within an organization. The illustration includes the original data, notes which are important to the decision-making process and a new calculation showing a revised cost estimate based on a relevant cost approach. In order to demonstrate the different issues involved in this calculation, we will discuss each item in turn.

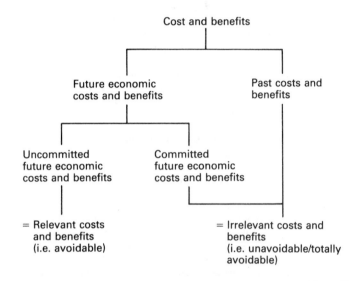

Figure 7.6 *Concepts of costs and benefits for decision-making. (Source: Coulthurst and Piper, 1986)*

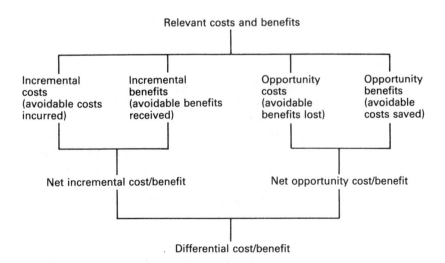

Figure 7.7 *Concepts in the analysis of decision relevant costs and benefits. (Source: Coulthurst and Piper, 1986)*

(a) **Terminology of costs and benefits** (relates to Figure 7.6)
Past
Costs/benefits which have already occurred or where a contractual obligation exists, i.e. committed by past actions (these are irrelevant i.e. unavoidable)

Future economic
Costs/benefits which have not yet occurred and where no contractual obligations exist

Committed future economic
Future economic costs/benefits that would/would not occur regardless of the decision under consideration (these are irrelevant i.e. unavoidable/totally avoidable)

Uncommitted future economic
Future economic costs/benefits whose occurrence depends upon the choice of alternative in the situation under consideration (these are relevant i.e. avoidable).

(b) **Terminology in analysis** (relates to Figure 7.7)
Incremental
Avoidable (i.e. uncommitted future economic) costs/benefits that would be incurred/received by taking a particular course of action

Opportunity
Avoidable (i.e. uncommitted future economic) costs/benefits that would be saved/lost by not taking a particular course of action

Differential
Incremental costs/benefits of taking a course of action, plus the opportunity cost (lost benefit)/opportunity benefit (cost saved) of not taking an alternative course of action

Figure 7.8 *Terminology of costs and benefits for decision-making. (Source: Coulthurst and Piper, 1986)*

Illustration 7.6 Use of relevant cost approach to decision-making (modified ACCA question)

A small contractor has been asked to quote for a contract which is larger than he would normally consider. The contractor would like to obtain the job as he does have surplus capacity.

The estimating and design department have spent 100 hours in preparing drawings and the following cost estimate:

Cost estimate	£	
Direct materials		
3,000 units of X at £10 (original cost)	30,000	See note 1
100 units of Y at £100 (original cost)	10,000	See note 2
Component to be bought in	12,000	See note 3

```
Direct labour
Skilled staff 3,000 hours at £8 per hour          24,000    See note 4
Trainees 500 hours at £3 per hour                  1,500    See note 5

Depreciation on machine
Annual depreciation (straight line)   26,000
4 weeks' depreciation                              2,000    See note 6

Sub-contract work                                 20,000    See Note 7
Supervisory staff                                  7,000    See Note 8

Estimating and design department
   100 hours at £12 per hour                        1,200    See note 9
                                                 _____
                                                 107,700

Administrative overhead @ 10% of above            10,770    See note 10
   costs
                                                 _____
                                                 118,470
                                                 ========
```

It is considered that any quotation higher than £100,000 will be unsuccessful.

You are required to prepare a revised cost estimate using a relevant cost approach.

Notes

1 A sufficient stock of direct material X is held in the stores. It is the residue of some old stock and, if this stock is not used on the prospective contract, it is unlikely that it will be used in the foreseeable future. The net resale value is thought to be £15,000.
2 Material Y is regularly used by the contractor on a variety of jobs. The current replacement cost of the material is £130 per unit.
3 This is the estimated cost of the required component.
4 Skilled staff are paid on a time basis for a 40 hour week. The present staff will work on the job although one additional worker will be required to be brought in. The additional worker accounts for 160 hours out of the 3,000 hours identified against the contract.
5 No additional trainees would be taken on.
6 The machine is normally fully occupied. If it is not being used by the contractor's own workforce it is being hired out at £1,000 per week.
7 This is the estimated cost for the work.
8 It is not considered that it would be necessary to employ any additional supervisory staff. The estimated cost of £7,000 includes an allowance of £1,000 for overtime which it may be necessary to pay to the supervisors.
9 The work on the drawings and plans has already been completed and the amount shown is for this work.
10 The additional overhead is a fixed cost. This is the established method of allocating the cost to specific contracts.

Relevant cost

Cost estimate	£
Direct material	
3,000 units of X at net realizable value	15,000
100 units of Y at £130 (replacement cost)	13,000
Bought in component	12,000
Direct labour	
Skilled staff 160 hours × £8 per hour	1,280
Trainees	—
Machine	
Rental foregone 4 weeks × £1,000 per week	4,000
Sub-contract work	20,000
Supervisory staff – overtime	1,000
Estimating and design – past cost	—
Administration overhead – fixed and unavoidable	—
Relevant cost	66,280

Direct material X has been in stock for some time and, if it is not used on this contract, it is unlikely that it will be used in the foreseeable future. The only alternative available for this material is to sell it for £15,000. The £15,000 therefore represents an opportunity cost and it is this cost which must be used in a relevant cost statement.

Direct material Y is regularly used by the contractor and, if it is used on this contract, it would need to be replaced at a replacement cost of £130. The original £100 cost is irrelevant because it is a past cost. The future economic cost is the number of units at £130 per unit and it is this cost which should be used in the relevant cost statement.

The cost of the component to be bought in is the relevant cost since it is an uncommitted future economic cost. The purchase of this component is dependent on the decision to go ahead with the contract.

The only avoidable cost, in terms of direct labour, is the cost of the additional skilled worker at 160 hours. The future economic cost of this additional worker is 160 hours at £8 per hour. The relevant cost is therefore £1,280. The other skilled workers and the trainees will represent a cost to the contractor even if the contract does not go ahead. They therefore represent unavoidable costs.

The depreciation cost on the machine is irrelevant because it relates to a charge which is based on a past cash outlay. The only relevant cost in this situation is the benefit foregone as a result of taking on this contract. If the contract is undertaken the contractor will forego the opportunity to hire the machine out at a rate of £1,000 per week. Since the machine will be used on this contract for four weeks, the relevant cost is the opportunity cost of £1,000 multiplied by four weeks. The relevant cost is therefore £4,000.

The cost of the sub-contractor is a relevant cost since it is an uncommitted future economic cost. The use of the sub-contractor is dependent upon the decision to go ahead with the contract.

The only avoidable cost, in terms of the supervisory staff, is the cost of the allowance of £1,000 for overtime which will be incurred if the contract goes ahead. The remaining supervisory staff cost figure of £6,000 will be incurred even if the contract does not go ahead. These costs therefore represent unavoidable costs.

The work done by the estimating and design department is already completed and therefore represents a past cost. The term *sunk cost* is often used to explain this type of cost. This cost will not change as a result of the decision since the work has been completed prior to the decision being taken.

The administrative overhead cost is irrelevant since it will not change as a result of the decision. The 10% charged merely represents a way of absorbing administrative costs into contracts. Administrative overhead costs will not change as a result of the decision and therefore they are unavoidable.

The revised relevant cost statement therefore suggests that the relevant cost of this contract is £66,280. The small contractor could therefore quote a figure under £100,000. The actual level of the quote will depend on the amount of profit which the contractor wishes to make out of the contract. As long as the contractor did not quote a figure below £66,280, the contract would make some contribution towards recovering fixed costs. The contractor would also need to take other issues into account when deciding on whether to quote for the contract. Issues such as implications for cash flows; implications for future business; possibility of other contracts which may be available. The relevant cost information is just part of the information required to make a particular decision. The use of accounting information for pricing decisions will be developed further in Chapter 9.

Having looked at an example of the use of relevant costs in a contracting decision, let us now look at other examples where relevant costs may be used to help the decision-making process.

Deleting a product

If a company produces a range of products, it is important to determine the profitability of each product in order to make decisions about the future of individual products. Illustration 7.7 shows an example of a decision-making situation involving a product profitability analysis.

The marginal cost analysis shows that product B does make a contribution to fixed costs. If the product is dropped, and the fixed costs remain the same, then company profitability would be reduced by £19,000. The crucial issue here is whether the fixed costs would fall as a result of the decision. We are concerned in this chapter with short-term decision-making and the assumption here is that we are looking at a period of up to one year. One of the assumptions underlying cost-volume-profit analysis is that fixed costs will remain fixed in the short term. We are therefore making the assumption that the fixed costs are unavoidable and will not change as a result of the decision. Using this approach it would not be advisable to drop product B. However, if as a result of dropping product B, fixed costs did reduce by an amount above £19,000, then the fixed cost reduction would be relevant and it may be decided that it is worth dropping the product. The key to this is a real understanding of what is happening in the specific organization in question and the timescale involved. We will return to this particular issue later when we go on to consider activity based costing. Another issue that needs considering in this situation is whether there is an alternative to producing product B. Is it possible to use the capacity to sell more of product A and product C? Are there other products which would be sold in place of product B? Again, we need to have a real understanding of what is happening in the organization in question and the alternative opportunities that are available to it.

Illustration 7.7 Deleting a product

The following is an analysis of the profitability of each product produced by Jones Ltd which has been produced on an absorption costing basis.

| | Product | | | |
| | A | B | C | Total |
	£	£	£	£
Sales revenue	170,000	100,000	150,000	420,000
Direct materials	30,000	25,000	35,000	90,000
Direct labour	20,000	25,000	24,000	69,000
Variable overheads	40,000	30,000	20,000	90,000
Apportioned fixed overheads	30,000	35,000	34,000	99,000
Total factory costs	120,000	115,000	113,000	348,000
Gross profit	50,000	(15,000)	37,000	72,000
Less selling and administration costs				40,000
Net profit				32,000

On the basis of this analysis the chief executive of Jones Ltd was about to make a decision to stop producing product B. His reasoning was that, since product B is making a loss, overall profitability would be improved by removing that product from the product portfolio. Debbie, the recently appointed accountant, told the chief executive not to be so hasty. She produced another analysis of the product profitability based on a marginal cost approach.

	Product A £	B £	C £	Total £
Sales revenue	170,000	100,000	150,000	420,000
Direct materials	30,000	25,000	35,000	90,000
Direct labour	20,000	25,000	24,000	69,000
Variable factory overhead	40,000	30,000	20,000	90,000
Variable selling and administrative overhead	2,000	1,000	1,500	4,500
Variable costs	92,000	81,000	80,500	253,500
Contribution	78,000	19,000	69,500	166,500
Less: Fixed factory overhead				99,000
Fixed selling and administrative costs				35,500
Net profit				32,000

Product B makes a contribution towards fixed costs of £19,000

If product B is dropped and the fixed costs remain the same, then the overall profitability of the company would drop by £19,000. The new profit figure for the company would then be £13,000.

The example shown relates to a product: similar analysis could be used for different cost objects, with examples being analysis by customer, by division or by distribution channel.

Make versus buy

Frequently managers are faced with a decision as to whether they should buy in a component or produce it themselves. Illustration 7.8 provides an example of this type of decision.

Illustration 7.8 Make or buy decision

A company is considering the alternative of either purchasing a component from an outside supplier or producing the component itself. The estimated costs to the company of producing the component are as follows:

	£
Direct labour	200
Direct materials	400
Variable overheads	100
Fixed overheads	300
	1,000

The outside supplier has quoted a figure of £800 for supplying the component.

A first glance at the information in Illustration 7.8 would seem to suggest that it would be worthwhile to purchase the components from outside. However, undertaking a relevant cost analysis of the situation would provide different information which would result in a different decision being taken. If we assume that the fixed costs are unavoidable, and therefore not relevant, the appropriate comparison is as follows:

	£
Relevant cost	
Direct labour	200
Direct material	400
Variable overhead	100
	700
	£
External supplier cost	800

It would therefore be cheaper to make the component internally than to buy it from an external supplier. Another assumption being made here is that the company is operating with spare capacity and that the production of the component is not being done at the expense of other products. If we relax this assumption and assume that the company is currently working to full capacity, then more information is required to make the decision. Let us assume that production of the component will require 30 scarce machine hours and that these scarce machine hours are currently being used to produce product X which yields a contribution of £7 per machine hour. Then, if the component is produced internally, there will be a lost contribution or opportunity cost of £210 which needs adding to the relevant cost. The new situation would then be:

	£
Relevant cost	
Direct labour	200
Direct materials	400

Variable overhead	100
Opportunity cost	210
	910
External supplier cost	800

The situation has now changed and the component should be purchased from outside, provided that issues such as quality and service are acceptable.

Having already introduced the idea of scarce resources, we will develop the idea further by looking at a decision-making situation where limiting factors exist.

Choice of a product where a limiting factor exists

We are looking here at a situation where there is a shortage of a key resource. Production output may be restricted by a shortage of labour, materials, equipment or factory space. When sales demand is greater than the productive capacity of a company, it is important for managers at that company to be aware of the profitability of each product in terms of the limiting factor. Illustration 7.9 provides an example of this situation.

Illustration 7.9 Choice of a product where a limiting factor exists

A company produces three products and current production capacity means that all sales cannot be met. Data related to each of the products is as follows:

	Product A	Product B	Product C
Selling price per unit (£)	20	30	40
Variable cost per unit (£)	10	15	32
Machine hours per unit	1	5	2
Estimated sales demand	10,000	5,000	12,000

Machine capacity is limited to 50,000 machine hours. You have been asked to advise as to which products should be produced during the period.

Calculation	Product A	Product B	Product C
Contribution per unit (£)	10	15	8
Contribution per machine hour (£)			

A 10 ÷ 1   10
B 15 ÷ 5   3
C 8 ÷ 2   4
Rank in order of contribution
    per machine hour   1   3   2

	Machine hours used	Machine hours left
Product A 10,000 × 1	10,000	40,000
Product C 12,000 × 2	24,000	16,000
Product B 3,200 × 5	16,000	—

Therefore the company can produce and sell:
    10,000 units of product A
    12,000 units of product C
    3,200 units of product B

The company would therefore be unable to meet the sales demand for product B by 1,800 units.

———

In Illustration 7.9 the limiting factor is machine hours. The company only has 50,000 machine hours available and the projected sales figures represent 59,000 hours of machine time. On the assumption that fixed costs will not change irrespective of which products are produced, the first stage in the decision-making process is to determine the contribution per limiting factor. This is done, as shown in Illustration 7.9, by dividing the contribution per unit for each product by the amount of machine time required to produce each unit of the product. The result of this calculation is that the contribution per limiting factor came out as follows:

	Contribution per machine hour	Ranking in order of contribution per machine hour
Product A	10	1
Product B	3	3
Product C	4	2

The first choice therefore would be to produce as much as possible of product A. Sales demand for product A is 10,000 units and this will use up 10,000 machine hours. As Illustration 7.9 shows, this leaves 40,000 machine hours to produce the other products. The next choice is product C, and the company should produce as much as possible of product C. Sales demand for product C is 12,000 units and this will use up 24,000 machine hours. As Illustration 7.9 shows, this leaves 16,000 machine hours to produce as much as possible of product B. The 16,000 machine hours which are left will allow the company to produce and sell 3,200 units of product B. This means that the company would be unable to meet the total sales demand for product B and there would be a shortfall of 1,800 units. In the short term, and this is the timescale we are currently considering, the company would have to let down customers for this particular product unless it could sub-contract the work to somebody else. In the longer term the company would have to decide whether to invest in new machinery to enable it to meet total customer demand. This type of long-term investment decision will be dealt with in Chapter 8.

We have dealt in this chapter with the concept of relevant costs and the way in which relevant cost information can be used in a number of different types of decisions. An important assumption we have made within the chapter is that all of the calculations are based on the short term. The other assumption we have is that, in the short term, fixed costs are unavoidable and therefore will not change as a result of the decision. There has been some criticism of this particular assumption, as illustrated in the following quote from Johnson and Kaplan:

> Despite the emphasis of most management accounting courses on computing relevant costs for short-term product decisions, there is a danger in using short-term variable costs for most decisions on product pricing, product introduction, product abandonment, order acceptance, product mix, and make versus buy. These decisions turn out to involve the commitment of the firm's capacity resources and should be made in the light of the long-term, not the short-term, variability of costs. The failure to recognize the long-term nature of most product related decisions has prevented cost accounting students, teachers and practitioners from understanding the cause of the rapid growth in the so called 'fixed costs' of the firm. (1987: 233)

The development from this particular criticism was the idea of activity based costing, and it is to this we now turn.

Activity based costing

The idea of activity based management was introduced in Chapter 4 and developed further in Chapter 6. Activity based costing was the first real development in the activity based management area. It concentrates on the need to make a more realistic allocation of overhead costs to products. It emphasizes the requirement to obtain a better understanding of the behaviour of overhead costs, and thus ascertains what causes overhead costs and how they relate to products. Cooper and Kaplan (1988) argue that activity based costing addresses the real issues of how and why overheads are being spent. The key is to identify the cost drivers for these overhead costs. The concept is that managers can only manage costs by managing the activities that cause the costs:

The goal of activity based costing is to understand what all the indirect costs in an organization are doing. We do not think of these indirect departments as overhead that needs to be eliminated (although this analysis may well result in productivity improvements because the various departments are examined closely). These departments are organizational resources that are providing useful and important activities that enable companies to design, make, sell and service their products. (Kaplan, 1988: 40)

Conventional

Stage 1: Overhead departmentalization

Stage 2: Application of absorption rates

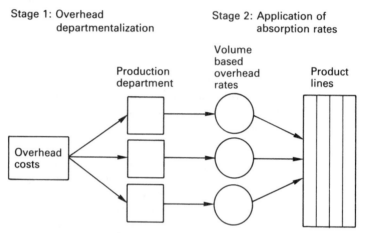

Activity based

Stage 1: Overhead pooling

Stage 2: Application of cost driver rates

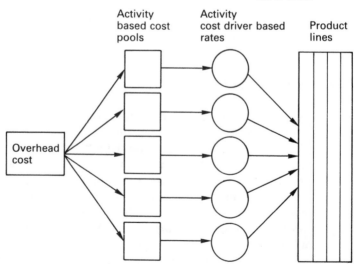

Figure 7.9 *Conventional versus activity based costing. (Source: Innes and Mitchell, 1990, p 6)*

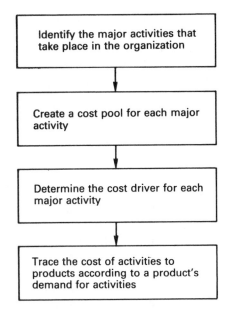

Figure 7.10 *An outline of an activity based costing system*

Mechanics of activity based costing

Figure 7.9, taken from the work of Innes and Mitchell (1990), compares activity based costing with the traditional method of applying overheads to products. As illustrated in Figure 7.9, activity based costing is based on a two-stage procedure. The first stage is to allocate overhead costs to a series of activity based cost pools. The second stage involves the derivation and use of appropriate cost driver based rates to attach the pooled costs to product lines. The design and operation of an activity based costing system is therefore dependent upon the choice of activity based cost pools and the choice of an appropriate cost driver for each cost pool. An outline of an activity based costing system is shown in Figure 7.10.

In order to understand the way in which activity based costing systems work, we will look at an example produced by Cooper and Kaplan (1988) shown here in Illustration 7.10.

Illustration 7.10 Allocating costs under an activity based system (This illustration is taken from Cooper and Kaplan (1988: 99) and slightly modified*)

The process of designing and implementing an activity based cost system for support departments usually begins with interviews of the department heads. The interviews yield insights into departmental operations and into the factors that trigger departmental activities. Subsequent analysis traces these activities to specific products.

The following example illustrates the activity based costing process for an inventory control department responsible for raw materials and purchased components. The annual costs associated with the department (mainly personnel costs) are £500,000.

Interview with Departmental Head
Q   How many people work for you?
A   Twelve.
Q   What do they do?
A   Six of them spend most of their time handling incoming shipments of purchased parts. They handle everything from documentation to transferring parts to the work-in-progress stockroom. Three others work in raw materials. After the material clears inspection, they move it into inventory and take care of the paperwork.
Q   What determines the time required to process an incoming shipment? Does it matter if the shipment is large or small?
A   Not for parts. They go directly to the work-in-progress stockroom, and unless its an extremely large shipment it can be handled in one trip. With raw materials, though, volume can play a big role in processing time. But there are only a few large raw material shipments. Over the course of a year, the time required to process a part or raw material really depends on the number of times it is received, not on the size of the shipments in which it comes.
Q   What other factors affect your department's workload?
A   Well, there are three people I haven't discussed yet. They disburse raw material to the shop floor. Again, volume is not really an issue, it's more the number of times material has to be disbursed.
Q   Do you usually disburse the total amount of material required for a production run all at once, or does it go out in smaller quantities?
A   It varies with the size of the run. On a big run we can't disburse it all at once — there would be too much raw material on the shop floor. On smaller runs — and I'd say that's 80% of all runs — we'd send it there in a single trip once set up is complete.

Design the system
After the interview, the system designer can use the number of people involved in each activity to allocate the department's £500,000 cost:

Activity	People	Cost in cost pool £
Receiving purchased parts	6	250,000
Receiving raw material	3	125,000
Disbursing material	3	125,000

The budget for 1993 is based on the company receiving 25,000 shipments of purchased parts and 10,000 shipments of raw materials. The factory plans to make 5,000 production runs. Dividing these totals into the cost pools associated with each activity yields the following costs per unit of activity.

Activity	Cost driver	Cost driver rate (£)
Receiving purchased parts	Number of shipments per year	£10 per shipment
Receiving raw material	Number of shipments per year	£12.50 per shipment
Disbursing material	Number of production runs	£25 per run

Attribute inventory control support costs to specific products
The company plans to produce 1,000 units of product A in 1993. Product A is a complex product with more than 50 purchased parts and several different types of raw material. The 1,000 units are planned to be assembled in ten different production runs requiring 200 purchased part shipments and 50 different raw material shipments. The amount of overhead charged to product A using an activity based cost approach, would be:

	£
Receiving purchased parts	
200 × £10 per shipment	2,000
Receiving raw material	
50 × £12.50 per shipment	625
Disbursing material	
10 × £25 per run	250
	2,875

A traditional overhead absorption rate would be based on labour hours. Product A is budgeted to use 1,000 hours of direct labour out of the factory's total of 400,000 hours. The overhead charged under the traditional method would be as follows:

$$\text{Direct labour overhead absorption rate} = \frac{£500,000}{400,000 \ \text{hours}}$$

$$= £1.25 \text{ per direct labour hour}$$

Product A uses 1,000 direct labour hours and the overhead absorbed by product A would be:

$$1,000 \text{ hours} \times £1.25 \text{ per direct labour hour} = £1,250$$

The amount of inventory control overhead attributed to product A would therefore differ between the two alternative methods used.

	Total overhead charged to product A £	Unit overhead cost to product A £
Activity based method	2,875	2.875
Conventional labour absorption method	1,250	1.25

The difference between the two methods reflects the fact that the complex, low volume product A demands a much greater share of inventory control resources than its share of factory direct labour hours.

The example in Illustration 7.10 follows the outline of the activity based costing system shown in Figure 7.10. The first is to identify the major activities taking place in the inventory control area. The three activities identified were receiving purchased parts, receiving raw materials and disbursing materials. The next stage is to create a cost pool for each of these activities. In this particular example, costs were identified as being mainly personnel type costs and therefore the number of people carrying out each activity is used to create the costs for each activity. The next stage of the process is to determine the cost driver for each major activity. The interviews provide the information required to determine the appropriate cost driver for each activity. Cost drivers were identified as follows:

Activity	*Cost driver*
Receiving purchased parts	Number of shipments per year
Receiving raw material	Number of shipments per year
Disbursing material	Number of production runs

The decision on cost drivers may involve some compromise. For instance, in the case of disbursement of materials, the point was made that on a big production run all of the material cannot be disbursed at once. On a smaller run, however, disbursement would take place in a single trip once the set up had been completed. Since smaller runs represented 80% of all runs, the decision has been taken to use the number of production runs as the appropriate cost driver for the disbursement of material. Such compromises have to be made for practical reasons.

The next stage is to trace the cost of activities to products, according to a product's demand for activities. The first step in this stage is to work out the rate per unit of cost driver. In order to explain this we will look at the receiving of purchased parts in Illustration 7.10. The company has budgeted for 25,000 shipments of purchased parts in 1993. In order to work out the rate per unit of cost driver we need to divide the total cost of the activity by the number of shipments of purchased parts for the year.

$$\frac{\text{Cost of activity}}{\text{Number of shipments}} = \frac{£250,000}{25,000}$$

$$= £10 \text{ per shipment of purchased parts}$$

The second step in this stage, once cost driver rates have been worked out, is to multiply the cost driver rates by the number of times a product uses the activities. For instance, in Illustration 7.10, product A requires 200 purchased part shipments. The costs associated with the receiving of purchased parts for product A are therefore as follows:

	£
Receiving purchased parts	
200 shipments × £10 per shipment	2,000

Illustration 7.10 shows how the other activity costs would be charged to product A resulting in an overhead charge of £2,875 for product A. The amount of overhead charged using a traditional overhead absorption rate based on direct labour hours would have been £1,250. Product A is a complex product and has been given a fairer share of the inventory control costs than it would have received under a traditional overhead absorption method. Product A has been attributed with a charge which more accurately reflects its consumption of the resources in the inventory control area.

Illustration 7.10 therefore provides an example of a situation where, under conventional overhead absorption systems such as direct labour hours, a low volume complex product may be being undercharged with overhead costs. It is likely that less complex high volume products will in fact be cross-subsidizing products such as product A. The obvious danger is that managers will take product mix decisions based on inappropriate cost information. Exponents of activity based costing systems argue, as shown in Illustration 7.10, that activity based costing will produce superior cost information for product mix decisions because it takes into account the real consumption of overhead activities by each product line. This point is further demonstrated in Illustration 7.11, which is based on a financial services organization. Activity based cost management appears to be well suited to the service area and the authors are aware of several activity based developments in the financial services area.

Illustration 7.11 Activity based costing in an insurance company

The insurance company has four products:

Personal pension
Term life policy

Group pension
Investment life policy

The following activities were identified as the major activities in the central administrative function of the company.

Activities	Costs associated with each activity (£)
New business processing	80,000
Policy administration	67,000
Receiving proposals	17,000
Processing claims/maturities	3,000
Processing surrenders/lapses	13,000

Appropriate cost drivers were identified for each activity and the total annual consumption of the cost driver was identified against each product.

Activity	Cost driver	Annual consumption of cost driving product				
		Personal	Term life	Group	Investment	Total
New business processing	Number of hrs on new business processing	200	500	300	3,000	4,000
Policy admin.	Number of hrs	600	500	1,250	1,000	3,350
Receiving proposals	Number of proposals received	10	115	10	115	250
Processing claims/ maturities	Number of claims/ maturities	2	20	3	5	30
Processing surrenders/ lapses	Number of terminations	1	1	1	10	13

Cost per unit of cost driver:

Activity	Total cost	Cost driver	Annual consumption of cost drivers	Cost driver rate
	£			£
New business	80,000	Number of hours on new business processing	4,000	20
Policy	67,000	Number of hours on policy administration	3,350	20
Receiving	17,000	Number of proposals received	250	68

Processing claims/maturities	3,000	Number of claims/ maturities	30	100
Processing surrenders/ lapses	13,000	Number of terminations	13	1,000

Costs allocated to each product using an activity based approach:

Activity	Cost driver rate	Personal	Term life	Group	Investment	Total
	£	£	£	£	£	£
New business processing	20	4,000*a	10,000	6,000	60,000	80,000
Policy admin.	20	12,000	10,000*b	25,000	20,000	67,000
Receiving proposals	68	680	7,820	680*c	7,820	17,000
Processing claims/ maturities	100	200	2,000	300	500*d	3,000
Processing surrenders/ lapses	1,000	1,000*e	1,000	1,000	10,000	13,000
		17,880	30,820	32,980	98,320	180,000

Example calculations:
*a 200 hours of new business processing × £20 per hour = £4,000
*b 500 hours of policy administration × £20 per hour = £10,000
*c 10 proposals received × £68 per proposal received = £680
*d 5 claims/maturities × £100 per claim/maturity = £500
*e 1 termination × £1,000 per termination = £1,000

Comparison of conventional cost allocation and activity based costing
Conventional overhead absorption system based on direct hours of new business processing:

	£
Total cost of central administration unit	180,000
Direct hours of new business processing	4,000
Overhead absorption rate per hour	45

Product	Direct hours of new business processing	Cost
		£
Personal pension	200	9,000
Term life policy	500	22,500
Group pension	300	13,500

Investment life policy	3,000	135,000
		——————
		180,000

Conventional versus activity based costing (ABC)

Product	Conventional	ABC	Difference (%)
Personal pension	9,000	17,880	+ 98.67%
Term life policy	22,500	30,820	+ 36.98%
Group pension	13,500	32,980	+ 144.30%
Investment life policy	135,000	98,320	− 27.17%

Illustration 7.11 demonstrates the cross-subsidization which has taken place between the products in the insurance company. If an activity based approach is used, investment life policy will be allocated a lower share of the overhead cost, which better reflects the actual consumption of the activities by the products.

Having illustrated the mechanics of an activity based costing approach, we will now go on to debate the merits of activity based costing.

Evaluation of activity based costing

A useful starting point would be to report on some of the results of a study carried out by Nicholls (1992) on activity based costing in the UK. This study suggested that 90% of respondent companies had implemented, were currently implementing or were investigating activity based costing (ABC) to determine suitability for their environments. 10% of companies (three out of six respondent companies from the financial/insurance sector) indicated that they had implemented ABC, while the majority of companies − 62% − were investigating ABC techniques to determine suitability and the remaining 18% were piloting ABC techniques.

The reasons given for initially considering ABC were as follows:

- Requirement to understand true product costs (65%).
- Not being entirely satisfied with current system (50%).
- Business requirement to identify and reduce product costs (45%).
- Increasing proportion of overhead as opposed to direct cost (32%).
- Improvements not financially recognized (7%).
- Make versus buy decisions (7%).

Respondents were asked about the benefits gained or hoped for from ABC. A summarized list of responses was as follows:

- Greater understanding of product costs (65%).
- Focused overhead reduction via activity analysis (60%).

- Greater understanding of customer profitability (47%).
- Anticipated change of product portfolio and/or pricing strategy (43%).
- Identification of non-value activities (40%).

Respondents were also asked about the problems and pitfalls of ABC implementation. A summarized list of responses was as follows:

- Unavailability of adequate detailed data (38%).
- Lack of resources (33%).
- Reluctance to change traditional accounting method (27%).
- Departmental resistance to change or provide information (25%).
- Lack of knowledge, training or information (17%).
- Lack of clear direction on how to implement (12%).

The results of the study by Nicholls (1992) suggest an increasing interest in the area of activity based costing within the UK. However, it is important to note that most of the organizations that responded were investigating ABC techniques and, therefore, any benefits mentioned were in the main ones which the organizations were hoping to achieve. Several of the respondents had also commented in detailed telephone conversations about some of the difficulties of implementing activity based costing.

Innes and Mitchell (1990: 27) provide a neat summary of the benefits and limitations of activity based costing:

Benefits

- Provides more accurate product line costings, particularly where non-volume-related overheads are significant and a diverse product line is manufactured.
- Is flexible enough to analyse costs by cost objects other than products such as processes, areas of managerial responsibility and customers.
- Provides a reliable indication of long-run variable product cost which is particularly relevant to managerial decision-making at a strategic level.
- Provides meaningful financial (periodic cost driver rates) and non-financial (period cost driver volumes) measures which are relevant for cost management and performance assessment at an operational level.
- Aids identification and understanding of cost behaviour and thus has the potential to improve cost estimation.
- Provides a more logical, acceptable and comprehensible basis for costing work.

Limitations

- Little evidence to date that ABC improves corporate profitability.
- Little is known about the potential behavioural, organizational and economic consequences of adopting ABC.
- ABC information is historic and internally orientated and therefore lacks direct relevance for future strategic decisions.
- Practical problems such as cost driver selection and cost commonalities are unresolved.
- Its novelty is questionable. It may be viewed as simply a rigorous application of conventional costing procedures.

It is important to note that exponents of activity based costing would probably wish to challenge many of the limitations listed above. However, it is important that the reader is aware of some of the concerns which have been expressed about ABC as well as the many positive things which have been said in its favour.

There has been considerable debate concerning comparisons between contribution costing and activity based costing with respect to decision-making issues. We have in fact included activity based costing in a chapter which is headed short-term decision-making. This was done deliberately, although one could argue that activity based costing is more concerned with long-run variable costs than the short-run variable costs normally associated with short-term decision-making. Activity based costing demands an understanding of cost behaviour and is designed to focus managerial attention on the long-term implications of product related decisions. Cooper (1990) emphasizes that activity based costing systems are designed to focus managerial attention and not to provide specific decision-relevant costs for individual independent decisions. Cooper states that ABC has evolved to support decisions where the number of products is large and decisions are not independent. In a real life setting it is important to have a number of different techniques which will complement each other in order to assist the decision making process.

Summary

This chapter has been concerned with short-term decision-making within organizations. Cost-volume-profit relationships were discussed and information for decision-making was presented in both mathematical and graphical form. The assumptions made in using cost-volume-profit analysis were identified. Relevant costs and revenues for decision-making were then considered. Relevant costs and benefits were identified as being uncommitted future economic costs and benefits. Information on relevant costs and benefits was used to illustrate decisions concerning the pricing of a contract, deletion of a product, make or buy decisions and choice of a product where a limiting factor exists.

The chapter then moved on to discuss the idea of activity based costing. The concept was introduced at this particular stage because of the criticism that failure to recognize the long-term nature of most product related decisions has prevented an understanding of the cause of the rapid growth in the so called 'fixed costs' of the firm. Exponents of activity based costing argue that managers can only manage cost by managing the activities that cause the costs. Activity based costing represents part of the move towards activity based management which was outlined in Chapter 6. It has been included in this chapter because, as stated before, in a real life setting it is important to have a number of different techniques which will complement each other in order to assist the decision-making process.

After reading this chapter you should be able to:

- Explain the nature of cost-volume-profit analysis and the assumptions that underpin it.
- Use formulae to calculate break-even point, contribution to sales ratio, level of sales to result in target profit and margin of safety ratio.
- Construct graphs to calculate break-even point, margin of safety and profit and loss areas.
- Identify relevant costs and benefits in a decision-making situation.
- Use relevant costs and benefits to make decisions about the pricing of a contract, the deletion of a product, make or buy decisions and choice of product where a limiting factor exists.
- Explain the concept of activity based costing and calculate product costs using an activity based costing approach.
- Debate the benefits and limitations of activity based costing.

References

Cooper, R. (1990) Explicating the logic of ABC. *Management Accounting*, November, pp. 58–60

Cooper, R. and Kaplan, R. S. (1988) Measure costs right: Make the right decisions. *Harvard Business Review*, September/October, pp. 96–103

Coulthurst, N. and Piper, J. (1986) The terminology and conceptual basis of information for decision making. *Management Accounting*, May, pp. 34–8

Innes, J. and Mitchell, F. (1990) *Activity Based Costing – Review with Case Studies*, Chartered Institute of Management Accountants, London

Johnson, H.T. and Kaplan, R.S. (1987) *Relevance Lost: The Rise and Fall of Management Accounting*, Harvard Business School, Boston, Mass.

Kaplan, R. (1988) Relevance Regained. *Management Accounting*, September, pp. 38–42

Nicholls, B. (1992) ABC in the UK: A status report. *Management Accounting*, May, pp. 22--3, 28

Further reading

Bhimani, A. and Pigott, D. (1992) Implementing ABC: a case study of organisational and behavioural consequences. *Management Accounting Research*, 3, 119–32

Drury, C. (1992) *Management and Cost Accounting*, 3rd edn, Chapman and Hall, London, Chapters 9, 10 and 11

Innes, J. and Mitchell, F. (1992) A review of activity based costing practice. In *Management Accounting Handbook* (ed. C. Drury), Butterworth-Heinemann in association with the Chartered Institute of Management Accountants. Oxford, Chapter 3

Piper, J.A. and Walley, P. (1990) Testing ABC logic. *Management Accounting*, September, pp. 37, 42

Piper, J.A. and Walley, P. (1991) ABC relevance not found. *Management Accounting*, March, pp. 42–4, 54

Wijeysinghe, B.S. (1993) Breakeven occupancy for a hotel operation. *Management Accounting*, February, pp. 32–3

Problems and discussion topics

1 A friend is deciding whether or not to start a business and discusses the matter with you. The business would involve assembling and selling a component that she has invented. She can obtain the parts required from various manufacturers.

She has estimated that she can sell 5,000 of these components a year at a selling price of £30 per unit. The variable costs of the component are £20 per unit and fixed costs would be £30,000 per annum. These fixed costs do not include a salary for your friend. She currently earns £25,000 per annum in her present job and would have to give this job up if she started her own business. Your friend is rather cautious and she is worried in case any of her estimates are incorrect.

You suggest that she uses cost-volume-profit analysis to help her make the decision and you are required to present examples of such analysis which may be useful to her. The information is to be presented in mathematical form.

2 The management of Springs plc is considering next year's production and purchase budgets. One of the components produced by the company, which is incorporated into another product before being sold, has a budgeted manufacturing cost as follows:

	£
Direct materials	20
Direct labour (4 hours at £6 per hour)	24
Variable overhead (4 hours at £4 per hour)	16
Fixed overhead (4 hours at £5 per hour)	20
	80 per unit

Trigger plc has offered to supply the above component at a guaranteed price of £70.

You are required to:
(a) Considering cost criteria only, advise management whether the above component should be purchased from Trigger plc. Any calculations should be shown and assumptions made, or aspects which may require further investigation, should be clearly stated.
(b) Explain how your above advice would be affected by each of the two separate situations shown below:

   (i) As a result of recent government legislation, if Springs plc continues to manufacture this component the company will incur additional inspection and testing expenses of £60,000 per annum. These additional expenses are not included in the above budgeted manu-facturing costs.
   (ii) Additional labour cannot be recruited and if the above component is not manufactured by Springs plc, the direct labour released will be employed in increasing the pro-duction of an existing product which is sold for £140 and which has budgeted manufacturing cost as follows:

	£
Direct material	20
Direct labour (8 hours at £6 per hour)	48
Variable overhead (8 hours at £4 per hour)	32
Fixed overhead (8 hours at £5 per hour)	40
	140 per unit

(c) The Production Director of Springs plc recently said: 'We must continue to manufacture the component as only one year ago we purchased some special grinding equipment to be used exclusively by this component. The equipment cost £100,000, it cannot be resold or used elsewhere and if we cease production of this component we will have to write off the written down book value which is £80,000.'

Draft a brief reply to the Production Director commenting on his statement.
(This is a modified ACCA question.)

3 Jones Ltd produces four products, namely P1, P2, P3 and P4. The following figures represent the budget information per unit of each product:

	Annual volume (units)	Material per unit £	Direct labour hours per unit	Selling price per unit £
P1	100	60	5	110
P2	1,000	60	5	110
P3	100	180	15	330
P4	1,000	180	15	330

The budgeted cost per direct labour hour is £5. The company currently absorbs overheads into products on the basis of a direct labour overhead absorption rate. The budgeted overhead for the year is £66,000 and the amount related to each activity is shown below:

Activity	Annual overhead cost (£)	Cost driver	P1	P2	P3	P4	Total
Setting up jobs	30,000	Number of set ups	2	10	5	13	30
Ordering material	15,000	Number of material orders	4	4	2	5	15
Material handling	21,000	Number of times material handled	6	50	20	24	100
	66,000						

The company uses a full cost plus pricing system. The sales manager of the company is currently worried about P4 since sales of this product seem to be under pressure from competitors in a market which is becoming particularly price sensitive.

You are required to:

(a) Calculate the unit cost per product using the company's traditional method of absorbing overheads into products.
(b) Calculate the unit cost per product using activity based costing as the method of absorbing overhead costs into the products.
(c) Discuss the results disclosed by a comparison between the two methods of absorbing overheads into the products and the implications for the company.

8 Investment appraisal

The aims of this chapter are to:

- Explain why capital investment decisions need a series of special techniques.
- Illustrate the process of capital investment within an organization.
- Present four capital investment evaluation techniques – net present value (NPV), internal rate of return (IRR), payback (PB) and accounting rate of return (ARR).
- Apply the four appraisal techniques to capital projects.
- Consider which techniques are used in practice and why.
- Explain how risk may be built into the appraisal techniques.
- Develop the post audit of capital investment decisions as a control mechanism.
- Introduce the idea of cost benefit analysis applicable to public sector and not-for-profit organizations.

Introduction

Capital investment within any organization is crucial for that organization's well-being and long-term survival. Capital investments are those which have long-term effects on the organization by providing benefits over a number of years. In terms of a company's balance sheet, capital investment is made up from fixed assets, current assets and current liabilities. While financial accountants use this classification, it would be equally valid to consider the balance sheet as a collection of on-going projects which are generating returns in the form of profits and cash flows. In fact any balance sheet is a collection of assets and liabilities relating to past capital investment decisions, which do not stop at each year end, as financial accountants would have us believe, but continue over several accounting periods (Figure 8.1).

The balance sheet at say 31/12/3 in Figure 8.1 represents the assets and liabilities that relate to projects A, B, C and D. A company like Ford (UK) does not consider itself an owner of assets but a producer of motor vehicles, so project A could represent a particular model of small car, project B a mid-range car, project C a tractor range, project E the new range of small cars to replace project A.

Balance sheet data

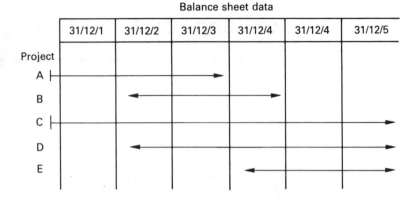

Figure 8.1   *Relationship between projects and year end balance sheets*

The acquisition of fixed assets and the working capital to make them operative may be very long-term indeed. Take, for example, a reservoir built by the Victorian Water Corporation still in use today, or a nuclear reactor producing electricity for National Power.

The decision-making process for investment in long-term assets is a part of the planning and control mechanism used by organizations to consider their future positioning in the market.

In Figure 8.2 the relationship between decision-making in the long term and planning and control is aimed specifically at equipping the organization to meet future challenges. The data collection system

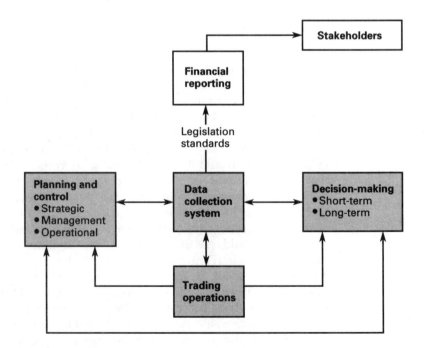

Figure 8.2   *Pricing decisions and policy*

appropriate to such decisions relating to long-term assets is based upon subjective estimates of the future, where the future estimates for profits or cash may be anything up to 20 or 30 years in advance. The Channel Tunnel is such a project, requiring heavy initial investment over several years before any profits and cash flows arise.

The basic question about capital investment is related to the sacrifices of current wealth, or consumption now, in the hope of reaping greater returns in the future. This question can be asked about a company building a new factory by reducing dividend payments in the short term; the same question is equally relevant to the acquisition of a house, or to the sacrifice of current leisure time to pursue a higher educational qualification which will be advantageous in the future. By the end of this chapter we should have some insights into the first two questions, but only you can answer the third.

Why have special techniques for capital investment decisions?

In the stated aims of this chapter four appraisal techniques were mentioned which may aid the decision-making process of whether to invest in a specific project or not. In addition, such decisions involve senior managers, usually at board or equivalent level. The reason for all this activity is that:

- Capital investment projects will have an impact on the organization for several years to come. It is worthwhile, and probably cost efficient, to put resources into the evaluation stage of such a decision before large sums of money are expended. Even if a project is rejected after the evaluation stage, the process of evaluation will have provided a useful learning exercise, and may have discovered issues not obvious at the earlier stages of consideration.
- Capital investment is dealing with major investments that will shape the future of an organization. Such decisions are of strategic importance and must be evaluated to enable the organization to justify to its stakeholders that it is pursuing the correct application of the strategic plan.
- Once a major project has received approval, and implementation is going ahead, it is usually very difficult to reverse the process without incurring significant costs. For example, a farmer may wish to convert some land into a golf course. Significant expenditure is required for planning permission, consultancy for course design, landscaping, club house construction etc., before any revenues are received. To abandon the project before fruition would be costly indeed.
- Because capital investment decisions involve the commitment of resources now, hopefully for future benefits, they are all subject to risk. If the future was known with certainty decisions regarding the

future would be simple, but because the future is unknown it is worthwhile attempting to forecast what may happen by evaluating the project before its inception.

Categories of capital investment

Capital investment decisions may be classified in two ways – by type of investment and by the monetary size of the investment.

By type

- *Replacement of existing facilities*. This is a relatively low risk decision as the consequences of replacement versus non-replacement are known and understood. For example, the replacement of a fleet of coaches for a Tour Operator can be evaluated with some measure of certainty as the extra maintenance costs of the old fleet and the fuel efficiencies of the new are known and understood.
- *Expansion of existing facilities*. Again the decision is not particularly risky, the market is understood and fairly reliable estimates can be made.
- *A new project*. This is where risk increases quite substantially as an organization is moving into unchartered water. Estimates of future profits and cash flows cannot be made using experience as a guide, but are the product of estimates and forecasts which will have greater risks attached.
- *Research and development* must be seen as the most risky venture as outcomes are highly uncertain, and the chance of a breakthrough may be many years ahead.
- *Welfare projects* do not fit into the risk classification of the other categories as they are usually required by legislation or are a part of employment costs, the benefits of which may be very difficult to measure.

High relative risk ↑   Research and development
                        New projects
                        Expansion
Low relative risk ↓   Replacement

Monetary size of investment

As with the responsibility accounting within budgetary control which we considered in Chapter 5, capital investment has different levels for approval of expenditure. Within a large company £10,000 may be spent without prior approval from head office by a division, but over this amount head office approval must be sought.

One large multinational distinguishes between projects that have been identified in the annual plan for approval and those in addition to the annual plan. A managing director of a division may approve a project within the annual plan of £200,000, but if the project is additional then the limit is restricted to £100,000.

We will return to the risk considerations of investment appraisal later in the chapter after the appraisal techniques have been introduced and the investment decision placed in an organizational context.

Context of capital investment

Anthony (1965) put forward a model which recognized three different levels of control within an organization. While the model is open to criticism, it does help in the understanding of integration of capital investment decision-making within the overall control of an organization. The levels of control, already presented on page 103 are:

- *Strategic planning*, which conceives the long-term objectives and goals of an organization and sets broad strategies about products and markets. It is usually done by the higher levels of management and should be constantly under review.
- *Management control*, which ensures the resources required to carry out the strategic plan are available and used effectively and efficiently. This level of control uses techniques like 5-year planning cycles, annual budgets and, what is relevant to us at this stage, capital budgeting techniques to plan how current resources can be best allocated to achieve future aims and objectives.
- *Operational control* is the process of seeing that specific tasks are carried out. It focuses on the short-term, daily and weekly routines of the organization's operations.

Anthony's model is useful because it sets the scene for capital budgeting by putting the investment decision within the management control level, with the aim of satisfying organizational aims and objectives. Figure 8.2 above links long-term decision-making and this notion of different control levels.

Capital investment appraisal is very much a part of and a product of strategic planning. The decision process can be considered within the Boston Consulting Group matrix approach to product management. The matrix links the market growth for a product and its relative market share.

The Boston matrix recognizes four types of product at any one time, they are:

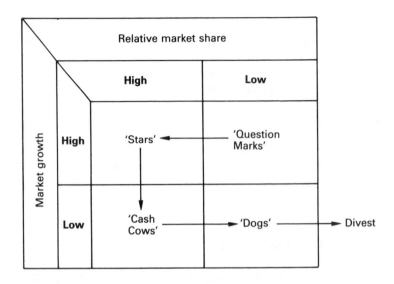

Figure 8.3   *Boston Consultancy Group product matrix and normal progression of product over time. (Source: Pike and Dobbins, 1986, p. 298)*

Stars	= high market share: high market growth
Cash Cows	= high market share: low market growth
Question Marks	= low market share: high market growth
Dogs	= low market share: low market growth

As each product progresses through its life cycle then the normal progression of a product over time is illustrated in Figure 8.3. If an investment strategy is superimposed on the matrix (Figure 8.4), then Cash Cows (high market share: low market growth) and Dogs

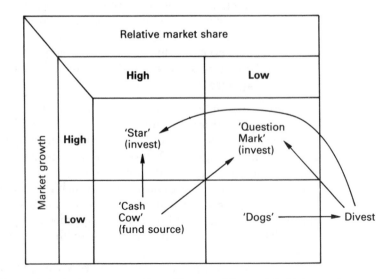

Figure 8.4   *Investment strategy. (Source: Pike and Dobbins, 1986, p. 298)*

(low market share: low market growth) should be used to finance Question Marks and Stars. Cash Cows should be retained and the cash generated from them used to finance the growing products, while Dogs should be disposed of and the resulting proceeds of sale used to finance Stars and Question Marks.

Objectives of capital investment

Capital investment decisions should allocate resources within the organization to offer the best potential of meeting its objectives. Two of the appraisal techniques to be considered take the maximization of shareholder wealth as objectives of investment. While this may be academically correct, the objectives set and decisions made in practice will be a function of the attributes and attitudes of the decision-makers. These decision-makers or managers may have a set of objectives which may not maximize the return to shareholders but will produce returns that will keep shareholders satisfied. Such policies may be because of risk aversion, resistance to change, individual aspirations etc., while stated objectives may be to:

- Maintain and improve profit performance.
- Maintain and increase market share.
- Achieve a balanced product portfolio.
- Grow by diversification.

These are not policies that will maximize shareholder wealth.

For non-profit-making organizations the objectives are much less clear. They might be to reduce suffering, enhance education, provide environmental services etc. The measurement of such objectives may be very difficult; at least the profit-making organization's objective is concerned with survival, profitability and returns to its owners.

Capital investment process

The process of capital investment can be considered to flow from strategic planning through a search for investment opportunities to meet that plan. The opportunities are screened, defined and evaluated for subsequent consideration by management. If the project is sanctioned then the investment is made, making sure cost overruns are not incurred, and the subsequent project is audited after completion as a control for the decision-makers. This process is illustrated in Figure 8.5.

The scheme shown in Figure 8.5 is described as a 'Normative' capital investment process; this represents an idealistic view of the way capital investment projects should be processed, while the reality may be something different (Northcott, 1991).

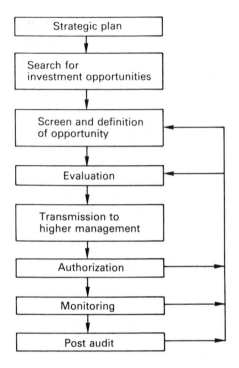

Figure 8.5 *Normative capital investment process. (Amended from Pike and Dobbins, 1986, p. 296)*

King (1975) suggests that the capital investment decision is 'a process of study, bargaining, persuasion and choice over many levels of the organization and over long periods'. Cooper (1975) maintains that the formal process may ignore the social and political interest which are part of any organization, while Kennedy and Sugden (1986) suggest such a process is just a ritual, the reality being moulded by political pressures within the organization.

While such comments may mitigate against the use of sophisticated evaluation techniques, there is evidence (Pike, 1989) to suggest the increased use of the four appraisal techniques to be considered.

Stakeholders, capital markets and the organization

We have already stated that management should seek to maximize the wealth of the owners of an enterprise, but have reflected that this may not always be the case. However, managers must ensure stakeholders maintain their investments in the enterprise by offering returns which are commensurate with returns elsewhere at that level of risk.

Shareholders and creditors invest capital or loan capital in an enterprise in the hope of gaining a return, and for creditors the

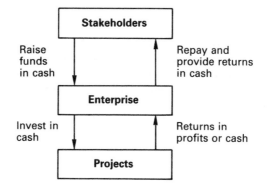

Figure 8.6 *Relationship between stakeholders, the enterprise and capital projects*

eventual return of their funds. The capital provided is channelled through the enterprise and invested in capital projects, which must generate returns commensurate with the expectations of the providers of capital.

In Figure 8.6, the left hand side demonstrates the flow of stakeholders' funds into the projects, while the right hand side illustrates the flow of funds to repay capital or service capital. The return from capital projects must be sufficient to maintain stakeholder involvement. Enterprises not providing adequate returns to stakeholders will find new funds very difficult to raise and will see the withdrawal of shareholders through the sale of shares.

The capital investment appraisal techniques to be considered below link the expected returns from the proposed projects with those required by stakeholders. The accounting rate of return measures the return in profit flows while the net present value *and* internal rate of return measure the return in discounted cash flows.

Techniques for appraisal of capital investment

There are four basic techniques:

- *Payback* (PB) measures the time taken for the project to recover its original cost in future cash flows.
- *Accounting rate of return* (ARR) measures the percentage return the project achieves over its life in terms of profitability.
- *Net present value* (NPV) compares the initial cost of the project with the future discounted cash flows it generates.
- *Internal rate of return* (IRR) measures the percentage return the project achieves over its lifetime in discounted cash flows.

Each will be considered in detail using numerical examples.

Payback

This simply measures the number of years it will take to recover the original investment from the net cash flows resulting from the project. For example, if a proposed project had an initial cost of £450, and net cash inflows over a future period of 5 years as follows:

    Year 1   100
    Year 2   200
    Year 3   100
    Year 4   100
    Year 5   220

Then the payback period would be approximately 3.5 years, in that it takes the net cash inflows for years 1, 2, 3 and part of year 4 to recover the initial £450 investment. (100 + 200 + 100 + 1/2 x 100).

The cash flows after the payback period would be ignored by this technique, so the £220 anticipated cash flow in year 5 would not be considered.

The answer obtained cannot be considered good or bad in isolation. The 3.5 year payback period may be considered inferior to a 2 year period and superior to a 4 year period, but the period cannot be compared to a measure of return required by stakeholders. It may be reasonable to assume stakeholders prefer shorter payback periods to longer ones, but how short, knowing that post-payback cash flows may be highly favourable but ignored? And while the return to stakeholders is ignored, so too is the profitability of the project, as payback does not equate to traditional accounting ideas of profits and capital employed.

The sheer simplicity of the payback method of investment appraisal makes it a useful and quick evaluation technique, but it assumes an amount of money received in year 1 is equal to the same amount of money received in year 2 etc. While this may be factually true, the opportunity cost of receiving money at different time intervals is the opportunity to invest cash received at an earlier time. This concept is known as the 'time value of money' and will be developed when the techniques of net present value and internal rate of return are considered. It is sufficient to say, at this point, that the payback technique ignores the time value of money by assuming amounts of money received at different time intervals can be simply added and subtracted from one another.

Accounting rate of return (ARR)

This appraisal technique compares the profits generated by the project with the original investment. The technique differs from payback as it considers future profit flows rather than cash flows. The main difference between cash flows and profit flows is depreciation.

If we return to the data given earlier, the original cost of the project was £450, the life of the asset was 5 years, and if we assume no residual value then the depreciation charge would be £90 per annum adopting a straight-line basis for depreciation. The annual figure can now be re-expressed as:

Year	Net cash inflow £	Depreciation £	Profit flows £
1	100	90	10
2	200	90	110
3	100	90	10
4	100	90	10
5	220	90	130

The accounting rate of return compares the average profits per annum with the average investment. The average profits are £54 per annum and the average investment is £225, i.e. half the original cost. Then the ARR is 24%.

It is common for this ratio to be varied by comparing average annual profit flows with the original cost, i.e. £54 divided by £450 giving an ARR of 12%. Because of the scaling involved, as long as consistency is applied both methods provide acceptable measures.

This technique complements the idea of return on capital employed (ROCE), which is used as a managerial and divisional performance measure, by relating profits to capital invested at the outset of the project.

The major reservation with this technique, like payback, is that it ignores the time value of money, by adding and subtracting profits (not cash, like payback) from different years, and assuming they are of equal value.

Before the two techniques involving the time value of money are introduced, it would be useful to consider two issues that are vital to the techniques. The first being the mathematics for the time value of money, known as compounding and discounting, and secondly the concept of a required rate of return for stakeholders.

Compounding and discounting – time value of money

Payback and accounting rate of return both ignored the time value of money or the preference to receive money earlier than later, because of the opportunity to invest the earlier received sums for the intervening period. The value of a future amount invested at a constant rate of interest can be calculated using the compound interest formula, which is:

$$An = P(1 + i)^n$$
where An = future amount in year n
P = amount invested now (at time, $n=0$)

$$i \ = \text{interest rate}$$
$$n \ = \text{number of years money is invested}$$

Very simply, if £100 is invested for 1 year at 10% then the future amount (An) will be £110 i.e. $100 (1 + 0.10)^1$. If £100 is invested for 2 years at 10%, then the future amount will be £121, i.e. $100 (1 + 0.10)^2$.

Compounding therefore converts present amounts into future sums, with capital investment appraisal, the opposite is required. Forecasting techniques have established the future cash flows which are estimated to arise from the investment in a particular project; it is the bringing of these future sums back to the present time that is required, so that all cash flows are expressed at the same time value of money, at the present time. This process is known as discounting and is the opposite of compounding.

The compounding formula linked a present amount when invested to a future amount. Discounting does the same but this time the future amount is known and the present amount (present value) needs to be established. Rearranging the compounding formula provides this:

$$P = \frac{An}{(1 + i)^n}$$

If £121 is received after 2 years, it has a present value of £100 if the interest rate is 10%, i.e.

$$\frac{121}{(1 + 0.10)^2}$$

Similarly £110 received after 1 year has a present value of £100. It may be useful to illustrate this as follows:

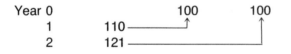

by moving the £110 and £121 respectively from future time periods to the present time we have considered the opportunity of funds or the time value of money.

The mathematics of this may seem daunting, especially if the project is generating cash flows 10 or 15 years into the future, but there are short cuts using discount tables which come to your aid. The £121 received in 2 years with an interest rate of 10% equated to £100 received now. The mathematics were

$$\frac{121}{(1.10)^2}$$

if this is expressed as

$$121 \times \frac{1}{(1.10)^2}$$

there are tables which express the second term for you. Using the discount tables in Appendix A, look down the first column until you find 2 years, and then across the rows until you find 10%. The resulting figure is 0.826, which is $1/(1.10)^2$. We will use these tables again when the two discounting techniques are introduced, after the *hurdle rate* issue has been resolved.

A hurdle rate for net present value and internal rate of return techniques

We have already introduced the idea of stakeholders requiring a return on their funds, and that investment projects within the firm should provide a return which is commensurate with these returns. To do this we need to establish the average required return by stakeholders. Consider the following example.

If a company has two major stakeholder groups, shareholders and long-term creditors, who supply finance in the ratio of 75% equity and 25% loan finance, and the opportunity cost of equity capital was 20%, and the after tax cost of loan finance was 9%, then the average return required would be 17.25%, calculated as follows.

	Weight		Opportunity cost (%)		Weighted average cost of capital (%)
Equity finance	0.75	×	20	=	15.00
Loan finance	0.25	×	9	=	2.25
	1.00				17.25%

The 17.25% is known as the weighted average cost of capital, and represents the average opportunity cost of funds for the company's stakeholders.

All projects for the above company must provide a return of at least 17.25%, as this is the minimum return which will keep both sets of stakeholders adequately compensated for investing within this particular company. If a project does not provide this level of return it is not worth pursuing, while a project providing a greater return will enhance the value of the firm by providing a return in excess of the average opportunity cost of funds.

Having established the idea of a hurdle rate, which is required to keep stakeholders satisfied, we can now turn to the two appraisal techniques which use discounted cash flows (DCF) as a measure for adoption or rejection of a project.

Net present value (NPV)

This technique, like internal rate of return which follows, brings together the concept of discounting and the weighted average cost of funds. The former is required to adjust for the time value of money while the latter provides an interest rate or discount rate to apply to the future cash flows.

Consider the project which we have already evaluated using payback and accounting rate of return. It may be useful to remind ourselves of the figures.

```
Initial cost      450
Cash flow Yr 1 100
          Yr 2 200
          Yr 3 100
          Yr 4 100
          Yr 5 220
Payback period = 3.5 years
Average accounting rate of return = 12%
```

If the opportunity cost of stakeholders funds was 10% then the estimated future cash flows would have present values, in £, as follows:

$$\frac{100}{1.10} + \frac{200}{(1.10)^2} + \frac{100}{(1.10)^3} + \frac{100}{(1.10)^4} + \frac{220}{(1.10)^5}$$

$$= 90.9 + 165.3 + 75.1 + 68.3 + 136.6$$

$$= £536.2$$

The initial cost was £450, giving a net present value of £86.2, which means the project generates 10% to maintain the stakeholders returns and gives a surplus of £86.2, i.e. the project gives a return in excess of 10% and therefore more than satisfies stakeholders.

An easier way to express this calculation is in a tabular form using the discount tables, as follows:

Time	Cash flow		Discount rate (10%)		DCF
0	(450)	×	1.000	=	(450)
1	100	×	0.909	=	91
2	200	×	0.826	=	165
3	100	×	0.751	=	75
4	100	×	0.683	=	68
5	220	×	0.621	=	137
					+ 86

It arrives at the same solution as the algebraic equation used above, but can now be applied easily to spreadsheets and other software packages.

To return to the net present value rule, if the project gives a positive net present value, then investing in it provides a return which will satisfy all the providers of funds (the stakeholders) and provide a surplus or additional return to the shareholders. If the net present value is negative then the project is not worth pursuing as the return does not satisfy the requirements of the stakeholders.

If the discount rate were raised to 20% then the net present value for the project would be minus £34 and not acceptable.

Year	Cash flow	Discount rate (20%)	DCF
0	(450)	1.000	(450)
1	100	0.833	83
2	200	0.694	139
3	100	0.579	58
4	100	0.483	48
5	220	0.402	88
			(34)

Internal rate of return

This is also known as the *discounted cash flow yield* method. It is given by the discount rate which equates the initial cost of a project with the discounted future inflows. For our project it can be expressed as follows:

$$0 = -450 + \frac{100}{(1 + r)} + \frac{200}{(1 + r)^2} + \frac{100}{(1 + r)^3} + \frac{100}{(1 + r)^4} + \frac{220}{(1 + r)^5}$$

where r = internal rate of return.

We have already established a relationship between the discount rate and the net present value for this project as follows:

NPV	10%	=	+86
NPV	20%	=	-34

The internal rate of return must be between 10% and 20%, as it is derived by establishing a discount rate which gives a net present value of zero.

The relationship can be graphed as shown in Graph 8.1. The dotted line crosses the horizontal axis when the net present value is zero. This will give the internal rate of return. Rather than draw a graph every time the same approximate answer can be derived mathematically by interpolation. The formula requires the discount rates for a positive and a negative net present value calculation, similar to the ones stated above.

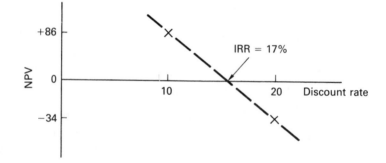

Graph 8.1 *IRR derived by graph*

IRR by interpretation =

Lower discount rate + $\dfrac{\text{NPV of lower discount rate}}{\text{NPV of lower rate} - \text{NPV}} \times \begin{array}{l}\text{Difference}\\ \text{in discount}\\ \text{rates}\end{array}$
$\qquad\qquad\qquad\qquad$ of higher rate

$$= 10\% + \left[\frac{86}{86 - (-34)}\,(20\% - 10\%)\right]$$
$$= 17.16\%$$

The resulting figure of 17.16% can now be compared with the weighted average cost of funds. If it is greater then the project is acceptable, if less, the project is not. In most cases the net present value rule and the internal rate of return rule will give the same recommendations.

Summary of discounted cash flow (DCF) methods

NPV
Discount project's cash flows at company's cost of capital:

> If NPV positive – acceptable
> If NPV zero – acceptable
> If NPV negative – reject

IRR
By trial and error find the discount rate which will produce a net present value of zero.

> If the discount rate found is greater than the cost of capital – acceptable.
> If the discount rate is less than the cost of capital – reject.

Illustration 8.1   Swanic

Swanic is considering whether to invest in the following project:

Life   5 years
Annual cash flows (receipts less payments)   £200,000
Initial cost   £660,000
Estimate scrap value   £60,000

Swanic uses the straight-line method for providing for depreciation and has an average cost of capital of 15%.
Calculate:

(i)   The accounting rate of return (over the project's life, using average accounting profit to average value of investment) to nearest 1%.
(ii)   The net present value.
(iii)   The internal rate of return (DCF yield) to nearest 1%.
(iv)   The payback period to one decimal place.

(i)   As the returns are stated in cash flows these need amending to profit flows before the accounting rate of return can be calculated. The main difference between cash flows and profit flows is depreciation; roughly

$$\text{Profit flows} = \text{cash flow} - \text{Depreciation}$$

$$\text{Depreciation p.a.} = \frac{660,000 - 60,000}{5 \text{ years}} = 120,000$$

$$\text{Average accounting profit} = 200,000 - 120,000 = 80,000$$

$$\text{Average investment} = \frac{660,000 - 60,000}{2} = £300,000$$

$$\text{ARR} = \frac{80,000}{300,000} = 27\%$$

(ii)

Cash flows (£000)

Time	Initial cost	Scrap	Annual cash flows	Net cash flows	15% discount factor	DCF
T_0	(660)			(660)	1.000	(660)
T_1	—		200	200	0.870	174
T_2	—		200	200	0.756	151
T_3	—		200	200	0.658	132
T_4	—		200	200	0.572	114
T_5	—	60	200	260	0.497	129
						+40

(iii) We already know that at a cost of capital of 15% the net present value was + £40,000. To produce a negative NPV we need to raise the discount rate, so try 20%.

Time	Cash flows	20% discounted rate	DCF
T_0	(660)	1.000	(660)
T_1	200	0.833	167
T_2	200	0.694	139
T_3	200	0.579	116
T_4	200	0.482	96
T_5	260	0.402	105
			−37

We now have the following information

Discount rate	NPV
15%	+40
20%	−37

A discount rate with an NPV of zero must be between 15% and 20%, and as +40 is as much above zero as −37 is below, it would suggest the IRR is approximately 17.5% (i.e. halfway between 15% and 20%), but to check, use interpolation.

$$15\% + \frac{40}{77} \times 5\% = 17.59\%$$

(iv) Payback period is 3.2 years.

Adoption of investment appraisal techniques

We have considered a range of appraisal techniques which varied from the relatively simple ideas of payback, through the profitability measure of accounting rate of return to the more sophisticated techniques of net present value and internal rate of return using discounted cash flow concepts. The usage of such techniques is quite common in large firms, as the trend analysis in Table 8.1 demonstrates. The trend analysis clearly shows growth in the use of the more sophisticated techniques, but also a steady growth in the use of payback. The analysis also shows that companies use more than one appraisal technique. This may be because each has some-thing to contribute to the establishment of a broader understanding of any investment project. Payback measures the time capital is at risk, accounting rate of return gives a measure of profitability while net present value and internal rate of return provide an indication of stakeholder returns.

Table 8.1 *Appraisal techniques: trend analysis in 100 UK large firms*

Technique	1986 (%)	1981 (%)	1975 (%)
Payback	92	81	73
Average accounting rate of return	56	49	51
Net present value	68	39	32
Internal rate of return	75	57	44

(Source: *Pike, 1989*)

Table 8.2 *Companies always using a specified investment appraisal technique*

Technique	%
Payback	47
Average accounting rate of return	18
Net present value	23
Internal rate of return	42

Pike pursued his survey further in 1989 and asked companies about the frequency of use of each technique. Responses indicated that the techniques were *always* used as shown in Table 8.2. This again demonstrates the use of more than one technique for any specific project. It also demonstrates the continued use of the internal rate of return technique and its dominance over the net present value rule despite the problems which will now be considered.

Net present value versus internal rate of return

In normal circumstances using the net present value rule and the internal rate of return will give the same recommendation (see Graph 8.2). As the discount rate increases in Graph 8.2 each term of the net present value equation decreases, as does the eventual net present value. The curve has a net present value of zero at point I which gives an internal rate of return of 0I. No conflict between the two techniques arises because any point on the curve AI will be accepted using the IRR or NPV rule, as the NPV is positive and the IRR is greater than the discount rate applied. Similarly, any point on IB would be rejected.

Using this illustration, it indicates there is no conflict between the NPV and IRR rules when applied to single investments with normal cash flows. However conflict does arise between the two techniques when:

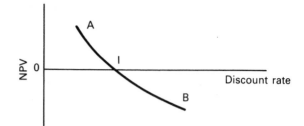

Graph 8.2 *NPV against discount rate*

- Projects have to be ranked each having differing outlays and different project lives.
- Cash flows are abnormal, resulting in the 'double zero problem'.
- In situations of capital rationing.

Ranking of projects

This applies to mutually exclusive projects, where the acceptance of one automatically leads to the rejection of the other. A typical example is the acquisition of a fleet of trucks and the decision whether to acquire say Mercedes or Iveco. The acquisition of either may have both positive net present values and internal rates of return greater than the cost of capital, but only one manufacturer's product must be acquired.
Consider the following data

	Yr 0 outlay	Yr 2 cash inflow	NPV 10%	IRR
Project 1	400	560	+62	18%
Project 2	200	290	+40	20%

While both projects would be acceptable, a decision has to be made which one to accept. If the NPV rule was adopted project 1 would dominate, while the IRR rule would favour project 2.

The conflict arises because project 1 is twice as large as project 2; it gives a higher absolute NPV of +62 but offers a relatively lower percentage return. IRR does not recognize scale, and suffers from the same problem as any percentage, in that 40% sounds superior to 25%, but if the 40% only relates to £100 of turnover, while the 25% relates to £10,000 of turnover, clearly the latter is preferable. Applying the same principle to our projects, project 1 is obviously superior as it produces a higher absolute return to shareholders.

Double zero problem

This arises when cash flows are as follows:

	£
Year 0 initial outlay	2,400
Year 1 cash inflow	8,000
Year 2 cash outlay	6,000

The example given is over-simplistic but reflects cash flows in the extraction industries, where a quarry or mine is commissioned, producing a series of cash inflows over a number of years and then finally the quarry or mine is decommissioned and the land reinstated, giving a cash outlay in the final year of the project.

The figures given above will produce a multiple answer to the IRR calculation; while both are correct they do not give a clear cut-off rate for decision-making. The problem is known as the 'double zero' one because such cash flows produce a curve that passes through the X-axis twice, that is, having two IRR solutions, or put another way, having two net present values of zero, as Graph 8.3 shows.

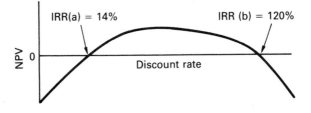

Graph 8.3 *Double zero problem*

The IRR calculations were as follows for IRR(a):

Year	Cash flow	Discount rate 14%	DCF
0	(2,400)	1.000	(2,400)
1	8,000	0.877	7,016
2	(6,000)	0.769	(4,614)
			+2

and for IRR (b):

Year	Cash flow	Discount rate 120%	DCF
0	(2,400)	1.0000	(2,400)
1	8,000	0.4545	3,636
2	(6,000)	0.2066	(1,240)
			−4

Sign changes like this are very common, as all projects subject to taxation produce tax payments in the final year of the enterprise, therefore producing the double zero problem for most tax-paying companies and their projects.

Capital rationing

This is where there is a limit on the amount of funds available for investment in capital projects. In such cases the best combination of projects must be selected to maximize returns to shareholders. While many projects may be offering positive net present values and internal rates of return above the cost of capital, only some may be selected.

The way to resolve this issue is to ignore the internal rate of return recommendation – we have already seen it does not recognize scale – and attempt to maximize the net present value per £1 invested by using a profitability index, which relates present value of cash inflows (outputs) to initial cost of project (input).

Consider the projects H and K

Project	Investment	Present value of cash inflows	Net present value
H	300	401	+101
K	1500	1637	+137

In the normal case, K would be superior as it provides a higher absolute net present value, but if investment capital is in short supply, then H produces the best ratio of inputs to outputs

$$\text{Profitability index (H)} \quad \frac{401}{300} \quad = 1.34$$

$$\text{Profitability index (K)} \quad \frac{1637}{1500} \quad = 1.09$$

and should be selected.

Illustration 8.2 Biddup

Biddup has a short-term capital rationing problem. It only has £650,000 available for capital investment in the next financial year yet has the following projects available:

Project	Investment required £	Internal rate of return %	NPV at 10% pa £
A	500,000	12	161,837
B	50,000	16	13,373

C	80,000	25	16,988
D	400,000	16	63,164
E	300,000	14	31,285
F	500,000	18	25,797

which projects should it adopt?

Using the maximization of net present value as the criterion, and as capital is restricted, then the profitability index (PI), linking initial investment to net present value will give the best solution.

The profitability index is calculated as follows:

	(a) Initial investment +	(b) NPV =	(c) Total discounted ÷ cash inflows	PI (a/c)	Ranking
A	500,000	161,837	661,836	1.32	1
B	50,000	13,373	63,373	1.27	2
C	80,000	16,988	96,988	1.21	3
D	400,000	63,164	463,164	1.15	4
E	300,000	31,285	331,285	1.10	5
F	500,000	25,897	525,797	1.05	6

If £650,000 is available, the selection will be as follows:

Project	Initial cost £	NPV £
A	500,000	161,837
B	50,000	13,373
C	80,000	16,988
	630,000	192,198
Surplus	20,000	nil
	650,000	192,198

If the IRR had been used for ranking purposes then the following would have resulted:

Project	Initial cost	NPV
C	80,000	16,988
F	500,000	25,787
B	50,000	13,373
	630,000	56,158
Surplus	20,000	nil
	650,000	56,158

which is inferior to the initial choice using the profitability index approach.

Many of the considerations discussed in this section on adoption of the different investment appraisal techniques are summarized in Tables 8.3 and 8.4.

Table 8.3   *Summary of discounted cash flow criteria and non-discounting criteria*

Payback	Accounting rate of return	DCF techniques
Advantages		
1 Uses cash flows	1 Recognizes whole life of project	1 Recognizes whole life of project
2 Stresses early cash generation	2 Commonly used as it relates to the impact of the project on the financial accounts	2 Uses net cash flows
3 Easily calculated, commonly used and understood		3 Recognizes the time value of money
Disadvantages		
1 Considers cash flows only up to the payback point	1 Does not use net cash flows	1 May be difficult to apply
2 Does not consider the time value of money	2 Many methods of calculation, e.g. different depreciation policies	2 May be costly to apply
3 Is not a measure of profitability	3 Does not consider the time value of money	3 Lacks consideration of short-term liquidity
	4 It is an average which may hide wide fluctuations	4 May not be easily reflected in financial accounts

Table 8.4   *Net profit value (NPV) versus internal rate of return (IRR)*

NPV	IRR
Advantages	
1 Absolute measure which deals with mutually exclusive projects	1 Ease of interpretation and understanding
2 Only produces a single answer	2 Useful for preliminary screening
3 Can cope with varying interest rates over time	
Disadvantages	
1 Difficult to interpret and understand	1 Can produce multiple answers
2 Not useful for preliminary screening	2 A relative measure which can fail to rank mutually exclusive projects correctly
	3 Cannot cope with varying interest rates

Relevant cash flows

The examples presented so far in this chapter have linked forecasted cash or profit flows to a time period, they have not attempted to explain how such forecasts have been derived as the emphasis has been on the evaluation stage with the calculation of net present values, accounting rates of return and internal rates of return. We now turn to the way in which forecasted flows are derived.

The process of establishing such estimated annual cash flows may be a product of many calculations involving sales volume, selling prices, cost prices, labour costs, advertising expenditure, etc., etc. It is crucial that such cash flows are incremental to the project being accepted. All the rules applicable to short-term decision-making relating to the relative cost and the decision equally apply to the long-term decision-making of capital investment appraisal. It may be useful to remind yourself of the ideas put forward in Chapter 7. The rules to follow are summarized below.

1 Only consider incremental cash flows (or profit flows).
2 Ignore depreciation charges if cash flows are being considered.
3 Exclude all financing expenses from the cash flows as these are taken into account when establishing the hurdle rate.
4 If resources are already held within the company and used up by the project, then charge the opportunity cost of these resources to the project.
5 Ignore sunk costs.

Illustration 8.3   Martan Company

Martan Company is considering acquiring a new machine which could be purchased for £100,000 with a life of 5 years and a scrap value of £5,000. The machine would produce 50,000 units per annum of a new product for which the estimated selling price is £3 per unit. Direct costs would be £1.75 per unit. Annual fixed costs, including depreciation, which is calculated on a straight-line basis, would be £40,000 per annum.

In years 1 and 2, special sales promotion expenditure, not included in the above costs, would be incurred amounting to £10,000 and £15,000 respectively. As a consequence of this particular project, investment by the company in debtors and stocks would increase, during year 1, by £15,000 and £20,000 respectively; creditors would also increase by £10,000. It should be assumed that at the end of the life of the machine, the debtors, creditors and stocks would revert to the amounts prior to introduction of the new machine.

Evaluate the project, using the NPV method of investment appraisal, assuming the company's cost of capital is 10%.

The calculation of net cash flows requires consideration of each item that generates or uses cash.

	Equipment	Contribution	Fixed cost	Adverts	Working capital	NCF	Disc. factors 10%	DCF
T_0	(100,000)					(100,000)	1.000	(100,000)
T_1		62,500	(21,000)	(10,000)	(25,000)	6,500	0.909	5,909
T_2		62,500	(21,000)	(15,000)	—	26,500	0.826	21,890
T_3		62,500	(21,000)	—	—	41,500	0.751	31,167
T_4		62,500	(21,000)	—	—	41,500	0.683	28,345
T_5	5,000	62,500	(21,000)	—	25,000	71,500	0.621	44,402
						NPV (10%)	=	+31,713

Workings

1 Contribution p.a.

SP 3.00
VC 1.75

$1.25 \times 50,000$ units $= \underline{62,500}$

2 Fixed costs   40,000
  less depreciation
  $\dfrac{100,000 - 5,000}{5}$ $\underline{19,000}$
                              $\underline{21,000}$

3 Working capital stocks   15,000
                  Debtors   20,000
                             $\overline{35,000}$
               Creditors   10,000
                             $\underline{25,000}$

Risk within capital investment appraisal

Risk is ever present in decisions dealing with future outcomes, and is particularly relevant to long-term decision-making. The ability to forecast with any accuracy will decrease the further that forecast is required to look into the future, yet the ability to make valid decisions is a product of those forecasted cash flows. There are different ways of handling risk: managers may concentrate on a few key variables, apply 'rules-of-thumb', 'mull-over' the position and then use judgement, hunch, instinct, intuition and other implicit techniques to arrive at a decision. There are several formal techniques that may help to handle risk within capital budgeting, and we return to the survey by Pike (1989) to highlight the usage of such techniques before considering them individually (Table 8.5).

Table 8.5 *Handling risk in capital investment evaluation: trend analysis in 100 UK large firms*

Technique	1986	1981	1975
Shorter payback period	61	30	25
Adjust discount rate	61	41	37
Sensitivity analysis	71	42	28
Formal analysis of risk	86	38	26

Note: While the techniques were used, they were only adopted rarely – probably only for large projects which may have a large impact on company performance and survival if they fail.
(Source: *Pike, 1989*)

Common methods of handling risk

Shorten payback

If the riskiness of the situation faced by an organization is characterized by a shortage of liquidity, then shortening the payback period may result in the selection of projects that ease the situation.

However, the payback period of a project is not a measure of profitability. If the problem of the organization is to achieve and maintain a satisfactory level of profitability, then shortening the payback period could be counterproductive. There is a relationship between payback period and profitability, but it is not straightforward on some projects and over some years of a project it may be inverse. In practice, few organizations would rely solely on payback period as the criterion for choice on larger projects. A profitability measure(s) and payback period would normally be used.

Risk-adjusted discount rates

Projects deemed to be higher risk than average are expected to provide a return higher than the normal cost of capital. Projects with lower than average risk are expected to provide a yield lower than the normal cost of capital. This is applicable as regards NPV, IRR, and ROCE. It is intuitively reasonable and fits in with management expectations – we expect a higher return on risky equity shareholdings than on safe building society investment accounts. Adjusting discount rates is a commonly used technique in organizations of all sizes and is usually tied in with the approach to project classification. For example:

Project classification	Risk classification	Required return (say)
1 Replacement	Low	10%
2 Expansion	Medium	20%
3 New product or diversification	High	30%

In favour of this approach are its ease of use and ready acceptance by managers, and it may recognize an existing informal approach to decision-making which managers use.

There are some difficulties, however. First, it does not consider the risks associated with a particular project in as rigorous and explicit a manner as may be desirable. It is very much a 'broad brush' approach. Secondly, the determination of the absolute values of the various hurdle rates can be done in a variety of ways from judgement through to more academic approaches. There are many practical and theoretical difficulties associated with the more formal approaches. Thirdly, raising the discount rate makes risk a function of time.

Conservative forecasts

In preparing forecasts, managers may attempt purposely to over-estimate costs and under-estimate revenues. An under-estimate of expected actual NPV, IRR or payback would then, hopefully, result. In smaller firms where the owners are doing the forecasting, this is feasible. However, the realities of the capital budgeting process in larger, perhaps divisionalized, organizations are that lower level managers will be competing to get their project proposals accepted, the forecasts of which are unlikely to be conservative. A further limitation is that it would be difficult to control the degree of conservatism of forecasting between managers, functions, divisions and from one project to another over time. A lack of consistency in forecasting (which will, however, always be present) may lead to project misranking.

Probability assignments

On sufficiently large or important projects managements may wish to explore more formally the possible patterns of future net cash flows and profits. Two or more forecasts may be made, for example:

'Pessimistic' forecast
'Most likely' forecast
'Optimistic' forecast

This approach moves away from the single point estimate which may have adjusted for risk implicitly at each level of aggregation.

This approach also clarifies exactly what figure a manager is supplying, as single point estimates could be the:

Mean	(average of a distribution)
or Mode	(occurring most)
or Median	(mid-point of a distribution).

Clearly aggregation of different ideas of average figures would be less than useful.

A three point estimate would look like the following:

	P	Forecast	Expected value
Optimistic	0.3	100,000	30,000
Most likely	0.6	75,000	45,000
Pessimistic	0.1	50,000	5,000
	1.0		80,000

From this three point estimate a full distribution may then be constructed, but this may be expensive and time consuming, the costs far outweighing the benefits.

Illustration 8.4   Binklim Chemicals

Binklim Chemicals is considering a major investment in a new acid plant. There is some debate amongst senior managers as to the size and productive capacity of such an installation. Because of the nature of the chemical process, once the basic plant is established, subsequent increases in capacity are very expensive.

The productive capacity required for the acid plant is a product of future demand which is highly dependent on the industrial solvents market.

The marketing and finance departments have provided the following estimates which may be useful in helping management in its decision.

The smaller plant will cost £3m, while the larger will cost £6m, with no scrap values after their expected life of 8 years.

Larger plant net cash inflows (£m)

	Probability	Years							
		1	2	3	4	5	6	7	8
Pessimistic	0.3	0.2	0.2	0.2	0.2	0.2	0.2	0.2	0.2
Most likely	0.5	1.6	1.6	1.6	1.6	1.4	1.4	1.4	1.4
Optimistic	0.2	2.0	2.0	2.0	2.0	1.6	1.6	1.6	1.6

Smaller plant net cash inflows (£m)

	Probability	Years							
		1	2	3	4	5	6	7	8
Pessimistic	0.4	0.2	0.2	0.2	0.2	0.2	0.2	0.2	0.2
Most likely	0.4	1.0	1.0	1.0	1.0	0.8	0.8	0.8	0.8
Optimistic	0.2	1.2	1.2	1.2	1.2	1.0	1.0	1.0	1.0

If the cost of capital is 10%, you are required to prepare statements which clearly give the financial implications of each project.

Because the cash flows are constant in years 1−4 and 5−8 the discount rates can be added together to speed the calculation.

Year	Discount rate 10%	
1	0.909	
2	0.826	
3	0.751	} 3.169
4	0.683	
5	0.621	
6	0.564	
7	0.513	} 2.165
8	0.467	

Larger plant

Years 1−4

P	£m	Expected value (£m)	Minimum £m	Maximum £m
0.3	0.2	0.06	0.2	
0.5	1.6	0.80		
0.2	2.0	0.40		2.0
		1.26		

Years 5−8

P	£m	Expected value (£m)	Minimum £m	Maximum £m
0.3	0.2	0.06	0.2	
0.5	1.4	0.70		
0.2	1.6	0.32		1.6
		1.08		

Discounting at 10%

Initial cost	(6.000)	(6.000)	(6.000)
Inflows 1−4	3.993	0.634	6.338
Inflows 5−10	2.338	0.433	3.464
NPV 10%	+0.331	−4.933	+3.802

Smaller plant

Years 1−4

P	£m	Expected value (£m)	Minimum £m	Maximum £m
0.4	0.2	0.08	0.2	
0.4	1.0	0.40		
0.2	1.2	0.24		1.2
		0.72		

Year 5–8

0.4	0.2	0.08	0.2
0.4	0.8	0.32	
0.2	1.0	0.02	1.0
		0.42	

Discounting at 10%			
Initial cost	(3.000)	(3.000)	(3.000)
Inflows 1–4	2.282	0.634	3.803
Inflows 5–10	0.909	0.433	2.165
NPV 10%	+0.191	−1.933	+2.968

Summarizing the outcomes − Net present values (£m)

	Larger plant	*Smaller plant*
Minimum	−4.933	−1.933
Expected value	+0.331	+0.191
Maximum	+3.802	+2.968

The outcomes are a product of subjective probabilities, which by their very nature are subject to risk, but the above summary does provide management with a decision tableau upon which to base their decision about plant size. Depending upon the risk preferences of managers either could be selected, but at least the parameters of their decision are explicit.

Sensitivity analysis

This technique is easy to use and can be quite revealing about the riskiness of a project. Of the techniques employed in practice, Pike's study (1989) revealed that the use of sensitivity analysis had increased markedly over the period of study. The techniques measure the sensitivity of changes in the net present value of a project by altering single variables and measuring their effect on the net present value. The appraisal of any project is a product of many variables and the estimates relating to them; even a relatively straightforward project will contain estimates for residual value, project duration, operating costs, selling price, market size, etc., etc.

If the project has a positive net present value, using single point estimates for all these variables, it would generally be accepted. However, sensitivity analysis would demonstrate how this general advice may be modified by changes in each variable; in other words sensitivity analysis indicates the margin of error that can exist in each variable before the project becomes unviable, i.e. has a net present value of zero.

Taxation within investment appraisal

There are three ways in which the UK taxation regime impacts on capital investment appraisal.

1   Tax relief is available on interest payments for borrowed money, in a similar manner to mortgage interest relief. This is adjusted for within the hurdle rate calculation in the establishment of the weighted average cost of capital. It does not effect the project cash flows.
2   Tax relief is available on capital expenditure through annual writing down allowances, known as Capital Allowances. The rates vary depending on the type of assets, for example:

Plant and machinery – 25% reducing balance
Industrial buildings – 4% straight line

The Chancellor may alter these in the annual budget if it is considered necessary.
3   A tax liability will arise on any taxable profits generated by a project. These are usually paid 9 months after the company's year end.

The latter two effects are drawn together in the following example which uses an after tax cost of capital as calculated using the approach specified in (1) above.

Illustration 8.5   Capital allowances – an example

A company is considering whether or not to purchase an item of machinery costing £40,000 in 1995. It would have a life of 4 years, after which it would be sold for £5,000. The machinery would create annual cost savings of £14,000.

The machinery would attract writing down allowances of 25% on the reducing balance basis which could be claimed against taxable profits.

The Corporation Tax rate is 35%.

The after-tax cost of capital is 8%.

Tax is paid 1 year after the financial year end to which it relates.

Should the machinery be purchased?

Taxable profits computation

| | *Accounting years* | | | |
	1	2	3	4
Savings (i.e. extra taxable profits)	14,000	14,000	14,000	14,000
less Capital allowances	10,000	7,500	5,625	4,219
less Balance allowance	–	–	–	7,656

Taxable profits	4,000	6,500	8,375	2,125
at 35%	1,400	2,275	2,931	744
payable one year in arrears i.e.	T_2	T_3	T_4	T_5

Net present value computation

Time	Equipment	Savings	Tax charge	NCF	Discount rate 8%	DCF
T_0	(40,000)			(40,000)	1,000	(40,000)
T_1		14,000		14,000	0.926	12,964
T_2		14,000	(1,400)	12,600	0.857	10,798
T_3		14,000	(2,275)	11,725	0.794	9,309
T_4	5,000	14,000	(2,931)	16,069	0.735	11,811
T_5			(744)	(744)	0.681	(507)
					NPV (8)%	4,375

Capital allowance computation

Cost	40,000		
Writing down allowance at 25% p.a.	10,000	Yr 1	
	30,000	Yr 1 written down value	
do.	7,500	Yr 2	
	22,500	Yr 2	do.
do.	5,625	Yr 3	
	16,875	Yr 3	do.
do.	4,219	Yr 4	
	12,656	Yr 4	do.
Residual value	5,000	Yr 4	
Balancing allowance	7,656	Yr 4	

The balancing allowance is produced because the residual value of the asset is less than its book value for taxation purposes. Had the residual value been greater than the book value a balancing charge would have arisen which would have increased the taxation for the final year of the project.

Investment appraisal in the public sector or not-for-profit sector

The development and application of the sophisticated appraisal techniques outlined so far in this chapter have their origins in the profit-making sectors of the economy. Where there is a profit motive it is clear that costs and benefits can be expressed in monetary terms and so appraisal techniques can be restricted to net cash or profit flows. Equally clear is the use of a discount rate which relates to the aspirations of the stakeholders through the opportunity cost of capital reflected within the weighted average cost of capital.

Within the public and not-for-profit sectors of the economy the clear profit objective is not applicable, so the cash flow measure is not wholly appropriate, and the cost of capital is highly problematic. It is because of these two issues that the costs and benefits relating to projects in these sectors cannot be restricted to cash flow only; a much wider approach is required.

Cost benefit analysis

Cost benefit analysis is much broader than cash or profit based analysis which deals with the economic, as it seeks to assess all the economic and social advantages (benefits) and disadvantages (costs) of a project and then attempts to quantify these in monetary terms. A new road may have clear economic monetary costs, but may also have social benefits in terms of time saved travelling, reduced congestion, reduction in accidents etc., while also incurring social costs in terms of disturbance to the environment through pollution, noise and destruction of habitat. Quite clearly some of the social costs and benefits are more easily quantified in monetary terms than others, in fact some are not capable of objective measurements, but the technique aims to provide an analysis of which projects provide the best value for money to society. Because no direct stakeholders are involved with such investments, the broadest view of stakeholders must be taken, i.e. whether society as a whole will be better off by pursuing a particular project.

As costs and benefits arise at different time periods it would be reasonable to use a discount rate which would equate them all in present value terms, but that leaves the question of which discount rate to use? There has been put forward the idea of a Social Time Preference Rate (STPR), while others suggest a Social Opportunity Cost Rate (SOCR). Present thinking is to use a test discount rate of 5% in real terms.

The whole area of cost benefit analysis and the appropriate discount rate is one that has been debated elsewhere and represents a very specialist area of study not appropriate for this text.

An example of cost benefit analysis in the public transport sector is offered in Illustration 8.5.

Illustration 8.5   Cost-benefit analysis: Victoria Line

Costs	Annual amount £m	Present value at 6% £m
Capital expenditure	—	38.81
Annual working expenses	1.413	16.16
Total costs	—	54.97

Benefits		
1 Traffic diverted to VL		
Underground: time saved	0.378	4.32
Underground: comfort/convenience	0.347	3.96
BR: time savings	0.205	2.93
Buses: time savings	0.573	6.58
Motorists: time savings	0.153	3.25
Motorists: savings in vehicle operating costs	0.377	8.02
Pedestrians: time savings	0.020	0.28
Sub-total (1)	2.055	29.34
2 Traffic not diverted to VL		
Underground: cost savings	0.150	1.72
Underground: comfort/convenience	0.457	5.22
Buses: cost savings	0.645	7.38
Road users: time savings	1.883	21.54
Road users: savings in vehicle operating costs	0.781	8.93
Sub-total (2)	3.916	44.79
3 Generated traffic		
Outer areas: time savings	0.096	1.37
Outer areas: fare savings	0.063	0.90
Outer areas: other benefits	0.375	5.36
Central area: time savings	0.056	0.80
Central area: fare savings	0.029	0.41
Central area: other benefits	0.203	2.90
Sub-total (3)	0.822	11.74
4 Terminal scrap value		0.29
Total benefits (1) + (2) + (3) + (4)	—	86.16
Net benefits		31.19

Source: *Jones and Pendlebury, 1992, p. 101*

Capital and revenue within public sector organizations

The way many public sector organizations are funded discriminates between a capital budget (for long-term assets) and a revenue budget (to meet current operational expenses). Because those budgets are separate with no provision to move funds from one budget to the other (i.e. no virements), then it is possible to have capital budgets under-spent because of the revenue consequences of spending these funds.

A hospital may have capital funds specifically allocated to fund a new maternity unit. The capital bid included all the latest baby care technology and a 'state of the art' premature unit. Such a unit will require extra, specially trained medical staff and technicians who will have to be paid from the revenue budget. If this budget is already under pressure to produce savings or greater efficiencies, the new maternity unit may not proceed because of these revenue consequences.

There may be funds available for public sector capital investments but this must be evaluated with regard to the consequences on the revenue budgets in addition to overall social benefits.

Post audit of capital investment projects

Once a project has been commissioned and running for a time it is useful to assess whether it is meeting the expectation promised at the evaluation stage, when the cash flows were estimated. Such audits may be routinely carried out after a year of operation or may be done on a random basis, or only done, in detail, for large projects. It is important post audits are carried out as they provide a link between estimated and actual performances, as in any feedback process.

Post audit provides a feedback loop for project appraisal and selection, thus ensuring that the process of project selection through to implementation can be improved. Post audit covers not only the performance of the project after commissioning but also the monitoring of expenditures during the building or acquisition stage.

Post audits perform three functions by establishing this feedback loop:

1 To improve the quality of investment decisions currently being considered. If managers know their decisions and procedures may be audited at some future time they may take greater care in the decision process. It may also inhibit the 'padding' of projects to make them acceptable.
2 To improve the quality of future investment decisions. By considering the project when it has been running for a while it is possible to reflect on the factors that have strongly affected its success or

failure. It may be that market size was critical to its success, if so, greater effort can be put into market forecasts for similar future projects.

3 To assist in taking corrective action for current projects. It may be that a current project is more or less profitable than was estimated at the appraisal stage. If more profitable, it may be useful to initiate an expansion of similar projects, while if less profitable, it may be abandoned or amended before more losses are incurred.

Summary

This chapter considered long-term decision-making, and after reading it you should be able to:

- Explain why such decisions need special techniques.
- Illustrate how the process of capital investment may be implemented.
- Using the NPV rate and the IRR rate recommend whether a project should be accepted.
- Using payback and the accounting rate of return rule indicate whether a project may be acceptable.
- Explain how cost benefit analysis is appropriate to public sector and not-for-profit organizations.
- Give three reasons why post audit is a useful feedback mechanism.

References

Anthony, R.N. (1965) In *Management Control Systems* (eds R.N. Anthony, J. Dearden and N.M. Bedford) (various editions), Irwin, Holmewood, Ill., Chapter 1

Cooper, D.J. (1975) Rationality in investment appraisal. *Accounting and Business Research*, Summer, 198−202

Kennedy, J.A. and Sugden, F. (1986) Ritual and reality in capital budgeting. *Management Accounting (UK)*, February, 34−7

King, P. (1975) Is the emphasis of capital budgeting misplaced? *Journal of Business Finance and Accounting*, 2(1), Spring, 69−82

Northcott, D. (1991) Rationality and decision making in capital budgeting. *British Accounting Review*, No. 23, 219−33

Pike, R.H. (1989) Do sophisticated capital budgeting approaches improve decision-making effectiveness? *The Engineering Economist*, 34(2), 149−61

Pike, R.H. and Dobbins, R. (1986) *Investment Decisions and Financial Strategy*, Philip Allan, London

Further reading

Jones, R. and Pendlebury, M. (1992) *Public Sector Accounting*, 3rd edn, Pitman, London, Chapter 6

Lumby, S. (1991) *Investment Appraisal and Financing Decisions*, 4th edn, Chapman and Hall, London

Puxty, A.G. and Dodds, J.C. (1991) *Financial Management Method and Meaning*, 2nd edn, Chapman and Hall, London, Chapters 4 and 5

Problems and discussion topics

1   The following is an extract from R.H. Pike (1989) 'Do Sophisticated Capital Budgeting Approaches Improve Investment Decision Making Effectiveness?' *The Engineering Economist*, 34(2), 149–61

Evaluation of control methods: trend analysis in 100 UK large firms.

Technique	1986	% usage 1981	1985
Payback	92	81	73
Average accounting rate of return	56	49	51
Internal rate of return	75	57	44
Net present value	68	39	32

The above trends suggest an increasing use of sophisticated techniques linked with an increase in payback.

You are required to explain and justify this trend, and outline its implications.

2   S.T. Ilton Co Ltd manufactures a special cheese, the current manufacturing cost and selling price of which is:

	£	£	
Selling price		200	(per 100 kg)
Variable manufacturing costs	160		
Fixed costs (based on annual output of 2,000,000 kg)	20	180	(per 100 kg)
Profit		20	(per 100 kg)

Because of the nature of the product it is only made to order. However, it is considered that the company could extend its current sales and output of 2,000,000 kg by investing in some special storage facilities. As a result, the company would be able to sell immediately from stock an additional 1,000,000 kg of cheese each year. Because the orders would be supplied immediately, the company may be able to charge a special sales premium over the existing selling price for the additional 1,000,000 kg. The premium is difficult to estimate with any certainty, it could be as high as 30% or it could be nil. The probability distribution shown below is the marketing director's best estimate of the possible sales premium likely to be obtained.

Selling price premium over current price %	Probability
0	0.20
10	0.30
20	0.30
30	0.20

The new storage facilities would incur additional fixed expenses each year of £100,000, and working capital required immediately would increase by £250,000. The total cost of the equipment would be £1,500,000, with an 8 year life and a nil scrap value.

You are required to evaluate the project to extend the storage facilities using the NPV method, assuming the company's cost of capital is 20%.

3 Bisket plc, a very large food processing company is considering a £6m. investment in one of its baked products factories. The cost includes purchase and installation of the equipment but excludes the training of operatives during the first year of operation. Training will be done on a rota basis and will cost £0.75m.

Acceptance of the project is expected to lead to massive reductions in labour cost amounting to £2m annually after year 1. More efficient operating conditions and improved quality will lead to stock reductions of £2.5m, while annual overheads will rise by £1m.

Sales are likely to be enhanced because of the firm's increased responsiveness to changes in demand and meeting specific customer requirements. Details of this and material costs are specified below.

Years	1	2	3	4	5	6
Additional sales (£m)	1.0	3.0	5.0	7.0	9.0	11.0
Additional material costs (£m)	0.5	1.5	2.5	3.5	4.5	5.5

A consultancy firm had been employed to advise on the technology and its correct implementation. The fees for this work are still outstanding and amount to £25,000.

Bisket plc pays Corporation Tax at 30%, which is paid approximately one year after the year in which the tax liability arises. Capital allowances at 25% reducing balance are available on the £6m investment, which is expected to have a 6 year life and have a residual value of £1.5m.

All figures are stated in current pounds unadjusted for expected inflation. Labour inflation is expected to be 8% p.a. while the price of other goods and services consumed by the company is expected to rise at 4% p.a. over the 6 year period. The company's monetary cost of capital is 15%, while average general inflation is expected to be 6% p.a. over the period. The current require-ment for projects is for them to provide a positive net present value.

You are required to advise the management of Bisket plc whether this opportunity should be adopted, stating any assumptions made.

9 Pricing

The aims of this chapter are to:

- Consider the environmental issues relating to pricing.
- Illustrate that price is only one variable within the marketing mix.
- Apply the different costing approaches of full cost pricing, marginal pricing and rate of return pricing to pricing issues.
- Evaluate the contribution accounting makes to the pricing decision within the organization.
- Consider different pricing objectives in relation to stages in product life cycles.
- Illustrate current developments in pricing.

Introduction

The pricing decision for any organization is crucial to its very survival. Regardless of whether that organization is producing goods or services, price multiplied by the volume of outputs sold generates turnover, or sales income, which in turn generates cash, the life blood of any organization.

While this chapter will consider the accountant's contribution to the pricing decision, it must be remembered that this only represents one partial approach to this decision. Economists and marketing specialists both have an important contribution to make to the decision of pricing a product or service, and while accounting figures may provide some of the basic input to both approaches, the actual price set is a product of many variables. The representation in Figure 9.1, which has been used in many of the chapters, is again developed here. This chapter explores the ideas of cost classification, introduced in Chapter 4, by applying the different cost models to arrive at selling prices. The Data Collection System holds information about costs which may be classified in various ways, direct and indirect or fixed and variable or controllable and uncontrollable, to mention only three. The process of accounting may assist in reaching decisions about selling prices based upon these different cost classifications. The pricing decision in the short term may differ from that in the longer term for some products; it is the use of accounting

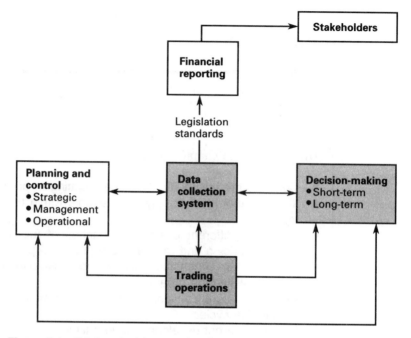

Figure 9.1 *Pricing decisions and policy*

cost data which may assist the marketing function to establish such selling prices, which over time generate surplus cash inflows and profits.

Marketing mix

Price is one of the four decisions which constitute the marketing mix, represented by the four Ps as follows:

- Product
- Place
- Promotion
- Price

Product considers issues around the design, quality and range of products or services provided. Compare any Japanese car with its full range of ancillary equipment, with VW or BMW which both offer basic equipment, but require ancillary extras to be specified at an extra cost.

Place considers where a product or service is sold and the most suitable distribution channels. Compare traditional banking through the branch networks of Lloyds or National Westminster with First Direct which has no branch infrastructure and offers 24 hour telephone banking.

Figure 9.2 *The marketing mix*

Promotion considers how and where a particular product or service may be best promoted and advertised. Designer label ladies fashions are heavily advertised in journals similar to *Vogue*, but not through *Woman's Weekly*. Similarly, professional and trade magazines are used to promote specialist services.

Price is an important factor in the marketing mix, it is not just a product of accounting, but a complex variable. Price may be perceived to be a proxy for quality, or expensive items may be seen as status symbols. The accounting numbers to be presented later in this chapter provide a guide to establishing prices for products, but these must be seen in the broader context of the marketing mix, as it is very difficult to isolate one variable from the mix.

The economist's view

The basic objective behind the literature of economics is to set a selling price which maximizes profits, and assumes that lower selling prices will generate larger volumes of sales, to provide a demand curve as depicted in Figure 9.3. Points Y and Z represent two

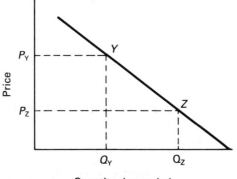

Figure 9.3 *Demand curve*

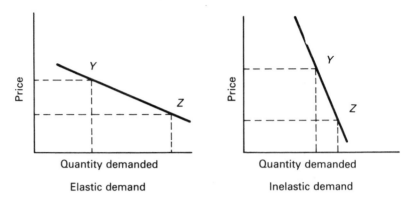

Figure 9.4   *Price elasticity of demand*

possible price and quantity combinations giving aggregate revenues of $P_Y Q_Y$ and $P_Z Q_Z$ respectively. The relationship between price changes and quantity demanded is known as the price elasticity of demand (Figure 9.4), and is reflected in the slope of the curve. If the slope of the demand curve is relatively shallow, small changes in price will produce large changes in the quantities demanded, probably because there are substitute products consumers can switch to. If the demand curve has a steep slope, consumers are reluctant to demand less even if the price has changed quite substantially.

The demand schedule for a product, if available, would be an invaluable tool for establishing optimal selling prices. While the schedule exists in economic theory, it is almost impossible to construct it in its entirety in reality. Small sections of the curve may be established by experience of operating in a particular market with a particular product, knowing how price changes affect the quantities demanded within a limited range.

If the demand curve is linked with a supply curve then an organization will be able to establish an optimal selling price and establish the quantity of goods to produce. While supply curves may be easier to establish than demand curves, the production of however many units can be sold at any particular selling price is highly problematic, the launch of a new product highlighting the problem.

Before the accountant's contribution to pricing is considered, it may be useful to look at broader issues relating to the price policy.

Factors to be considered in the pricing problem

Firm's objectives

While the economic model of supply and demand assumes profit maximization as its target, such an objective may not be pursued by individual organizations. Different objectives may be sales turnover

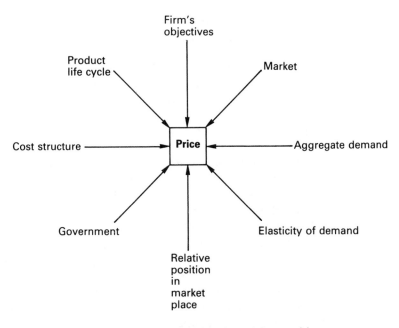

Figure 9.5 *Factors to be considered in the pricing problem*

growth, market share targets, or others relating to management, rather than other stakeholder objectives. It may be that some organizations do have profit as their main objective, others like the Co-operative Wholesale Society, while being a huge retailer, operating superstores across the country, prides itself by providing value for money shopping for its members. The issue of organizational objectives stated by marketing executives when pricing their products will be considered later in the chapter.

The market for the product or service

While some near monopoly suppliers exist in the UK, for example, British Telecom and British Gas, their prices are controlled by watch-dog bodies – Oftel and Ofgas respectively – which currently only allow them to raise prices by figures less than annual general inflation. Most companies operate in markets which have much greater competition than these two, including large companies which set the level of prices (price makers) that other smaller companies follow (price takers), or there may be many small companies operating in geographic competition, like domestic plumbers and electricians.

Aggregate demand within the economy

The British and world economies are subject to movements in the trade cycle which produce booms and slumps in aggregate demand.

The changes in aggregate demand for organizations and companies will vary with the ability to finance new acquisitions, either from cash resources or borrowing, and the perception that such acquisitions are affordable. This latter variable is a function of whether the future will provide an improvement in the individual's or company's financial position or not.

Elasticity of demand for the product

As already explained, elasticity of demand is the change in quantities demanded relative to price changes. If demand does not change relative to price the product is said to have an inelastic demand curve, while large changes in demand relative to price would indicate a highly elastic demand curve.

An example of relatively elastic products would be white kitchen appliances: because so many similar products are available, price changes making one relatively more expensive, or cheaper will mean consumers change brand, therefore making price a very important factor in this particular market. A relatively inelastic product would be gas for heating purposes: while changes in price may make consumers more economic with their use of this energy, it is hardly likely to make them switch to electricity, oil or solid fuel with the change of boiler that may require. Ofgas is not only important because of the monopoly of British Gas, it is also important because of the nature of the product and its demand curve, which could lead to high prices with only small drops in demand.

Relative position of the firm in the market place

We have already seen that some companies are price makers and others price takers, the former usually goes with large market share while the latter with small market share.

The government

Legislation of all kinds will have an effect on the cost and price of many products. While taxes on alcoholic drinks, cars, cigarettes etc. are obvious to see, welfare legislation for employees and environmental codes of conduct will produce costs that have to be recovered through revenues and profits.

Cost structure of the firm

In Chapter 7, on short-term decision-making, we considered the concept of cost-volume-profit analysis, which presented the idea of a break-even level of activity. If a company has high fixed costs its break-even activity will be high relative to a company with low fixed costs. Because a company must at least break even to survive, it is crucial that price, and hence contribution per unit are set so that break-even activity levels are reached.

Product life cycle

Within the marketing literature there is a concept of products having a finite life, and that over their life cycle, they go through different stages of development. The analysis used in this chapter will highlight four stages:

1 Introduction
2 Growth
3 Maturity
4 Saturation and decline

Pricing policies and objectives may vary with the life cycle of the product, and this specific issue will be developed after the accountant's contribution to the pricing decision has been illustrated.

Accountant's contribution to the pricing of products through cost based pricing approaches

The approaches put forward in this section relate to costing ideas developed in Chapters 4 and 7. If you need clarification of the terminology or methodology it may be useful quickly to revise these chapters.

The three methods of cost based pricing are:

- Full cost pricing
- Rate of return pricing
- Marginal pricing

Each is calculated using accounting data relating to the product cost, whether it be manufactured or within the service sector.

The most widely used approaches are, full cost pricing and rate of return pricing, which are known collectively as *cost-plus pricing*. The 'plus' element is to add a figure to cost thus ensuring the firm is selling products at a price greater than cost. These two approaches are traditional and widespread. Atkin and Skinner (1975) found that the most popular method of pricing is by the addition of a percentage (the 'plus') to cost, while Mills (1988) found that cost-related pricing methods were again most popular, being 71% in manufacturing and 68% in service companies. Mills did find, however, a 'greater tendency to modify cost-based prices by market considerations, typically with reference to competitor's prices'.

Full cost pricing

This relies on the absorption method of product costing, which attempts to charge all cost, by a series of allocations, apportionments and absorption rates to products and services. The formula for this approach is basic, while the process of calculation is cumbersome and often arbitrary.

The basic formula is as follows, using figures for illustrative purposes only:

	£ per unit
Labour costs	17.00
Material costs	15.00
Prime cost	32.00
Production overhead	
(400% of labour costs)	68.00
Production cost	100.00
Administration, selling and	
finance overhead (50% of cost)	50.00
Total cost	150.00
Mark-up (25% of total cost)	37.50
Selling price	£187.50

The derived selling price of £187.50 per unit is a product of various percentages being added to the cost to cover production and other overheads. As these overhead allocations, apportionments and absorption rates and their subsequent costs are highly dependent on capacity, the basis for the ultimate price being accurate is questionable.

In this particular example, production overheads have been charged at 400% of direct labour cost. This typifies the problem of this approach, as direct labour costs only represent a small percentage of total production costs, yet are used as a basis for charging much larger production overheads. To remedy this situation, activity based costing (ABC) approaches may be used but the basic arbitrary nature of overhead allocations remains.

The final 25% mark-up for profit is highly arbitrary and varies from industry to industry and customer to customer. It is quite common to calculate a catalogue price of £187.50 and then offer discounts to attract business.

Rate of return pricing

This is a specific application of full cost pricing, the only difference being the setting of the mark-up, or 'plus' percentage. If the performance of a company or division is assessed using return on capital employed (ROCE), then it would be sensible to set selling prices which generate the target return on capital employed required. Quite clearly, such an approach broadens the pricing objective to complement that of the organization.

If the example already quoted is developed further, we already know that the total cost per unit of production was calculated at £150.00 and sales are 1,200 units per annum. What is now required is a mark-up which provides the target return on capital employed figure. To calculate this an estimate of the value of capital employed for each type of product is required. Assuming this can be done, and if the relevant figure is £170,000 with a target return of 20%, the selling price would be as follows:

$$\% \text{ mark-up on cost} = \frac{\text{Capital employed}}{\text{Annual costs}} \times \text{target ROCE}$$

$$= \frac{£170,000}{£150 \times 1,200} \times 20\%$$

$$= 18.9\%$$

Checking back to the original selling price:

	per unit £	1,200 units £
Total cost	150.00	180,000
Mark-up at 18.9%	28.35	34,020
Selling price/revenue	£178.35	£214,020

$$\text{ROCE} = \frac{\text{Profit}}{\text{Capital employed}} = \frac{£34,020}{£170,000} = 20\%$$

Before considering marginal pricing it may be useful to highlight the problems with the two cost-plus pricing techniques. Sizer (1972) argues that accountants in multi-consumer product companies should not simply provide management with 'full unit cost estimates for evaluating alternative selling prices' because of the following drawbacks associated with both full cost and rate of return pricing.

Drawbacks of full cost and rate of return pricing

- Assumes price is a product of cost and therefore ignores demand.
- Provides no consideration of competitors' prices for similar products.
- Gives the impression that overhead allocation and capital employed are precise concepts, yet both are arbitrary.
- Costs, especially fixed costs, are long term, yet price may have to be short term in response to environmental changes.
- Ignores the non-price variables of place, promotion and product.

In fact, Sizer (1972) was reflecting earlier criticism put forward by Baxter and Oxenfelt (1968):

> the inability to estimate demand accurately and in time, scarcely excuses the substitution of cost information for demand information ... as cost gives remarkably little insight into demand.

Partly to remedy these criticisms, accountants have another approach to product cost, known as marginal pricing. This approach has already been described in Chapter 7 on short-term decision-making, where it was associated with cost-volume-profit analysis and break-even charts.

Marginal pricing (contribution costing)

As already stated, this applies the ideas of cost-volume-profit analysis to pricing decisions. The firm sets prices that will maximize contribution (sales revenue less variable costs) on the basis that fixed costs are fixed in the short term. Such an approach does not compare total cost with selling price. If volumes are sufficient to generate an adequate contribution to cover fixed costs then profit is assured, but if volumes are lower than break-even capacity then losses will be incurred.

Marginal pricing is quite often used to generate additional business to full cost business. For example, London Hotels offer cheaper week-end breaks, yet retain their week-day full cost business; British Rail, and most airlines, discount tickets to ensure capacity is taken up. Because the fixed cost base of many operations cannot be reduced, it is better to price competitively to ensure capacity is maximized.

Marginal costing if used in the above manner complements one of the tenets of marketing management: price discrimination, by selling the same product in different markets at different prices.

Mills (1988) found the highest use of marginal costing (contribution costing) by both manufacturing and service companies related to special orders which could be met from existing capacity but the

Table 9.1 *Linking sales volume and prices*

		Sales volume units				
		1,000	1,200	1,400	1,600	1,800
Price	(£)	50	49	45	40	35
Variable cost	(£)	20	20	20	20	20
Contributions per unit	(£)	30	29	25	20	15
Aggregate contribution	(£)	30,000	34,800	35,000	32,000	27,000

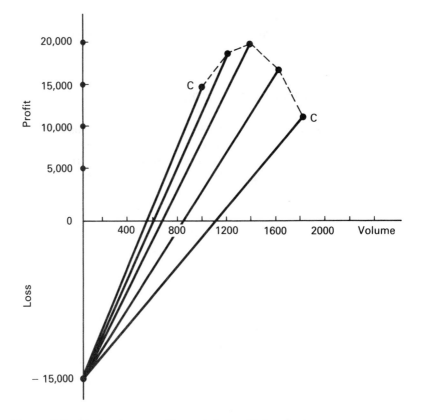

Figure 9.6 *Cost-volume-profit graph for multiple prices*

use of such a technique was not as 'high as we might be led to believe from many management accounting textbooks'.

Unlike full cost pricing, marginal pricing does make an explicit link between price and demand. Sizer (1972) develops this idea further by considering a profit-volume chart at different sales prices (and thus different contributions) for the same product and links them to estimated demand levels (see Table 9.1).

A selling price of £45 would generate the highest contribution. If fixed costs were estimated to be £15,000, then the cost-volume-profit graphs for the different prices and volume would be as shown in Figure 9.6. The aggregate profit at the different sales volume levels is represented by curve CC, the highest contribution is given by selling 1,400 units at £45 each, generating revenue of £63,000, variable costs of £28,000 and a profit of £20,000. The profit is not highly sensitive to price changes between £49 and £45 but is highly sensitive elsewhere.

This approach assumes a demand curve can be established, which we know is problematic, but it also provides management with a simple model which can be modified for changes in the two important short-term variables — sales price and sales volume. It can also be argued that such subjective estimates of a range of likely outcomes, based on the experience of managers will be superior to single value estimates for decision-making.

Illustration 9.1   Convex Ltd

Convex Ltd produces various low-priced consumer products, disposable cameras being produced in a newly acquired factory in Bridgend. The following budget has been established for the current 12 months for that factory, assuming 100,000 units can be produced.

	100,000 units £000	per unit £
Direct costs		
materials	60	0.60
labour	40	0.40
	100	1.00
Production overheads	100	1.00
Factory costs	200	2.00
Administrative and marketing		
costs	50	0.50
Full costs	250	2.50
Profit	50	0.50
Revenue	£300	£3.00

Production overheads are absorbed on the basis of 100% of direct cost, 50% being fixed, while the remainder are variable. The administrative and marketing overheads are based on 25% of factory costs and do not vary with variations in activity. Each product within Convex Ltd must provide a 20% profit margin, which is considered to provide a fair return on assets and sufficient profit for its investors. It is felt the £3.00 derived from these cost-plus calculations gives a fair and competitive selling price.

Halfway through the current year it became obvious to the senior managers of Convex Ltd that the Bridgend factory was only going to reach 75% of its expected capacity. This shortfall was not a result of production difficulties but as a result of high price competition and low general consumer spending on such 'frivolous' items.

At the same time as the sales shortfall became apparent, a national chain of newsagents approached Convex Ltd to purchase 25,000 cameras which would be sold under the chain's brand name of THIMS. The cameras would be more basic than Convex's normal product. The materials have been estimated to cost £12,000 and the labour £8,000 for the 25,000 units required.

What price should be set for the special order from the newsagent?

There are several prices which may be appropriate:

- Full cost pricing.
- Price which would enable the budgeted profit to be maintained.
- Marginal cost approach.
- If absorption rates were applied on a unit costs basis.

(a) *Full cost pricing*

	£	
Direct costs		
Materials	12,000	
Labour	8,000	
	20,000	
Production overhead	20,000	(100% × £20,000)
	40,000	
Administration and overhead	10,000	(25% × £40,000)
	50,000	
Profit	10,000	(20% × £50,000)
Selling price	£60,000	

Per unit   £60,000 ÷ 25,000 = £2.40 each

(b) *Price which would enable the budgeted profits to be maintained*

	Fixed budget	Flexed budget	Special order
Units	100,000	75,000	25,000
Direct costs			
Materials	60,000	45,000	12,000
Labour (£)	40,000	30,000	8,000
	100,000	75,000	20,000
Fixed production overhead (£)	50,000	50,000	—
Variable production overhead (£)	50,000	37,500	10,000
	200,000	162,500	30,000
Admin. and marketing (all fixed costs) (£)	50,000	50,000	—
	250,000	212,500	30,000
Profit (£)	50,000	12,500	37,500
Revenue (£)	300,000	225,000	67,500
Price per unit	£3.00	£3.00	£2.70

The figure of £2.70 is sufficient to recover the lost profit on the 75% capacity considered realistic. The behaviour of cost is recognized within the flexed budget, the fixed costs being charged to the 75% capacity as they are unavoidable within the year under consideration. The profit figures of £12,500 from existing operations and the £37,500 from the special order generate £50,000, which was required initially.

(c) *Marginal cost approach*

	£	£ per unit
Direct costs		
Materials	12,000	0.80
Labour	8,000	
	20,000	
Variable overhead	10,000	0.40
Total variable cost	30,000	1.20

Selling price to achieve break-even £30,000 ÷ 25,000 = £1.20. The selling price must be above the £1.20 if any profit is to be gained.

(d) *If absorption rates were applied on a unit basis*, the total overhead is £100,000 for production and £50,000 for administration and marketing, so the budgeted overhead rate per unit is £150,000 ÷ 100,000 units or £1.50 per unit.

For the 25,000 unit special order the costs would be:

	£	
Direct costs		
Material	12,000	
Labour	8,000	
	20,000	
Overhead	37,500	(£1.50 × 25,000 units)
	57,500	
Profit	11,500	(£57,500 × 20%)
	69,000	
Selling price	£2.76	

From the above Illustration it is clear that accounting calculations can calculate an array of prices:

  £

(a) 2.40

(b) 2.70
(c) 1.20
(d) 2.76

This range provides useful parameters for the price to be negotiated around. The marginal cost of £1.20 must be exceeded if any profit is to be made, while the £2.70 represents the price needed to attain the overall profit target of £50,000. The £2.76 can be used to demonstrate the costing procedures to the client, who may believe them to be appropriate, and feel a price of £2.70 may be fair.

The Convex case demonstrates that the accountant's contribution to the pricing decision provides limits in which negotiations about price may be conducted by supplier and customer, but other attributes of delivery, product, terms of payments may be equally important factors.

Before continuing with pricing within the private sector it may be useful to consider how pricing may be used within the public sector.

Pricing (tendering) within the public sector

Pricing (or tendering) for products and services within the public sector, and particularly within local authority direct labour organizations (DLO), has grown in importance since 1980. DLOs existed within local authorities to undertake maintenance and construction work using actual cost as a recharge for client departments within that local authority. Since the Local Government Planning and Land Act 1980, each DLO has had to operate independently from its local authority, keeping separate books of accounts and having to earn a 'real' return of 5% on the capital it employs.

Monies allocated by local authorities for maintenance and construction work cannot be used to finance DLO activities automatically, as any DLO must compete openly for local authority contracts against private sector companies. Hence the importance of pricing within DLO organizations and the use of rate of return pricing in particular.

Following the introduction of pricing and tendering for DLOs there has been a series of developments in the public sector which has necessitated the use of accounting techniques to price services that have been offered to tender against private companies. Examples include school cleaning and maintenance contracts, catering services, laundry services, refuse collection and hospital X-ray services.

In parallel with the competitive tendering for public sector work there has been the devolution of budgetary control within the sector through initiatives like the local management of schools (LMS), fund holding for GPs and the devolution of local authority tertiary colleges from local government control. These provisions have led to DLOs, National Health Service departments etc. having to tender

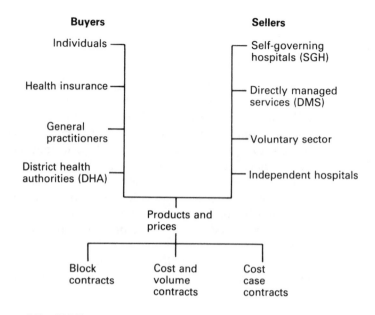

Buyers   **Sellers**

Individuals   Self-governing
                               hospitals (SGH)

Health insurance   Directly managed
                               services (DMS)

General   Voluntary sector
practitioners

District health   Independent hospitals
authorities (DHA)

Products and
prices

Block   Cost and   Cost
contracts   volume   case
                 contracts   contracts

Figure 9.7 *Bidding system*

for work at much lower levels within organizations. For example, the DLO of a local authority may in the past have tendered for *all* the school cleaning and maintenance within that local authority, but must now tender on a school by school basis, as each has its own budget and governing body to make such decisions.

The pricing of health care within the NHS is an interesting example of the use of accounting data to provide both buyers and sellers the costs of treatment-related or diagnosis-related health care. The costings for treatments will be used by district health authorities (DHAs) and general practitioners as a basis of whether to accept or reject tenders from individual suppliers of medical services; whether they are Directly Managed Services (DMS); Self Governing Hospital Trusts (SGHs) or other providers of health care. The bidding system, with its buyers and sellers, is summarized in Figure 9.7.

Having won contracts each provider will be required to ensure financial viability by linking the medical services provided with a product costing system.

Block grants: These will be for the provision of
                                a defined block of service in return
                                for an annual fee. (It is envisaged
                                that this type of contract will be
                                used to cover those care services
                                which every DHA must provide.)
Cost and volume contracts: With this type of contract, SGHs
                                and DMSs will secure a defined
                                sum for the provision of a baseline

level of activity. Beyond that level, payment will be on a cost per case basis.

Cost per case contracts: Payment will be on the basis of a sum for each case treated.

Regardless of the contract applied for, each DMS or SGH must have a sound basis upon which to base their unit costs, expenditures, prices and income levels. Instead of having conventional budgetary information dealing with expenditure over time, this will have to be related to unit costs and prices. At the heart of this is the notion that each patient who is treated in hospital must carry the cost of that treatment, which will be funded by the DHA. The cost can be generated using a database linked to the financial control system either by individual patient or ultimately by treatment or diagnosis group.

While only a basic introduction to pricing within the public sector has been possible here, its growing importance has been illustrated.

Target pricing

This technique has been widely adopted in Japan. It could be known as 'reverse costing', as a target price is suggested by marketing management prior to the product being designed and introduced. The target price is set to be competitive with existing products, or for a new product at a skimming or penetration price, but the important aspect is to set the price to achieve desired market share and volume. From the target price a profit margin is deducted to arrive at the *target cost*.

The target cost is seen as a goal to achieve at the design stage. A product development team comprising manufacturing engineers, designers, marketing, production and accountants will be charged to develop the product which will meet the desired target cost and subsequent price. The approach means that cost is engineered into the product at the design stage knowing the price will be competitive. Target pricing therefore avoids the problem of having to establish a price by cost plus pricing which may have to be modified to meet market conditions.

Pricing policies

The price decision within the marketing mix may be particularly crucial at the launch of a new product. Once the product has been launched then price becomes less crucial and becomes just one of the tactical decision variables to keep the product or service relatively competitive with its nearest rivals. If a company is selling a standard product, like central heating oil, then that company will almost certainly be a 'price taker', accepting the price given by the market place. If this is the case then the emphasis is upon efficient production rather than pricing policies.

On the launch of a new product or service a company might adopt a *price penetration* or *price skimming* policy.

Price penetration policy

A penetration pricing policy is where low prices are charged initially with a view to gaining a large market share, through rapid acceptance by consumers. Past examples of this are Bic biro pens and Bic disposable razors, while more recent examples are disposable cameras and spectacles through companies like Vision Express. Such a policy is useful when there are similar products but the market is easy to enter with a cheaper substitute. Once the company has established a large market share at the low penetration price this will deter new entrants into the market.

Price skimming policy

This is the opposite to penetration pricing. The concept is to charge high initial prices to take full advantage of the uniqueness of the product. Once this price band has been fully exploited then the price can be reduced to attract further sales and so on. It is easy to think of this type of pricing policy as 'sliding down the demand curve', initially high prices are set to attract low volumes, and gradually the price is lowered to attract extra volume over time.

Quite clearly, this policy would not be possible in a highly competitive market; the product must be unique and either (probably) be protected by patents or require vast amounts of initial capital to develop. If the latter two situations were not present, then competitors would see the high profits being made and attempt to enter the market. Recent examples of such a pricing policy have been the launch of CD players and personal computers, both now relatively inexpensive.

Having considered pricing policies at the launch of a product, it may be useful now to consider the pricing decision within the product life cycle.

Product life cycle

Products and services typically go through a series of distinct phases, from introduction, to growth, through maturity and eventually to saturation and decline. These phases are termed the *product life cycle* (Figure 9.8).

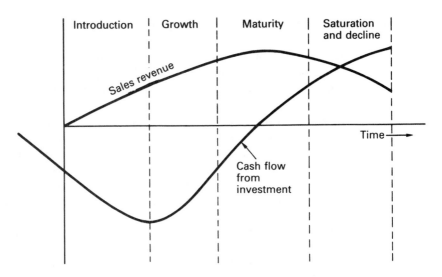

Figure 9.8 *Product life cycle*

The concept of the product life cycle has several major characteristics:

- That products have limited lives, and that a product's life can be depicted by a curve tracing its sales history.
- That clear stages in the sales history can be recognized.
- That profit per unit will vary over the life cycle, probably falling after the 'growth' stage.
- That the cash recovery from the investment in the product complements the long-term decision-making process through techniques like payback and net present value.

Table 9.2 *Features of the stages within the product life cycle*

	Introduction	Growth	Maturity	Saturation and decline
Sales	Low	Rising rapidly	Sales peak	Decline
Cash flow	Negative initially	Positive cash flows	Positive cash flows	Positive cash flows
Prices	High	Falling	Low	Falling
Competitors	Few	Growing number	Competition amongst rivals	Declining numbers
Profit per unit	Negative	High and rising	Average	Declining

Pricing objectives and the product life cycle

The concept of the product life cycle links into pricing issues by considering the pricing objectives being pursued at any particular phase and the resulting market share that price generates.

Japanese companies have a tendency to use penetration pricing when entering new markets to gain initial market share. Once established they then amend their objectives to become more profit orientated. It makes sense to have the objective of gaining market share in the new, growth markets, where most companies are experiencing growth, but not in a mature market where any gain in market share for one company can only be achieved by the loss of market share of another.

Both situations illustrate the link between price and market share. The former may be better illustrated by considering the Honda sales policy in the UK. Both Honda motor cycles and motor cars were introduced at relatively cheap prices from the early 1970s onwards but since the mid 1980s the products and their prices have changed. Honda are now selling relatively expensive motor cycles and motor cars in the UK and experiencing high profits per unit.

There have been numerous surveys linking pricing objectives and the relative phase of the product life cycle. A UK study by Jobber and Hooley (1987) is worth considering. Their study was based on a questionnaire sent to members of the Institute of Marketing, in which respondents were asked to rank the main pricing objectives and the relative nature of the major market in which they operated. The pricing objectives were:

Profit maximization
Market share attainment
Maximize current sales revenue
Ensure adequate cash flow
Target profit attainment

The results are presented in Table 9.3.

Table 9.3 demonstrates that profit maximization is the dominant objective followed by target profit attainment. Within each phase of the product life cycle these two objectives generally hold, although the latter – target profit attainment – is more dominant for products after the emerging phase.

Shipley (1981), when considering pricing objectives of British manufacturing firms, found that most firms had more than one pricing goal, like the Jobber and Hooley study, and that two-thirds specified a target profit or return on capital employed as their principle objective. He also found that a popular pricing goal was a 'price fair to the firm and the customer'.

Table 9.3 *Prime pricing objectives*

	All	By stage of market evolution				By size of firm (£m)		
					% Respondents			
		Emerging	Growth	Mature	Decline	Below 2.50	2.5 to 20	Above 20
Profit maximization	40.2	41.3	40.9	38.8	41.8	45.3	44.9	39.2
Market share attainment	16.6	11.9	16.8	17.7	15.2	13.0	16.0	22.3
Maximize current sales revenue	9.1	13.0	5.7	9.4	12.4	9.7	11.1	8.6
Ensure adequate cash flow	8.0	17.4	8.7	5.6	9.8	13.9	6.3	5.5
Target profit attainment	26.0	16.3	27.8	28.4	20.7	22.3	27.0	32.7

(Source: *Jobber and Hooley, 1987*)

Summary

In this chapter we have seen that any pricing decision is complex and only one part of the total product mix. The financial manager's contribution to the pricing decision may help set price parameters for marketing experts to work within. To adopt accounting techniques in isolation from other factors will result in prices that are unrelated to the market in general and to competitors' prices in particular.

After reading this chapter you should be able to:

- Illustrate the environmental issues relating to product pricing.
- Consider pricing within the broader ideas of the marketing mix.
- Apply the different costing approaches of absorption, marginal and return on capital employed to pricing issues.
- Evaluate how accountants may contribute to the pricing decision.
- Explain how pricing objectives may vary with the phases of the product life cycle.
- Consider current pricing issues of companies and organizations with relation to the issues raised within this chapter.

References

Atkin, B. and Skinner, R. (1975) *How British Industry Prices*, Industrial Market Research Ltd.

Baxter, W.T. and Oxenfelt, A.R. (1968) Approaches to pricing: economist versus accountant. Reprinted in G.J. Benston (1977) *Contemporary Cost Accounting and Control*, 2nd edn.

Jobber, D. and Hooley, G. (1987) Price behaviour in the UK manufacturing and service industries. *Managerial and Decision Economics*, 8 (2), pp. 167–71

Mills, R.W. (1988) Pricing decision in UK manufacturing and service companies. *Management Accounting (UK)*, November, pp. 38–9

Shipley, D.D. (1981) Pricing objectives in British manufacturing industry. *Journal of Industrial Economics*, 29, pp. 429–43

Sizer, J. (1972) Accountants, product managers and selling price in multi-consumer product firms. *Journal of Business Finance*, Spring (summarized in Size, J. *An Insight into Management Accounting*, Penguin, Harmondsworth, various editions, 1969 onwards)

Further reading

Arnold, J. and Hope, T. (1990) *Accounting for Management Decisions*, 2nd edn., Prentice Hall, Englewood Cliffs, NJ, Chapter 7

Dorward, N. (1987) *The Pricing Decision: Economic Theory and Business Practice*, Harper and Row, New York

Problems and discussion topics

1 Hisec plc is a divisionalized manufacturer and assembling company in which each division is regarded as a profit centre. The Digital Measurement Division is one of six divisions and is headed by a Divisional Managing Director, who reports directly to the main board of Hisec plc.

   The division manufactures three main products which provide detailed electronic measurement devices for manufacturing processes and outputs. Because of the rapidly changing technology within microelectronics and computer applications the Digital Measurement Division is particularly conscious of its product offering.

   The budget committee within the division has just received the following initial draft master budgets for the next financial year. This usually forms a basis for negotiation within the division before an agreed budget is submitted to the main board of Hisec plc.

Initial draft master budget by product

	Product MXR	E210	Omega	Total
Sales (units)	1,000	400	100	–
	£000	£000	£000	£000
Sales	4,000	3,200	800	8,000
Variable costs	–	–	–	–
Materials	800	320	120	1,240
Labour	640	400	160	1,200
Overheads	160	80	40	280
	1,600	800	320	2,720

Contribution	2,400	2,400	480	5,280
Fixed costs				
Manufacturing				840
Administration				720
Selling and distribution				480
Research and development				80
				2,120
Profit				3,160

At the meeting of the budget committee, it was decided that revisions should be made to the initial draft budget in the light of information submitted by the marketing manager, who maintains that the product market is becoming more competitive, particularly with the development of European companies entering the UK market.

MXR was introduced on to the market several years ago and although it is still a well-established product, it is considered to be approaching the decline stage of its life cycle. A decision is made to manage MXR as a 'Cash Cow' and maximize the profit it makes. Market research indicates that price elasticity of demand only applies to price increases. If the price is reduced, this is likely to provoke a price war. However, for every £100 increase in price, demand is likely to diminish by 50 units.

E210 is becoming well established in the market where demand is increasing, although competition is beginning to have some impact. A policy of price skimming has been in operation since the launch of E210. The market is expanding but is subject to increasing competition and management feel the time is now right for a price reduction. Market research indicates that every price reduction of £500 per unit would increase demand by 50 units, although this level of elasticity would only apply up to a 50% increase above the levels in the draft budget. Above this level, competitors are likely to retaliate. The decision is made to manage E210 as a 'Rising Star' and expand sales units by 50% by reducing the price.

Omega is a newly developed product that was recently launched by the division. Although competition is currently insignificant, it is expected to increase in the next year and a decision is made to adopt a policy of price penetration. The selling price is to be adjusted to give a contribution/sales ratio of 70%. Demand is expected to fall, resulting in a 5% reduction of original units.

As a result of the above changes, fixed costs are expected to be changed as follows:

Manufacturing overheads	5% decrease
Administration	No change
Selling and distribution	10% increase
Research and development	No change

You are required to:

(a) Outline the scope and purpose of the annual budget of the Digital Measurement Division in the context of the company's long-term planning, decision-making and control.
(b) Use the information provided to:
   (i) prepare a statement to show for each product: the selling price, variable cost and contribution per unit;
   (ii) calculate the sales volumes needed to comply with the decisions made at the budget committee meeting;
   (iii) re-draft the master budget to incorporate these decisions for submission to the next budget committee meeting.
(c) Briefly comment on the proposed revisions.

2 Fred Pearson was pleased with his new appointment as Management Accountant to Woodhouse Ltd. It was his first really important job since qualifying and at the final interview he had been impressed by the progressive attitude of Mr McKay, the Managing Director.

Mr McKay had developed a thermostat for use in industrial heating systems, and had founded Woodhouse to manufacture it. This single product formed the whole of the business of Woodhouse. A similar product, however, was produced by two other companies in Britain. In spite of this competition, Woodhouse had achieved steady growth in sales volume and profitability, due in no small part to Mr McKay's managerial expertise.

After the May budget meeting, Mr McKay took Fred to one side and expressed satisfaction with the improvements Fred had incorporated into the accounting information system at Woodhouse. Mr McKay then began to outline his plans for the firm's future. He pointed out that the present rate of growth was expected to continue into the foreseeable future, and that total demand for thermostats in the industrial field had only been partially fulfilled, even though Woodhouse's competitors had, between them, the largest share of the market.

He told Fred that the board of directors had reached a critical stage in their deliberations about the future and were undecided whether to continue the present policy of gradual sustained growth, or to follow Mr McKay's recommendation, which was to seize market leadership in price and volume as soon as possible. The board, added Mr McKay, agreed that this plan would involve greater risk, but as the firm was working at full capacity now, an expansion of the present production facilities was inevitable, and if the present growth rate was to be maintained.

If a final decision were not delayed too long, any new building work which might need to be done could be completed and the new plant could be ready for operation within 18 months, which would be March 1994.

Finally, Mr McKay stated that he had asked the Marketing Department to prepare some forecasts of sales quantity and prices based on a number of possible alternatives. The study was nearing completion and would need to be evaluated financially.

Fred was then told that he would be expected to carry out the evaluation when the information from the Marketing Department became available. Within a week from the day of the conversation, Fred received the following letter from Mr McKay.

WOODHOUSE LIMITED
Internal Memo

From: N McKay   August 1992
To: F Pearson
Subject: Expansion Plans

During our talk after the Budget meeting last week, I mentioned that the Marketing Department would soon be completing their sales forecast study.

This has now been accomplished and four alternative courses of action are possible; these are:

PLAN A
Continue operations as at present, utilizing existing facilities and producing 500,000 units (the same as the current sales level) with no change in the present selling price of £5 per unit.
PLAN B
Expand sales by 7% to 535,000 from January 1993 and maintain the present selling price of £5 per unit. The increased production demand would be met by working at weekends, which will naturally increase the cost of both operating and supervisory labour.
PLAN C
Increase output by 15% to bring annual sales up to 575,000 by a small expansion of our production facilities and reduce the selling price to £4.8 in order to sell all the units produced. This plan could commence from October 1993.
PLAN D
Carry out an intensive modernization programme as well as expanding the size of our present factory to bring production up to 600,000 units. Selling price would be reduced to £4.7 per unit so

that a much greater share of the market can be captured. Modernization should bring about substantial savings in labour costs and some reduction in material prices should be possible due to larger purchases. During modernization Plan A would have to operate.

Could you prepare a report outlining the comparative advantages/disadvantages of each plan? Which plan would you recommend, and why? How would each alternative affect our break-even position?
I know that there are other factors to be considered apart from the pure financial ones with which we are presently concerned; could you let me have your views on this aspect too.
Mr Johnson in the Work Study Department will give you all the information you need about labour requirements, and Mr Hayes in Production Engineering possesses full details of building costs and the type of equipment we expect to use (including capital and operating costs).
If you need any further information let me know.

N McKay
Managing Director

Fred got down to the task at once and produced the following analysis of the current year's profit and loss account:

	£	£	
Sales		2,500,000	
Direct materials	400,000		
Direct labour	500,000		
Prime cost	900,000		100%
Production overhead	750,000		33.3%
Factory cost	1,650,000		
Administrative overhead	400,000		12.5%
Cost of finished goods	2,050,000		
Selling and distribution overhead	200,000		25%
Cost of sales		2,250,000	
Profit		£250,000	

The percentages on the right are Fred's estimate of the degree of variability of the items concerned in relation to sales volume.
The effect on cost of the alternative plans could not be calculated until after discussions with Work Study, Production

Engineering, etc. However, Fred expected to have all the relevant cost information available by September 1992.

Fred collected the relevant cost details of the alternative plans:

PLAN B: There would be a 10% increase in labour costs per unit because of increases in rates and bonuses to achieve the increase in production. There would also be a £20,000 per annum increase in fixed production overhead due to extra pay to supervisors, service staff etc.

PLAN C: There would be no effect on costs apart from an annual increase of £100,000 in production overhead fixed costs.

PLAN D: The use of up-to-date production equipment would reduce material and labour costs per unit by 25% and 20% respectively. Additional depreciation and production overhead would increase annual fixed costs by £260,000. The additional capital investment necessary for Plan D would be £600,000.

You are required to prepare Fred Pearson's report to Mr McKay. Your report should incorporate.

(i) The relative profitability of each option.
(ii) The break-even point and margin of safety.
(iii) Details of other information (particularly for Plan D) you consider necessary before a decision can be made on the best option.
(iv) A recommendation, with brief notes of explanation, on which plan would be most advantageous to the firm.

3 Dartmoor Ltd is able to produce four products, and is planning its production mix for the next period. Estimated costs, sales, and production data are given below:

	Product			
£ per unit	W	X	Y	Z
Direct materials	12	36	14	24
Direct labour	9	6	18	15
Variable overhead	9	8	9	11
Selling price	36	60	50	60

Total fixed costs are estimated to be £150,000 per annum which are anticipated to be absorbed at £7.50 per unit of each product.

Resources/unit				
Labour (hours)	3	2	6	5
Materials (kg)	1	3	2	2

Maximum demand has been estimated by the sales manager at 5,000 units for each product.

(a) Calculate the profit Dartmoor Ltd would earn if the company sold the maximum possible of each product.

(b) The particular labour skill required is in short supply and it is not anticipated that further employees could be recruited and trained in the following year, consequently the labour hours available are restricted to 72,000 per annum.

    (i) Calculate the optimum sales volume that would maximize profit subject to this constraint — what would this profit be?

    (ii) How much per hour would it be worth to obtain additional labour?

(c) Consider how you would calculate the cost to the company of one hour's worth of wasted or idle time.

(d) Exmoor Ltd (a small engineering company) has agreed to supply 5,000 units of product X at a fixed price of £48 each.

    (i) Is the offer worth pursuing and why?

    (ii) What non-monetary factors should be considered in adopting such a contract?

10 Performance measurement and transfer pricing in divisionalized organizations

---

The aims of this chapter are to:

- Introduce the ideas of differentiation and decentralization.
- Provide an understanding of why organizations form divisions and the nature of such divisions.
- Introduce and explain traditional accounting measures of divisional performance.
- Illustrate and explain the limitations of the traditional accounting measures of divisional performance.
- Develop the idea of using non-financial measures of performance together with financial measures of performance in order to provide a balanced view of performance.
- Promote the idea that measures of performance should be linked to the strategy of the organization.
- Illustrate issues of performance measurement in service and public sector organizations.
- Introduce and explain the nature of a transfer pricing system within organizations.
- Identify the objectives of a transfer pricing system and the difficulty of meeting all of the objectives with any one transfer pricing method.
- Evaluate the suggested methods of transfer pricing for organizations.

Introduction

This chapter concerns itself with performance measurement and transfer pricing issues within divisionalized organizations. In Chapter 5 we introduced the idea of a management control system made up of a management control structure and a management control process. Management control structure focuses on various types of responsibility centres (cost centres, revenue centres, profit centres, investment centres or strategic business units). The management control process involves both formal and informal communication and interaction between managers. Chapter 5 concentrated on the budgeting part of the management control process. In this particular chapter we are looking at issues of both structure and process as well as the inter-relationship between the two. The discussion on structure will concentrate on a divisional organization. Discussion on process revolves around the development, within a divisionalized structure, of both performance measurement and transfer pricing systems. We will start by looking at the two key concepts of differentiation and decentralization.

Differentiation and decentralization

Differentiation is concerned with the way in which an organization structures itself and decentralization is concerned with the way in which the organization allocates responsibility for decision-making. An organization differentiates into sub-units so that each faces a more homogeneous and manageable environment. Differentiation can take many forms but the two most popular forms are differentiation by function and differentiation by product. Differentiation determines organizational structure, the scope of each unit and its potential range of activities. However, another key element in describing the activities of any responsibility unit is the extent to which it is allocated responsibility. Thus, while differentiation determines what each responsibility unit is potentially capable of doing, it is decentralization that determines what decisions it is accountable for.

Decentralization determines the range of discretion allowed each sub-unit. It is also important to recognize that an organization's planning and control system is highly dependent on the structure of that organization and the degree of responsibility assigned to the sub-units that comprise it. Therefore, the type of differentiation and the degree of decentralization are important factors which determine management control structure. This relationship is shown in Figure 10.1.

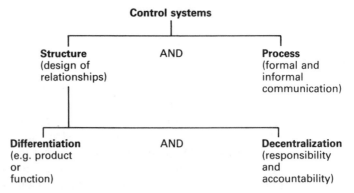

Figure 10.1 *Management control system*

Having identified the importance of differentiation and decentralization in determining management control structure, we are now going to take the concept a stage further by introducing the idea of divisionalization.

Divisionalization

Early in the chapter we identified that organizations can differentiate in numerous ways, with the most popular probably being by function and product. In order to develop the topic further we will start off with a small organization producing one product. In this situation the organization will probably be structured in a functional way (Figure 10.2).

It is easier to look at a simple functional organization structure initially and then move on to a more complex divisionalized structure. In this particular situation the owner/managing director will have to decide what decisions he or she will delegate to the managers of the different functional departments (Production, Sales, Finance and Personnel). For instance, the production department could be classed as a cost centre with the manager being allowed to take decisions relating to costs within the responsibility unit. The sales department may be classed as a revenue centre with the manager taking responsibility for revenue generation within the organization. Another important issue is the relationship between the nature of the reponsibility centre and the measures used to judge the performance of the manager.

At this stage we are concentrating only on financial measures of performance and it is necessary to match the financial measure of performance with the appropriate degree of decentralization. To place a manager in charge of a cost centre implies that their performance will be evaluated largely in terms of some measure of cost. It will rarely be possible to achieve a perfect measure of managerial performance since financial measures of performance are necessarily limited in scope and also have a short-term stress associated with them. The extent to which decentralization is feasible will in part depend on whether satisfactory measures of performance can be developed for managers so that control can be exercised. A key issue here is the fact that the benefits derived from delegating the decisions should exceed the potential costs associated with such delegation.

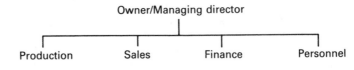

Figure 10.2 *Functional organization*

We started off with a small organization producing one product which has been structured on the basis of the different functions within the organization. A feature of functional organizations is that they usually have a fairly limited degree of diversification. However, the further a functional organization attempts to diversify, the more likely that the organization will become less effective. As diversification proceeds in a functional organization, each function of the business becomes more and more complex. This increases the difficulty of inter- and intra-functional coordination, and decision-making becomes increasingly formalized and committee based. Any conflicts between functions must be resolved by top management. The effect of this may be a slow response to environmental change owing to slow and cumbersome decision-making procedures. Figure 10.3 shows a situation where the Functional structure is maintained even though the organization is now producing and selling more than one product.

An alternative way of dealing with this situation would be to divisionalize the organization on the basis of product groups. In this situation each divisional general manager is responsible for all operations relating to his or her product. Within each division it is likely that there will be a functional structure. This situation is shown in Figure 10.4.

By combining the closely related production and marketing activities of a product group under a divisional general manager, it is potentially easier to identify the responsibilities of the divisional general manager and thereby achieve accountability. Generally, a divisionalized organizational structure will lead to a decentralization of the decision-making process.

The only functions shown in Figures 10.3 and 10.4 are marketing and production. This is obviously an over-simplification and other functional areas would need to be included within the organizations depicted. The functions of finance and personnel would need to be included somewhere within the organization structure. An interesting issue here would surround the level of decentralization of decisions about finance and personnel within the organization. If each of the divisions are classified as profit centres or investment

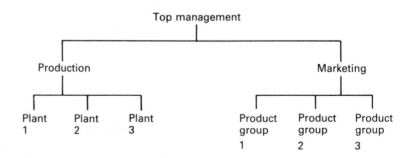

Figure 10.3 *Complex functional structure*

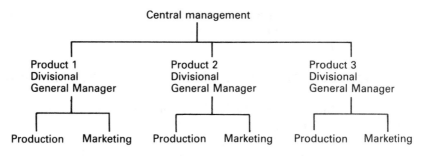

Figure 10.4 *Divisional organization*

centres there would need to be agreement on the appropriate level of support within the divisions in terms of financial and personnel support.

Earlier we mentioned that a decision needs to be taken on whether the benefits derived from delegating the decisions exceed the potential costs associated with such delegation. This particular issue will now be developed by looking at the advantages and problems associated with divisionalization.

Advantages and problems associated with divisionalization

Divisionalization can improve the decision-making process both from the point of view of the speed of the decision and the quality of the decision. Speed is improved because decisions can be taken at a divisional level without the need to pass all decisions on to a central management function. Quality of decision-making is improved because decisions are made by managers who are more familiar with the product area and the related environment. Motivation is improved because managers are given more responsibility. It is also argued that central management can spend more time concentrating on strategic issues for the group as a whole.

There are, however, potential problems associated with divisionalization. Divisionalization may result in duplication of job functions between the various divisions and the centre. This obviously needs careful planning to ensure that appropriate support levels are available where they are required. Another problem with divisionalization is that sub-optimal decisions may be taken within the divisions. Divisional managers may be encouraged to take action which will increase their own profits at the expense of the profits of other divisions and the organization as a whole. This is an issue we will develop further when we look at both financial measures of performance and transfer pricing.

Divisionalization therefore has both potential benefits and problems and it is up to the management team to decide on the appropriate degree of differentiation and decentralization within a particular organization. For our part, we will continue to assume that a divisional structure is in place and go on to look at the traditional accounting measures of performance.

Traditional accounting measures of divisional performance

In this section we will assume that an organization is divisionalized and that each division is considered to be either a profit centre or an investment centre.

If the responsibility unit is a profit centre, then absolute profit is an appropriate measure of performance. There are, however, problems concerning profit measurement, and issues such as common costs, common revenues and transfer prices have to be looked at when measuring the profit performance of a profit centre in a divisionalized company. There are also problems of definition since absolute profit can be defined in many ways.

The profit used could be the *divisional profit* before taxes. There are arguments which suggest that, if we are measuring the performance of a divisional manager, the profit used should be the *controllable profit* which only takes into account items that the manager can control. Another suggestion is that *contribution* should be used rather than profit. It can therefore be seen that there are problems with this measure and this has led to other measures being used.

Another profit measure suggested for profit centres is the use of *percentage profit margin*. This is often referred to as *return on sales* and refers to profit as a percentage of sales revenue. This measure has the advantage of relating profit to sales but has the disadvantage of being a ratio rather than an absolute amount. It also suffers from similar problems to absolute profit in terms of common costs, common revenues and transfer prices. It also suffers from the same problem of definition as absolute profit.

It is interesting to note though that, in a survey of Japanese management accounting by Scarborough *et al.* (1991), profit was the primary financial measure of performance in Japanese companies. Return on sales was the next most popular measure and the authors of that particular study suggested that there was a close link between the use of return on sales as a performance measure and target costing as a planning tool. The least favoured financial measure of performance in Japan, according to Scarborough *et al.*, was *return on investment*. Return on investment, which is popular in the West, was found to be used by less than 20% of Japanese companies in the survey.

Return on investment (ROI)

ROI is suggested as an appropriate financial measure of performance when the responsibility unit is designated as an investment centre.

It is calculated by dividing the profit into the capital invested in the division.

	Division A	Division B
Capital invested (£000)	1,000	5,000
Divisional profit (£000)	200	750
Return on investment (ROI)	20%	15%

Return on capital employed (ROCE) was introduced in Chapter 3; ROI is basically the same calculation. ROI is a popular measure of divisional performance in the United Kingdom. Its popularity is probably due to the following factors:

- It is a financial measure which is widely used and understood by managers.
- As a ratio, it can be used for inter-division and inter-firm comparisons. ROI for a division can be compared with the return from other divisions within the group or with companies outside the group.
- It focuses attention on both assets and profits.
- It is a comprehensive measure – all decisions are eventually reflected in it.

Despite these advantages, ROI does have many problems and limitations:

- ROI is a ratio and usually a divisional general manager is required to maintain or improve on his ROI target. A divisional general manager may be able to maintain his ROI by replacing assets as necessary and making process improvements. There is no strong encouragement for him to make the division grow in size. One of the possible reasons why many companies still rely on absolute profits as a measure of performance may be the incentive for growth which it brings. Absolute measures may generate a stronger incentive for growth than relative ones.
- As with profits, problems of definition arise when calculating ROI. Woodward (1991) discusses this particular issue at length and raises many interesting points. Is total assets, net assets (total assets less total liabilities) or fixed assets plus current assets the correct interpretation of divisional investment? Should fixed assets be included at historic cost, net book value or an 'appraised' value. How does one deal with central assets which are shared between the divisions? Should the investment base be calculated at the beginning or end of the period, or is an average figure more appropriate? What is the most appropriate profit figure to use? Since there are numerous possible definitions, care has to be taken when using ROI for comparison purposes.

- ROI can lead to sub-optimization of decisions. Divisional managers may reject projects which are in the company's best interests (e.g. projects that give a positive net present value) because of the effect that project would have on the divisional return on investment. This particular situation is highlighted in Illustration 10.1.

Illustration 10.1 P Division of Seago Company

The managers of P division of Seago Company produced the following budgeted profit statement for the next financial year:

P Division budgeted profit statement for the year ended
31 December 1993

	£000
Sales	1,000
Variable costs	500
Contribution margin	500
Fixed costs	300
Profit	200
Capital invested in the division	1,000
ROI	20%

Divisional managers at Seago Company are paid a bonus based on meeting their budgeted ROI target. Therefore at P Division the division must achieve an actual ROI of 20% to obtain a bonus at the end of the year.

The managers of P Division are now considering a new capital investment opportunity which was not included in the original budget for 1993. Details of the capital investment project are as follows:

	£000
Capital investment cost	150
Annual profit	25

The asset will have a 4 year life and the company cost of capital is 15%.

Consider whether, as the manager of P Division, you would accept or reject the investment opportunity; and as the Chief Executive of Seago Company, whether you would accept or reject the investment opportunity.

From a divisional manager's perspective, if everything else goes as budgeted and the investment opportunity is taken by the managers of P Division, the actual results for P Division for 1993 would be as follows:

	Budget £000	New investment £000	Actual £000
Profit	200	25	225
Capital invested	1,000	150	1,150
ROI	20%		19.57%

The inclusion of the new investment opportunity would mean that divisional managers in P Division would not receive their bonus. This is because the ROI figure for the division has reduced from 20% to 19.57%. Since many capital investment opportunities are initiated from the division, it is likely that the Seago central management team may never become aware of the investment opportunity.

If the Chief Executive of Seago had become aware of the investment opportunity, the factor to be considered would be the net present value of the project.

			£000
Cash outflow	Year	0	(150)
Cash inflows	Year	1	62.5
		2	62.5
		3	62.5
		4	62.5

Present value of cash inflows = 62,500 × 2.855
= £178,437.5

Net present value = £28,437.5

Since the project gives a positive net present value, the Chief Executive of Seago Company would consider the project to be a good one and worth undertaking.

Explanatory notes on net present value calculation:

Annual cashflow = Profit and depreciation
= 25,000 + (150,000 ÷ 4)
= 62,500

The cumulative present value factor for 4 years at a 15% cost of capital is 2.855.

As shown in Illustration 10.1, the divisional managers at P division of Seago Company would probably reject the opportunity to invest in the new project because of the adverse effect it would have on the divisional ROI. On the other hand, the Chief Executive of Seago Company would probably approve of the project because of the positive net present value. In the calculation of ROI, depreciation has been charged against the profits for the year while the capital invested in the division has been valued at

beginning of year figures. Over time, because of the nature of the ROI calculation, the ROI will improve because the asset value will go down as it is further depreciated and the profit figure will remain the same. However, it is the impact on the first year which is all important and, as shown in our example, dysfunctional decisions can take place as a result of the use of ROI as a divisional performance measure.
- ROI encourages managers to pursue short-term goals.
- ROI is just one measure of performance and as such presents a narrow view of objectives. This particular aspect will be developed later in the chapter.

One proposed solution to the difficulties outlined above is to change the basis of evaluation from ROI to *residual income,* which we will now consider.

Residual income

Residual income is defined as the difference between the divisional profit and an imputed interest charge based on the assets used in the division. The imputed interest charge is a cost of capital charge on the assets used in the division. An example of the residual income calculation is shown below.

	Division A	Division B
Capital invested (£000)	1,000	5,000
Divisional profit (£000)	200	750
Cost of capital 15%		
Divisional profit	200	750
Cost of capital charge		
15% × 1,000	150	
15% × 5,000		750
Residual income	50	—

Residual Income has a number of advantages and these are listed below:

- If residual income is used as the financial measure of performance, there is a greater possibility that managers will be encouraged, when acting in their own best interests, also to act in the best interests of the company as a whole. This is highlighted in Illustration 10.2, which uses the data from Illustration 10.1.

Illustration 10.2 Residual income calculation of P Division of Seago Company

Using the data presented in Illustration 10.1, the budgeted residual income calculation for P Division is as follows:

	£
Budgeted profit	200,000
Cost of capital charge	
15% × £1,000,000	150,000
Budgeted residual	
income	50,000

Inclusion of the capital project would result in the following actual figures:

	Budget £	New investment £	Actual £
Profit	200,000	25,000	225,000
Cost of capital charge			
15% of £1,150,000			172,500
Actual residual income			52,500

The residual income has therefore improved as a result of the inclusion of the new project and therefore the divisional managers would be encouraged to make the same decision as the Chief Executive of Seago Company.

Goal congruence has therefore occurred in this particular situation. It is important to note, however, that short-run residual income may not always give the same decision advice as net present value. An example of such a situation where consistency does not occur is included in the problems and discussion topics at the end of the chapter.

- The performance measure is now in absolute terms and growth is encouraged.
- Long-run residual income is the counterpart of the net present value rule.
- Different cost of capital charges can be applied to different assets. The residual income measure enables different risk-adjusted cost of capital charges to be incorporated into the calculation.

Despite these advantages, residual income also has some problems and limitations:

- As mentioned above, short-run residual income may not always be the counterpart of the net present value rule. A lot depends on the timing of the cashflows and the method of depreciation used.
- The calculation favours bigger divisions when divisions are being ranked.
- Residual income has the same problems of definition as occurred for ROI.
- It has the same short-term stress as other financial measures of performance.
- Residual income is just one measure of performance and as such presents a narrow view of objectives. This particular aspect will be developed later in the chapter.

Having considered four main financial measures of performance it is now useful to re-emphasize some of the general problems associated with such measures.

Limitations of financial measures of performance

Financial measures of performance tend to concentrate on the short term (i.e. the effect of actions on one year's profits, ROI or residual income). Projects that harm short-term financial performance are likely to be held back by the divisional management team unless specific provision is made for them in the capital budgeting process. Financial texts place much stress on the achievement of goal congruence by which is meant that the divisional managers make decisions which are consistent with the achievement of a corporate financial objective. This idea ignores the fact that organizations, and units of them, have multiple objectives with many of these objectives not being easily measurable in financial terms. To use one key measure of financial performance is almost sure to produce dys-functional behaviour as regards one or more other objectives. Other objectives may relate to sales growth, market share, employee relations, quality or social responsibility.

So far we have implicitly considered those companies and divisions where decentralization is still relatively restricted to operating decisions and some capital expenditure. When the company is still small enough, this degree of decentralization may be satisfactory. However, many large companies have grown in size through con-centric diversification and conglomerate diversification. Concentric diversification involves similar customer/new product and new customer/related technology. Conglomerate diversification involves a move into areas of unrelated products or customers. When a company indulges in such extreme forms of diversification, problems are created for central management as regards strategic decision-making.

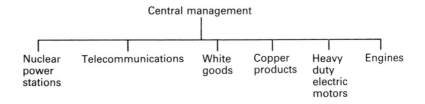

Figure 10.5 *Conglomerate organization*

- It becomes impossible to acquire sufficient knowledge of each industry and industrial sector to be able to decide the research and development, marketing, production and purchasing strategies for each division.
- To get involved in such strategy decisions for each different division may involve central management losing control of the general direction of the group as a whole. Figure 10.5 highlights the organization chart for an organization in such a position.
- In such circumstances central management are forced to delegate a degree of strategic decision-making. The large and more diversified the group, the more must be delegated. To cope with this degree of decentralization, a responsibility centre above that of an investment centre has been created – the strategic business unit (SBU). In the case of a strategic business unit, performance should be measured on the basis of the strategy being followed by that particular division. It is likely that the sole use of a financial measure of performance would be inappropriate in such a situation.

We first made reference to the use of non-financial measures of performance in Chapter 5, when we were looking at budgeting. It is to the use of these non-financial measures of performance that we will now turn. Such measures need to relate to the strategy of the organization or division concerned and are often associated with the idea of world class performance.

Non-financial measures of performance

As mentioned in Chapter 1, Johnson and Kaplan (1987) expressed concern about the way management accounting had lost its way. They argued that management accounting had lost its relevance to modern day manufacturing and that techniques and ideas developed early in the twentieth century were still being used today in an unmodified form. The need to produce performance measurement systems that support world class performance initiatives within organizations has become a major topic of concern for managers within organizations. Contact with part-time postgraduate students over the past few years has reinforced the view that this is a key area of development need within organizations.

The need to bring non-financial measures into the performance measurement area was highlighted as early as 1979 in work by Parker:

> If accountants recognize that the performance of divisions can only be judged in relation to the whole corporate goal set, then they must be prepared to reject any divisional profit measure as a sole test of performance. (1979: 313)

Parker suggested that organizations should move beyond a single divisional profit based index to provide an expanded number of measures of divisional performance, which accounts for a broader range of success criteria. He suggested the following as possible additions to the profit/ROI measure:

- Financial management ability – stock and asset turnover, gearing ratio, sources and applications of funds, fixed asset statistics such as age, maintenance expenditure, depreciation policies.
- Profit before interest and tax per employee.
- Marketing – sales volume, market share, sales effort, indicators (e.g. visits per customer).
- Research and development cost to sales; research and development cost per employee, project performance indicators.
- Social responsibility – social budget, narrative report.
- Employee relations – lost time accidents, lost hours to total hours.

Other writers have suggested before and since that profit/ROI is too narrow a view, but Parker's points are that there is a plurality of objectives for the company and its divisions and that there must therefore be a more balanced view of performance and the indicators used to appraise it. This idea of a balanced view has been taken up by Kaplan and Norton (1992). They introduced the idea of a balanced scorecard which represents a set of measures that give top managers a fast but comprehensive view of the business.

> The balanced scorecard includes financial measures that tell the results of actions already taken. And it complements the financial measures with operational measures on customer satisfaction, internal processes, and the organization's innovation and improvement activities – operational measures that are the drivers of future financial performance. (Kaplan and Norton, 1992: 71)

An example of Kaplan and Norton's balanced scorecard is shown in Figure 10.6.

An important feature of this approach is that it is looking at both internal and external matters concerning the organization. In Chapter 4 we introduced the concept of strategic management accounting and emphasized the need for management accounting to become more externally focused. The balanced scorecard introduces the idea of competitor benchmarking in relation to new product introductions and technology capability. Another important feature is that it is related to the key elements of a company's strategy. Dif-

Financial perspective	
GOALS	MEASURES
Survive	Cash flow
Succeed	Quarterly sales growth and operating income by division
Prosper	Increased market share and ROI

Customer perspective	
GOALS	MEASURES
New products	Percent of sales from new products
	Percent of sales from proprietary products
Responsive supply	On-time delivery (defined by customer)
Preferred supplier	Share of key accounts' purchases
	Ranking by key accounts
Customer partnership	Number of cooperative engineering efforts

Internal business perspective	
GOALS	MEASURES
Technology capability	Manufacturing geometry vs competition
Manufacturing excellence	Cycle time Unit cost Yield
Design productivity	Silicon efficiency Engineering efficiency
New product introduction	Actual introduction schedule vs plan

Innovation and learning perspective	
GOALS	MEASURES
Technology leadership	Time to develop next generation
Manufacturing learning	Process time to maturity
Product focus	Percent of products that equal 80% sales
Time to market	New product introduction vs competition

Figure 10.6 *The balanced scorecard. Reprinted by permission of* Harvard Business Review. *An exhibit from 'The balanced scorecard – measures that drive performance' by Kaplan, Robert S. and Norton, David P., Jan–Feb 1992. Copyright © 1992 by the President and Fellows of Harvard College; all rights reserved*

ferent divisions may be following different strategies and as such the items in the balanced scorecard would need to reflect these differences. A final important feature is the fact that financial and non-financial measures are linked together. Kaplan and Norton do not suggest that financial performance measures should be discarded altogether. They suggest that they have an important role to play alongside the non-financial measures of performance. Periodic financial statements remind managers that improved quality, response time, productivity or new products only benefit the company when they are translated into improved sales and market share, reduced expenses, or higher asset turnover.

Kaplan and Norton conclude by stating that:

> This new approach to performance measurement is consistent with the initiatives under way in many companies: cross functional integration, customer supplier partnerships, global scale, continuous improvement, and team rather than individual accountability. By combining the financial, customer, internal process and innovation, and organizational learning perspectives, the balanced scorecard helps managers understand, at least implicitly, many interrelationships. This understanding can help managers transcend traditional notions about functional barriers and ultimately lead to improved decision-making and problem-solving. The balanced scorecard keeps companies looking – and moving – forwards instead of backwards (1992: 74).

It can be seen therefore that both financial and non-financial measures of performance have a role to play in the measurement of divisional performance. These measures must be linked to the organization's strategy. If different divisions of the organizations are following different strategies then the performance measurement system should be specifically related to the strategic needs of individual divisions. Consideration must be given as to whether the organization is measuring the performance of the individual divisional manager, or the division as an economic unit. The issue here is one of controllability, and in the case of a divisional manager, it is argued that performance should only be measured against the items which are under the manager's direct control. Divisional performance measurement is therefore a complex issue but one which is of major importance to divisional organizations. The issues discussed so far should give the reader a good understanding of the main areas of concern when considering the design of a divisional performance measurement system.

The chapter so far has tended to introduce manufacturing examples. However, performance measurement is equally important in both service and public sector organizations. As mentioned in Chapter 5, recent developments in the public sector have focused on the need to attempt to measure the outputs of such organizations. British Rail, schools, local authorities and hospitals are all required to produce output type information. First, however, we will look at performance measurement in service businesses.

Performance measurement in service businesses

While we have used some manufacturing examples earlier in the chapter, all of the issues already raised are very relevant to the service sector. The use of non-financial measures and the need to link performance measurement to organization strategy are just as important in a service business as they are in a manufacturing organization. It is, however, important to recognize any differences between the two and take these into account when designing an appropriate performance measurement system.

Fitzgerald *et al.* (1989) identify four unique characteristics of services: intangibility, heterogeneity, inseparability and perishability:

- *Intangibility* − for example, in travelling on a particular airline the customer will be influenced by the comfort of the seat, the meals served, the attitudes and competence of the cabin staff, the boarding process and so on. Is the customer buying the journey or the treatment? Intangibles are an integral part of the service package that the customer buys.
- *Heterogeneity* − there can be a great deal of variability in the performance of a single firm, or even of a single service employee from day to day. Consistent behaviour from personnel is difficult to assure, yet crucially affects what the customer receives.
- *Inseparability* − the production and consumption of many services are inseparable: for example, having a haircut or taking a rail journey. As a result, most services cannot be tested and verified in advance of sale to assure quality. Designing quality into a service process is even more difficult because of the presence of the customer in the process.
- *Perishability* − services cannot be stored. A hotel for example, has a fixed number of rooms available each night. If a room is not occupied that sales opportunity is lost for ever. Services do not have the stock buffer used by manufacturing to cope with fluctuation in demand and the problems of inventory control are replaced by those of peak scheduling.

Fitzgerald *et al.* (1989) were working on a CIMA funded research project looking at performance measurement in profit based service business. An output of this research was produced by Brignall *et al.* in 1991. Recognizing the four unique characteristics of services described above, they advocated the measurement of service business performance across six dimensions. They proposed that managers of every service organization need to develop their own set of performance measures across the six dimensions to monitor the continued relevance of their competitive strategy. The six dimensions and associated performance measures are shown in Figure 10.7.

Brignall *et al.* emphasize that the six generic performance dimensions fall into two conceptually different categories. Competitiveness and financial performance reflect the success of the chosen strategy. The other four are factors which determine competitive success. The authors also emphasize that there are different types of service organization and that the performance measurement system needs

	Dimensions of performance	Types of measure
Results	Competitiveness	Relative market share and position Sales growth Measures of the customer base
Results	Financial performance	Profitability Liquidity Capital structure Market ratios
Determinants	Quality of service	Reliability Responsiveness Aesthetics/appearance Cleanliness/tidiness Comfort Friendliness Communication Courtesy Competence Access Availability Security
Determinants	Flexibility	Volume flexibility Delivery speed flexibility Specification flexibility
Determinants	Resource utilization	Productivity Efficiency
Determinants	Innovation	Performance of the innovation process Performance of individual innovations

Figure 10.7 *Performance measures across six dimensions. (Source: Brignall et al., 1991, p. 36)*

to be related to the particular service type. In summary, they suggest that the design of a balanced range of performance measures should be completed in relation to a company's service type, competitive environment and chosen strategy.

There are obvious similarities between the work of Brignall *et al.* (1991) and Kaplan and Norton (1992). Both pieces of work recognize the need for a balanced approach to performance measurement. Both speak of possible trade-offs between different parts of the performance scorecard. Both highlight the need to link performance measures to the strategy which the organization is following. Finally, both recognize the need to link financial and non-financial performance measures together in order to create a powerful performance measurement system for an organization.

Performance measurement in the public sector

As mentioned in Chapter 5, recent developments in the public sector have focused on the need to attempt to measure the outputs of such organizations. British Rail, schools and local authorities for instance are all required to produce output information. The published league table of results for GCSE and A levels is an example of the move in this direction which has taken place throughout the public sector. The Education Secretary explained the reasons for the league table thus:

> Of the many responsibilities parents have, choosing a secondary school for their child is perhaps one of the most important. For some, it is also one of the most bewildering or confusing tasks.
>
> The tables I am publishing . . . are among the first fruits of the Parent's Charter. They are the start of an information revolution that will bring to an end a system that has too often denied parents the right to know how schools are performing and prevented them from making informed choices about where they want their children educated. Not only will parents be able to make better informed decisions but, along with pupils, employers, and the wider community, they will also be able to call to account the schools and local education authorities that are not delivering the high standards of education that parents demand.
>
> When choosing a secondary school for their children parents have a number of priorities. They want a school where their own child will reach his or her full educational potential, will develop socially and will be able to pursue particular interests outside the classroom. They want to visit the school and talk to the head and the hard working teaching staff.
>
> However, before they look at this sort of detail, they want information about how local schools compare and what pupils of all ranges of ability have achieved by the key ages of 16 and 18. That is what the new tables tell them.
>
> . . . This year's tables are only the beginning. Next year, as well as covering all independent schools, we shall be including information about national curriculum assessment results, truancy rates, and the choices made by pupils once they reach school leaving age. (*Times*, 19 November 1992)

When the league table of results was published there was a lot of debate about the merits of such tables. Several voices have argued that 'value added' results, which take the pupils' background and their previous attainment into account, are superior to the new data which were used in the first set of league tables produced. Arguments are also presented which suggest that league tables are not the best way of measuring the effectiveness of a school. The problem of measuring effectiveness in the whole public sector area has been the subject of much debate in academic journals. People tend to have differing views about the objectives for many public sector bodies and, since they are in the public sector, there are a wide range of interested stakeholders. It is certain therefore that there

---

Patient's Charter (introduced 1 April 1992)
National charter standards – your health authority will publish information about performance against the standards annually.

Local charter standards – your district health authority will publish an annual report of achievement against its local standards.

Information to be produced on health services including quality standards and maximum waiting times.

British Rail Passenger's Charter (introduced 6 January 1992)

Standards to be set and performance to be measured against these standards.

Example of standards:
Intercity standards – Punctuality: 90% of trains (Monday–Saturday) to arrive within 10 minutes of scheduled time.*
– Reliability: 99% of services to run.
Regional railways standards – Punctionality: on long distance routes 90% of trains (Monday–Saturday) to arrive within 10 minutes of scheduled time.*
– Punctuality: on short distance routes 90% of trains (Monday–Saturday) to arrive within 5 minutes of scheduled time.*
– Reliability: 99% of services to run.

* Measured at the end of the route

Figure 10.8 *Examples from the Patient's Charter and the British Rail Passenger's Charter*

will be continuing debate in the area. It also seems certain though, that the momentum for public sector performance measurement schemes will continue. Figure 10.8 shows examples from the Patient's Charter and the British Rail Passenger's Charter. It highlights some examples of the performance measurement systems which are being used within the public sector. These basically represent a development alongside the traditional desire for 'value for money' in the sector. Value for money in the public sector means providing a service to the required standard: a way which is economical, efficient and effective. Economy, efficiency and effectiveness are defined as follows:

- *Economy* – attaining the appropriate quantity and quality of resources (input) at lowest cost.
- *Efficiency* – relationship between goods or services produced (outputs) and the resources used to produce them.
- *Effectiveness* – the extent to which the organization is achieving its policy objectives or other intended effects.

It has often been argued that, in the past, there has been an over-concentration on economy and efficiency at the expense of effectiveness. While there may be difficulties in getting a consensus view on the objectives of such organizations, it is important that effectiveness is seen as an important part of the performance measurement process.

Transfer pricing

We will now turn our attention in this chapter to transfer pricing issues which arise when goods or services are transferred between divisions. Transfer pricing takes place when there is interdependence between divisions. Some organizations use allocation of costs to deal with this interdependence, but many organizations use transfer pricing systems. In a transfer pricing situation between two divisions, the revenue of the supplying division becomes a cost to the receiving division.

Supplying division	1,000 units of an intermediate product transferred at a transfer price of £10 per unit →	Receiving division
Revenue 1,000 × £10 = £10,000		Cost to receiving division 1,000 × £10 = £10,000

Transfer pricing can take place in any organization where you have a divisional structure. Most of the literature in the area seems to concentrate on the transfer of intermediate products in a manufacturing organization. However, it is important to realize that transfer pricing can take place in any organization where goods or services are transferred between divisions. Halford (1992) provides an interesting illustration of transfer pricing at St Bartholomew's Hospital, London. Reorganization into clinical directorates has necessitated the development of a transfer pricing system within the hospital. Transfer prices will be the standard cost of resources provided by the facility directorates to user directorates. Halford concludes with the following statement:

> The introduction of flexible budgets, standard costing and transfer pricing is new to the NHS and appears to have a momentum independent of political concern with provider and purchaser splits, trusts and GP fund-holders. The creation of relatively autonomous clinical directorates inevitably brings into focus the potential for conflict between the aims of the service provider and user directorates and the aims of the organization as a whole. In general it seems that any transfer pricing mechanism will reflect these conflicts but when particular methods are applied these conflicts may be exacerbated. (1992: 57)

As illustrated in the quotation above, it is important, when considering transfer pricing systems within organizations, to consider organizational and behavioural implications as well as the technical aspects of such a system. The type of transfer pricing system used will have an impact on any divisional performance measurement system that is being operated within an organization. The degree of such impact will depend on the level of interdependency existing between the divisions of an organization. In considering transfer pricing within organizations, the first issue to consider is the objectives of a transfer pricing system.

Objectives of a transfer pricing system

Any transfer pricing system should attempt to support:

- Goal congruence
- Objective performance evaluation
- Divisional autonomy
- Managerial motivation

We will now look at each of these in turn.

Goal congruence

The system should facilitate decision-making and avoid sub-optimal decisions taking place. Divisional general managers should be encouraged by the system to take the same decision as a member of the headquarters staff would do in a given situation.

Illustrations 10.3 and 10.4 highlight situations where there is a possible conflict between the central position and the divisional position.

Illustration 10.3   Transfer pricing and goal congruence

Incremental cost of Intermediate Product = £200
Additional further costs of receiving division = £80
Supply division − not at full capacity
Market price of final product = £320
Transfer price   = £260

Central view	£	Division R view	£
Incremental revenue	320	Incremental revenue	320
Incremental cost	280	Incremental cost	340
	40		(20)
Accept		**Reject**	

Illustration 10.4   Transfer pricing and goal congruence: Smith Company

The tool division of Smith Company produces tools which are sold both externally and internally. One-third of the division's output is sold to the household products division of Smith, and the remainder is sold to outside customers. The tool division's budgeted results for the coming year appear below.

	Internal sales to household products £	External sales £
Sales	150,000	300,000
Variable costs	(100,000)	(200,000)
Fixed costs	(30,000)	(60,000)
Profit	20,000	40,000
Unit sales	100,000	200,000

The fixed costs are allocated on a per unit basis and are all unavoidable. The household products division has the opportunity to buy 100,000 tools of identical quality at £1.25 per unit. The tool division cannot increase its outside sales.

We must determine whether it is in Smith Company's best interest for the household products division to buy tools outside.

Tool division's variable cost is £1.00 per unit, which is either of the variable cost figures divided by the appropriate volume (£100,000/100,000 or £200,000/200,000).

Outside price		£1.25
Tool division variable cost		1.00
Loss per unit		£0.25
Units	100,000	
Total loss	£25,000	

By accepting the outside price of £1.25 instead of an internal transfer at the minimum transfer price of £1.00, the company as a whole loses £25,000. It is therefore not in Smith Company's best interest for the household products division to buy tools outside.

In both of the Illustrations, the divisional managers would not, given the opportunity, make the same decision as the central management team. If we consider Illustration 10.3, the problem here is that, in the eyes of the receiving division, the transfer price of £260 becomes an incremental cost. This amount is added to the receiving division's own incremental costs and the two are added together. Therefore, from the point of view of the receiving division, it has total incremental costs of £340 and incremental revenue of only £320. The divisional managers at the receiving division will feel that the transaction is not in the best interests of the division. However, if you consider the situation from a central perspective, the total incremental cost is only £280 and the incremental revenue is £320. Therefore, from a central management perspective, the transaction is profitable for the company as a whole. The problem in this particular situation surrounds the transfer price of £260 and the fact that the supplying division is not working at full capacity.

In a situation where the supplying division is not operating at full capacity, the technically correct transfer price to be used would be one based on variable cost. If variable cost is used, both the central management team and the receiving division's management team would be using the same incremental cost figure. As a result, goal congruence would exist because both parties would take the same decision. The supplying division management team would probably not be happy and we will pick up on this issue later.

A similar situation exists in Illustration 10.4 within Smith Company. If the household products division purchased its tools from outside the company, the company as a whole would be worse off by £25,000. Since the tool division cannot sell the products it currently sells internally on the external market, there would be spare capacity in the supplying division and the use of a variable cost transfer price would ensure goal congruence between the centre and the household products division. As, in the previous example, however, the tool division would not be happy with the situation and this is an issue we will turn to later.

Objective performance evaluation

The transfer pricing system needs to be seen to be fair and equitable, particularly if the performance evaluation is linked to a bonus scheme. As indicated earlier, when goods or services are transferred from one division to another, a portion of the revenue of the supplying division becomes a portion of the cost of the receiving division. This means that the price at which goods or services are transferred can influence each division's reported profits. Performance in a particular division may either increase or decrease as a result of any change in transfer pricing system. If the change is not recognized in any target set for that particular divisional management team, they will feel that the system does not provide a fair measure of performance in a situation where the change results in a reduction in profits. In Illustration 10.4, the divisional managers of the tool division would not be happy if they were forced to transfer the tools at the variable cost figure of £1 per item. The divisional managers at household products division would obviously be very pleased with such a situation.

Divisional autonomy

Any interference from the centre in a transfer pricing dispute may destroy divisional autonomy. If the centre interfered in the situations highlighted in Illustrations 10.3 and 10.4, the divisional managers might be unhappy with the situation. In Illustration 10.4, if the divisional managers at household products division were told that they could not buy from an external source and were forced to continue buying at £1.50 per unit, they would not be happy. They would argue that they were being denied the right to operate as a truly autonomous unit. In the same example, the divisional managers at the tool division would be unhappy if they were made to drop their transfer price to the variable cost figure of £1. Illustration 10.5 highlights an interesting example of this particular debate within Electrolux.

Illustration 10.5   Transfer pricing within Electrolux*

Some Italian managers are experiencing considerable difficulty adjusting to the ambiguous matrix structure, which has been introduced since the Zanussi acquisition to bind it and Electrolux together and to enable them to manage a complex network of cross-frontier product flows between factories in one country and sales companies in others.

Faced with the need still to report to a (very) strong Italian white goods 'country manager' while also being coordinated by a manager from the product line's Stockholm headquarters, the head of several of the Italian units are finding it hard to adjust.

Things are made more complicated by the fact that since the beginning of last year the Italian factory managers − 70 per cent of whose revenues come from exports − have joined their other European counterparts within Electrolux in becoming 'product division managers', and gaining what is supposed to be direct control over a third dimension: the negotiation of sales volumes and transfer prices with Electrolux marketing companies throughout Europe.

This arm's-length relationship is a fundamental part of the Electrolux system of breaking down its organization into small operational units with as full responsibility as possible for their own profitability and balance sheet.

But since Italy was brought fully into this structure during last year, the result has been a tense time for everyone concerned: for the Italian product division managers themselves; for marketing and sales company managers (especially in the UK, one of the prime customers of the Italian factories, but also in Italy itself); for the country manager in Italy and his counterpart in Britain; and for central management of the white goods product line in Stockholm.

---

* *Source*: *Financial Times*, 23 June 1989

Since last autumn Stockholm has had to adjudicate several times in serious transfer price disputes, for instance between the Italian product divisions and the UK sales companies when the Italian country manager insisted that raw material cost increases could not be absorbed by his local factories. Something similar came to a head in February when the Italian sales companies resisted a new round of price rises from their local factories.

So it is not surprising that the question of how to avoid constant disputes over transfer prices is currently exercising the minds of managers throughout the white goods product line, even if Leif Johansson, who heads it, says 'the issue has been blown out of all proportion; the system is working well, except in Italy'. Several Italian executives have suggested that the system should be changed, so that all transfer prices are set centrally, by Stockholm and the 'Marketing Europe' coordination unit it established two years ago. This would require the unit, which is based in Italy under an old Zanussi hand, Sergio Pusca, to be given stronger powers – something which many Electrolux managers across Europe consider necessary for other reasons too.

Mario Vischi, the tough Italian country manager for white goods, says 'the key in this complex international organization is to have active mechanisms in place to create – and force – the necessary integration'. (Force is a word that is rarely heard in the Electrolux culture.)

With 1992 in mind, and even today, Vischi says that Marketing Europe 'needs more authority, for example clear control over the promotion of particular brands.' On that point, Johansson agrees – but not with the notion of imposed authority.

One of the would-be centralizers of transfer price decisions is Aldo Sessegolo, who heads the four-brand Electrolux/Zanussi marketing arm in Italy. He complains that, because of the number of European product divisions which supply him, and the frequency of price changes, 'I'm losing at least 40 per cent of my time discussing transfer prices – not just once a year but continually. This kind of organization is only possible if the group is below a certain size.'

Sessegolo also complains that giving the product division managers a degree of responsibility for marketing 'is like handing a copy of *Playboy* to a 14 year old – they're getting far too concerned about it, instead of paying attention to keeping down their product costs and their price to us'.

But Leif Johansson holds firmly to the principle of giving division managers as direct contact as possible with market pressures. And he continues to resist exercising his authority to intervene on transfer prices, except in extreme cases. 'Our greater decentralization than competitors on internal pricing gives us a faster speed of reaction in the market place,' he claims. He also suspects that much of the time people say they spend on transfer price arguments is not internal wrangling, but actually valuable debate about what he calls 'real business issues': market strategy, competitors and so on.

Johansson hopes the system will settle down after it has operated in Italy for a little longer: 'It's a question of maturity,' he says. He also agrees with Mario Vischi that 'the tension should be released a bit' by a change in accounting procedures this autumn which will give each product division manger quarterly data on the profit which every sales company makes on products bought from that manager's factories. Such a process already operates in the reverse direction, enabling each country manager to know what profit a division has made on a sale to the sales companies in his territory.

In Sweden and some other long-standing parts of the Electrolux group, managers' interest in the profitability of other units with which they have dealings is fostered by the consolidation of such transfer profits with their own local results. When Electrolux can settle all the international complexities involved, it plans to extend this principle to managers throughout the white goods product line.

In the meantime the transfer price debate rumbles on. Occupying a rather different position in it from Leif Johansson is Lennart Ribohn, the group's deputy managing director and chief financial officer. Ribohn, who is known to some of his colleagues as 'the class monitor' (literally, 'the one who keeps order'), is in favour of Stockholm placing a percentage 'cap' on potential price increases, while leaving the two sides freedom to negotiate beneath it.

Ribohn denies that this would require many – if any – extra central staff, but Johansson dislikes the proposal on the grounds that 'it would kill some of the businessmanship which is developing in the company, by 'eroding the feeling of control which the units now have over their business'. He also suspects it would tend to push all price rises right up to the level of 'cap'.

Anders Scharp, Electrolux's Chief Executive, is well aware of all the arguments but says 'It's up to Leif'. Whatever happens, he is determined that any changes in transfer price system should not slow down the company's ability to react quickly to marketplace changes. 'In future, speed will become increasingly important,' he says. If unit managers had to consult Stockholm, via two country managers in between, 'It would slow things down tremendously'.

The Electrolux example illustrates a number of the issues surrounding divisional autonomy within organizations. Concern is expressed on the one side that too much time is being spent on negotiation. On the other hand, the feeling within the company is that the autonomy that divisional managers are given is crucial in terms of the company's ability to react to changes in the market place.

Managerial motivation

A measure of the suitability of any particular transfer pricing system depends on the way it motivates managers within the organization.

Examples have already been given of situations where managerial motivation may be harmed. Interference, or conversely lack of interference, from the centre can cause managers to be demotivated. The feeling that their performance is being measured unfairly because of the transfer pricing system being used can obviously lead to demotivation.

As indicated in the discussion of the objectives of a transfer pricing system, the problem with designing such a system is how to satisfy all of these objectives at once. It is in fact very difficult to do this, and in designing the system, it is nearly certain that an organization will be forced into a compromise between these objectives. Attempts have been made to arrive at theoretically correct transfer prices but these tend not to take into account the organizational and behavioural implications for organizations.

Methods of transfer pricing

The three most common methods of transfer pricing available for use are:

- Market price
- Cost based
- Negotiation

We will also briefly consider *dual pricing* and *linear programming* as methods of transfer pricing. When considering transfer pricing between divisonalized organizations there are obvious similarities between this chapter and Chapter 9, which considered the accountant's contribution to the pricing decision for external sales. Market price, price based on full cost and price based on marginal cost are all ideas that were introduced in Chapter 9. It is therefore important that you bring with you ideas from Chapter 9 when considering transfer pricing issues within this chapter.

Illustration 10.6 gives an example of a situation where transfer prices are calculated using market price, standard full cost and standard variable cost. The issues surrounding the choice of transfer price are also discussed in Illustration 10.6.

Illustration 10.6 Beck plc

Beck plc prides itself on being a growing, prosperous company, its success being partly due to a good management team which fully participates in its development via a decentralized control system.

This statement was questioned at a meeting which took place between John Saunders, group finance director of Beck plc and Paul Rush, divisional general manager of the Southern Division of Beck plc. The surprise came when Paul revealed that he did not believe he was responsible for his division's profitability. This he claimed was due to the company's transfer pricing policy. Paul went on to give reasons for his concern about the transfer pricing policy.

Paul was upset because he is forced to buy components from the company's Northern Division for use in the production of his own division's output. The Head Office of Beck plc therefore prevents Southern Division buying the components from any other supplier. The company operates a full cost transfer pricing system for transfers between Northern Division and Southern Division. Full cost is defined as variable cost plus absorbed standard fixed cost and does not include any allocation of profit. Paul is particularly upset because he feels that he could sell a further 40,000 units of his own product if Northern Division transferred the components at variable cost.

After the meeting John Saunders discussed the matter with Peter Barnes divisional general manager of the Northern Division. Peter Barnes was very hostile to the idea of making transfers at variable cost and suggested that market price may be the better alternative.

Northern Division produces component A which is used by Southern Division to produce product B. Each unit of product B requires one unit of component A. Southern Division has first call on component A but Northern Division can sell the balance of its output outside the group. Northern Division has a maximum capacity of 170,000 units of component A. Southern Division has a maximum capacity of 150,000 units of product B. Budgeted information for 1993 is as follows:

Northern Division

Budgeted output of component A	170,000 units
Open market price of component A	£50 per unit
Variable cost of component A	£25 per unit
Fixed cost of component A	£15 per unit (based on budgeted output)

Southern Division

Budgeted output of product B	110,000 units
Selling price of product B	£80 per unit
Variable cost of product B (excluding transferred-in cost of component A)	£20 per unit
Fixed cost of product B	£10 per unit (based on budgeted output)

The extra sales of 40,000 units mentioned by Paul Rush are not included in the budgeted figures for Northern Division and Southern Division. Market research has suggested that if product B were sold at £70 per unit, annual sales would be 150,000 units and this confirms the 40,000 unit increases that Paul Rush mentioned.

We will look at three aspects of this case.

(a) We will calculate the budgeted profit figures for Northern Division and Southern Division using:
   (i) Transfer price based on market price.
   (ii) Transfer price based on full cost.
   (iii) Transfer price based on variable cost.
(b) We will calculate the impact on the profits for Northern Division and Southern Division of the suggestion by Paul Rush that product B is sold at £70 per unit.
(c) We will discuss the issues highlighted by the calculations in (a) and (b).

Abbreviations used:
   TP   Transfer price
   TIC Transferred in cost
   VCs Variable costs
   FCs Fixed costs

(a) **Budgeted profit figures**
   (i) *Market price TP*

| | | Northern | | | Southern |
	Units	*£000*		*Units*	*£000*
Sales					
Internal	110,000	5,500			
External	60,000	3,000		110,000	8,800
		8,500			*£000*
		£000	TIC	5,500	
VCs		4,250	VCs	2,200	
FCs		2,550	FCs	1,100	
		6,800			8,800
Profit		1,700			—

   (ii) *Full cost TP*

| | | Northern | | | Southern |
	Units	*£000*		*Units*	*£000*
Sales					
Internal	110,000	4,400			
External	60,000	3,000		110,000	8,800
		7,400			*£000*
		£000	TIC	4,400	
VCs		4,250	VCs	2,200	
FCs		2,550	FCs	1,100	
		6,800			7,700
Profit		600			1,100

(iii) *Variable cost TP*

		Northern			Southern
	Units	£000		Units	£000
Sales					
Internal	110,000	2,750			
External	60,000	3,000		110,000	8,800
		5,750			£000
VCs	£000		TIC	2,750	
FCs	4,250		VCs	2,200	
	2,550		FCs	1,100	
		6,800			6,050
Profit/loss		(1,050)			2,750

(b) **If product B were sold at £70**
   (iv) *Variable cost TP*

		Northern			Southern
	Units	£000		Units	£000
Sales					
Internal	150,000	3,750			
External	20,000	1,000		150,000	10,500
		4,750			£000
	£000		TIC	3,750	
VCs	4,250		VCs	3,000	
FCs	2,550		FCs	1,100	
		6,800			7,850
Profit		(2,050)			2,650

(c) **Discussion**

One of the key factors in Beck plc is the capacity situation in Northern Division. Northern Division can sell the balance of its output outside the group and is therefore operating at full capacity. Part (b) above shows that company profits as a whole would decrease since Northern Division is denied the opportunity of selling 40,000 units of component A externally. Since the supplying division is operating at full capacity, the appropriate transfer price is the market price. There may be benefits from selling internally and, as such, an adjustment might be made to the market price for internal transfers. A question mark must be raised over the profitability of product B since buying at market price and selling at £70 per unit would result in a significant loss for that division. This however assumes that Paul Rush cannot buy the component externally at less than £50. While the market price is quoted at £50 it may be that Paul Rush can negotiate a lower price with an external supplier. The market may in reality not be perfectly competitive. There may be quality and service differences. There may also be some suppliers with capacity problems who are willing to sell at lower prices. Paul Rush has not been allowed to test the market situation.

The range of profits for the two divisions in part (a) highlights the behavioural issues associated with transfer pricing. The transfer prices used can have a significant impact on divisional profits if there is a high level of interdependence between divisions. Issues of fairness and motivation need considering. The fact that Paul Rush is denied the opportunity to look at external suppliers goes against the idea of divisional autonomy. The transfer pricing debate may in fact hide a real problem in Southern Division.

Market price

Theoretically, if a perfectly competitive market exists for an intermediate product then the current market price is the most suitable basis for setting the transfer price. In such a situation, divisional profits are likely to be similar to the profits that would be calculated if the divisions were separate organizations. Consideration must be given, however, to the capacity situation, and we will return to this later.

A competitive market is one where the supplying division can sell as much of the product as it wishes to external customers and the receiving division can buy as much as it wishes from external suppliers without the price of the intermediate product being affected. If the transfer price is set at the current market price, the receiving division will be indifferent as to whether the intermediate product is obtained internally or externally. The use of market prices has the advantage of preserving the autonomy of the divisional managers.

In practice there may be a saving on selling expenses when a supplying division sells internally. As a result of this, many organizations modify the market price rule for pricing inter-divisional transfers and deduct a margin to take into account the savings in selling expenses.

It would seem, then, that a market price provides a suitable solution to the transfer pricing problem for organizations. In practice, however, there are a number of problems associated with market based transfer pricing systems:

- The market may not be perfectly competitive — a particular consideration here is that internal and external products may not be compatible. Quality, delivery, service and characteristics of the products may be slightly different.
- The supplying division may not be operating at full capacity. If the supplying division has spare capacity then the theoretically correct transfer price should be variable cost (i.e. the marginal cost of

production). The use of market price in this situation would result in a lack of goal congruence for the organization as a whole.

- If idle capacity exists in the industry then companies may be selling products at distress prices. This again means that the market conditions do not hold and, if the supplying division is operating with spare capacity, adherence to the market price rule would result in divisional managers taking decisions which are not in the best interests of the company as a whole.
- There may be no external market for the intermediate product.

As can be seen from the above, there are problems associated with market based transfer pricing systems. As a result, many organizations use cost based transfer pricing systems.

Cost based

Cost based transfer prices can take numerous forms:

- Transfer at variable cost (actual or standard).
- Transfer at full cost (actual or standard).
- Transfer at variable cost (actual or standard) plus a profit margin.
- Transfer at full cost (actual or standard) plus a profit margin.
- Transfer at variable cost plus a lump sum to cover fixed costs.

In reviewing these different cost based transfer pricing methods it is useful to evaluate them against the objectives of a transfer pricing system which were identified at the beginning of this section. Illustration 10.6 above also provides discussion on some of the arguments that may be used in a practical situation.

Transferring at variable cost, in a situation where the supplying division has spare capacity, may support the goal congruence objective but it will not lead to management motivation on the part of the supplying division. The supplying division management will only cover variable costs under this arrangement and will therefore make no contribution towards fixed costs. Transferring at full cost would allow the supplying division to cover its fixed costs but would not give rise to any profit. Transferring at actual costs would mean that the supplying division could pass any inefficiencies on to the buying division. Transferring at standard costs may lead to arguments about standards and lead to central interference. This would then destroy the divisional autonomy which is again one of the objectives identified for a transfer pricing system. If a profit margin is added to the costs, then one has to decide on the level of the profit margin. Rate of return pricing, introduced in Chapter 9, may be used to determine the profit margin. As a final point, all of these cost based transfer prices totally ignore the market situation and the opportunities available to either the supplying division or the buying division.

We have seen there are difficulties with market based transfer pricing systems and cost based systems. We shall now look at negotiation as a method of arriving at an agreed transfer price.

Negotiation

Where markets are not perfectly competitive, or where cost based systems are considered inappropriate, it is argued that negotiation may be the way forward. Negotiation supports the idea of divisional autonomy and managerial motivation. The use of negotiation is dependent on managers being allowed freely to negotiate and make buying and selling decisions externally. The extract from Electrolux in Illustration 10.5 above provides an interesting example of negotiated transfer pricing in action.

The arguments in favour of negotiation of Electrolux were that this negotiation involved valuable debate about real business issues which gave the organization a competitive advantage compared with its competitors. Those who were not happy with the situation at Electrolux complained that they spent a lot of their time negotiating, time which they considered not to be well spent. Other problems can exist with negotiation: it can lead to sub-optimal decisions; it can lead to conflict between divisions; it can be dependent on the negotiating skills of the managers involved; it can tend to be time consuming for the managers involved. There is also the danger that divisional disputes will result in the centre intervening through arbitration and this could destroy the objective of divisional autonomy.

The three major methods of transfer pricing have been discussed. There are two other possible methods, and we will discuss these briefly.

Dual pricing

In this situation there is no single transfer price being used. For example, the supplying division could be credited with the market price and the buying division could be charged with the variable cost of production. The advantage this particular technique has over other systems is that it enables the organization to achieve goal congruence more easily by setting prices individually for both parties so motivating them both to act in the best interests of the organization and at the same time to charge prices which will be competitive for each unit and so enable fair performance measurement. However, a problem with dual pricing systems is that they are rather complex. Adjustments have to be made centrally when reconciling divisional accounts to take into account duplication of profits. There is also a feeling that the figures that are arrived at are fairly artificial.

Linear programming

Linear programming models can be developed to arrive at theoretically correct transfer prices. However, linear programming models are developed with a variety of basic assumptions which make them difficult to apply in a practical situation. A linear programme solution will give the optimal corporate solution which, while satisfying the goal congruence objective, will not satisfy the objectives of divisional autonomy, management motivation and fair performance assessment.

The section on transfer pricing has hopefully illustrated the difficulties associated with arriving at appropriate transfer prices for the transfer of goods or services between divisions. It is one of the most contentious issues facing divisional organizations, particularly where the level of interdependence between divisions is high.

Summary

This chapter has been concerned with performance measurement and transfer pricing issues within divisionalized organizations. The nature of differentiation and decentralization was discussed and developed through the vehicle of divisionalization. The nature and limitations of traditional accounting measures of performance were examined. Non-financial measures of performance have been introduced and the idea of using these non-financial measures, together with financial measures of performance, to form a balanced approach to performance measurement was developed. Issues of performance measurement in service organizations and public sector organizations were introduced. Recent developments in the public sector have focused on the need to attempt to measure the outputs of such organizations. The use of transfer prices to deal with interdependence between divisions was developed from both a technical and behavioural perspective. Objectives for a transfer pricing system were identified and different methods of transfer pricing were evaluated against these objectives.

After reading this chapter you should be able to:

- Understand the terms differentiation, decentralization and divisionalization.
- Explain and calculate return and investment and residual income.
- Explain the limitation of traditional accounting measures of divisional performance.
- Provide examples of appropriate non-financial measures of performance and link those non-financial measures with financial measures in order to create a balanced approach to performance measurement.

- Explain, calculate and recognize the problems associated with the different transfer pricing methods that can be used within organizations.
- Recognize the need to link performance measures to the strategy of the organization.
- Recognize the link between transfer pricing and performance measurement within organizations.

References

Brignall, T.J., Fitzgerald, L., Johnston, R. and Silvestro, R. (1991) Performance measurement in service businesses. *Management Accounting*, November, pp. 34–6

Fitzgerald, L., Johnston, R., Silvestro, R., Steele, A. and Voss, C. (1989) Management control in service industries. *Management Accounting*, April, pp. 44–6

Halford, R. (1992) Transfer pricing comes to Barts. *Management Accounting*, May, pp. 34–5,57

Johnson, H.T. and Kaplan, R.S. (1987) *Relevance Lost: The Rise and Fall of Management Accounting*, Harvard Business School, Boston, Mass.

Kaplan, R.S. and Norton, D.P. (1992) The Balanced Scorecard: measures that drive performance. *Harvard Business Review*, January/February, pp. 71–79

Parker, L.D. (1979) Divisional performance measurement: beyond an exclusive profit test. *Accounting and Business Research*, pp. 309–19

Scarborough, P., Nanni Jr, A.J. and Sakurai, M. (1991) Japanese management accounting practices and the effects of assembly and process automation. *Management Accounting Research*, 2 (1), pp. 27–46

Woodward, D. (1991) Back to basics with divisional performance measurement. *Management Accounting*, May, pp. 26–9

Further reading

Brignall, T.J., Fitzgerald, L., Johnston, R. and Silvestro, R. (1992) Linking performance measures and competitive strategies in service business: three case studies. *Management Accounting Handbook* (ed. C. Drury), Butterworth-Heinemann in association with the Chartered Institute of Management Accountants, Oxford, Chapter 9

Ezzamel, M. (1992) *Business Unit and Divisional Performance Measurement*, Academic Press in association with the Chartered Institute of Management Accountants, London, Chapters 2, 5

Wilson, R.M.S. and Chua, W.F. (1993) *Managerial Accounting: Method and Meaning*, Chapman and Hall, 2nd edn, London, Chapter 11

Problems and discussion topics

1 Narrow View plc is a large, long established, and now widely diversified company mainly manufacturing industrial products in more than ten divisions. Divisional managers are paid a bonus which is largely dependent on the division meeting its budgeted return on investment (ROI) target. One of the divisions in the group is the Forgings Division. The budgeted ROI figure for Forgings in 1993 is 13.2%. The budgeted profit is £10m and

the capital employed is £76m. A new opportunity for investment has arisen in Forgings and this opportunity was not included in the 1993 budget. Before looking at the specific investment opportunity it is worth just briefly looking at some background to the Forgings Division.

Traditionally, the Forgings Division had produced a high volume, low value-added product range. However, the strategic emphasis of the division was changed some years ago and it now concentrates on highly specialized, large size, high quality, lower volume products for two main related groups of customers. Demand is more predictable in these market areas and there is less competition but the market is still subject to major cyclical fluctuations. The division enjoys formally recognized status as a high quality supplier with several of its major customers. Each new product needs expensive specially developed design work and tooling which is carried out under contract for a customer. Because of this there is a need to maintain the design and technical capability of the division. Only one other company in the world has a plant to match the new investment made by this division. More recently the division has made significant investments in computer aided design and integrated automated manufacture of dies. The engineering manager is now arguing for the acquisition of a major new investment in forging equipment which would give a world lead to the company. However the rest of the divisional management team are resisting the proposal and have decided not to support it. Details of the new investment proposal are as follows.

The new proposed equipment would provide the division with a technical forging capability unmatched by any other company in the world and would help to develop markets for precision production of large part sizes which have been beyond the range of existing equipment. The financial projections are as follows:

	£m
Initial investment	20
Net cash flows	
Year 1	4
Year 2	5
Year 3	15
Year 4	15
Year 5	15
Net present value at 15%	13.16

You are required to discuss the use of divisional financial measures of performance using the information given for the Forgings Division as the basis for the discussion.

2 The following represents small extracts from the British Rail annual reports and accounts 1991/2.

QUALITY OF SERVICE
Intercity

	Objective	Performance 90/1	Performance 91/2
Punctuality: trains arriving on time or within 10 min	90%	85%	84.1%
Reliability: percentage of services to run – at least	99.5%	97.8%	97.8%
Train enquiry bureau: percentage of calls answered within 30 s	95%	78.7%	84.9%
Ticket offices: maximum queuing time:			
Off peak	3 min	95%	96%
Peak	5 min	91%	92%
Carriage cleaning:			
Interior – daily clean	100%	98%	97%
Exterior – daily wash	95%	95%	95%
Heavy interior – every 28 days	95%	90%	90%

PERFORMANCE INDICATORS
Intercity

	1987/8	1988/9	1989/90	1990/1	1991/2
Profit(loss) as a percentage of receipts (%)	(12.4)	7.9	6.0	4.6	0.5
Receipts per train mile (£)	17.76	18.03	18.05	17.65	16.59
Receipts per passenger mile	10.47	10.77	11.23	11.25	11.02
Passenger miles per loaded train mile (average train load) (passengers)	175	174	167	162	155
Total operating expenses per train mile (£)	19.04	16.80	18.04	17.34	16.95
Percentage of trains arriving within 10 min of booked time (%)	86	87	84	85	84
Percentage of trains cancelled (%)	0.5	1.5	2.0	2.2	2.2

Monetary items have been converted to 1991/2 price levels using the GDP deflator.

> INTERNATIONAL PERFORMANCE
> Indicators

The latest international performance indicators are shown below. The Community of European Railways (CER) consists of Austria, Belgium, Denmark, Eire, France, Great Britain, Greece, Holland, Italy, Luxembourg, Northern Ireland, Portugal, Spain, Switzerland and West Germany. Great Britain is excluded from the average.

	Year to 31 March 1991		Year to 31 March 1990	
	British Rail	*Average of other CER Railways*	*British Rail*	*Average of other CER Railways*
Train km (loaded and empty) per member of staff employed	3,289	2,320	3,422	2,301
Average passenger train loading (passenger km divided by loaded and empty passenger train km)	89	144	92	144
Average freight train loading (freight tonnes km divided by loaded and empty freight train km)	268	322	217	311
Support from public funds as a proportion of Gross Domestic Product (%)	0.14	0.68	0.12	0.70

You are required to discuss the value of this type of information for managers within a public sector organization.

3 The Northern Division of the Sherer Group of companies manufacturers one product, product X, which it sells for £500 per unit. Northern Division has budgeted to manufacture and sell 100,000

units of product X in 1993. Unit data for the product is as follows:

	£
Direct labour	100
Component part	150
Other variable costs	50
Fixed overheads	100
Profit	100
Selling price	500

The component part used in the manufacture of product X is supplied to Northern Division by another division of the Sherer Group, Southern Division. The cost of £150 for the component part represents the transfer price from Southern Division to Northern Division. The transfer price of £150 is calculated, on a full cost-plus basis, by Southern Division as follows:

	£
Variable costs:	
Direct labour	20
Direct material	60
Expenses	20
Fixed overheads	20
Profit	30
	150

Southern Division produces other components as well as the type transferred to Northern Division. However, it does have sufficient capacity to meet all of Northern's requirements and even after meeting their requirements, it will still be working with spare capacity. If the component is not produced at Southern, there is no opportunity for further work to replace it.

Sherer Group has set a target of 25% return on investment (ROI) and Northern Division and the managers of Northern Division will only receive an annual bonus if this figure is achieved. The capital employed of Northern Division in 1993 is £50m. The General Manager of Northern Division realizes that the budgeted ROI does not meet the group's requirements. As a result of this, the General Manager has been looking at ways of improving the profitability of his division. One of the options being considered is the purchase of the component part used in product X from an external supplier. Robo plc, a company which is not part of the Sherer Group, can supply the component part to Northern Division at a price of £125 each.

You are required to:

(a) Calculate the effect of purchasing the component from Robo plc on Northern Division's profits and comment on the likely reaction of the General Manager of Northern Division to this option.

(b) Calculate the effect of the purchase of the component from Robo plc on the group's overall profits and comment on the likely reaction of the Group management team.

(c) Critically evaluate the method of transfer pricing being used in the Sherer Group.

Answers to problems

Chapter 1

Problem 1

The stated objectives may be summarized as:

- Above average return to shareholders.
- Satisfy existing and emerging worldwide customers by producing high quality goods, services etc.
- Good working environment for employees.
- Enrich the community.
- Due consideration to impact on environment.

Compatibility issues:

- Above average returns suggest greater efficiency than its competitors, or the company is operating as a monopoly and not subject to market pressures.
- The satisfying of the other objectives may be incompatible with the first − this may suggest a hierarchy of objectives.

Communication process:

- The first objective is the only truly measurable one and can be communicated through the published annual accounts, the receipt of dividends and the appreciation of the share price.
- The other objectives are less easily measured:

  - customer satisfaction may be measured by repeat business;
  - working environment by no prosecutions by the Health and Safety Executive in the UK;
  - enrich community: donations to charity!
  - environmental impact: green audit.

Problem 2

The answers will vary from reader to reader.
(a) As an employee useful information may be:
    profit for year;
    dividend per year;

directors' salaries;
ownership of the company;
chairperson's statement;

(b)   share price movements over the period;
profits of major competitors;
forecasted profits for the next year;
major expansion/divestment plans.

Problem 3

The answer to this question is highly personal to you as an employee of a particular organization. Issues may include:

- Budget holder
- Cost centre manager
- Profit centre manager
- Investment manager
- Effect of cost cutting exercises
- Implementation of cost control measures

Chapter 2

Problem 1 Erika Gladwell

Income statement for the period up to 30 June (£)

Income[1] Sale of herbs			2,900
Sales to florist			4,800
			7,700
Seed purchases	500		
Herb plant purchases	970		
	1,470		
Less costs of standing crops[2]	780		690
			7,010
Less expenses			
Fencing contractor[3]		1,850	
Manure and fertilizer[4]		690	
Van and rotavator expenses		760	
Wages		650	
Depreciation[5]			
Van	700		
Rotavator	205		
Harrow	100	1,005	4,955

Profit before drawings	2,055
Less drawings	2,600
Reduction in capital	545

Notes

1 Realized income only.
2 It is assumed this is valued at the lower of cost or net realizable value.
3 This could be depreciated over its useful life but prudence suggests it should be charged in the first period as an expense.
4 It is assumed there is no closing stock of this item.
5 Erika will have to make a decision as to a depreciation policy. The figures given assume a life of 5 years for all mechanical assets with no estimated residual values after that time.

Balance sheet as at 30 June (£) (but not required)

Fixed assets	Cost	Depreciation to date	Net book value
Van	7,000	700	6,300
Rotavator	2,050	205	1,845
Harrow	1,000	100	900
			9,045
Current assets (standing crops)		780	
Current liabilities (bank overdraft)		370	410
			£9,455
Capital			
Opening capital		1,000	
Reduction in capital after drawings		545	£9,455

Problem 2 The football clubs

Pembroke City view the acquisition and disposal of players during any one year as an expense or revenue of that year. The accounting treatment is prudent by adopting a treatment which charges for the asset acquired during one accounting period. It goes against the concept of matching revenues with appropriate expenses.

Pembroke United view the acquisition and disposal of players during any one year as an acquisition or disposal of a company asset. The player's acquisition cost is not charged against current revenues of the year, but capitalized in the balance sheet, the benefit for the future use of the player being charged as depreciation each year of playing. This approach applies the matching principle by charging for the use of an asset (player) against receipts from ownership (gate receipts).

The balance sheet of both companies may not reflect the value of the team, the concept is ignored by City and while accounted for through the balance sheet of United, may not reflect a true value.

Both approaches are acceptable, the former being more prudent than the latter. Generally employees are not seen as assets and are not accounted for unless represented in the goodwill.

Problem 3   Tracey and Melanie

Income statements for year to 31 December

		(£)
	Tracey	*Melanie*
Sales (2,000 units × £150)	300,000	300,000
Less cost of sales		
Opening stock	nil	nil
Purchases (2,000 × £50 + 2,000 × £100)	300,000	300,000
Enclosing stock[1] (2,000 × £100)	200,000	200,000
	100,000	100,000
Gross profit	200,000	200,000
Less expenses		
Depreciation[2]	80,000	40,000
Research and development[3]	5,000	50,000
	85,000	90,000
Net profit	115,000	110,000

Notes

1   Valued on a first in first out basis, i.e. of the 2,000 units remaining, these are valued as being the last items received (other methods are equally applicable).

2   For Tracey £400,000 ÷ 5 = 80,000 p.a.
   For Melanie £400,000 ÷ 10 = 40,000 p.a.

3   Tracey £50,000 ÷ 10 = £5,000.
   It is very strange both retailers view the R + D so differently; Tracey must consider that it has some future benefits if it is to be charged to future periods. Melanie has taken the prudent approach, assuming no measurable future benefit.

Chapter 3

Problem 2(a)   Standardization of costs per FTE numbers

	H	L	S	T
Academic staff	1.79	1.64	1.61	1.65
Professional and other academic				
support staff	0.58	0.47	0.62	0.54
Premises	0.56	0.36	0.43	0.46
Supplies and services	0.31	0.17	0.25	0.30
Transport	0.05	0.04	0.06	0.07
Establishment expenses	0.18	0.15	0.12	0.13
Agency services	—	—	0.02	—
Miscellaneous expenses	0.06	0.04	0.08	0.05
Miscellaneous income	(0.06)	(0.04)	(0.03)	(0.05)
Catering services (net deficit)	—	0.03	0.03	0.02
Residences (net deficit)	0.04	0.03	0.07	0.02
Debt charges etc.	0.53	0.25	0.35	0.30
Redundancy etc.	0.04	0.09	0.07	0.06
Total expenditure	4.09	3.23	3.67	3.56

Problem 2(b)

- Halifax has very high premises cost.
- Southsea has the cheapest academic staff but the highest support staff.
- Southsea has high supplies and services, and miscellaneous costs. With a highest residences deficit.
- Overall Halifax is the most costly, stemming from academic staffing and debt charges.

Problem 2(c)

Measurements of efficiency are not measurements of effectiveness. The ratios presented in (a) imply the quality of education provided in these four establishments is equal. Not-for-profit organizations inputs and outputs are not truly measurable in economic terms.

Problem 3(a)

Company A has 17% of its total assets invested in other fixed assets, and 44% invested in stocks and work-in-progress. Company A is number 4, the contractor in the civil engineering industry. In this type of industry, contracts usually span over a long period of time, and it is not unusual for such companies to have huge stocks and work-in-progress. The funds invested in other fixed assets is material, because civil engineering companies use lots of heavy machinery for their work.

Company B has an unusual net asset structure, i.e. low fixed assets, no stocks and high trade debtors and trade creditors. These are features one would expect a bank to have because banks mainly borrow on a short-term basis and lend on a short-term basis as well. Company B is therefore number 3, the commercial bank with a network of branches.

Company C has high investment in land and buildings practically no debtors, a sizable proportion of creditors and stocks. These features would fit in with the expected position of a supermarket chain. Supermarkets usually occupy prime sites and hence their high investment in land and buildings. Company C is number 1, the operator of a chain of retail supermarkets.

Company D has 1% of its total assets invested in stocks and 73% invested in other fixed assets. Such asset structure could fit in with a company which is involved in a service industry. The lorry transport operator is therefore company D. It has funds invested in lorries which would help in its transport operation.

Problem 3(b)

The major limitations of ratio analysis are:

(i) Calculations based on conventional historic cost accounts will not reflect current values of assets and may therefore be of less use if used to predict future performance.
(ii) If the rate of inflation is not taken into account, when measuring performance the wrong conclusions may be drawn, e.g. a return of investment of 20% (before tax) appears satisfactory against a background inflation rate of 4% but if inflation is running at 30%, it would clearly not be as satisfactory.
(iii) Comparability between companies is difficult because of the application of different accounting policies, methods and rates used of depreciation and stock valuation.
(iv) The information available about a company may itself limit the quality of the ratios calculated, e.g. year end figures for capital employed may have to be used for calculating ROCE where a weighted or even simple average of capital employed would provide a more meaningful figure.

Problem 4

(i) Useful ratios
Candidates need not provide all these for a correct solution.

		1988	1989	1990	1991	1992
ROCE	(%)	19.1	18.4	17.9	18.1	18.4
Op. profit/sales	(%)	13.6	12.1	11.6	12.4	13.1
Asset Utilization		1.40	1.52	1.54	1.46	1.39
CA/CL		1.72	1.50	1.58	1.91	1.77
CA-Stock/CL		0.79	0.70	0.75	0.87	0.89
Gearing D/E		0.49	0.62	0.55	0.45	0.63
Stock turnover (days)		153	151	140	145	160
Debtors turnover (days)		98	83	92	106	123
Creditors turnover (days)		(65)	(74)	(69)	(73)	(78)
WC turnover (days)		186	160	163	178	205
Net profit/equity	(%)	16.0	14.4	13.7	12.0	11.8
Dividend cover	(X)	3.8	3.2	3.3	2.7	2.5
Interest cover	(X)	4.4	4.7	3.5	3.3	2.8
EPS	(p)	37.7	42.2	42.2	42.2	42.2
Market price	(p)	380	420	378	370	320
P/E ratio	(X)	10.1	9.9	8.9	8.7	7.6
P/E industry	(X)	10	10	14	15	18

Abbreviations: ROCE, return on capital employed; Op. profit/sales, operating profit/turnover; CA/CL, current ratio; CA-Stock/CL, quick ratio; Gearing D/E, long-term loans/shareholders' funds; WC turnover, working capital turnover.

Main features of the figures:

ROCE is fairly constant.
Liquidity is not strong but short-term borrowings support liquidity.
Gearing is increasing over the period – there is a worrying emphasis on short-term borrowings – the repayment/renegotiation dates are fast approaching.
Stock turnover and debtors turnover are gradually worsening – especially debtors.
Creditors turnover is worsening to our benefit.
Net profit to equity is falling.
Dividend and loan cover are also falling.

Therefore: general demise over the past 5 years – but sector is doing very well with average P/E ratios suggesting growth way above that of this company.
Problem of £30m for new assets!

(ii)   Consolidate short-term debt into long-term debt.
Dispose of investments to repay same debt.
Management must be replaced to generate growth in line with sector – get away from dormant investment image.
Tighten up control ratios.

Chapter 4

Problem 1

The answer to parts (a) and (b) can be taken directly from the chapter. The answer to part (c) is specific to the reader's own choice of organization and the cost objects chosen. An important point is that the reader has attempted to identify a wide range of cost objects within their own organization. The next important point to remember, is that the classification of costs into direct and indirect will depend on the nature of the cost object that has been chosen. The cost object could, for example, be a responsibility centre, a product, a customer or a distribution channel. These are just some examples and do not form a comprehensive list.

Problem 2

Item of expenditure	Basis of apportionment	Machine Shop A £	Machine Shop B £	Stores £
Indirect wages and supervision	Allocation	150,000	100,000	30,000
Indirect materials	Allocation	100,000	50,000	10,000
Rent	Apportion by area	40,000	10,000	10,000
Light and heat	Apportion by area	20,000	5,000	5,000
Insurance for machinery	Apportion by book value of machinery	15,000	5,000	–
		325,000	170,000	55,000
Stores	Stores issues	35,000	20,000	(55,000)
		360,000	190,000	
Budgeted Machine Hours		36,000	9,500	

(a) Budgeted overhead absorption rate Machine Shop A

$$\frac{360,000}{36,000}$$

$$= £10 \text{ per machine hour}$$

(b) Budgeted overhead absorption rate Machine Shop B

$$\frac{190,000}{9,500}$$

= £20 per machine hour

(c) Product X

	£
Machine Shop A: 6 × 10	60
Machine Shop B: 3 × 20	60
	120

Notes

(i) Rent – the budgeted rent cost is £60,000 and the factory covers 30,000 square metres. The cost per metre is therefore £2 and apportionment of rent costs would be as follows:

	£
Machine Shop A 20,000 sq m × £2 =	40,000
Machine Shop B 5,000 sq m × £2 =	10,000
Stores 5,000 sq m × £2 =	10,000

(ii) Light and heat – the budgeted lighting and heating cost is £30,000 and the factory covers 30,000 square metres. The cost per square metre is therefore £1 and apportionment of the light and heating costs would be as follows:

	£
Machine Shop A 20,000 sq m × £1 =	20,000
Machine Shop B 5,000 sq m × £1 =	5,000
Stores 5,000 sq m × £1 =	5,000

(iii) Insurance for machinery – the budgeted insurance cost is £20,000 and the book value of the machinery is £80,000. The cost per £ of book value is therefore £0.25 and apportionment of the insurance costs would be as follows:

	£
Machine Shop A £60,000 × £0.25 =	15,000
Machine Shop B £20,000 × £0.25 =	5,000

(iv) Stores are apportioned on the basis of the value of the direct and indirect materials issued by the stores department. The cost of the stores department has worked out at £55,000 and the total value of material issued is £550,000. The cost per £ of material issued is therefore £0.10 and apportionment of stores department costs would be as follows:

£

Machine Shop A £350,000 × £0.10 =	35,000
Machine Shop B £200,000 × £0.10 =	20,000

Problem 3

Since this was a question based on the reader's own choice of organization there is no specific answer to be given. The important learning objective is to create an awareness of the nature of quality costs within the reader's own organization. Some of those reading this book will work in organizations where a quality costing system already exists. Other readers will be starting the exercise from the beginning. This will not be an easy exercise since we have only briefly touched on the ideas behind quality costs in this book. However, it is hoped its inclusion will stimulate interest and the sources of additional reading at the end of the chapter should help those interested to develop the ideas further.

Chapter 5

Problem 1

The case describes a situation where decision-making has been delegated to local management. Potentially, many of the advantages of delegation should therefore occur. However, behavioural problems have arisen because of the feeling that the measurement of performance within the organization is unfair. There are a number of main issues arising out of the case and these will be dealt with in turn.

Strategy

Many readers will feel that there has been an abrogation of duties by the senior managers in their failure to produce long-term plans and their apparent delegation of strategy-making to the branch managers. Others may feel, however, that there needs to be careful consideration of this issue. Mike Collins states that the board is concerned with decisions such as where to open a new branch. They might also consider such issues as branch closure or product market diversification. This strategic agenda may be wholly or partially hidden from branch management and outsiders. It is possible that the delegation of many responsibilities to branch managers has, in fact, freed time for the board to consider strategic issues. Some may also argue that the directors influence strategy via the control system and their involvement in judging budgets sub-mitted by branch managers. The negotiation surrounding these two events may have an important part to play in the strategic develop-ment process.

Level of participation in budget setting

Some readers may argue that the system of setting budgets is one which is highly participative. A couple of the branch managers (John Nelson and Iain Reed) talk about having a lot of freedom. Branch managers submit their own budgets and it would appear that the only people who alter their budgets, after negotiation, are the branch managers themselves. As suggested in the main text, there is a wealth of literature on the impact of participation and some of it is contradictory. However, there is a reasonable consensus concerning the benefits of participation (for example, increased like-lihood of budget acceptance by managers involved, more positive attitude to budgets, more accurate budgets). Some readers may, however, feel uneasy about the situation and may suggest that branch managers are under enormous pressure to produce figures required by head office. Mike Collins, for example, makes the point that branch managers are aware that head office takes a dim view of them if they attempt to set themselves easy targets. Some readers may point out that in the majority of circumstances where branch managers' budgets are challenged by the budget committee, the budgets are modified. A key issue then, surrounds the severity of the pressure on branch managers to meet head office expectations and, therefore, the true level of participation involved.

Fairness of the control system

The branch managers involved put forward a variety of different attitudes towards the control system. Their perspective seems to vary according to the local environmental conditions facing their particular branch. Where market conditions are favourable, and targets are consequently easy to achieve, the local manager seems satisfied with the operation of the control system. But where market conditions are unfavourable, the managers are not so happy with the control system. The manager of the Wolverhampton branch has been held accountable for what appears to be relatively poor perfor-mance. However, given the recession in the local engineering sector, this may be an unfair assessment and it may be that the branch manager at Wolverhampton has performed well in highly unfavour-able circumstances. The situation may be made worse by the lack of any mechanism to revise budgets. The result is that the manager is demotivated by the control system being used at CALSCO No matter how hard he and his staff work, targets become impossible to meet because of circumstances beyond their control. This is compounded by the implicit assumption made by Head Office that Harding is trying to 'cheat' the system. The system, as it currently operates, fails to take into account the impact of external factors beyond the control and influence of branch staff.

The system currently operating involves only single loop learning. Double loop learning would entail the development of processes that facilitate a re-evaluation of the original budgets in the light of varying local conditions.

The use of budgets in performance evaluation

Many readers may recognize evidence that the company is using a 'budget constrained' style of performance evaluation. There is also evidence of some of the dysfunctional behaviour which has been associated with this particular style. There is some manipulation of actual data, together with the biasing of budgeted data in order to create easier targets. Associated job tension is evident in the case of Harding, the branch manager at Wolverhampton.

The role of the management accountants

The management accountants in this particular company are required to perform two seemingly contradictory roles. On the one hand they are responsible for providing assistance with branch decision-making. To be effective this necessitates involvement in branch affairs and requires the confidence of branch management. On the other hand, the management accountants are responsible for the accuracy of financial reporting and for the integrity of internal controls. Perceptions of the accountants acting as the 'eyes and ears' of the board of directors may lead branch managers to view them with suspicion. There are obvious behavioural issues involved in this role conflict. It can be argued that each branch, or alternatively each region, should have its own accounting staff which would be in addition to the centrally based accountants. The cost of providing this additional resource would have to be looked at against the benefits that might arise from such a change. The important point, at the end of the day, is that the accountants are seen to be part of a team which manages the organization.

Suggested changes

There are a number of possible responses to the issues raised in the case. Some people may argue for the introduction of double loop learning by means of quarterly forecasting. Others may suggest a change to a profit conscious style of evaluation. These are just two examples of possible responses. It is important to recognize that any suggested changes may bring about different types of problems.

Problem 2

The discussion will probably draw upon examples from the main text and the question itself. The move towards delegated budgets has affected the nature of accountability and control over the use of resources. There has been a move away from a traditional bureaucratic model, which concentrated on input control, towards accountability based on performance and, in particular, on whether the required outputs are produced for a given allocation of resources. It has been recognized that a lot of progress has been made in the area of budgetary control systems within central government organizations. The argument in favour of delegated budgets within all sectors of the public sector is that the flexibility associated with delegation has enabled resources to be used better. It is argued that the delegation of budgets to schools has enabled heads and governors to manage the budget in a way which meets the needs of a particular school. Similarly, in the case of GP fund holders, it is argued that practice budgets offer GPs an opportunity to improve the quality of service on offer to patients, to stimulate hospitals to be more responsive to the needs of GPs and their patients and to develop their own practices for the benefits of their patients.

It is important to point out, however, that many people have expressed concern about some of the management control developments in the public sector in recent years. Many of these concerns relate to the fear that efficiency and economy may be promoted at the expense of effectiveness. Supporters of these reforms would counter by reference to the new systems of performance measurement in the public sector which are discussed in Chapter 10. Concerns with regard to the health service relate to the fact that cost may become the overriding consideration rather than the need to treat patients. The counter-argument is that there will always be a constraint on the amount of money that can be spent on the health service, and the changes brought about by the NHS internal market will ensure that the money that is available will be used in the most efficient and effective manner. Another area of debate surrounds the amount of time that doctors and headteachers are spending on finance matters rather than clinical or teaching activities. This is obviously an area where many differing views are expressed. It can be argued though that the involvement of doctors and teachers is essential in order to take into account the need to offer an effective service in both situations.

In Chapter 4 we looked at the use of quality costing in the health service to provide an illustration of the way in which accounting systems can be used positively to help meet the needs of patients while at the same time providing value for money. To conclude, it is worth repeating the point made on several occasions in this book, that it is essential to link management control systems to the strategies being followed by the organization. This is the same for all the different sectors we have talked about in this book.

Chapter 6

Problem 1(a) Flexing the budget

	Original budget £000		Flexed budget £000
Sales revenue		Sales revenue	
30,000 × £280	8,400	28,000 × £280	7,840
Direct material		Direct material	
30,000 × 10 kg ×		28,000 × 10 kg ×	
£8 per kg	2,400	£8 per kg	2,240
Direct labour		Direct labour	
30,000 × 8 hr ×		28,000 × 8 hr ×	
£7 per hr	1,680	£7 per hr	1,568
Variable production		Variable production	
overheads	1,200	overheads	
		28,000 × 8 hr ×	
		£5 per hr*a	1,120
Fixed production overheads	2,100	Fixed production overheads	2,100
Profit	1,020		812

*a Variable production overhead absorption rate per direct labour hour

$$= \frac{1,200,000}{30,000 \times 8}$$

$$= £5 \text{ per direct labour hour}$$

The difference between the flexed budget and the original budget is explained by a volume variance.

Volume variance (using absorption costing)

	£	
Sales volume profit variance		
(30,000 × 34) − (28,000 × 34) =	68,000	(Adverse)
Fixed production overhead volume variance		
(28,000 × 70) − 2,100,000 =	140,000	(Adverse)
	208,000	(Adverse)

Volume variance (using marginal costing)

Sales volume contribution variance
(30,000 × 104) − (28,000 × 104) =   208,000 (Adverse)

Problem 1(b) Variance analysis explaining the difference between the flexed budgeted profit and the actual profit

	Variances Adverse £000	Variances Favourable £000	£000
Flexed budget profit			812
Variances			
Direct labour rate			
(196,000 × 7) − (196,000 × 7)	—	—	
Direct labour efficiency			
(224,000 × 7) − (196,000 × 7)		196	
Direct material price			
(252,000 × 8) − (252,000 × 9)	(252)		
Direct material usage			
(280,000 × 8) − (252,000 × 8)		224	
Variable production overhead expenditure			
(196,000 × 5) − 1,110,000	(130)		
Variable production overhead efficiency			
(224,000 × 5) − (196,000 × 5)		140	
Fixed production overhead expenditure			
2,100,000 − 2,100,000	—	—	
Sales price			
(28,000 × 280) − (28,000 × 270)	(280)		
	(662)	560	
			(102)
Actual profit			710

Notes

(i) Standard margins per unit

	£
Sales price	280
Variable costs	
Direct materials 10 kg × £8 per kg	80
Direct labour 8 hr × £7 per hr	56
Variable production overhead 1,200,000 ÷ 30,000	40

Standard contribution per unit	104
Fixed production overhead 2,100,000 ÷ 30,000	70
Standard profit per unit	34

(ii) Standard hours of actual production
28,000 units × 8 hr = 224,000 hr

(iii) Standard quantity of material specified for actual production
28,000 units × 10 kg = 280,000 kg

(iv) Variable production overhead absorption rate per direct labour hour
1,200,000 ÷ (30,000 × 8) = £5 per direct labour hour

(v) Standard absorbed fixed production overhead cost
28,000 units × £70 per unit = 1,960,000

Problem 2

The answer is specific to the reader's own choice of organization. Examples of some of the issues which may be raised were given in the question itself. Other issues are important and will be mentioned here.

Behavioural issues, which were dealt with in Chapter 5, may form the basis of many answers to this question. The speed of feedback and the complexity of the systems being used may feature in many of the responses. The impact of traditional variance analysis on organizations using a just-in-time philosophy may form the basis of some responses. Differences between sectors may, or may not, come out of an analysis of responses from readers. It is obviously very important that the variance analysis meets the particular needs of the organizations concerned and recognition of this should be an important feature of responses to the question.

Problem 3

Since this was a question based on the reader's own choice of organization there is no specific answer to be given. The important learning objective here is to create an awareness of the nature of the activities taking place in the reader's own organization and an understanding of the links between different activities within the overall business process. Once this awareness takes place it is then possible to think about the next stage, which is business process redesign. This involves an examination of the flow of activities and information that make up the key business processes in an organization with a view to simplification, cost reduction or improvement in quality or flexibility (Morrow and Hazell, 1992). Morrow and Hazell (1992: 38) provide examples, in the form of little case study illustrations, of the redesign of business processes.

Chapter 7

Problem 1

$$\text{Contribution per unit} = \text{Sales price} - \text{Variable costs}$$
$$= 30 - 20$$
$$= £10 \text{ per unit}$$

$$\text{Break-even point in units} = \frac{\text{Fixed costs}}{\text{Contribution per unit}}$$
$$= \frac{30,000}{10}$$
$$= 3,000 \text{ units}$$

$$\text{Break-even point in £ sales} = \frac{\text{Fixed costs} \times \text{Sales price per unit}}{\text{Contribution per unit}}$$
$$= \frac{30,000 \times 30}{10}$$
$$= £90,000$$

$$\text{Profit} = \text{Contribution} - \text{Fixed costs}$$
$$= (5,000 \times 10) - 30,000$$
$$= £20,000$$

It is important to note at this stage that the fixed costs do not include any salary for the owner of the business. The owner of the business currently earns £25,000 per annum and it can be argued that this is the amount of profit which she would like to make. This can be looked at in two different ways:

(i)   As a further fixed cost to the company.
(ii) As the target profit required by the company.

(i)   If we look at it as a further fixed cost to the company, the impact would be as follows:

$$\text{Break-even point in units} = \frac{\text{Fixed costs}}{\text{Contribution per unit}}$$

$$= \frac{30,000 + 25,000}{10}$$

$$= \underline{\underline{5,500 \text{ units}}}$$

$$\text{Break-even point in £ sales} = \frac{\text{Fixed costs} \times \text{Sales price per unit}}{\text{Contribution per unit}}$$

$$= \frac{55,000 \times 30}{10}$$

$$= \underline{\underline{£165,000}}$$

$$\text{Profit} = \text{Contribution} - \text{Fixed costs}$$

$$= (5,000 \times 10) - 55,000$$

$$= \underline{\underline{£(5,000) \text{ Loss}}}$$

(ii) If we look at it as the target profit required by the company:

Level of sales to result in target profit

$$= \frac{\text{Fixed costs} + \text{Target profit}}{\text{Contribution per unit}}$$

$$= \frac{30,000 + 25,000}{10}$$

$$= \underline{\underline{5,500 \text{ units}}}$$

£ level of sales to result in target profit

$$= \frac{(\text{Fixed cost} + \text{Target profit}) \times \text{Sales price per unit}}{\text{Contribution per unit}}$$

$$= \frac{30,000 + 25,000}{10}$$

$$= \underline{\underline{£165,000}}$$

From the calculations above it is obvious that, if your friend requires the same return from her business as she did from her salaried employment, the projected level of sales are insufficient. She would then have to consider ways around the problem. For instance, is it possible to increase sales to 5,500 units? Is it possible to reduce variable costs by 5% since a 5% reduction in variable costs would give the required return on the original sales projection of 5,000 units:

Contribution per unit = Sales price − Variable costs
$$= 30 - (20 \times 95\%)$$
$$= 30 - 19$$
$$= \underline{\underline{£11 \text{ per unit}}}$$

Assuming the £25,000 is an additional fixed cost

$$\text{Break-even point in units} = \frac{\text{Fixed costs}}{\text{Contribution per unit}}$$

$$= \frac{55,000}{11}$$

$$= 5,000 \text{ units}$$

This represents the original sales figure projections.

The question suggested that your friend is concerned as to whether any of her estimates are incorrect. As already demonstrated, cost-volume-profit analysis is a powerful tool for looking at the impact of different assumptions. We have only briefly considered a few of the options that can be looked at. Different assumptions could be made about sales price, sales volume, variable costs and fixed costs. The information could be put on to a computer spreadsheet and the impact of certain charges could be calculated in a very short space of time. Sensitivity analysis could be carried out on the computer with very little difficulty.

It is important to conclude by saying that your friend, as the decision-maker, must take the decision herself. The information provided by cost-volume-profit analysis will help the decision-making process but is not the sole factor in that process. Your friend must decide on the basis of a whole variety of issues which may be important. Starting a business may, or may not be, riskier than her current employment. She may be happier working for herself than working as an employee in another organization. Many factors need to be taken into account, but cost-volume-profit analysis is a very useful tool to aid the decision-making process.

Problem 2(a)   Springs plc

	£ per unit
Purchase price of component from Trigger plc	70
Variable manufacturing cost	60
Saving if component manufactured internally	10

It is therefore in the best interests of Springs plc to manufacture the component themselves.

Assumptions made/aspects which may require further investigation include:

(i) Assume direct labour is a variable cost.
(ii) Assume fixed overheads will be incurred whether or not the component is manufactured. If fixed overheads can be saved then the extent of the savings would need to be compared with the additional variable cost of purchasing.
(iii) Assume that continuing to manufacture the component will not restrict the production of a more profitable product.
(iv) Assume that quality and service are the same for both sources of supply.
(v) Investigations should be undertaken to establish the period over which supplies of the component will continue to be required and for how long the required quantity may be obtained from the outside supplier.
(vi) Some assessment of the period over which the guaranteed purchase price is applicable would also be necessary.

Problem 2(b) Springs plc

(i) $\dfrac{\text{Additional fixed costs of manufacturing}}{\text{Additional purchasing costs}}$

$$= \frac{£60,000}{£10}$$

$$= 6,000 \text{ units}$$

If the quantity of components manufactured each year is less than 6,000 units then it would be cheaper to purchase from the outside supplier.

(ii)

	Additional sales of existing product £	Continue manufacture of existing component £
Selling price	140	
Purhase price		70
Variable manufacturing costs	100	60
Contribution earned per unit:		
By additional sales	40	
By manufacturing component		10
Contribution earned per direct labour hour:		

By additional sales

$$\frac{40}{8}$$
$$= £5 \text{ per direct labour hour}$$

By manufacturing component

$$\frac{10}{4}$$
$$= £2.50 \text{ per direct labour hour}$$

Since labour is restricted, the key aspect to consider is the contribution per direct labour hour (i.e. contribution per limiting factor). Additional sales of an existing product gives a higher contribution per limiting factor than the internal manufacture of the existing component. The recommendation would therefore be that additional products should be manufactured and the components purchased from Trigger plc.

Problem 2(c)   Springs plc

The reply should indicate that the book value of the grinding equipment is irrelevant to the decision as to whether the company should purchase or continue to manufacture the components. Springs plc incurred the £100,000 cost one year ago and this therefore represents a past cost which is not relevant to the decision.

Problem 3(a)   Jones Ltd

The first stage is to calculate the budgeted annual direct labour hours:

Product	Annual volume	Direct labour hours per unit	Total budgeted direct labour hours
P1	100	5	500
P2	1,000	5	5,000
P3	100	15	1,500
P4	1,000	15	15,000
			22,000

Therefore the direct labour overhead absorption rate is:

$$\frac{£66,000}{22,000}$$
$$= £3 \text{ per hour}$$

The unit cost per product is therefore:

Product	Material £	Labour £	Overhead £	Total £
P1	60	25*(a)	15*(b)	100
P2	60	25	15	100
P3	180	75	45	300
P4	180	75	45	300

*(a) 5 hours per unit × £5 per hour
*(b) 5 hours per unit × £3 per hour

Problem 3(b)   Jones Ltd

The first stage is to calculate the cost per unit of cost driver:

Activity	Total cost £	Cost driver	Annual consumption of cost driver	Cost driver rate £
Setting up jobs	30,000	Number of set ups	30	1,000
Ordering material	15,000	Number of material orders	15	1,000
Material handling	21,000	Number of times material handled	100	210

The unit cost per product is therefore:

		£
P1	Direct materials	60
	Direct labour	25
	Overhead costs	
	Setting up jobs $\frac{2 \times 1,000}{100}$	20
	Ordering material $\frac{4 \times 1,000}{100}$	40
	Material handling $\frac{6 \times 210}{100}$	12.6
		157.60

		£
P2	Direct materials	60
	Direct labour	25
	Overhead costs	
	Setting up jobs $\frac{10 \times 1,000}{1,000}$	10

$$\text{Ordering material } \frac{4 \times 1,000}{1,000} \qquad\qquad 4$$

$$\text{Material handling } \frac{50 \times 210}{1,000} \qquad\qquad \underline{10.5}$$

$$\underline{\underline{109.50}}$$

		£
P3	Direct materials	180
	Direct labour	75
	Overhead costs	

$$\text{Setting up jobs } \frac{5 \times 1,000}{100} \qquad\qquad 50$$

$$\text{Ordering material } \frac{2 \times 1,000}{100} \qquad\qquad 20$$

$$\text{Material handling } \frac{20 \times 120}{100} \qquad\qquad \underline{42}$$

$$\underline{\underline{367}}$$

		£
P4	Direct materials	180
	Direct labour	75
	Overhead costs	

$$\text{Setting up jobs } \frac{13 \times 1,000}{1,000} \qquad\qquad 13$$

$$\text{Ordering material } \frac{5 \times 1,000}{1,000} \qquad\qquad 5$$

$$\text{Material handling } \frac{24 \times 210}{1,000} \qquad\qquad \underline{5.04}$$

$$\underline{\underline{278.04}}$$

Problem 3(c)   Jones Ltd

Comparison of two methods of allocating overheads:

	Cost per unit (£)		
	Traditional method	Activity based costing	Difference
P1	100	157.60	(57.60)
P2	100	109.50	(9.50)
P3	300	367.00	(67.00)
P4	300	278.04	21.96

The results show that, when using a traditional approach to overhead absorption, Product 4 subsidizes the other three products. Product 4 is charged with a greater share of the overheads than is appropriate when considering the use made by each of those products of the overhead resources. The traditional system has particularly under-charged the lower volume products, P1 and P3. The traditional volume based system ignores the differences in relative consumption of overhead resources.

This issue is particularly important for this company since the sales of P4 seem to be under pressure from competitors in a market which is becoming particularly price sensitive. The company uses a cost-plus method of pricing (an issue which is dealt with in detail in Chapter 9), and the traditional approach to overhead absorption may be the reason that the product is overpriced. The activity based costing approach suggests that P4 is overcosted in terms of the amount of overhead resources it actually uses. This means that the company could look at reducing the selling price of P4 in order to meet the prices being charged by the competition. It is also worth noting, however, that the position of P1, P2 and P3 also needs reviewing. These have tended to be undercosted by the traditional method and the company may think that these products are making a profit when in fact they may not be doing so. A review of these products needs to be undertaken to ensure that the selling price of these products is a realistic one bearing in mind the costs of the product and the price that the customers are willing to pay.

Chapter 8

Problem 1

Multiple use of evaluation techniques by large firms:

- Payback measures time initial capital investment takes to be received.
- Average accounting rate of return parallels the ratios used for performance evaluation measuring profit against capital employed.
- NPV and IRR both measure wealth creation potential of the project over its lifetime.

These three measures therefore link time, profit and wealth if used together.

Payback has survived because it handles risk and capital rationing, yet it is the most naive of the techniques.

IRR is a weaker technique than NPV, yet its survival and growth in usage is because it is simple to communicate to other managers.

All sophisticated techniques have gained in importance because of management education over the period and a greater level of uncertainty in the environment makes managers seek greater sophistication, while also using the simplest of the techniques as a yardstick.

Problem 2   S.T. Ilton

'Mean' selling price premium − 15%
Therefore selling price may be £230
Could be as high as £260 or low as £200
Variable manufacturing costs £160
Most likely contribution £70 per 100 kilos.

Cap. inv.	W. cap.	Additional fixed costs	Additional contribution	Net cash flow	Disc. factor 20%	PV
Yr 0 (1,500,000)	(250,000)			(1,750,000)	1.00	(1,750,000)
1		(100,000)	700,000	600,000	0.83	498,000
2		(100,000)	700,000	600,000	0.69	414,000
3		(100,000)	700,000	600,000	0.58	348,000
4		(100,000)	700,000	600,000	0.48	288,000
5		(100,000)	700,000	600,000	0.40	240,000
6		(100,000)	700,000	600,000	0.34	204,000
7		(100,000)	700,000	600,000	0.28	168,000
8	(250,000)	(100,000)	700,000	850,000	0.23	195,500

NPV +605,500

Notes

1   $1,000,000 \times \dfrac{£230 - £160}{100} = £700,000$

2   Exploring the impact of a change in assumptions re. selling price premium.

If 10% premium then £100,000 reduction in contribution p.a., i.e. 3.84 × 100,000 lost NPV but still worthwhile, NPV = 605,000 − 384,000 = +221,500.

If 5% premium then £200,000 reduction in contribution p.a., i.e. 3.84 × 200,000 lost NPV, now not worth proceeding as NPV = 605,500 − 768,000 = −162,500.

Premium must be $\dfrac{221,500}{221,500 + 162,500} \times 5\% + 5\% = 7.88\%$

for positive NPV.

Problem 3   Bisket plc

Cash flow statement

	T0	T1	T2	T3	T4	T5	T6	T7
Sales (6%)		1.06	3.37	5.96	8.83	12.04	15.60	
Costs (40%)		(0.52)	(1.62)	(2.81)	(4.09)	(5.48)	(6.96)	
Working capital								
Training (6%)		(0.80)						
Labour (8%)		nil	2.33	2.52	2.72	2.93	3.17	
Savings								
overheads (4%)		(1.04)	(1.08)	(1.12)	(1.17)	(1.22)	(1.26)	
		(1.30)	3.00	4.55	6.29	8.27	10.55	
Taxation			0.98	(0.65)	(1.29)	(1.98)	(2.73)	(3.72)
initial cost	(6.00)						1.50	
Working capital	2.50							
	(4.50)	(1.30)	3.98	3.90	5.00	6.29	9.32	(3.72)
Disc. rate 15%	1.000	0.870	0.756	0.658	0.572	0.497	0.432	0.376
DCF	(4.50)	(1.13)	3.00	2.56	2.86	3.13	4.02	(1.40)
NPV (15%) = £8.54m								

Tax computation

	T0	T1	T2	T3	T4	T5	T6	T7
As above		(1.30)	3.00	4.55	6.29	8.27	10.55	
CA		1.50	1.13	0.84	0.63	0.48	(0.08)	
Taxable profits		(2.80)	1.87	3.71	5.66	7.79	10.63	
at 35%		(0.98)	0.65	1.29	1.98	2.73	3.72	
Payable		T2	T3	T4	T5	T6	T7	

CA computation

T1	6.00
	1.50
	4.50
T2	1.13
	3.37
T3	0.84
	2.53
T4	0.63
	1.90
T5	0.48
	1.42
T6	0.36
	1.06
Disposal	1.50
BC	0.44

Assumptions:
Inflation rate for
particular costs
of revenues

0.08 Balancing charge

Chapter 9

Problem 1   Hisec plc

(a)   Reasons for producing budgets are as follows:

- To aid the planning of annual operations.
- To coordinate the activities of the various parts of an organization and to ensure that the parts are in harmony with each other.
- To communicate plans to the various responsibility centre managers.
- To motivate managers to achieve organizational goals.
- To evaluate the performance of managers.

(b)

	MXR	E210	Omega
Selling price (£)	4,000	8,000	8,000
Variable cost (£)	1,600	2,000	3,200
Contribution	2,400	6,000	4,800

MXR

Price (£)	Variable cost (£)	Contribution (£)	Volume (units)	Total contribution (£000)
4,000	1,600	2,400	1,000	2,400
4,100	1,600	2,500	950	2,375
4,200	1,600	2,600	900	2,340

E210

8,000	2,000	6,000	400	2,400
7,500	2,000	5,500	450	2,475
7,000	2,000	5,000	500	2,500
6,500	2,000	4,500	550	2,475
6,000	2,000	4,000	600	2,400

Optimum selling price is £7,000 given sales of 500 units, therefore not feasible to increase production by 50%.

Omega

Contribution ratio must equal 70%.

Let S = selling price, variable cost per unit = £3,200

$$\therefore 0.70 = \frac{S - 3,200}{S}$$

$$0.70S = S - 3,200$$
$$-0.30S = -3,200$$
$$S = £10,667 \text{ [old price per unit} = £8,000]$$
∴ new selling price is £10,667 per unit

Price	10,667
Variable costs	3,200
Contribution	7,467
Volume 100 × 0.95	95

£709,365	say	£709,000

Master budget

		£000	£000
Contributions	MXR		2,400
	E210		2,500
	Omega		709
			5,609
Less fixed costs			
Manufacturing overhead		798	
Administration		720	
Selling and distribution		528	
Research and development		80	2,126
Revised profit			3,483

(c) Risks with the estimates
Assumptions about the competitors' reactions. MXR not really a 'Cash Cow', produces little volume from price reductions. E210 not really a 'Rising Star', volume increases of 50% have not been required. Omega, real benefits can be made here.

Problem 2   Woodhouse Ltd

(i) and (ii)

Plan A

	£	£ per unit	
Direct materials	400,000	0.80	
Direct labour	500,000	1.00	
Prac: OHD	250,000	0.50	(33.3% × 750,000)
Admin: OHD	50,000	0.10	(12.5% × 400,000)
S×D: OHD	50,000	0.10	(25% × 200,000)
Total variable cost	1,250,000	2.50	
Sales	2,500,000	5.00	
Contribution	1,250,000	2.50	

Fixed cost   1,000,000

                     250,000 p.a.

$$\text{BEP} = \frac{1,000,000}{2.5} = 400,000 \text{ units}$$

Margin of safety = (500,000 − 400,000) units = 100,000 units.

Plan B

Sales units   535,000

	£	
Selling price	5.00	
New variable cost	2.60	(Labour now £1.10)
Contribution	2.40	

Aggregate contribution 535,000 × £2.40 = 1,284,000
Less fixed costs (£1,000,000 + £20,000)   1,020,000

                           £264,000 p.a.

$$\text{BEP} = \frac{1,020,000}{2.40} = 425,000 \text{ units}$$

Margin of safety (535,000 − 425,000) = 110,000 units.

Plan C

Sales units   575,000

	£	
Selling price	4.80	
Less variable costs	2.50	(As in A)
Contribution	2.30	

Aggregate contribution 575,000 × £2.30   = 1,322,500
Less fixed costs (£1,000,000 + £100,000)   1,100,000

Profit   £222,500 p.a.

$$\text{BEP} = \frac{1,100,000}{2.30} = 478,260$$

Margin of safety (575,000 − 478,260) = 96,740 units.

Plan D

Sales units   600,000

	£	
Selling price	4.70	
Less variable costs	2.10	(materials now 0.60 and
Contribution	2.60	labour 0.80)

Aggregate contribution 600,000 × £2.60 = 1,560,000
Fixed costs (£1,000,000 + £260,000)   = 1,260,000

Profit   300,000 p.a.

$$BEP = \frac{1,260,000}{2.60} = 484,615 \text{ units}$$

Margin of safety (600,000 − 484,615) = 115,385 units.

(iii) Plan D Extra information required

- Feasibility of Plan A while modernization is taking place.
- Competitor actions to a price reduction.
- Capital investment appraisal.
- Pessimistic, most likely, optimistic forecasts.
- Increased administrative activity, e.g. production planning.
- Reliability of cost/efficiency forecasts.
- Management and workforce cooperation.
- Alternative investments (opportunity cost of pursuing this plan).

(iv)

	A	B	C	D
Profit (p.a.)	£250,000	£264,000	£222,500	£300,000
BEP (units)	400,000	425,000	478,260	484,615
Margin of safety (units)	100,000	110,000	96,740	115,385

B over A: annual profit 5.6% increase but with a higher risk 6.25% on BEP

C over A: no, C procedures level profits, higher BEP and lower margin of safety

D over A: increase in profit by 20%, increase in BEP by 21.15%, needs capital investment. If a 10% ROCE is required and the extra profit is £50,000 on an investment of £600,000, i.e. 8.3% − then the investment is not worthwhile

Forecast B looks best BUT may be only a short-term solution and competitive advantage may be sacrificed. Can we afford not to do D?

Problem 3   Dartmoor Ltd

		Products		
	W	X	Y	Z
Selling price (£)	36	60	50	60
Less variable costs				
Materials (£)	12	36	14	24
Labour (£)	9	6	18	15
Overhead (£)	9	8	9	11
	30	50	41	50
Contribution £	6	10	9	10

(a) *Maximum profit*

Sales (units)	5,000	5,000	5,000	5,000
Contribution (£)	30,000	50,000	45,000	50,000
Aggregate				
contribution (£)		175,000		
Less fixed costs (£)		150,000		
Profit		25,000		

(b) (i)

	W	X	Y	Z
Contribution	£6	£10	£9	£10
Limiting factor	3 hr	2 hr	6 hr	5 hr
	£2	£5	£1.50	£2
Ranking	=2	1	4	=2

Therefore restrict production of Y

Units sold	5,000	5,000	3,667	5,000
Hours used	15,000	10,000	22,000	25,000
Contribution (£)	30,000	50,000	33,003	50,000
Aggregate contribution			163,003	
Revised profit			13,003	

(b) (ii) If extra labour was available it could only be usefully employed making Y, as there are sales volume constraints on the other products.

Y produces a contribution of £1.50 per labour hour and labour is £3.00 per hour, therefore labour could be hired in at a maximum rate of £4.50 per hour.

(c) Any lost labour hours would mean £3.00 labour cost wasted plus any contribution that could have been made in the hour.

(d) (i)

Buy-in-price	£48
Variable cost of manufacture	£50
Benefit from buying in	£ 2

(d) (ii)

- Dependency
- Long-term or short-term price
- X is the most profitable product, therefore reluctance for others to manufacture it and eventually cut out Dartmoor from the market.

Chapter 10

Problem 1 Narrow View plc

The main reason for the decision of the divisional management team not to support the proposal is probably the impact of the proposal on the first year's ROI figures. It is important to remember that the divisional managers have a reward system which is based on the achievement of the budgeted ROI. It is not just the monetary award associated with this but also the tremendous pressure which is put on managers from external forces to achieve short-term financial performance. The impact of the investment proposal on the division's ROI would be as follows:

Annual depreciation (straight line depreciation based on a five year life)

$$= \frac{20}{5}$$

$= £4m$ per annum

Profit in year 1 = Cash flow − depreciation

$$= \quad 4 \qquad\qquad 4$$

$$= \quad 0$$

Impact on ROI:

	Profit (£m)	Capital employed (£m)	ROI(%)
1993 budget	10	76	13.2
1st year impact of project	–	20	–
ROI after impact of project	10	96	9.6

Performance in the second year is also poor and it is not until year 3 that a dramatic improvement in performance would be shown. Even without the large improvement in cash flow, the nature of the ROI calculation would mean improvement in ROI performance over the years.

The nature of the financial performance measure has therefore resulted in the rejection of investment opportunity which gives a very positive net present value over the life of the asset. (Net present value, as described in Chapter 8, is the technique used to judge the worth of a capital investment.) The proposed capital project is worth investing in from a long-term financial point of view. There are also strong arguments in favour of going ahead with the proposal from a strategic point of view. It would seem to give the division a strong competitive advantage and the opportunity to make products that were previously beyond the range of existing equipment. It can be argued that sole concentration on financial measures of performance is not in the best interest of the organization from a strategic point of view. The use of a more balanced approach to performance measurement, for example the balanced scorecard approach of Kaplan and Norton (1992), may be more appropriate in today's competitive environment. Obviously financial issues are very important and this balanced scorecard approach attempts to ensure the long-term financial strength of the organization.

Problem 2   British Rail

The extracts demonstrate the wide range of performance measures which are produced by one public sector organization. The measures include both financial and non-financial measures of performance. There are also measures which compare the performance of British Rail with the average performance of other European railways.

The quality of service measures compare performance against both the target and the previous year's performance. The general performance indicators show a trend of performance over the past five years. Trends indicate either an improvement or a deterioration in the level of performance over a period of time. In order to make real comparisons, monetary values have been converted to 1991/2 levels. Managers can use these measures to determine the success or otherwise of the organization and to trigger corrective action if necessary.

As with any type of organization, it is important that managers are aware of their customers' expectations and whether those expectations are being met. The quality of service measures highlight expectations and ensures that management attention is focused upon them. Other measures enable managers to look at the efficiency of the organization. The figures for operating expenses per train mile seem to have gone down since 1987/8. However, receipts per passenger mile and receipts per train mile have gone down in 1991/2 compared with 1990/1. Also, the profit as a percentage of receipts has gone down from 7.9% in 1988/9 to 0.5% in 1991/2. The statistics can therefore be used in a very similar way to the ratios that were discussed in Chapter 3.

It can be argued that British Rail is more like a private sector organization than many of the other activities in the public sector. The plans to privatize British Rail lend particular weight to that theory. However, some people argue that British Rail has a public role to play as part of a national transport policy. Such arguments highlight the social concerns of many public sector organizations and the need to recognize these concerns in the objectives of the organization. Once these objectives are recognized, then the performance measurement system should report on the success of the organization in terms of meeting those objectives. Such measures of performance would be measures of effectiveness.

Problem 3   Sherer Group

(a) *Current planned ROI for Northern Division*:

    Profit   £100 × 100,000 = £10m
    Capital employed   = £50m
            Current ROI = 20%

If component purchased from Robo plc the ROI will be:

    Profit per unit = £125
    Total profit   = 125 x 100,000 units
                    = £12½m
            ROI = 25%

The General Manager of Northern Division would be happy with the reduction in cost of the component part because it would ensure that Northern Division achieved its target and he will receive a bonus.

(b) The cost of £125 from Robo plc is a variable cost to the group. The variable costs of Southern Division are only £100 and Southern Division has spare capacity. The overall profit of the Group will therefore reduce by

    100,000 x £25 = £2½m

Profit with Southern producing component parts

	£m
Northern £100 × 100,000 units of product X	10
Southern £30 × 100,000 component parts	3
	13

Profit with Robo plc producing component parts

	£m
Northern £125 × 100,000 units of product X	12½
Southern fixed costs not recovered 20 × 100,000	(2)
	10½

The Group management team would not be happy with a loss in profit for the group of £2½m. However, the Group management team would need to recognize the dysfunctional effect that a decision to stop Northern purchasing from Robo plc would have on the management team at Northern Division.

(c) The current method of transfer pricing is *full cost-plus* (25%). When critically evaluating transfer prices one should always bear in mind the objectives of a transfer pricing policy – goal congruence, objective performance evaluation, divisional autonomy and management motivation.

The full cost-plus method has the advantage of providing some incentive to the supplying division since they do make some profit on the transaction. However, as shown in part (b), the transfer price from the supplying division becomes the variable cost of the receiving division. This can cause dysfunctional decisions as highlighted in (a) and (b) since goal congruence would not be observed.

A problem with full cost-plus pricing is that the receiving division is not given satisfactory information for decision-making. A crucial point in this situation is that Southern Division has spare capacity and will not replace the capacity used in the production of the component part. In this situation it can be argued that the most appropriate transfer price is the standard variable cost of the supplying division. This, however, also causes problems from the supplying division's point of view – lack of autonomy and poor management motivation.

Appendix A Discount tables

Table A.1 *Present value of £1 due at end of* n *years*

n	1%	2%	3%	4%	5%	6%	7%	8%	9%	10%	n
1	0.99010	0.98039	0.97007	0.96154	0.95238	0.94340	0.93458	0.92593	0.91743	0.90909	1
2	0.98030	0.96117	0.94260	0.92456	0.90703	0.89000	0.87344	0.85734	0.84168	0.82645	2
3	0.97059	0.94232	0.91514	0.88900	0.86384	0.83962	0.81630	0.79383	0.77218	0.75131	3
4	0.96098	0.92385	0.88849	0.85480	0.82270	0.79209	0.76290	0.73503	0.70843	0.68301	4
5	0.95147	0.90573	0.86261	0.82193	0.78353	0.74726	0.71299	0.68058	0.64993	0.62092	5
6	0.94204	0.88797	0.83748	0.79031	0.74622	0.70496	0.66634	0.63017	0.59627	0.56447	6
7	0.93272	0.87056	0.81309	0.75992	0.71068	0.66506	0.62275	0.58349	0.54703	0.51316	7
8	0.92348	0.85349	0.78941	0.73069	0.67684	0.62741	0.58201	0.54027	0.50187	0.46651	8
9	0.91434	0.83675	0.76642	0.70259	0.64461	0.59190	0.54393	0.50025	0.46043	0.42410	9
10	0.90529	0.82035	0.74409	0.67556	0.61391	0.55839	0.50835	0.46319	0.42241	0.38554	10
11	0.89632	0.80426	0.72242	0.64958	0.58468	0.52679	0.47509	0.42888	0.38753	0.35049	11
12	0.88745	0.78849	0.70138	0.62460	0.55684	0.49697	0.44401	0.39711	0.35553	0.31863	12
13	0.87866	0.77303	0.68095	0.60057	0.53032	0.46884	0.41496	0.36770	0.32618	0.28966	13
14	0.86996	0.75787	0.66112	0.57747	0.50507	0.44230	0.38782	0.34046	0.29925	0.26333	14
15	0.86135	0.74301	0.64186	0.55526	0.48102	0.41726	0.36245	0.31524	0.27454	0.23939	15
16	0.85282	0.72845	0.62317	0.53391	0.45811	0.39365	0.33873	0.29189	0.25187	0.21763	16
17	0.84438	0.71416	0.60502	0.51337	0.43630	0.37136	0.31657	0.27027	0.23107	0.19784	17
18	0.83602	0.70016	0.58739	0.49363	0.41552	0.35034	0.29586	0.25025	0.21199	0.17986	18
19	0.82774	0.68643	0.57029	0.47464	0.39573	0.33051	0.27651	0.23171	0.19449	0.16351	19
20	0.81954	0.67297	0.55367	0.45639	0.37689	0.31180	0.25842	0.21455	0.17843	0.14864	20
21	0.81143	0.65978	0.53755	0.43883	0.35894	0.29415	0.24151	0.19866	0.16370	0.13513	21
22	0.80340	0.64684	0.52189	0.42195	0.34185	0.27750	0.22571	0.18394	0.15018	0.12285	22
23	0.79544	0.63414	0.50669	0.40573	0.32557	0.26180	0.21095	0.17031	0.13778	0.11168	23
24	0.78757	0.62172	0.49193	0.39012	0.31007	0.24698	0.19715	0.15770	0.12640	0.10153	24
25	0.77977	0.60953	0.47760	0.37512	0.29530	0.23300	0.18425	0.14602	0.11597	0.09230	25

Note: $PV = £1/(1 + r)^n$

Table A.1 *(continued)*

n	11%	12%	13%	14%	15%	16%	17%	18%	19%	20%	n
1	0.90090	0.89286	0.88496	0.87719	0.86957	0.86207	0.85470	0.84746	0.84034	0.83333	1
2	0.81162	0.79719	0.78315	0.76947	0.75614	0.74316	0.73051	0.71818	0.70616	0.69444	2
3	0.73119	0.71178	0.69305	0.67497	0.65752	0.64066	0.62437	0.60863	0.59342	0.57870	3
4	0.65873	0.63552	0.61332	0.59208	0.57175	0.55229	0.53365	0.51579	0.49867	0.48225	4
5	0.59345	0.56743	0.54276	0.51937	0.49718	0.47611	0.45611	0.43711	0.41905	0.40188	5
6	0.53464	0.50663	0.48032	0.45559	0.43233	0.41044	0.38984	0.37043	0.35214	0.33490	6
7	0.48166	0.45235	0.42506	0.39964	0.37594	0.35383	0.33320	0.31392	0.29592	0.27908	7
8	0.43393	0.40388	0.37616	0.35056	0.32690	0.30503	0.28487	0.26604	0.24867	0.23257	8
9	0.39092	0.36061	0.33288	0.30751	0.28426	0.26295	0.24340	0.22546	0.20897	0.19381	9
10	0.35218	0.32197	0.29459	0.26974	0.24718	0.22668	0.20804	0.19106	0.17560	0.16151	10
11	0.31728	0.28748	0.26070	0.23662	0.21494	0.19542	0.17781	0.16192	0.14756	0.13459	11
12	0.28584	0.25667	0.23071	0.20756	0.18691	0.16846	0.15197	0.13722	0.12400	0.11216	12
13	0.25751	0.22917	0.20416	0.18207	0.16253	0.14523	0.12989	0.11629	0.10420	0.09346	13
14	0.23199	0.20462	0.18068	0.15971	0.14133	0.12520	0.11102	0.09855	0.08757	0.07789	14
15	0.20900	0.18270	0.15989	0.14010	0.12289	0.10793	0.09489	0.08352	0.07359	0.06491	15
16	0.18829	0.16312	0.14150	0.12289	0.10686	0.09304	0.08110	0.07078	0.06184	0.05409	16
17	0.16963	0.14564	0.12522	0.10780	0.09393	0.08021	0.06932	0.05998	0.05196	0.04507	17
18	0.15282	0.13004	0.11081	0.09456	0.08080	0.06914	0.05925	0.05083	0.04367	0.03756	18
19	0.13768	0.11611	0.09806	0.08295	0.07026	0.05961	0.05064	0.04308	0.03669	0.03130	19
20	0.12403	0.10367	0.08678	0.07276	0.06110	0.05139	0.04328	0.03651	0.03084	0.02608	20
21	0.11174	0.09256	0.07680	0.06383	0.05313	0.04430	0.03699	0.03094	0.02591	0.02174	21
22	0.10067	0.08264	0.06796	0.05599	0.04620	0.03819	0.03162	0.02622	0.02178	0.01811	22
23	0.09069	0.07379	0.06014	0.04911	0.04017	0.03292	0.02702	0.02222	0.01830	0.01509	23
24	0.08170	0.06588	0.05322	0.04308	0.03493	0.02838	0.02310	0.01883	0.01538	0.01258	24
25	0.07361	0.05882	0.04710	0.03779	0.03038	0.02447	0.01974	0.01596	0.01292	0.01048	25

Table A.2 *Present value of annuity of £1 for n years*

n	1%	2%	3%	4%	5%	6%	7%	8%	9%	10%	n
1	0.9901	0.9804	0.9709	0.9615	0.9524	0.9434	0.9346	0.9259	0.9174	0.9091	1
2	1.9704	1.9416	1.9135	1.8861	1.8594	1.8334	1.8080	1.7833	1.7591	1.7355	2
3	2.9410	2.8839	2.8286	2.7751	2.7232	2.6730	2.6243	2.5771	2.5313	2.4868	3
4	3.9020	3.8077	3.7171	3.6299	3.5459	3.4651	3.3872	3.3121	3.2397	3.1699	4
5	4.8535	4.7134	4.5797	4.4518	4.3295	3.2123	4.1002	3.9927	3.8896	3.7908	5
6	5.7955	5.6014	5.4172	5.2421	5.0757	4.9173	4.7665	4.6229	4.4859	4.3553	6
7	6.7282	6.4720	6.2302	6.0020	5.7863	5.5824	5.3893	5.2064	5.0329	4.8684	7
8	7.6517	7.3254	7.0196	6.7327	6.4632	6.2098	5.9713	5.7466	5.5348	5.3349	8
9	8.5661	8.1622	7.7861	7.4353	7.1078	6.8017	6.5152	6.2469	5.9852	5.7590	9
10	9.4714	8.9825	8.5302	8.1109	7.7217	7.3601	7.0236	6.7101	6.4176	6.1446	10
11	10.3677	9.7868	9.2526	8.7604	8.3064	7.8868	7.4987	7.1389	6.8052	6.4951	11
12	11.2552	10.5753	9.9539	9.3850	8.8632	8.3838	7.9427	7.5361	7.1607	6.8137	12
13	12.1338	11.3483	10.6349	9.9856	9.3935	8.8527	8.3576	7.9038	7.4869	7.1034	13
14	13.0038	12.1062	11.2960	10.5631	9.8986	9.2950	8.7454	8.2442	7.7861	7.3667	14
15	13.8651	12.8492	11.9379	11.1183	10.3796	9.7122	9.1079	8.5595	8.0607	7.6061	15
16	14.7180	13.5777	12.5610	11.6522	10.8377	10.1059	9.4466	8.8514	8.3125	7.8237	16
17	15.5624	14.2918	13.1660	12.1656	11.2740	10.4772	9.7632	9.1216	8.5436	8.0215	17
18	16.3984	14.9920	13.7534	12.6592	11.6895	10.8276	10.0591	9.3719	8.7556	8.2014	18
19	17.2261	15.6784	14.3237	13.1339	12.0853	11.1581	10.3356	9.6036	8.9501	8.3649	19
20	18.0457	16.3514	14.8774	13.5903	12.4622	11.4699	10.5940	9.8181	9.1285	8.5136	20
21	18.8571	17.0111	15.4149	14.0291	12.8211	11.7640	10.8355	10.0168	9.2922	8.6487	21
22	19.6605	17.6580	15.9368	14.4511	13.1630	12.0416	11.0612	10.2007	9.4424	8.7715	22
23	20.4559	18.2921	16.4435	14.8568	13.4885	12.3033	11.2722	10.3710	9.5802	8.8832	23
24	21.2435	18.9139	16.9355	15.2469	13.7986	12.5503	11.4693	10.5287	9.7066	8.9847	24
25	22.0233	19.5234	17.4131	15.6220	14.0939	12.7833	11.6536	10.6748	9.8226	9.0770	25

Table A.2 *(continued)*

n	11%	12%	13%	14%	15%	16%	17%	18%	19%	20%	n
1	0.0009	0.8929	0.8850	0.3772	0.8696	0.8621	0.8547	0.8475	0.8403	0.8333	1
2	1.7125	1.6901	1.6681	1.6467	1.6257	1.6052	1.5852	1.5656	1.5465	1.5278	2
3	2.4437	2.4018	2.3612	2.3216	2.2832	2.2459	2.2096	2.1743	2.1399	2.1065	3
4	3.1024	3.0373	2.9745	2.9137	2.8550	2.7982	2.7432	2.6901	2.6386	2.5887	4
5	3.6959	3.6048	3.5172	3.4331	3.3522	3.2743	3.1993	3.1272	3.0576	2.9906	5
6	4.2305	4.1114	3.9976	3.8887	3.7845	3.6847	3.5892	3.4976	3.4098	3.3255	6
7	4.7122	4.5638	4.4226	4.2883	4.1604	4.0386	3.9224	3.8115	3.7057	3.6046	7
8	5.1461	4.9676	4.7988	4.6389	4.4873	4.3436	3.2072	4.0776	3.9544	3.8372	8
9	5.5370	5.3282	5.1317	4.9464	4.7716	4.6065	4.4506	4.3030	4.1633	4.0310	9
10	5.8892	5.6502	5.4262	5.2161	5.0188	4.8332	4.6586	4.4941	4.3389	4.1925	10
11	6.2065	5.9377	5.6869	5.4527	5.2337	5.0286	4.8364	4.6560	4.4865	4.3271	11
12	6.4924	6.1944	5.9176	5.6603	5.4206	5.1971	4.9884	4.7932	4.6105	4.4392	12
13	6.7499	6.4235	6.1218	5.8424	5.5931	5.3423	5.1183	4.9095	4.7147	4.5327	13
14	6.9819	6.6282	6.3025	6.0021	5.7245	5.4675	5.2293	5.0081	4.8023	4.6106	14
15	7.1909	6.8109	6.4624	6.1422	5.8474	5.5755	5.3242	5.0916	4.8759	4.6755	15
16	7.3792	6.9740	6.6039	6.2651	5.9542	5.6685	5.4053	5.1624	4.9377	4.7296	16
17	7.5488	7.1196	6.7291	6.3729	6.0472	5.7487	5.4746	5.2223	4.9897	4.7746	17
18	7.7016	7.2497	6.8399	6.4674	6.1280	5.8178	5.5339	5.2732	5.0333	4.8122	18
19	7.8393	7.3658	6.9380	6.5504	6.1982	5.8775	5.5845	5.3162	5.0700	4.8435	19
20	7.9633	7.4694	7.0248	6.6231	6.2593	5.9288	5.6278	5.3527	5.1009	4.8696	20
21	8.0751	7.5620	7.1016	6.6870	6.3125	5.9731	5.6648	5.3837	5.1268	4.8913	21
22	8.1757	7.6446	7.1695	6.7429	6.3587	6.0113	5.6964	5.4099	5.1486	4.9094	22
23	8.2664	7.7184	7.2297	6.7921	6.3988	6.0442	5.7234	5.4321	5.1668	4.9245	23
24	8.3481	7.7843	7.2829	6.8351	6.4338	6.0726	5.7465	5.4509	5.1822	4.9371	24
25	8.4217	7.8431	7.3300	6.8729	6.4641	6.0971	5.7662	5.4669	5.1951	4.9476	25

Appendix B Extracts from the published accounts of WH Smith Group plc*

Chairman
Sir Simon Hornby

Directors
Edward Elson
Sir Malcolm Field
Jeremy Hardie
Stanley Honeyman
Dr Janet Morgan
John Napier
David Roberts
The Hon Philip Smith
Neil Thomas
Peter Troughton
Peter Wilmot-Sitwell
Lord Windlesham

Secretary
Christopher Rule

Company number
471941 (England)

Registered Office
Strand House
7 Holbein Place
London SW1W 8NR

Auditors
Touche Ross & Co
Hill House
1 Little New Street
London EC4A 3TR

Solicitors
Herbert Smith
Exchange House
Primrose Street
London EC2A 2HS

Registrars
Barclays Registrars Limited
Bourne House
34 Beckenham Road
Beckenham, Kent
BR3 4TU

Stockbrokers
Cazenove & Co
12 Tokenhouse Yard
London EC2R 7AN

Merchant Bankers
Baring Brothers & Co Limited
8 Bishopsgate
London EC2N 4AE

Contents

Financial Highlights

	52 weeks to 1 June 1991 £m	52 weeks to 2 June 1990 £m
Turnover	1,970.6	2,130.8
Trading profit including associated undertakings	117.2	110.7
Profit on ordinary activities before taxation	89.0	86.0
Extraordinary items	(13.7)	27.4
Profit for the financial period	45.8	86.5
Total capital and reserves	252.8	294.3
Per 50p Ordinary Share:		
Ordinary dividends	12.5p	11.5p
Earnings	29.8p	29.9 p
Asset value	124.8p	147.8p
Dividend cover before extraordinary items (times)	2.2	2.6

Financial Calendar

Results
Interim (6 months) results announced late January
Final results announced end August

Dividends and interest payments
Ordinary dividends
   Interim paid early April
   Final paid mid October

Preference dividends
   Paid end March, September

7⅛% Convertible Subordinated Bonds 2002 interest
   Paid March

Debenture and Loan Stock interest
   8% Redeemable Debenture Stock
   5⅛% Redeemable Loan Stock
   7¾% Redeemable Loan Stock
   Paid early January, early July

Capital gains tax
For capital gains tax purposes, market values on 31 March 1982 were as follows:

'A' Ordinary Shares of 50 pence each	85½p
'B' Ordinary Shares of 10 pence each	16¼p

Ordinary share market values have been adjusted for a scrip issue on 15 July 1983.

5¾% Cumulative Preference Shares of £1 each	42½p
7¾% Redeemable Loan Stock	£59¼
3¾% Cumulative Redeemable Preference Shares of £1 each	28½p
5⅛% Redeemable Loan Stock	£33¼

Five Year Review

Sales £ m

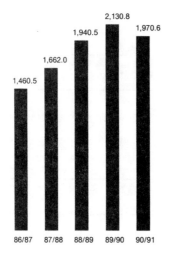

Profit before tax £ m

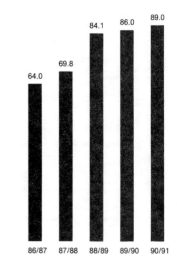

Dividend per 50p ordinary share p

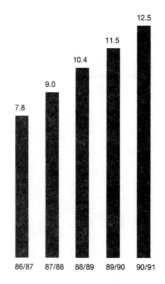

Earnings per 50p ordinary share p

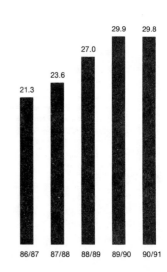

Report of the Directors

The Directors of WH Smith Group PLC present their forty second annual report to shareholders, together with the audited financial statements for the 52 weeks to 1 June 1991

Principal Activities

The principal activities and future prospects of the Group are set out in the Chairman's Statement on pages 4 and 5 and in the Review of Operations on pages 14 to 29.

Group Results

The Group profit and loss account for the 52 weeks to 1 June 1991 shown on page 42 includes the following details:

	52 weeks to 1 June 1991	52 weeks to 2 June 1990
	£m	£m
Trading profit including associated undertakings	117.2	110.7
Profit on ordinary activities before taxation	89.0	86.0
Profit retained	18.4	63.6

An analysis of turnover and trading profit by activity and by geographical area is shown in Note 2 to the financial statements on page 46.

Dividends

The Directors recommend the payment of final dividends for the year of 8.5 pence per 'A' Ordinary Share of 50 pence and 1.7 pence per 'B' Ordinary Share of 10 pence on 18 October 1991 to members on the register at the close of business on 17 September 1991.

These final dividends, together with the interim dividends of 4.0 pence per 'A' Ordinary Share and 0.8 pence per 'B' Ordinary Share paid on 3 April 1991, make total dividends of 12.5 pence per 'A' Ordinary Share and 2.5 pence per 'B' Ordinary Share for the year compared with 11.5 pence per 'A' Ordinary Share and 2.3 pence per 'B' Ordinary Share for the year to 2 June 1990.

Share Capital

The authorised and issued share capital of the Company, together with details of all the shares issued during the year, are shown in Note 21 on page 54.

Since the year end the Company has successfully completed a rights issue of 'A' Ordinary Shares to raise approximately £149.0 million (net of expenses), the details of which are set out in Note 30 on page 60.

Fixed Assets

Details of tangible fixed assets and capital expenditure for the year are shown in Note 12 to the financial statements on page 49.

The most recent valuation of the Group's properties in the United Kingdom, other than those containing provision for rent reviews at seven year intervals or less and those freehold properties which it was intended to dispose of, was made by Messrs. Edward Erdman, Surveyors, as at 2 June 1990 in the adjusted sum of £192.5m. The valuation of the properties was made on the basis of their open market value within their existing use and with vacant possession of those properties which were in the Group's occupation but otherwise subject to lettings then existing. The resulting surplus of £31.3m over book value was incorporated in the 1990 financial statements. The Board believes that the value of the Group's properties on 1 June 1991 was not substantially different from the value of those properties on 2 June 1990.

Subsidiaries, Associated Undertakings and Businesses

During the period and subsequent to the period end, the Group:

(i) agreed with The Boots Company PLC in June 1990 to merge the 'Do It All' and 'Payless' DIY businesses of the Group and Boots respectively. The new company, Do It All Limited, is owned 50 per cent by Boots and 50 per cent by W H Smith.

(ii) acquired in November 1990 49 recorded music shops in the USA from the Wall to Wall chain for a cash consideration of US$23 million.

Disposals in the period and subsequent to the period end were:

(i) in August 1991 the Group's television business (excluding the Group's investment in Yorkshire Television Holdings plc) was sold to a consortium of ESPN Inc (80% owned by Capital Cities/ABC Inc. and 20% owned by Hearst Corporation), Canal Plus and Compagnie Generale des Eaux – for £45m in cash. The Group will assume the net debt of the Group's television business of approximately £4m.

(ii) in August 1991 the Group reached agreement with A T Mays Limited/Carlson Travel Network for the sale of a large part of the Group's W H Smith Travel business.

Further information on Post Balance Sheet Events is given in Note 30 on page 60.

Employment Policies

The Company believes that employees are motivated and committed to the objectives of the business for which they work if they are involved in the decision-making process and have the opportunity to communicate their views. Employees receive regular briefings and presentations about the Group and the business in which they work and on matters which affect them and are encouraged to comment either through the formal channels which exist or at the informal meetings with directors which are organised in different parts of the country. The Group publishes a staff newspaper which provides information on the businesses and a forum for staff to comment on any matter.

Staff Committees have been extended within the Group; there has been a re-organisation of the Staff Associations to provide a closer alignment with the individual businesses and greater harmony has been established in the relationship with trade unions representing employees.

The training and development of its staff remains a priority for the Group since it believes that well-trained employees feel their efforts are recognised and that they can perform their jobs better. Also, with an established staff development policy and well-trained staff the Group can respond quickly to changes in the business environment and introduce the new systems and technologies required for the Group to remain competitive.

The Group is committed to providing equal opportunities for all irrespective of sex, ethnic origin, religion or disability. Initiatives in the past year have been the introduction of creche facilities at the Retail Head Office, the equalisation of retirement ages and the extension of pension benefits to some part-time employees.

The Group recognises its responsibility to encourage and assist in the employment, training, promotion and career development of disabled people and employs them where suitable opportunities arise. Wherever practicable, arrangements are made to continue the employment of persons who become disabled during their service with the Group.

The Group believes that staff commitment and performance is enhanced by the opportunity to acquire shares in the Company and operates two schemes by which members of staff can obtain shares – a Share Ownership Scheme and an SAYE Share Option Scheme.

As at 1 June 1991 some 12,600 past and present employees were participating in the Share Ownership Scheme and some 3,500 current employees were participating in the SAYE Share Option Scheme.

Health and Safety at Work

The Company believes that the introduction and maintenance of high standards of health and safety at work is essential and has a Group Health and Safety Department to provide an integrated approach to matters concerning the well-being of employees and members of the public.

Political and Charitable Donations

Charitable donations during the period totalled £251,000 (52 weeks to 2 June 1990 £342,000). There were no political donations.

Directors

The names of the Directors of this Company are set out on page 1.

Mr J D Smith retired on 4 September 1990.

Mr P J C Troughton was appointed a director on 2 April 1991 and pursuant to the Articles of Association retires but, being eligible, offers himself for re-appointment. Mr Troughton has a contract of service which may be terminated by the Company giving three years' notice.

Sir Malcolm Field, Mr J A Napier, Mr C J M Hardie and Lord Windlesham retire by rotation but, being eligible, offer themselves for re-election.

Sir Malcolm Field, who is Group Managing Director, has been a director since 1974. Sir Malcolm has a contract of service which may be terminated by the Company giving three years' notice.

Mr J A Napier, who is Group Finance Director, has been a director since 1989. Mr Napier does not have a contract of service.

Mr C J M Hardie has served the Company as a non-executive director since 1988. Mr Hardie does not have a contract of service.

Lord Windlesham has served the Company as a non-executive director since 1986. Lord Windlesham does not have a contract of service.

Details of the interests of Directors and their families in the share capital of the Company are shown on pages 39 and 40.

Significant Contracts

In the period from 3 June 1990 to the date of this report no director had an interest in any significant contract relating to the business of the Company or its subsidiaries, other than the contracts of service of executive directors.

Company Shareholders

An analysis showing the spread of ordinary shareholders in the Company and details of substantial shareholdings is shown on page 41.

Insurance of Directors and Officers

Insurance is maintained by the Group in respect of liability attaching to directors and officers arising out of their employment by the Group.

Income and Corporation Taxes Act 1988

The Company is not a close company for the purposes of this Act.

Auditors

It is proposed to re-appoint Touche Ross & Co. as auditors and a resolution to re-appoint them and to authorise the directors to fix their remuneration will be proposed at the Annual General Meeting.

By Order of the Board

C S Rule
Company Secretary
29 August 1991

Directors' interests as at 7 August 1991

in shares, share options, debentures and unsecured loan stocks.

The interests of each Director, as recorded in the Company's Register of Directors' Share Interests as at 7 August 1991, are summarised below and incorporate changes in holdings of 'A' Ordinary Shares and in Share Options which have arisen since 1 June 1991 as a result of the Rights Issue. There have been no changes in holdings of 'B' Ordinary Shares since 1 June 1991.

| | Shareholdings | | Share Options |
	'A' Ordinary Shares	'B' Ordinary Shares	'A' Ordinary Shares
Beneficially			
E E Elson	23,232	464,641	–
Sir Malcolm Field	40,832	42,500	268,832
C J M Hardie	1,250	–	–
S H Honeyman	548	10,000	–
Sir Simon Hornby	54,916	1,091,192	170,391
Dr J P Morgan	250	–	–
J A Napier	1,273	–	160,955
D J M Roberts	2,366	–	118,520
The Hon P R Smith	194,280	35,682,047	–
R N Thomas	3,961	–	114,226
P J C Troughton	2,273	40,150	96,463
P S Wilmot-Sitwell	5,000	–	–
Lord Windlesham	3,186	–	–
As Trustees			
Sir Malcolm Field, Sir Simon Hornby, J A Napier, R N Thomas, *note (i)*	–	905,210	–
Sir Simon Hornby	97,257	253,730	–
D J M Roberts	4,759	450,000	–
The Hon P R Smith *note (ii)*	556,145	5,365,441	–
P J C Troughton	–	1,000,000	–

Notes:
i) Sir Malcolm Field and his co-trustees also had an interest in £10 5⅛% Redeemable Unsecured Loan Stock at 7 August 1991.
ii) Shareholdings in which The Hon P R Smith was interested both as a beneficiary and as a trustee as at 7 August 1991 have been excluded from his trustee figures to avoid duplication, as follows:

'A' Ordinary Shares	'B' Ordinary Shares
126,528	17,936,607

Profit and loss account

	52 weeks to 1 June 1991 £m	52 weeks to 2 June 1990 £m
Turnover note 2	**1970.6**	**2,130.8**
Cost of sales	(1404.7)	(1,499.9)
Gross Profit	565.9	630.9
Other net expenses note 3	(453.7)	(520.3)
Trading profit	**112.2**	**110.6**
Share of profits of associated undertakings note 2	5.0	0.1
Trading profit including associated undertakings	**117.2**	**110.7**
Net interest note 4	(28.2)	(24.7)
Profit on ordinary activities before taxation note 5	**89.0**	**86.0**
Tax on profit on ordinary activities note 6	(27.8)	(28.9)
Profit on ordinary activities after taxation	**61.2**	**57.1**
DIA preference dividend note 7	(2.8)	–
Minority interests	1.1	2.0
Profit before extraordinary items	**59.5**	**59.1**
Extraordinary items note 8	(13.7)	27.4
Profit for the financial period note 9	**45.8**	**86.5**
Dividends note 10	(27.4)	(22.9)
Transfer to reserves note 22	**18.4**	**63.6**
Earnings per 50p Ordinary share note 11	**29.8p**	**29.9p**

Total reserves

	52 weeks to 1 June 1991 £m	52 weeks to 2 June 1990 £m
At beginning of the period	194.4	182.0
Profit retained for the period	18.4	63.6
Other movements in the period:		
Realisation of revaluation surplus	(3.0)	(1.6)
Exchange movement	(0.7)	(0.7)
Surplus on revaluation of properties	–	31.3
Premium on 'A' Ordinary Shares issued	9.1	3.7
Goodwill	(66.9)	(83.9)
At the end of the period	151.3	194.4

An analysis of movements in reserves is given in note 22 to the financial statements on page 55.

	Group 1 June 1991 £m	Group 2 June 1990 £m	Company 1 June 1991 £m	Company 2 June 1990 £m
Fixed assets				
Tangible fixed assets *note 12*	404.8	455.0	–	–
Investments *note 13*	44.6	11.4	258.0	258.0
	449.4	**466.4**	**258.0**	**258.0**
Current assets				
Stocks *note 14*	221.4	262.3	–	–
Debtors *note 15*	100.7	157.7	73.9	59.0
Assets in the course of disposal *note 16*	45.3	–	–	–
Cash at bank and in hand	34.1	51.7	–	–
	401.5	471.7	73.9	59.0
Pension prepayment *note 17*	37.6	8.4	–	–
Creditors: amounts falling due within one year *note 18*	(417.9)	(445.5)	(46.1)	(28.5)
Net current assets	**21.2**	**34.6**	**27.8**	**30.5**
Total assets less current liabilities	**470.6**	**501.0**	**285.8**	**288.5**
Creditors: amounts falling due after more than one year *note 19*	(193.8)	(188.7)	(41.1)	(54.5)
Provisions for liabilities and charges *note 20*	(19.3)	(12.6)	–	–
Minority interests	(4.7)	(5.4)	–	–
Total net assets	**252.8**	**294.3**	**244.7**	**234.0**
Called up share capital *note 21*	101.5	99.9	101.5	99.9
Share premium account *note 22*	30.9	21.8	30.9	21.8
Revaluation reserve *note 22*	74.4	77.4	58.1	58.1
Other capital reserve *note 22*	–	–	33.4	33.4
Profit and loss account *note 22*	46.0	95.2	20.8	20.8
Total capital and reserves	**252.8**	**294.3**	**244.7**	**234.0**

These financial statements were approved by the Board of Directors on 29 August 1991.

Signed on behalf of the Board of Directors

Sir Simon Hornby
Chairman

John A Napier
Director

	52 weeks to 1 June 1991	52 weeks to 2 June 1990
	£m	£m
Operating Activities:		
Profit before tax and extraordinary items excluding associated undertakings	84.0	85.9
Depreciation charged	33.1	42.4
Pension credit	(11.2)	(3.7)
Decrease (increase) in debtors	5.0	(26.9)
Increase in creditors	24.2	4.1
Increase in stock	(25.4)	(34.6)
Effect of other deferrals and accruals of operating		
activity cash flows	3.8	4.5
Corporation tax paid	(30.3)	(38.6)
Cash flow from operating activities	**83.2**	**33.1**
Investing Activities:		
Purchase of businesses *note 22*	(30.0)	(98.9)
Purchase of fixed assets	(70.5)	(91.9)
Sale of businesses	–	61.8
Sale of fixed assets	15.3	14.3
Other	(2.2)	(0.5)
Cash flow from investing activities	**(87.4)**	**(115.2)**
Financing Activities:		
Increase in borrowings	4.3	125.5
Proceeds from shares issued	5.3	4.3
Payment of dividends	(23.0)	(21.0)
Cash flow from financing activities	**(13.4)**	**108.8**
Net decrease in cash and cash equivalents	(17.6)	26.7
Cash and cash equivalents at 2 June 1990	51.7	25.0
Cash and cash equivalents at 1 June 1991	**34.1**	**51.7**

The Group has adopted a new cash flow statement format this year. Prior year figures have been restated for comparative purposes.

1 Accounting Policies

The financial statements have been prepared in accordance with statements of standard accounting practice issued by UK accountancy bodies.

a Accounting convention

The financial statements are prepared in compliance with the Companies Act 1985 and under the historical cost convention with the exception of certain fixed assets and investments which are stated at revalued amounts. Prior year figures have been restated for comparative purposes (see note 8).

b Basis of consolidation

The Group financial statements consolidate the financial statements of the parent company, its subsidiaries and the Group's share of associated undertakings and include, from the date of acquisition, the results of subsidiaries, associated undertakings and new businesses acquired during the period. Goodwill, representing the excess of the purchase consideration over the fair value of the net tangible assets of acquired businesses, is written off against reserves.

c Fixed asset investments

In the consolidated accounts, shares in associated undertakings are accounted for using the equity method of accounting. The consolidated profit and loss account includes the appropriate share of the results of the associate and the investment is shown, in the consolidated balance sheet, at the group's share of net assets, excluding goodwill.

d Foreign currencies

Assets and liabilities denominated in foreign currencies are translated into sterling at rates prevailing at the balance sheet date. Profit and loss account items denominated in foreign currencies are translated at the average exchange rates for the period. Differences on exchange arising as follows are taken directly to reserves:

(i) The retranslation at closing rates of the opening net investment in overseas subsidiary companies, less related long term foreign currency borrowings raised to finance such investments.

(ii) The difference between the profit and loss account of overseas subsidiary companies translated at average rates and at closing rates.

All other profits and losses on exchange are credited or charged to the profit and loss account.

e Depreciation

(i) Freehold and long leasehold properties are not depreciated where, in the opinion of the Directors, the residual value of these properties is such that any depreciation charge would be immaterial. Other freehold and long leasehold properties are depreciated by equal instalments over 50 years.

(ii) Short leasehold and rack rent properties are amortised by equal instalments over the estimated period of the leases or their estimated remaining working lives if less.

(iii) Integral plant, shopfronts and structures included within properties are depreciated by equal instalments over periods of 6 to 10 years, or over the term of the lease if less.

(iv) Other assets are depreciated by equal instalments over their estimated lives at appropriate rates generally varying from 10% to 33%.

f Deferred taxation

Deferred taxation is provided on the liability method, to the extent that it is probable that a liability or asset will crystallise in the future. It is provided on items of income and expenditure included in the profit and loss account in different years from those in which they are assessed for taxation purposes.

g Stocks

Stocks are stated at the lower of purchase cost and net realisable value. The cost of finished goods and goods for resale is arrived at using the first in, first out method of valuation.

h Pension costs

Pension costs are recognised on a systematic and rational basis over the period of employees' service in accordance with Statement of Standard Accounting Practice 24. Details of pensions costs and pension funding are provided in note 25 on page 58.

1 Accounting Policies (continued)

i Leases

(i) Operating leases

Rental costs under operating leases are charged to the profit and loss account in equal annual amounts over the periods of the leases.

(ii) Finance leases

The cost of assets held under finance leases is included under tangible fixed assets and depreciation is provided in accordance with the Group's accounting policy for the class of asset concerned. The capital element of future lease payments is included in creditors. The interest cost is allocated to accounting periods based on the capital element of the leases outstanding.

2 Analysis of turnover and trading profit including associated undertakings

	Turnover		Trading profit including associated undertakings	
By activity	52 weeks to 1 June 1991	52 weeks to 2 June 1990	52 weeks to 1 June 1991	52 weeks to 2 June 1990
Retailing	£m	£m	£m	£m
News, books, stationery, recorded music, video etc	1,184.6	1,084.3	87.8	87.6
Do it yourself	214.2	252.2	10.4	9.6
Distribution				
News, office supplies, books etc	838.2	771.7	24.3	24.1
	2,237.0	2,108.2	122.5	121.3
Less: Intra group turnover	(72.3)	(73.5)	–	–
Continuing business	2,164.7	2,034.7	122.5	121.3
Discontinued businesses *note*	44.5	136.2	(5.3)	(10.6)
	2,209.2	**2,170.9**	**117.2**	**110.7**
Analysed as				
Group companies	1,970.6	2,130.8	112.2	110.6
Share of associated undertakings	238.6	40.1	5.0	0.1
	2,209.2	**2,170.9**	**117.2**	**110.7**
By geographical area				
United Kingdom and Europe	2,142.7	2,021.8	118.5	115.3
USA	94.3	86.4	4.0	6.0
	2,237.0	2,108.2	122.5	121.3
Less: Intra group turnover	(72.3)	(73.5)	–	–
Continuing business	2,164.7	2,034.7	122.5	121.3
Discontinued businesses *note*	44.5	136.2	(5.3)	(10.6)
	2,209.2	**2,170.9**	**117.2**	**110.7**

Note:

The trading results of the W H Smith Travel and WHSTV businesses have been consolidated to 1 December 1990, at which time the decision to dispose of these interests was taken. The trading results of those businesses since that date have been treated as extraordinary.

3 Other net expenses

	52 weeks to 1 June 1991	52 weeks to 2 June 1990
	£m	£m
Selling and distribution costs	440.6	508.8
Central administrative expenses		
Audit fees and expenses	0.7	0.7
Other	12.4	10.8
	13.1	11.5
	453.7	**520.3**

4 Net interest

	52 weeks to 1 June 1991 £m	52 weeks to 2 June 1990 £m
Payable		
On borrowings repayable within 5 years		
Bank overdrafts and loans	26.2	22.1
Debentures and loan stock	0.2	0.2
On borrowings repayable after 5 years		
Convertible bonds	3.4	3.6
Debentures and loan stock	0.1	0.1
Finance lease charges	0.7	1.5
	30.6	27.5
Receivable		
Bank deposits	(2.4)	(2.8)
	28.2	**24.7**

**5 Profit on ordinary activities before taxation
is stated after charging/(crediting)**

	52 weeks to 1 June 1991 £m	52 weeks to 2 June 1990 £m
Depreciation	33.1	42.4
Operating lease rentals:		
Land and buildings	83.6	93.2
Hire of plant and machinery	2.7	3.1
Pensions *note 25*	(11.2)	(3.7)
Operating lease rental income on land and buildings	(5.8)	(4.7)

6 Tax on profit on ordinary activities

	52 weeks to 1 June 1991 £m	52 weeks to 2 June 1990 £m
UK corporation tax at 33.8% (1989/90 – 35%)		
Current	20.3	25.3
Adjustment for prior years	(1.1)	(0.5)
Deferred	4.6	3.0
	23.8	27.8
Share of taxation on profits of associated undertakings	3.5	1.4
Overseas taxation	0.5	(0.3)
	27.8	**28.9**

7   DIA preference dividend

Do It All Limited is a joint venture owned 50 per cent by W H Smith Limited and 50 per cent by The Boots Company PLC who have merged the businesses of W H Smith Do It All Limited and Payless DIY Limited in accordance with the joint venture agreement dated 5 June 1990. The new merged company has issued cumulative preference shares to W H Smith and Boots. The Group's share of the cost of the preference dividend payable by the new merged company to The Boots Company PLC is shown separately in the profit and loss account.

8   Extraordinary items

	52 weeks to 1 June 1991 £m	52 weeks to 2 June 1990 £m
(Losses)/profits on disposal or closure of discontinued businesses	(24.7)	26.3
Pension surplus attributable to the merger of Do It All	12.3	–
Disposal of property	1.3	3.7
Share of extraordinary items in Yorkshire Television Holdings plc	(1.1)	1.9
	(12.2)	31.9
Related taxation	(1.5)	(4.5)
	(13.7)	**27.4**

Profits and losses on disposal of property are now being treated as extraordinary as it is not the policy of the Group to purchase property with a view to resale. Comparatives have been restated.

9   Profit for the financial period

As permitted by section 230 of the Companies Act 1985, the profit and loss account of the Company is not presented as part of these financial statements. The consolidated profit of £45.8m (1990–£86.5m) includes £27.4m (1990–£22.9m) which is dealt with in the accounts of the Company.

10   Dividends

	52 weeks to 1 June 1991 £'000	52 weeks to 2 June 1990 £'000
Preference Shares	20	20
'A' and 'B' Ordinary Shares		
Interim	8,024	7,930
Final	19,350	14,930
	27,374	22,860
	27,394	**22,880**

The final dividend includes the dividends payable on the new shares issued after the period end under the terms of the rights issue as detailed in note 30.

11   Earnings per 50p ordinary share

	52 weeks to 1 June 1991	52 weeks to 2 June 1990
The calculation of earnings per share is based on:		
Earnings (£m)	59.5	59.1
Weighted average ordinary shares in issue (m)	200.0	197.8

Earnings per share are based on both 50p 'A' Ordinary and 10p 'B' Ordinary Shares and are expressed in terms of a 50p 'A' Ordinary Share.

12 Tangible fixed assets

	Freehold properties £m Note (i)	Land and Buildings — Long-term £m Note (i)	Leasehold properties — Short-term £m	Rack rent £m Note (ii)	Fixtures and fittings £m	Equipment and motor vehicles £m Note (iii)	Total £m
Group							
Cost or valuation							
2 June 1990							
At valuation	177.6	8.0	6.9	–	–	–	192.5
At cost	8.7	0.1	18.9	141.1	154.4	108.1	431.3
	186.3	8.1	25.8	141.1	154.4	108.1	623.8
Subsidiaries acquired	–	–	–	–	0.6	–	0.6
Capital expenditure	6.2	0.5	2.2	19.9	21.4	20.3	70.5
Disposals	(13.9)	(1.9)	(0.1)	(4.0)	(8.1)	(6.4)	(34.4)
Subsidiaries sold	–	–	–	(26.5)	(51.4)	(11.3)	(89.2)
Transfer from stock	6.1	1.6	–	–	–	–	7.7
Transfer to assets in course of disposal	–	–	(1.3)	(2.4)	(4.4)	(23.8)	(31.9)
1 June 1991	**184.7**	**8.3**	**26.6**	**128.1**	**112.5**	**86.9**	**547.1**
Aggregate depreciation							
2 June 1990	0.4	0.1	9.3	42.7	62.7	53.6	168.8
Depreciation charged	0.1	–	2.1	5.9	11.1	13.9	33.1
Disposals	–	–	(0.2)	(2.2)	(6.0)	(5.6)	(14.0)
Subsidiaries sold	–	–	–	(6.1)	(19.5)	(2.9)	(28.5)
Transfer to assets in course of disposal	–	–	(0.4)	(0.7)	(1.0)	(15.0)	(17.1)
1 June 1991	**0.5**	**0.1**	**10.8**	**39.6**	**47.3**	**44.0**	**142.3**
Net book value							
At valuation note (iv)	166.3	7.6	7.0	–	–	–	180.9
At cost	17.9	0.6	8.8	88.5	65.2	42.9	223.9
1 June 1991 note (v)	**184.2**	**8.2**	**15.8**	**88.5**	**65.2**	**42.9**	**404.8**
2 June 1990	185.9	8.0	16.5	98.4	91.7	54.5	455.0

Notes:

(i) Freehold properties and long-term leasehold properties at 1 June 1991 includes assets not depreciated at cost or valuation of £154.7m and £8.2m respectively.

(ii) Rack rent properties are those held under leases containing provision for regular rent reviews at seven year intervals or less.

(iii) Equipment and motor vehicles includes assets held under finance leases:

	Cost £m	Depreciation £m	Net book value £m
At 2 June 1990	24.6	11.3	13.3
Movement in period	(17.1)	(8.2)	(8.9)
At 1 June 1991	7.5	3.1	4.4

(iv) The valuation of the properties was made as at 2 June 1990 on the basis of open market value for existing use and with vacant possession of those properties, or parts of properties, which were in the Group's occupation but otherwise subject to the existing lettings.

(v) If the Group's properties had not been revalued they would have been included at cost or earliest known valuation as shown below.

	Freehold properties £m	Leasehold properties — Long-term £m	Short-term £m	Total £m
Cost or earliest known valuation	88.2	5.6	25.1	118.9
Accumulated depreciation	(9.4)	(0.8)	(12.0)	(22.2)
At 1 June 1991	78.8	4.8	13.1	96.7
At 2 June 1990	83.9	4.2	12.9	101.0

13 Investments	Equity	Loans	Total
	£m	£m	£m
Group investments in associated undertakings			
Cost			
At 2 June 1990	16.2	2.1	18.3
Transfer to assets in the course of disposal	(9.8)	(2.1)	(11.9)
Additions	78.8	–	78.8
At 1 June 1991	**85.2**	**–**	**85.2**
Reserves			
At 2 June 1990	(6.3)	(0.6)	(6.9)
Transfer to assets in the course of disposal	12.4	0.6	13.0
Share of retained profits for the period	(0.1)	–	(0.1)
Other movements	0.5	–	0.5
Dividends received	(0.9)	–	(0.9)
Goodwill	(46.2)	–	(46.2)
At 1 June 1991	**(40.6)**	**–**	**(40.6)**
Net book value at 1 June 1991 *note (i)*	**44.6**	**–**	**44.6**
Net book value at 2 June 1990	9.9	1.5	11.4

Notes:
(i) Net book value at 1 June 1991 analysed as:

	Equity	Loans	Total
Listed *note (ii)*	10.0	–	10.0
Unlisted	34.6	–	34.6
	44.6	–	44.6

(ii) The cost and market value of listed investments as at 1 June 1991 are £6.4m and £20.2m respectively.

(iii) The Group's principal associated undertakings are listed in note 29.

(iv) The Group's share of the profits of Yorkshire Television Holdings plc is based on the most recent published financial statements which are for the period to 31 March 1991. The year end of Yorkshire Television Holdings plc is 30 September.

(v) The Group's share of the profits of Do It All Limited is based on the most recent audited financial statements which are for the period to 28 February 1991 and the unaudited management accounts for the subsequent period from 1 March 1991 to 1 June 1991.

	1 June 1991	2 June 1990
	£m	£m
Company		
Investment in W H Smith Limited		
Shares	116.0	116.0
Loans	142.0	142.0
	258.0	**258.0**

14   Stocks

	1 June 1991 £m	2 June 1990 £m
Group		
Finished goods and goods for resale	221.4	254.6
Property in the course of development	–	7.7
	221.4	**262.3**

15   Debtors

	Group 1 June 1991 £m	Group 2 June 1990 £m	Company 1 June 1991 £m	Company 2 June 1990 £m
Amounts falling due within one year:				
Trade debtors	53.6	62.9	–	–
Amounts owed by associated undertakings	2.7	5.7	–	–
Amounts owed by subsidiaries	–	–	60.2	47.4
Advance corporation tax	7.4	6.7	7.3	6.7
Other debtors	13.8	8.6	–	–
Prepayments and accrued income	16.7	31.8	–	–
Total debtors due within one year	**94.2**	**115.7**	**67.5**	**54.1**
Amounts falling due after more than one year:				
Tax recoverable *note (i)*	6.4	6.4	6.4	4.9
Prepayments and accrued income	0.1	35.6	–	–
Total debtors after more than one year	**6.5**	**42.0**	**6.4**	**4.9**
Total debtors	**100.7**	**157.7**	**73.9**	**59.0**

Notes:
(i) Tax recoverable after more than one year includes:

Advance corporation tax	6.4	4.9	6.4	4.9
Other timing differences *note (ii)*	–	1.5	–	–
	6.4	6.4	6.4	4.9

(ii) The deferred tax on other timing differences is included in provisions for liabilities and charges in note 20.

16   Assets in the course of disposal

Assets in the course of disposal represent the net assets of the WHSTV business and W H Smith Travel operations. Details of the disposals are set out in note 30.

17	Pension prepayment	52 weeks to 1 June 1991
		£m
	At 2 June 1990	8.4
	Cash contributions to funds	0.9
	Pension credit *note 25*	11.2
	Share of surplus attributable to	
	disposals and Do It All merger	17.1
		37.6

Notes:

(i) The pension prepayment is not refundable in cash and will be offset against pension costs charged to the profit and loss account after more than one year.

(ii) Deferred tax of £12.3m (1990 – £2.8m) has been provided on the prepayment as set out in note 20.

18	Creditors	Group	Group	Company	Company
	Amounts falling due within one year	1 June 1991	2 June 1990	1 June 1991	2 June 1990
		£m	£m	£m	£m
	Bank loans and overdrafts *note (i)*	62.8	80.0	9.0	–
	8% Redeemable Debenture Stock secured 1987/92 *note (ii)*	1.4	–	1.4	–
	7⅛% Convertible Subordinated Bonds 2002 in the course				
	of conversion	6.7	–	6.7	–
	Trade creditors	196.7	209.3	–	–
	Corporation tax	25.8	38.4	8.9	7.4
	VAT, payroll tax and social security	15.1	15.5	–	–
	Dividends	19.3	14.9	19.3	14.9
	Obligations under finance leases	1.3	4.1	–	–
	Other creditors	38.6	20.8	–	5.0
	Accruals and deferred income	50.2	62.5	0.8	1.2
	Total creditors due within one year	**417.9**	**445.5**	**46.1**	**28.5**

Notes:

(i) Bank loans and overdrafts include Sterling Commercial Paper of £9m (1990 £ nil).

(ii) The 8% Debenture stock 1987/92 is redeemable at the Company's option at par. The Debenture stock is secured by a floating charge on the undertaking, property and assets of the Company and certain of its wholly owned UK subsidiaries.

19 Creditors
Amounts falling due after more than one year

	Group 1 June 1991 £m	Group 2 June 1990 £m	Company 1 June 1991 £m	Company 2 June 1990 £m
Medium Term (1-5 years)				
Mortgage	–	0.4	–	–
8% Redeemable Debenture Stock secured 1987/92	–	1.4	–	1.4
7¾% Redeemable Unsecured Loan Stock 1988/93 *note (i)*	0.8	0.8	0.8	0.8
Bank loans *note (ii)*	149.5	121.6	–	–
Obligations under finance leases	3.3	10.5	–	–
Other creditors	–	0.6	0.1	–
Total medium term	**153.6**	**135.3**	**0.9**	**2.2**
Long Term (over 5 years)				
Mortgage	–	1.1	–	–
7⅛% Convertible Subordinated Bonds 2002 *note (iii)*	37.9	50.0	37.9	50.0
5⅛% Redeemable Unsecured Loan Stock *note (iv)*	2.3	2.3	2.3	2.3
Total long term	**40.2**	**53.4**	**40.2**	**52.3**
Total creditors due after more than one year	**193.8**	**188.7**	**41.1**	**54.5**

Notes:

(i) The 7¾% Loan stock 1988/93 is redeemable at the Company's option at par.

(ii) The medium term bank loans bear interest linked to London interbank rates and comprise:

(a) short term bills of exchange or advances, which can be replaced at the Group's option for further bills of exchange or advances under a committed facility available until February 1995; and

(b) foreign currency advances drawn under committed facilities repayable in July 1991, £10.5m (1990 – £11.9m) and June 1994, £29.5m (1990 – £29.8m)

(iii) The 7⅛% Convertible Subordinated Bonds 2002 are in denominations of £1,000. They are convertible prior to the close of business on 14 March 2002 at 335p per 'A' Ordinary Share. (Following the rights issue detailed in note 30 the conversion price has been adjusted to 325p). If the price of 'A' Ordinary Shares is equal to or greater than 436p (423p subsequent to the rights issue) for a continuous period of 30 days prior to 14 March 1993 then the Company may redeem the Bonds in £1,000,000 tranches at the following respective percentages of their principal amount during the 12 months indicated below:

12 months beginning 14 March 1991 102

1992 101

and thereafter at par.

Subsequent to 14 March 1993 the Company's option to redeem the bonds is not dependent upon the share price.

(iv) The 5⅛% Loan stock is redeemable at the Company's option at par.

20 Provisions for liabilities and charges

	Deferred taxation £m	Acquisition provisions £m	Total £m
Group			
At 2 June 1990 *note*	(1.5)	12.6	11.1
Utilised during the period	0.4	(0.5)	(0.1)
Profit and loss account	4.6	–	4.6
Extraordinary items	3.7	–	3.7
At 1 June 1991	**7.2**	**12.1**	**19.3**

52 weeks to 1 June 1991

Analysis of deferred taxation provision:

	1 June 1991 £m	2 June 1990 £m
Pension prepayment	12.3	2.8
Acquisition provision	(3.1)	(3.5)
Other timing differences	(2.0)	(0.8)
	7.2	**(1.5)**

Note:
The deferred taxation asset was included in debtors in 1990.

21 Called up share capital

	1 June 1991 Authorised £m	Allotted and fully paid £m	2 June 1990 Authorised £m	Allotted and fully paid £m
169,072 5¾% Cumulative Preference Shares of £1 each	0.2	0.2	0.2	0.2
260,620 3¾% Cumulative Redeemable Preference Shares of £1 each *note*	0.3	0.3	0.3	0.3
225,000,000 'A' Ordinary Shares of 50 pence each	112.5	87.1	112.5	85.5
155,000,000 'B' Ordinary Shares of 10 pence each	15.5	13.9	15.5	13.9
	128.5	**101.5**	**128.5**	**99.9**

Note:
The 3¾% Cumulative Redeemable Preference Shares are redeemable at the Company's option at par.

Movement in allotted share capital

	Number 'A' Ordinary shares	Number 'B' Ordinary shares	£m
At 2 June 1990			
Ordinary Shares, fully paid:	171,005,002	139,218,750	99.9
on conversion of Convertible Bonds	1,599,992	–	0.8
under Share Ownership Scheme	842,021	–	0.4
under SAYE Share Option Scheme	292,466	–	0.1
under Senior Executive Share Option Scheme	548,154	–	0.3
At 1 June 1991	**174,287,635**	**139,218,750**	**101.5**

52 weeks to 1 June 1991

Options granted at 1 June 1991:

(i) SAYE Share Option Scheme
3,668,844 'A' Ordinary Shares exercisable between June 1991 and October 1996 at between 244.8 pence and 327.6 pence per share.

(ii) Senior Executive Share Option Scheme
3,519,000 'A' Ordinary Shares exercisable between June 1991 and January 2001 at between 178.0 pence and 406.0 pence per share.

22 Reserves

	Share premium account £m	Revaluation Reserve £m	Other capital reserve £m	Profit and loss account £m	Total £m
Group					
At 2 June 1990	21.8	77.4	–	95.2	194.4
Profit retained	–	–	–	18.4	18.4
Realisation of revaluation surplus	–	(3.0)	–	–	(3.0)
Exchange movement	–	–	–	(0.7)	(0.7)
Premium on 'A' Ordinary Shares issued	9.1	–	–	–	9.1
Goodwill *note (i)*	–	–	–	(66.9)	(66.9)
At 1 June 1991	**30.9**	**74.4**	**–**	**46.0**	**151.3**
Company					
At 2 June 1990	21.8	58.1	33.4	20.8	134.1
Profit retained	–	–	–	–	–
Premium on 'A' Ordinary Shares issued	9.1	–	–	–	9.1
At 1 June 1991	**30.9**	**58.1**	**33.4**	**20.8**	**143.2**

Notes:

	52 weeks to 1 June 1991 £m
(i) Purchase consideration – cash	30.0
– net assets contributed to Do It All Limited	78.0
Total consideration	108.0
Less: fair value of net assets acquired *note (ii)*	(41.1)
Goodwill	66.9

	£m
Analysed as follows:	
Do It All Limited	46.2
Wall to Wall	15.4
Other acquisitions	5.3
	66.9

(ii) Fair value of net assets acquired is as follows:

	Book value at acquisition £m	Fair value adjustments £m	Fair value to the group £m
Investment in associated undertaking	52.0	(19.4)	32.6
Wall to Wall and other acquisitions:			
Tangible fixed assets	0.6	–	0.6
Stock	9.5	–	9.5
Debtors	–	–	–
Creditors	(1.6)	–	(1.6)
	8.5	–	8.5
	60.5	(19.4)	41.1

(iii) Goodwill of approximately £200 million has previously been written off to the profit and loss account relating to continuing businesses.

23	**Directors**		52 weeks to 1 June 1991 £'000	52 weeks to 2 June 1990 £'000
	Company Directors' emoluments:			
	Fees		100	100
	Salaries and pension contributions		923	864
	Profit related bonuses		–	–
	Pensions and pension contributions relating to former Directors		36	33
			1059	**997**
	Remuneration of the Chairman		181	159
	Remuneration of the highest paid Director		206	186

Number of other Directors of the Company whose remuneration was within the scale:

£	52 weeks to 1 June 1991 Number	52 weeks to 2 June 1990 Number
10,001 – 15,000	6	6
20,001 – 25,000	2	1
25,001 – 30,000	1	–
70,001 – 75,000	–	1
120,001 – 125,000	–	1
125,001 – 130,000	–	1
130,001 – 135,000	2	1
180,001 – 185,000	1	–

24   Staff

Analysis of staff by activity

The average number of persons employed by the Group analysed by activity was as follows:

	52 weeks to 1 June 1991 Number	52 weeks to 2 June 1990 Number
Retailing		
Books, stationery, news, recorded music, video etc	22,859	22,765
Distribution		
News, office supplies, books, etc	6,182	6,403
	29,041	29,168
Do it yourself	–	4,638
Discontinued businesses	1,095	1,325
	30,136	**35,131**

Analysis of staff by geographical area

The average number of persons employed by the Group analysed by geographical area was as follows:

United Kingdom		
Full time	16,771	19,384
8 – 29 hours per week	7,535	9,569
Less than 8 hours per week	3,186	2,792
	27,492	31,745
Europe	108	104
USA	2,536	2,349
Canada	–	933
	30,136	**35,131**

	52 weeks to 1 June 1991 £m	52 weeks to 2 June 1990 £m
Staff costs		
Wages and salaries	233.7	252.2
Social Security costs	20.0	21.1
Other pension costs *note 25*	(11.2)	(3.7)
Staff share ownership scheme	3.0	3.2
	245.5	**272.8**

25   Pension costs

The Group operates a number of pension schemes. The major schemes, which cover over 90% of members, are of the defined benefit type and are contracted-in to the State Earnings Related Pension ("SERPS") scheme. The assets of the schemes are held in separate funds administered by trustees.

The most recent formal actuarial valuations of the schemes were undertaken at 31 March 1988 adopting the attained age method. The market value of the assets of the UK schemes was £311.8m and the actuarial value of the assets was sufficient at that date to cover 129% of the benefits that had accrued to members after allowing for expected future increases in earnings. The principal actuarial assumptions used for the valuations were as follows:

Investment return	9.0% pa compound
General increase in earnings	7.5% pa compound
Pensions increase	4.0% pa compound

The surplus of the actuarial valuation of assets over the benefits accrued to members is being eliminated by a reduction in employer contributions.

The pension cost relating to the UK schemes has been assessed in accordance with the advice of a qualified actuary based on the same actuarial method and assumptions as for the actuarial valuations, updating them to 1 June 1991. The pension cost charged in the profit and loss account is as follows:

Major UK Schemes	52 weeks to 1 June 1991 £m	52 weeks to 2 June 1990 £m
Regular cost	18.2	15.3
Variation from regular cost	(29.4)	(19.3)
	(11.2)	(4.0)
Other schemes	–	0.3
Credit for the period	**(11.2)**	**(3.7)**

The variation from regular cost for the period represents the amortisation of the estimated surplus at the beginning of the period spreading it by equal instalments of capital and reducing elements of interest over the estimated service lives of the existing members taken as 9 years. The pension costs relating to overseas schemes are immaterial.

The social security costs shown in note 24 above include SERPS contributions of approximately £3.5m (1990 – £3.2m).

26   Capital commitments

	Group 1 June 1991 £m	Group 2 June 1990 £m
Group		
Future capital expenditure approved by the Directors and not provided in these financial statements is as follows:		
Contracts placed	12.4	23.9
Contracts not placed	31.3	4.9
Total capital commitments	**43.7**	**28.8**

27 Contingent liabilities

	Group 1 June 1991	Group 2 June 1990	Company 1 June 1991	Company 2 June 1990
	£m	£m	£m	£m
(a) Guarantees given by the Group in the normal course of business	3.0	7.5	2.0	–
(b) Guarantees in respect of associated undertakings	17.2	–	17.2	–
(c) Bank and other loans guaranteed by the Company	–	–	159.3	121.6
(d) The amounts of deferred taxation not provided in these financial statements are:				
Capital allowances in excess of depreciation	7.9	13.6	–	–
Chargeable gains *note (i)*	16.0	12.9	–	–
Less: other timing differences	(0.8)	(0.9)	–	–
	23.1	25.6	–	–

Notes:

(i) Estimated tax on chargeable gains, including those which would arise if freehold and leasehold properties were realised at balance sheet values.

(ii) No amount has been included for taxation that would arise in the event of certain overseas subsidiaries and associated undertakings distributing the balance of their reserves.

(iii) In addition to the timing differences noted above there are tax losses available in North America of £5.2m (1990 – £4.5m).

28 Annual commitments under operating leases

	1 June 1991 Land and Buildings	1 June 1991 Other	2 June 1990 Land and Buildings	2 June 1990 Other
	£m	£m	£m	£m
At 1 June 1991 the Group had annual commitments under operating leases which expire:				
Within one year	1.4	0.4	1.1	0.6
Between 2 and 5 years inclusive	17.0	1.9	10.2	1.5
Over 5 years	63.7	0.5	82.3	0.5
	82.1	2.8	93.6	2.6

29 Principal subsidiary companies and associated undertakings

Principal subsidiary companies

Name	Activity	Class of share	Effective group interest %	Country of incorporation where operating abroad
Held directly				
W H Smith Limited	Retailing Wholesaling	Ordinary	100.0	
Held indirectly				
Our Price Music Limited	Retailing	Ordinary	100.0	
Waterstone Investments Limited	Retailing	Ordinary	66.7	
W H Smith Group (USA) Inc	Retailing	Common	100.0	USA
W H Smith Amsterdam BV	Retailing	Ordinary	100.0	Holland
W H Smith (Belgium) SA	Retailing	Ordinary	100.0	Belgium
W H Smith SA	Retailing	Ordinary	100.0	France
Pentagon Group Limited	Wholesaling	Ordinary	100.0	
Satex Group PLC	Wholesaling	Ordinary	100.0	
Sandhurst Marketing PLC	Wholesaling	Ordinary	100.0	
Cartwright Brice Holdings Limited	Wholesaling	Ordinary	100.0	

29 Principal subsidiary companies and associated undertakings (continued)

Principal associated undertakings

Held indirectly

		Ordinary and	
Do It All Limited	Do it yourself	preference	50.0
Yorkshire Television Holdings plc	Television	Ordinary	19.92

Notes:

(i) The shares of Yorkshire Television Holdings plc are listed on a recognised investment exchange.

(ii) A list of interests in all subsidiaries is filed with the Annual Return.

(iii) The above companies are registered in England except for those operating abroad.

30 Post balance sheet events

(i) On 22 May 1991 the Group announced a proposed rights issue of new "A" Ordinary Shares at 300p. The bases were 1 new "A" Ordinary Share for every 4 "A" Ordinary Shares of 50 pence each and 1 new "A" Ordinary Share for every 20 "B" Ordinary Shares of 10 pence each.

On 7 June 1991 the necessary resolutions were approved by the shareholders to authorise the Directors to implement the rights issue and to increase the Company's authorised capital from £128,429,692 to £185,000,000 by the creation of 113,140,616 additional "A" Ordinary Shares of 50 pence each.

Under the terms of the rights issue, 50,945,267 new "A" Ordinary Shares of 50 pence each have been issued at a premium of 250 pence. The net proceeds available to the Group were £149 million.

As a result of the rights issue, the conversion price of the $7\frac{1}{8}$% Convertible Subordinated Bonds 2002 was adjusted from 335 pence per "A" Ordinary Share to 325 pence. The Company's redemption option price was also adjusted from 436p to 423p.

At 7 August 1991 there were outstanding £37.9 million nominal Convertible Bonds.

(ii) On 24 June 1991 the Group announced plans to merge the business of W H Hayden, one of six commercial stationery companies within the Office Supplies Division, so that existing customers are supplied by either Satex in London or Sandhurst in Horsham.

(iii) On 24 July 1991 the Group issued US $75 million (£44.8 million) 9.54% Senior Notes due 25 May 1998.

(iv) On 31 July 1991 W H Smith Limited signed an agreement with A. T. Mays Limited effective from 1 August 1991 for the sale of a large part of the W H Smith Travel business. The Group agreed with A. T. Mays Limited for the orderly closure of the balance of the W H Smith Travel business by 31 August 1991.

(v) On 2 August 1991 agreements were signed for the sale of the Group's satellite and cable television business, WHSTV, to a consortium of ESPN Inc., Canal Plus and Compagnie Generale des Eaux. The consideration is £45.35 million payable in cash on completion. In addition, the Group will assume the net debt of WHSTV of approximately £4 million. Completion of the sale is subject to certain regulatory and third party approvals.

Report of the Auditors

Auditors' Report to the Members of W H Smith Group PLC

We have audited the financial statements on pages 42 to 60 in accordance with Auditing Standards.

In our opinion the financial statements give a true and fair view of the state of affairs of the Company and of the Group at 1 June 1991 and of the profit and cash flows of the Group for the 52 weeks then ended and have been properly prepared in accordance with the Companies Act 1985.

Touche Ross & Co.
Chartered Accountants
Hill House
1 Little New Street
London EC4A 3TR
29 August 1991

Profit and loss account

	Year end May *note (i)*				
	1990/91	1989/90	1988/89	1987/88	1986/87
	£m	£m	£m	£m	£m
Turnover	1,970.6	2,130.8	1,940.5	1,662.0	1,460.5
Profit					
Continuing business	122.5	121.3	96.9	72.3	61.6
Discontinued businesses	(5.3)	(10.6)	0.7	6.2	8.4
Trading profit including associated undertakings	**117.2**	**110.7**	**97.6**	**78.5**	**70.0**
Exceptional item	–	–	(2.5)	–	–
Net interest	(28.2)	(24.7)	(11.0)	(8.7)	(6.0)
Profit on ordinary activities before taxation	**89.0**	**86.0**	**84.1**	**69.8**	**64.0**
Tax on profit on ordinary activities	(27.8)	(28.9)	(32.3)	(24.7)	(23.5)
Profit on ordinary activities after taxation	**61.2**	**57.1**	**51.8**	**45.1**	**40.5**
DIA preference dividend	(2.8)	–	–	–	–
Minority interests	1.1	2.0	1.1	0.1	(0.3)
Profit before extraordinary items	**59.5**	**59.1**	**52.9**	**45.2**	**40.2**
Extraordinary items after taxation	(13.7)	27.4	48.4	1.1	0.6
Profit for the period	**45.8**	**86.5**	**101.3**	**46.3**	**40.8**
Dividends	(27.4)	(22.9)	(20.5)	(17.5)	(14.8)
Transfer to reserves	**18.4**	**63.6**	**80.8**	**28.8**	**26.0**

Summary of balance sheets

Fixed assets *note (ii)*	449.4	466.4	387.2	354.0	288.6
Pension prepayment	37.6	8.4	–	–	–
Assets in the course of disposal	45.3	–	–	–	–
Other current (liabilities)/assets	(61.7)	26.2	23.5	21.3	35.2
Creditors falling due after more than one year	(193.8)	(188.7)	(127.2)	(136.2)	(95.3)
Provisions for liabilities and charges	(19.3)	(12.6)	–	–	–
Minority interests	(4.7)	(5.4)	(2.6)	(3.9)·	(1.1)
Total net assets	**252.8**	**294.3**	**280.9**	**235.2**	**227.4**

Called up share capital	101.5	99.9	98.9	96.9	95.4
Reserves	151.3	194.4	182.0	138.3	132.0
Total capital and reserves	**252.8**	**294.3**	**280.9**	**235.2**	**227.4**

Statistics per 50p ordinary share *note (iii)*

Asset value *note (ii)*	124.8p	147.8p	142.5p	121.8p	119.5p
Earnings per share	29.8p	29.9p	27.0p	23.6p	21.3p
Dividend	12.5p	11.5p	10.4p	9.0p	7.8p
Gross dividend equivalent	16.7p	15.3p	13.9p	12.1p	10.8p
Dividend cover before extraordinary items (times)	2.2	2.6	2.6	2.6	2.7

Notes:

(i) The accounts are prepared to the nearest Saturday to 31 May. Figures for 1988/9 are for the 53 weeks ended 3 June 1989.

(ii) The property revaluations in 1986/7 and 1989/90 increased fixed assets and reserves by £51.8m (27.2p per share) and by £31.3m (15.7p per share) respectively.

(iii) Statistics per share are based on both 50p 'A' Ordinary and 10p 'B' Ordinary Shares and are expressed in terms of a 50p 'A' Ordinary.

(iv) Figures have been restated on a comparable basis.

Appendix C   WH Smith Group plc: financial ratio analysis of results for the year ended 1 June 1991*

1   Financial highlights

Turnover decrease		− 7.5%
Gross profit decrease		−10.3%
Profit before taxation increase		+ 3.5%
Shareholders' funds £294.3m to £252m		−14.1%
Capital expenditure (properties and other tangible assets)	£466.4m to £449.4m	− 3.6%
Longer term loans	£193.8m from £188.7m	+ 2.7%

2   Measures of profitability

2.1   Return on capital employed

$$= \frac{\text{Operating profit}}{\text{Total assets less current liabilities}}$$

1981	*1990*
117.2	110.7
470.6	501.0
= 24.9%	= 22.1%

This return on the investment may seem satisfactory, but:

(i) It has increased by only 2.8% points in 1991 with inflation in excess of this figure.
(ii) The defects of historical cost accounting should be noted because they will have overstated this return.
(iii) This can be compared directly with the return from alternative investments.
(iv) The performance can be viewed positively as other net expenses is a lesser percentage of turnover than 1990.

2.2 Operating profit margin

		1991	1990
$=$	$\dfrac{\text{Operating profit}}{\text{Turnover}}$	$\dfrac{117.2}{1970.6}\%$	$\dfrac{110.7}{2130.8}\%$
	$=$	5.9%	5.2%

2.3 Activity ratio

$$= \frac{\text{Turnover}}{\text{Total assets less current liabilities}}$$

1991	1990
$\dfrac{1970.6}{470.6}$	$\dfrac{2130.8}{501.0}$
$= \quad 4.18$ times	$= \quad 4.25$ times

2.4 Operating expenses to sales

	1991		1990	
	£m	%	£m	%
Cost of sales	1404.7	71.3	1499.9	70.4
Distribution and selling costs	440.6	22.4	508.8	23.9
Administration etc.	13.1	0.6	11.5	0.5
Other (income)/ expenses	(5.0)	(0.2)	(0.1)	—
	1853.4	94.1	2020.1	94.8
Operating profit	117.2	5.9	100.7	5.2
Turnover	1970.6	100.0	2130.8	100.0

2.5 Asset usage

This examines, in further detail, the relationship between turnover and each major class of asset.

	1991	1992
$\dfrac{\text{Turnover}}{\text{Fixed assets}}$	$\dfrac{1970.6}{449.4}$	$\dfrac{2130.8}{446.4}$
	$= \quad 4.4$ times	$= \quad 4.6$ times
$\dfrac{\text{Turnover}}{\text{Net current assets}}$	$\dfrac{1970.6}{21.2}$	$\dfrac{2130.8}{34.6}$
	$= \quad 93.0$ times	$= \quad 61.6$ times

While (on the basis of book value) the use of fixed assets to generate turnover has fallen slightly, the major influence on the changed return on capital employed is the greater efficiency of net current assets.

3 Measures of solvency

3.1 *Current ratio*

		1.6.91	2.6.90
$= \dfrac{\text{Current assets}}{\text{Current liabilities}}$		$\dfrac{401.5}{417.9}$	$\dfrac{471.7}{445.5}$
		$=\quad 0.96$	$=\quad 1.06$

3.2 *Liquid/quick ratio*

$= \dfrac{\text{Debtors and cash}}{\text{Current liabilities}}$		$\dfrac{180.1}{417.9}$	$\dfrac{209.4}{445.5}$
		$=\quad 0.43$	$=\quad 0.47$

In a traditional sense both the above ratios are inadequate.

3.3 *Debtors Turnover*

$= \dfrac{\text{Trade debtors} \times 365}{\text{Turnover}}$		$\dfrac{100.7}{1970.6}$	$\dfrac{157.7}{2130.8}$
		$=\quad 19\quad \text{days}$	$=\quad 27\quad \text{days}$

A significant reduction of 8 days.

3.4 *Creditors turnover*

		1991	1990
$= \dfrac{\text{Trade creditors} \times 365}{\text{Cost of sales}}$		$\dfrac{417.9}{1404.7}$	$\dfrac{445.5}{1499.9}$
		$=\quad 109\quad \text{days}$	$=\quad 108\quad \text{days}$

Again no significant change.

3.5 *Stock turnover*

		1991	1992
$= \dfrac{\text{Stock} \times 365}{\text{Cost of sales}}$		$\dfrac{221.4}{1404.7}$	$\dfrac{262.3}{1499.9}$
		$=\quad 58\quad \text{days}$	$=\quad 64\quad \text{days}$

Stock turnover	58	64
Debtors turnover	19	27
	77	77
Less creditors turnovers	109	108
Working capital turnover	(32)	(17)

This reduction in the working capital cycle must mean that less cash is required to operate the business – but would be expected on a lower turnover figure.

4 Measures of financial structure

4.1 Gearing (claims based)

The 'lower half' of the two balance sheets in summary form are as follows:

	1.6.91		2.6.90	
	£m	%	£m	%
Long-term creditors	198.5	42.1	194.1	38.7
Provisions for liabilities	19.3	4.2	12.6	2.6
	217.8	46.3	206.7	41.3
Capital and reserves	252.8	53.7	294.3	58.7
	470.6	100.0	501.0	100.0

Borrowings have increased over the 2-year period, while capital and reserves have fallen slightly, reflecting the 1991 reduced profits.

Gearing (income based) – Interest cover

		1991	1990
$=$	$\dfrac{\text{Operating profit}}{\text{Interest on loans}}$	$\dfrac{117.2}{28.2}$	$\dfrac{110.7}{24.7}$
		= 4.2 times	= 4.5 times

4.3 Dividend cover

	1991	1990
$\dfrac{\text{Profit interest and tax}}{\text{Dividends}}$	$\dfrac{45.8}{27.4}$	$\dfrac{86.5}{22.9}$
	= 1.67 times	= 3.77 times

4.4 *Return on shareholders' equity*

$$= \frac{\text{Profits available to ordinary shareholders}}{\text{Shareholder's equity}}$$

1991	1990
45.8	86.5
252.8	294.3
= 18%	= 29%

The return on shareholders' equity has decreased significantly over the 2-year period.

Index